THE INDIGENOUS WORLD 2002-2003

IWGIA
Copenhagen 2003

GN
380
.I57
2002-
2003
c.1

THE INDIGENOUS WORLD 2002-2003

Compilation and editing: Diana Vinding
Regional editors:
  The Circumpolar North & North America: Kathrin Wessendorf
  Mexico, Central America & the Circumcaribbean: Diana Vinding
  South America: Alejandro Parellada
  Australia and the Pacific: Diana Vinding
  Asia: Christian Erni and Sille Stidsen
  Middle East: Diana Vinding
  Africa: Marianne Wiben Jensen
  Indigenous Rights: Lola García-Alix

Cover, typesetting and maps: Jorge Monrás
English translation: Elaine Bolton
English proofreading: Elaine Bolton & Birgit Stephenson

Prepress and Print: Eks-Skolens Trykkeri, Copenhagen, Denmark
ISSN 0105-4503   ISBN 87-90730-74-7

The Indigenous World is published annually in English and Spanish by IWGIA
Director: Jens Dahl
Deputy Director: Lola García-Alix
Administrator: Karen Bundgaard Andersen

*This book has been produced with financial support from the Danish
Ministry of Foreign Affairs and the Norwegian Agency for
Development Cooperation.*

**INTERNATIONAL WORK
GROUP FOR INDIGENOUS AFFAIRS**
IWGIA
Classensgade 11 E, DK 2100 - Copenhagen, Denmark
Tel: (+45) 35 27 05 00 - Fax: (+45) 35 27 05 07
E-mail: iwgia@iwgia.org - www.iwgia.org

CONTENTS

Editorial 8

About our contributors 11

PART I - Region and country reports

The Circumpolar North
The Arctic Council 22
Greenland 26
Sápmi
    Norway 31
    Sweden 35
    Finland 38
Russia 40
Alaska 47
Nunavut 52
Nunavit 55

North America
Canada 58
The United States of America 64

Mexico and Central America and the Circumcaribbean
Mexico 70
Guatemala 77
Nicaragua 83
Costa Rica 91
Panama 96
The Circumcaribbean 102
    Belize 102
    Trinidad & Tobago 106
    The Guyanas 109

South America
Colombia 114
Venezuela 122
Ecuador 129
Peru 133
Bolivia 143

Brazil 157
Paraguay 163
Argentina 169
Chile 177

Australia and the Pacific
Australia 186
The Pacific region 193
Occupied nations 201
    Guahan (Guam) 202
    West Papua 202
    Kanaky (New Caledonia) 204
    Te Ao Maohi (French Polynesia) 208
    Bougainville 208
    Northern Mariana Islands (CNMI) 210
Independent countries 210
    Fiji 211
    Kiribati 211
    Marshall Islands and FSM 212
    Papua New Guinea 212
    Solomon Islands 214
    Tonga 214
    Vanuatu 215

East Asia & Southeast Asia
Japan 218
Tibet 222
Taiwan 227
Philippines 233
Timor Lorosa'e 239
Indonesia 245
Malaysia 252
Thailand 257
Cambodia 263
Vietnam 269
Laos 276
Burma 283
Nagalim 291

South Asia
Bangladesh 298
Nepal 308
India 315
Sri Lanka 330

Middle East

The Bedouins of Israel 336

North and West Africa

The Amazigh People 344

The Touareg People 350

The Horn of Africa and East Africa

Ethiopia 358

Kenya 364

Tanzania 372

Central Africa and Cameroon

The Great Lakes Region 382

Rwanda 384

Burundi ...:... 387

Democratic Republic of Congo 395

Republic of Congo 391

Cameroon 392

Southern Africa

Namibia 398

Botswana 403

South Africa 409

PART II - Indigenous Rights

8th Session of the Working Group
on the Draft Declaration 416

First session of the Permanent Forum 427

The UN Special Rapporteur visits the Philippines 431

Report from the African Commission 440

French Guiana: making good use of the UN System: 442

PART III - IWGIA publications and general informations 446

EDITORIAL

The struggle for land and resource rights remained the major concern of indigenous peoples throughout 2002-2003.

A number of legal victories were recorded such as the adoption by the Nicaraguan parliament of Law No.445 on indigenous communal lands, and two landmark rulings on indigenous land rights - one by the Supreme Court of India regarding the removal of settlers from tribal reserves on the Adaman Islands, the other by the High Court in Peninsular Malaysia in favour of the Orang Asli's customary and property rights.

Unfortunately, however, 2002 also provided examples of the fact that new legislation, High Court decisions and international commitments are either not always followed up by implementation, or often suffer setbacks. In Nicaragua, the government did not fulfil the rulings of the Inter-American Court of Human Rights (IACHR) in favour of Awas Tingni; in Kerala (India), the government failed to comply with the much-acclaimed land agreement made in 2001 with indigenous organisations; and in Bolivia, the land titling process was in some cases stalled because of obstruction by farmers and livestock rearers.

On the whole, therefore, the land issue situation remained critical. The most vulnerable groups were, as usual, hunter-gatherers and forest dwellers. The Wanniyala-Aetto (Sri Lanka), the forest-dwelling Adivasis (India), the San, the Hadzabe and the Ogiek (Africa) were all faced during 2002 with either denied access to their ancestral lands or eviction from them in order to make way for commercial hunting, environmental conservation or logging interests. Another exposed group was the pastoralists, who suffered similar hardships in Ethiopia and Tanzania where land dispossession increasingly threatened their livelihood. Even the Saami reindeer pastoralists of northern Europe – often considered to be the most privileged indigenous peoples in the world - experienced a set-back. In several instances, land issues triggered off violence, gross human rights abuses and even massacres.

Social issues such as poverty, unemployment (often a corollary of land and resource deprivation) and high morbidity rates due to a lack of adequate health services were another major concern. These issues were seen as undermining the social fabric of indigenous communities, threatening their cultural as well as their physical survival. One stark example is that of the Evenk Autonomous Okrug (Russia) where the indigenous population has fallen by almost half over the last 7 years. Life expectancy is 20 years lower than among Russians in general and, while tuberculosis is a main killer, many deaths are alcohol-related. This, unfortunately, is the case in many other indigenous societies but, as a rule, not something openly acknowledged as a problem. This also used to be the case in Alaska although the high rates of suicides, accidents and domestic violence were known to be alcohol and drug related. A new approach building on local solutions has changed this situation and communities are now for the first time openly addressing the problems linked to alcoholism and drug abuse.

An overarching and recurrent theme of many of the articles, however, is globalisation and its different aspects, which appears to be increasingly affecting indigenous peoples worldwide.

One foremost example, of course, was the global impact of George W. Bush's "war against terrorism" and the conflict in Iraq. From Chile to India and the Pacific, governments eagerly used the pretext of anti-terrorism to clamp down on indigenous individuals and organisations that were simply asserting their rights. The build-up to the Iraq conflict meant that attention was diverted from other events, making it possible for certain governments to intensify their repression of marginalized population groups, without attracting any significant international concern. A case in point was the situation in the Negev desert (Israel), where the Israeli government not only stepped up its anti-Bedouin policy of house demolitions but also introduced a new strategy: crop destruction by toxic spraying. Other examples were the Indonesian government's military intervention in Aceh, and the increased military presence in Chiapas (Mexico).

Indigenous peoples also felt the increased impact of economic globalisation processes. Not only through the activities of multinational corporations but equally through the proliferation of free trade agreements and regional development plans, like the North American Free Trade Agreement (NAFTA), the Plan Puebla Panama,and the forthcoming Free Trade Agreement for the Americas (FTAA) that were seen as new threats to indigenous territories and resources. In other parts of the world, like Cameroon, Cambodia and Namibia, indigenous peoples feared the impact of cross-border developments (e.g. pipe-lines and hydroelectric dams) that would affect their livelihood.

Globalization, however, is multifaceted, and although it has become a negatively laden concept for many indigenous peoples, it can also be beneficial to them. 2002-2003 saw many examples of this.

The Permanent Forum held its first session that confirmed its potentially important role. It also became institutionalised with the establishment of its permanent Secretariat in New York. The UN Special Rapporteur, Rodolfo Stavenhagen, delivered two much praised reports from his missions to Guatemala and the Philippines to the

Commission on Human Rights. With these two new "global" institutions, the concern and the responsibility of the United Nations system towards indigenous peoples have been considerably furthered

At regional level, the process underway in the African Commission on Human and Peoples' Rights towards the recognition of indigenous peoples in Africa, and the active role played by the Inter-American Court on Human Rights (IACHR) in most Latin American countries, should also be seen as the result of international efforts to ensure a global view of indigenous issues. The Arctic Council is another regional effort with a strong indigenous participation and focus. In the Pacific, the Pacific Islands Forum has emerged as a united voice of the Pacific Islands, and 2002 witnessed the consolidation of the Pacific peoples into a stronger, more cohesive community, able to face challenges together. This included a framework legislation to protect Pacific intellectual property rights, and a joint strategy in dealing with the EU.

Finally, this volume also documents how globalization has made it possible for indigenous peoples to make themselves known worldwide by organizing international meetings, exchange visits and academic conferences; and by sharing their various cultural expressions whether films, books, music, or handicrafts.

However, to fully benefit from what the Paraguay report calls "this context of a new universal legal awareness that recognises [indigenous peoples'] participation in forming a new model of social, legal and political relations in their own right, on an equal footing with the societies with whom they live alongside, within the borders of nation states", indigenous peoples' organisations need to be strong so they can play a major and decisive role. It is therefore positive to note that 2002 saw several initiatives in South America to further the unity between indigenous organisations. It is to be hoped that this trend will continue in 2003-2004.

Diana Vinding
Coordinating editor

IWGIA would like to extend warm thanks to the following people and organisations for having contributed to *The Indigenous World 2002-2003*. We would also like to thank those contributors who have wished to remain anonymous and are therefore not mentioned below. A special thanks goes to those who took the initiative and have contributed to our two new sections - the Circumcaribbean and the Middle East (the Bedouins of Israel.) Without the help of all these people this book would not have been published.

PART I

The Circumpolar North & North America

This section has been compiled and edited by Kathrin Wessendorf, Arctic Program Coordinator, IWGIA

Kathrin Wessendorf is an anthropologist and IWGIA's Arctic Programme Coordinator.(*Arctic Council*)

Mette Uldall Jensen is an eskimologist from the University of Copenhagen. She has been an active member of the IWGIA local group in Denmark for many years. (*Greenland*)

Rune Fjellheim is an economist and works for the Saami Council as head of the Arctic and environmental unit. He is also co-owner of and senior advisor for Jaruma AS, a company working with Saami and Indigenous Peoples issues. (*Sápmi - Norway*)

Stefan Mikkaelson is a reindeer owner from northern Sweden. He has been a board member of the Saami Council since 1996 and its vice-president since 2001. He is a member of the Indigenous Peoples Secretariat's board. (*Sápmi - Sweden*)

Leif Rantala is a teacher of Saami language and culture at the University of Lapland, in Rovaniemi, Finland. (*Sápmi - Finland*)

Olga Murashko is an anthropologist and co-founder of the IWGIA local group in Russia. She works in close collaboration with RAIPON on indigenous peoples and legal rights in the Russian Federation. *Thomas Køhler* has a MA in Russian and

Political Science from Denmark and works as a consultant on indigenous issues in Russia. (*Russia*)

Jim La Belle is an Inupiaq and a MA student on the Rural Development Programme at the University of Alaska Fairbanks. He uses his 25 years of experience in Alaska Native corporations and state government to assist and promote capacity building among Alaska's indigenous leaders. *Mary Jane Nielsen*, a Sugpiaq/Alutiiq from South Naknek, has been the general manager of five Alaska Native Land Claims villages, which have been merged into the Alaska Peninsula Corporation since 1980. She will receive her Master's Degree in Rural Development in spring 2003. *Gloria Simeon* is Yup'ik and Athabascan and has worked for more than twenty years in Native organizations. She expects to complete her baccalaureate degree in Rural Development this May. (*Alaska*)

Jack Hicks lives in Iqaluit, Nunavut, where he works for the government of Nunavut. (*Nunavut*)

Gérard Duhaime is a sociologist and political scientist at Université Laval, Québec, Canada. The author of numerous books on Arctic issues, he holds the Canada Research Chair on Comparative Aboriginal Condition, where the METRINORD databank on social issues is located. Contact: Gerard. Duhaime@fss.ulaval.ca (*Nunavik*)

Michael Posluns is a consultant on Canadian parliamentary relations and legislative history. He maintains a watching brief on discussions on First Nations matters in the Canadian Parliament.(*Canada*)

Martha McCollough works as an assistant professor of cultural anthropology at the Anthropology and Ethnic Studies Department at the University of Nebraska. Her research interests include the relationship between states and non-state societies. (*USA*)

Mexico, Central America and the Circumcaribbean

This section has been compiled and edited by Diana Vinding, Programme Coordinator for Mexico, Central America & Pacific, IWGIA.

Gabriel Baeza Espejel is an ethnohistorian. He is a professor at the Mexican National School of Anthropology and History (ENAH) and an assistant researcher at the Colegio de México. *Abel Barrera Hernández* is an anthropologist and the director of the

Centre for Human Rights of the Montaña region in Guerrero, an NGO based in Tlapa, Mexico. Web page: www.tlachinollan.org *(Mexico)*

Santiago Bastos and Manuela Camus are social anthropologists and researchers at FLACSO-Guatemala, and the authors of *Entre el mecapal y el cielo. Desarrollo del movimiento maya en Guatemala*. 2003. Guatemala: Cholsamaj and FLACSO-Guatemala. Contact: mango@conexion.com.gt *(Guatemala)*

Dennis Williamson Cuthbert is an economist and the director of the Research and Investigation Centre of the Atlantic Coast of Nicaragua, CIDCA. Contact: cidca@ibw.com.ni *(Nicaragua)*

Gilbert González Maroto is an indigenous Brunca and the director of the Centre for Indigenous Development (CEDIN S.C). cedin@cedin.iwarp.com *(Costa Rica)*

Atencio López is a Kuna lawyer. He is President of the NGO "Napguana". *(Panama)*

Joseph O. Palacio is Garifuna and holds a doctorate in social anthropology from the University of California at Berkeley (1982). He is Resident Tutor and Senior Lecturer at the University of the West Indies School of Continuing Studies in Belize, a position he has held for twenty years. He has undertaken extensive research and published widely on the indigenous peoples of Belize, notably the Garifuna people. Contact: uwiret@btl.net *(Belize)*

Maximilian Forte is an Australian-trained anthropologist whose doctoral research and publications have focused on the history and cultural revitalization of the Caribs of Arima, Trinidad. He currently serves on the editorial boards of two online information resources, the Caribbean Amerindian Centrelink (www.centrelink.org), and Kacike: The Journal of Caribbean Amerindian History and Anthropology (www.kacike.org). He also currently serves as the Arima Caribs' Webmaster. *(Trinidad)*

Fergus MacKay is a US-trained lawyer and the coordinator of the Legal and Human Rights and Three Guyanas Projects for the Forest Peoples Programme, UK. *(The Guyanas)*

South America

This section has been compiled and edited by Alejandro Parellada, IWGIA's South American Programme Coordinator and General Editor of IWGIA's quarterly journal, *Asuntos Indígenas*.

José Domingo Caldón is an indigenous Kokonuco from Cauca and a well-know leader of the Regional Indigenous Council of the Cauca, CRIC. He is currently a member of the National Indigenous Council for Peace. (*Colombia*)

José Gregorio Díaz Mirabal is the General Coordinator of the Regional Organisation of Indigenous Peoples of Amazonas (ORPIA). (*Venezuela*)

Jorge Agurto is Technical Secretary of the Permanent Conference of the Indigenous Peoples of Peru, COPPIP, and in charge of the Indigenous Information Service SERVINDI ,which publishes an electronic bulletin specialising in indigenous and environmental issues. Contact: coppip@amauta.rcp.net.pe; servindi@yahoo.com . (*Peru*)

CEJIS, the Centre for Legal Studies and Social Research is a non-governmental organisation that provides legal assistance to indigenous and farmer organisations in the lowlands of Bolivia. *Ana Cecilia Betancur* is a lawyer for the Dutch Development Cooperation Service, SNV, and a consultant on indigenous peoples' rights for CEJIS. (*Bolivia*)

Paulo Celso de Oliveira belongs to the Pankararu people. He is a lawyer and works in the NGO Warä Instituto Indígena Brasileiro. (*Brazil*)

Andrés Ramírez is a member of Tierraviva's legal department and responsible for submitting cases to the Inter-american Commission on Human Rights and the Inter-American court of Human Rights on behalf of three indigenous communities. He is a former intern-scholar at the IACHR. (*Paraguay*)

Morita Carrasco is an anthropologist and lecturer at the University of Buenos Aires, specializing in the field of hunter gatherers and their rights. She works at the Centre for Legal and Social Studies (CELS) forming part of the team of technical/legal advisors supporting the Lhaka Honhat organisation in its lawsuit before the Inter-American Commission for Human Rights. (*Argentina*)

Alvaro Bello is Chilean and holds a Master's Degree in Social Sciences. He conducts research and works as an international consultant on indigenous affairs for various international bodies such as CEPAL and GTZ. Presently he lives in Mexico where he is preparing his doctorate. (*Chile*)

Australia and the Pacific

This section has been compiled and edited by Diana Vinding, Central America & Pacific Programme Coordinator,IWGIA .

Peter Jull is Adjunct Associate Professor, School of Political Science & International Studies, University of Queensland, Brisbane, Australia. (*Australia*)
Motarilavoa Hilda Lini is the Director of the Pacific Concerns Resource Centre (PCRC) based in Fiji. Born in Vanuatu, she has a degree in journalism and was for many years a Member of Parliament in Vanuatu. She has also been part of the government on several occasions, and last held the portofolio of Minister of Justice, Culture, Religion and Women. *Jimmy Nâunââ*, from Kanaky (New Caledonia), is the former Assistant Director - Decolonisation & Indigenous Rights at PCRC in Suva, Fiji Islands. Web site: www.pcrc.org .fj (*The Pacific*)

Asia

This section has been compiled, edited and partially written by Christian Erni, Asia Programme Coordinator, and Sille Stidsen, Assistant Asia Programme Coordinator, IWGIA.

East and Southeast Asia

Tomek Bogdanowicz is doing research on an Ainu video-collaboration project. He occasionally contributes articles on Ainu affairs to English-language publications. Regrettably, this contribution was submitted without any active Ainu participation in the wake of the untimely death of Masahiro Konaka, a regular IWGIA contributor on Ainu affairs. (*Japan*)
Charlotte Mathiassen is a social anthropologist and a consultant on development projects. She has worked with Tibetan communities in the Himalayas and on Tibetan issues in general for many years. She is an active member of the Danish Tibet Support Committee and a member of the Network for Indigenous Peoples in Denmark.(*Tibet*)
Shunling Chen is a non-indigenous volunteer staff member of the Association for Taiwan Indigenous Peoples' Policies (ATIPP),

15

an NGO established and run by Taiwan indigenous activists. ATIPP works for the empowerment of Taiwan indigenous peoples, and as a research group, seeks to promote the rights of Taiwan indigenous peoples through policy-making, bill lobbying and other means. *(Taiwan)*

Christian Erni, IWGIA Asia Programme Coordinator, has compiled and partly written the article on the Philippines, with contributions from *Crissy Guerrero*, Coordinator, NTFP-Exchange Programme for Southeast Asia, *Milet Mendoza*, Executive Coordinator, Tabang Mindanaw, *Jocelyn Villanueva*, LRC-Cagayan de Oro and *Joan Carling*, Chairperson, Cordillera Peoples Alliance. *(The Philippines)*

Torben Retbøll teaches history and Latin at Aarhus Katedradralskole, a junior college, in Aarhus, Denmark. He has written and edited several books on international affairs and the mass media, including three IWGIA documents (1980, 1984 and 1998). He visited Timor Lorosa'e on a networking trip for IWGIA in July 2001. *(Timor Lorosa'e)*

Emilianus Ola Kleden is the Information and Communication Manager of the Secretarial Office of the Indonesian national indigenous peoples' umbrella organisation AMAN (Alyansi Masyarakat Adat Nusantara). *(Indonesia)*

Jannie Lasimbang is Kadasan from Sabah, Malaysia. She is co-founder of the local indigenous organisation PACOS. She is currently working as the Secretary General of the Asia Indigenous Peoples Pact Foundation (AIPP), based in Chiang Mai, Thailand. *(Malaysia)*

Helen Leake has worked with IMPECT in indigenous and tribal communities in Thailand for over six years. She is currently working at the International Secretariat of the International Alliance of the Indigenous and Tribal Peoples of the Tropical Forests in Chiang Mai, Thailand. *(Thailand)*

Graeme Brown is an Australian volunteer who has been working in Ratanakiri province since 1999, supporting community-based natural resource development and an indigenous advocacy network. *(Cambodia)*

Tu Kien Dang is a Vietnamese student of environmental science at the Australian National University. She has been working at the Centre for Human Ecology Studies of the Highlands. *(Vietnam)*

Ian Baird, originally from Canada, has been working on natural resource management and indigenous issues in mainland Southeast Asia for 16 years, and has been living in Laos for the last 11 years. He is President of the Global Association for People and the Environment, a Canadian NGO active in Laos. *(Laos)*

Michele Keegan, (American) Altsean-Burma's Research Officer, has been working with the Free Burma Movement for six years. Altsean-Burma (Alternative Asian Network on Burma) is a Southeast Asian network of groups and individuals supporting human rights and democracy in Burma. *(Burma)*

Luingam Luithui, a Tangkhul Naga, is a human rights advocate. For twenty-five years, he has been actively involved in local and regional networking of indigenous peoples and building alliances with NGOs. *(Nagalim)*

South Asia

The Jumma Peoples Network (JUPNET) is an organisation established and run by indigenous Jummas based in various countries of Europe and elsewhere. JUPNET seeks to promote the rights of the indigenous Jummas through dialogue, negotiation and other peaceful means. *Sanjeeb Drong,* a Garo from northern Bangladesh, is the Secretary General of the Bangladesh Indigenous Peoples Forum, a national forum representing 45 different indigenous communities in Bangladesh. He has published extensively on indigenous issues through books and the print media in Bangladesh. *(Bangladesh)*

Balkrishna Mabuhang is a lecturer at the Central Department of Population Studies at Tribhuvan University, Kathmandu. He has been active in the Nepal Federation of Nationalities (NEFEN) for a number of years. NEFEN is a national umbrella organization for indigenous peoples in Nepal. Balkrishna Mabuhang has been the General Secretary of the organization since 2000. *(Nepal)*

C. R. Bijoy is a human rights activist based in Tamil Nadu, South India. For the past sixteen years he has been involved in and associated with indigenous issues and organisations in India and has written about these and associated matters. *Samar Bosu Mullick* is a political activist, teacher and researcher who has been working in solidarity with the indigenous peoples of Jharkhand for the last quarter of a century. He was one of the frontline people in the Jharkhand separate state movement. He has compiled the article on Jharkhand in cooperation with the following people and organizations: **People's Union for Civil Liberties, Tony Herbert,**

Kumar Rana, and Souparna Lahiri. *Linda Chhakchhuak* is a journalist based in Shillong, Meghalaya, northeast India, and publisher of Grassroots Options, North East India's first magazine on people, environment and development. *(India)*

Wiveca Stegeborn, is a Cultural Anthropologist (M.A. from Washington State University) attached to the University of Tromsoe, Norway, where she will defend her Ph.D dissertation. She has conducted research among the Wanniyala-Aetto of Sri Lanka since 1977. She speaks the major language of the country and the indigenous people's language. In 1996 she served as their interpreter at the annual WGIP meeting at the UN. *(Sri Lanka)*

The Middle East

The article on the Bedouins of Israel has been compiled and partly written by *Diana Vinding*, IWGIA Programme Coordinator, with contributions from *Devorah Brous* and *Adam Keller*. *Devorah Brous* is the founder and director of Bustan L'Shalom, a grassroots social/environmental justice organization that works with indigenous and marginalized sectors in Israel/Palestine, raising public awareness around issues of systemic discrimination through actions of resistance. She has a Master's Degree in Conflict Resolution and Israel Studies. Contact: bustanlshalom@yahoogroups.com. *Adam Keller* is an Israeli peace activist and the spokesperson of Gush Shalom (Peace Bloc) - a grassroots peace movement founded in 1992, advocating Israeli-Palestinian peace. He is the editor of *The Other Israel*, a newsletter published by the Israeli Council for Israeli-Palestinian Peace (founded in 1975), and the author of *"Terrible Days - Social Divisions and Political Paradoxes in Israel"* (1986). Contact: keller@actcom.co.il *(Israel)*

Africa

This section has been compiled and edited by Marianne Wiben Jensen, IWGIA Africa Programme Coordinator and General Editor of IWGIA's quarterly journal, *Indigenous Affairs*.

Hassan Idbalkassm is an Amazigh from Morocco. He is a lawyer and President of the Amazigh association "Tamaynut", which he founded in 1978. He is also the Vice-President of the "Congrès Mondial Amazigh", which has a membership of more than 70 Amazigh associations in North Africa and Europe. (*The Amazigh people*)

Melakou Tegegn is Ethiopian and Director of Panos Ethiopia. He is currently the chairman of the board of the Pastoralist Forum Ethiopia. He has worked in the Middle East, North Africa, South East Asia and Europe as coordinator for various NGO capacity building and advocacy projects. He is a Ph. D-candidate at the University of South Africa and conducts research on the link between the state of democratization/civil society and poverty in Ethiopia. He also teaches political science at Addis Ababa University. (*Ethiopia*)

Naomi Kipuri is a Maasai from Kajiado district of Kenya. She is an anthropologist by training. Naomi Kipuri taught at the University of Nairobi and is now a development consultant. She conducts research and development and is keen on development concerns and issues relating to human rights and the rights of indigenous peoples. (*Kenya)*

Benedict Ole Nangoro, is a Maasai from Kiteto, in Tanzania. He currently works with CORDS, a local NGO working with the indigenous Maasai people in collective land demarcation, mapping, registration and titling. (*Tanzania*)

Dorothy Jackson is the Africa Programme Coordinator for the Forest Peoples Programme and its charitable wing, the Forest Peoples Project. **Lucy Mulvagh** is FPP's Project Support Officer. **John Nelson** is FPP's Policy Advisor. FPP is working with Pygmy peoples in Cameroon and the Great Lakes region to support their capacity building and advocacy work. Contact: info@fppwrm.gn.apc.org ; fpproject@gn.apc.org; www.forestpeoples.org (*Central Africa and Cameroon*)

Robert K. Hitchcock is a Professor of Anthropology and Geography at the University of Nebraska-Lincoln, USA. His forthcoming book is about *Organizing to Survive: Indigenous Peoples' Political and Human Rights Movements.*(*Botswana and Namibia*)

Megan Biesle has long worked with Ju | 'hoan San communities in Botswana and Namibia as an advocate and documentarian. She is the President of the Kalahari Peoples Fund. (*Namibia)*

Nigel Crawhall is an activist for indigenous peoples' rights. He has worked with the Indigenous Peoples of Africa Co-ordinating Committee (IPACC) and is project manager on an indigenous knowledge and cultural resources management and training project with the South African San Institute (SASI). (*South Africa*).

PART II

Indigenous Rights

This section has been compiled and edited by Lola García-Alix, Human Rights Programme Coordinator, IWGIA.

Andrea Muehlebach is a board member of IWGIA and a Ph.D candidate in the Department of Anthropology of the University of Chicago. She has followed and published on the international indigenous movement, and is currently exploring the procedural aspects of indigenous activism at the UN. (*Report on the 8th Session of the Working Group on the Draft Declaration*)

Lola García Alix is Coordinator of Human Rights Activities, IWGIA. (*The First Session of the UN Permanent Forum on Indigenous Peoples*)

Raymundo D. Rovillos is a research coordinator of Tebtebba (Indigenous Peoples' International Centre for Policy Research and Education). He is also an Assistant Professor in History at the University of the Philippines College in Baguio and a Ph.D-candidate in History at the University of the Philippines. As a researcher, Rovillos has done extensive work on indigenous peoples and development, indigenous education and conflict resolution. (*The UN Special Rapporteur visits the Philippines*)

Marianne Wiben Jensen is the Coordinator of IWGIA's Africa Programme. (*The African Commission on Human and Peoples' Rights*)

Alexis Tiouka is an indigenous leader from French Guiana, and the Coordinator / delegate of F.O.A.G. (*French Guiana: Making good use of the UN system*)

20

PART I

REGION AND
COUNTRY REPORTS

THE CIRCUMPOLAR NORTH

THE ARCTIC COUNCIL

The Arctic Council (AC) is an intergovernmental organisation comprising 8 member states with territories in the Arctic realm. These are: Canada, the USA, the Russian Federation, Finland, Sweden, Norway, Denmark/Greenland and Iceland. Six indigenous organisations are also Permanent Participants to the AC. These are: the Aleut International Association (AIA), the Arctic Athabaskan Council (AAC), the Gwich'in Council International (GCI), the Inuit Circumpolar Conference (ICC), the Russian Association of Indigenous Peoples of the North (RAIPON) and the Saami Council. The AC also has a number of observers, including states (France, Poland, Germany, the Netherlands and the United Kingdom), international organisations and NGOs. IWGIA received observer status in 2002. The more technical and scientific work is carried out by the working groups: the Arctic Monitoring and Assessment Programme (AMAP); Protection of Arctic Marine Environment (PAME); Conservation of Arctic Flora and Fauna (CAFF); and the Sustainable Development Working Group (SDWG). The SDWG, for example, is involved in projects on sustainable reindeer husbandry, sacred sites, co-management of marine resources, etc.

2002 was a particularly active year for the Arctic Council, due to several major events that took place. Under the chairmanship of Finland, the AC has, over the last two years, put particular efforts into raising its profile internationally.

The AC in the WSSD process

On a global level, the AC concentrated on the World Summit on Sustainable Development (WSSD) that took place in August 2002. Canada took the lead in strategising for actions during the meeting. The Arctic has become recognised as an indicator of global environmental health, as issues such as Persistent Organic Pollutants (POPs) and climate change are of particular concern to the Arctic but also of global importance. However, despite many efforts by Arctic indigenous organisations and Arctic states, the only two references that were included in the final Plan of Implementation are in Paragraph 36(i) in relation to climate change and in Paragraph 74 in relation to regional initiatives. Nowhere is the Arctic mentioned as an indicator region.

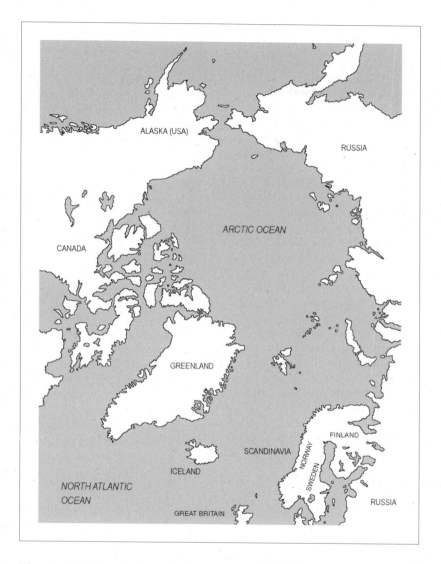

The Arctic Climate Impact Assessment (ACIA) was presented at a fringe event at the WSSD and was very well attended and successful. Furthermore, two Arctic states, Canada and the Russian Federation, announced at the meeting that they would ratify the Kyoto Protocol (Canada ratified the protocol on 17 December 2002, Russia has so far not followed up on its promise).[1]

Capacity building and gender

Alongside this high level involvement, the Arctic Council also tried to further outline its general principles and implementation strategies for the recommendations from its Capacity Building workshop of 2001. The outcome of the conference on capacity building led to further discussions in the Senior Arctic Officials' (SAO) meetings in May and October 2002. A report on a capacity building strategy, presented by Canada was rejected but Canada received a mandate to review how capacity building could be implemented in the practical activities of the Arctic Council. From the beginning, the Permanent Participants of the Arctic Council (the indigenous organisations) stressed the importance of including indigenous peoples in the drafting of a strategy and implementation of capacity building components.

A conference on gender equality and women in the Arctic, "Taking Wing", took place in early August in the very north of Finland with around 200 participants, mostly women, from all Arctic countries. The three main topics of the conference were: "Women and Work", "Gender in the Self-determination of Indigenous Peoples" and "Violence against Women". The second theme was suggested by the Permanent Participants and issues such as land rights, self-government, indigenous organisations, etc, were considered, all with a view to gender equality although particular indigenous angles were also discussed. The need for further support for the self-determination of indigenous peoples was stressed, along with the need to ratify ILO Convention 169.

The recommendations of the conference put emphasis on the need to mainstream gender equality in the Arctic Council.

The Ministerial Meeting

In 2002, another biannual Ministerial Meeting took place to discuss the past two years of work and establish guidelines for the future work of the Arctic Council. The Inari Declaration (named after the municipality where the meeting was convened) formalises the decisions made by the ministers. The meeting endorsed the need for a strong capacity building component to be included in all Arctic Council activities. A similar decision was taken by the ministers concerning the outcomes and recommendations of the Taking Wing conference.

At the end of the meeting, Iceland took over the chairmanship of the AC for the next two years from Finland. A new country chairing the council always implies new priorities for its work and Iceland is particularly interested in the human dimension of the council's work. This is interesting as it has not been a priority of the AC so far. However, given that Iceland is the "only truly Arctic country" (someone once stated that countries such as the US, Russia and even Scandinavian countries are psychologically not 'Arctic countries' as most of their population lives in the south), this focus is not particularly surprising but nevertheless very encouraging.

Iceland's main priority is the Arctic Human Development Report (AHDR), a new project under the Sustainable Development Working Group that was approved by the Ministers in Inari. The "Report on the State of Sustainable Human Development in the Arctic: Challenges and Opportunities" will draw on available data and other projects under the auspices of the AC and includes chapters such as: "Arctic Economies", "Arctic Environments and Resource Governance in the Arctic", "Arctic Political Systems" (including self-government of indigenous peoples), "Arctic Legal Issues", "Globalisation and the Arctic" and many more. A steering group was set up in 2002 and, by February 2003, the lead authors of the individual chapters had been chosen.

The other priorities of the Icelandic chairmanship are: information technology (a conference will take place in 2003) and research cooperation. ❑

Note and Sources

1   Kyoto Protocol, Status of ratification:
    www.unfccc.int/resource/kpstats.pdf (as per 20 March 2003).

Arctic Council: www.arctic-council.org/index.html
Indigenous Peoples' Secretariat: www.arcticpeoples.org/
    (see especially IPS Update).
Taking Wing. Conference Report. Ministry of Social Affairs and Health, Helsinki 2002.

GREENLAND

Politics

In 1999, the Home Rule Government in Greenland established a self-government commission to investigate the possibilities for taking over more responsibilities from the Danish State. The commission presented a report in August 2002 and it was emphasised that alternative sources of income, development of trade and industry and a better educational level would be needed to create the basis for more independence. Until an alternative exists to the yearly grant (about 3 billion) from the Danish state, the Commission will not recommend further independence unless living standards can be guaranteed.

An internal struggle within the largest government party, Siumut (the Social Democratic Party), during 2001 led to the appointment of a new party leader, Hans Enoksen. This created a situation whereby the Home Rule Premier, Jonathan Motzfeldt, was no longer leader of his own party. The problems continued during 2002 as Hans Enoksen and Jonathan Motzfeldt represented two different wings of the party. With Hans Enoksen, Siumut has adopted a strategy for the equal development of all parts of Greenland. However, this might clash with the party's wish for more independence from Denmark, as keeping the outlying districts alive is a costly affair.

By the autumn, the crisis inside Siumut had worsened, as three members of the Home Rule Government were accused of violating the law and of using too much money. This made the right-wing party, Atassut, threaten to leave the coalition with Siumut while the left-wing IA (Inuit Ataqatigiit) threatened to bring a vote of no confidence.

The power struggle inside Siumut, combined with the charges against the members of the Home Rule Government, finally led to elections for the Home Rule Parliament in December 2002. The elections resulted in a coalition between Siumut and IA, with Hans Enoksen as the new Premier of Greenland. Only a few weeks after the elections, however, the new Home Rule Government faced severe internal problems because Siumut had replaced a number of civil servants in the Home Rule administration with party colleagues and because of a healing ceremony that took place within the Home Rule Government's offices in order to rid it of negative energies. The healing and the camaraderie made IA demand that Hans Enoksen step down. Consequently Hans Enoksen denounced the coalition agreement with IA and began negotiations with Atassut to form a new coalition. In January 2003, Siumut and Atassut formed a new Government.

Map labels:
Qaanaaq (Thule)
Upernavik
Ittoqqortoomiit (Scoresbysund)
Uummannaq
Saqqaq
Qeqertarsuaq (Godhavn)
Ilulissat (Jakobshavn)
Aasiaat (Egedesminde)
Qasigiannguit (Christianshåb)
Kangaatsiaq
Sisimiut (Holsteinsborg)
Kangerlussuaq
Maniitsoq (Sukkertoppen)
Tasiilaq (Angmagssalik)
Nuuk (Godthåb)
Paamiut (Frederikshåb)
Ivittuut
Narsaq
Qaqortoq (Julianehåb)
Nanortalik

KALAALLIT NUNAAT
GREENLAND

In foreign politics, 2002 saw the U.S.A. promise to return the old hunting area, Dundas, close to the US airbase in Thule (northern Greenland) to its original occupants. The Thule hunters were forced to move in 1953 due to a military agreement between the US and

Denmark. In recent years, they and their descendants have intensified their fight to regain the title to the whole Thule air base – and not just Dundas. The restitution of Dundas became effective in early 2003. It was later revealed that the US had used the site as a military waste dumping ground, causing serious pollution problems. Whose job is to clean up? The US or Denmark? The debate continues...

Mineral and oil resources

The Greenland Home Rule places great expectations on the investigation of both oil and minerals as a means of improving the economy and thereby making the country more self- reliant and independent from Denmark. Concerning oil, the prospects have not been too good, since the search for oil outside Nuuk in 2001 turned out to be negative.

With regard to gold, prospecting has been going on in the area of Nanortalik (southern Greenland) since the 1980s. The Greenlandic company, NunaMinerals, and the Canadian Crew Development Corporation have created the production company, Nalunaq Goldmine A/S, and hope to start mining in the spring of 2003. The ore will be shipped to Canada for processing in order to reduce the construction expenses in Greenland. In terms of the income from the gold, this has to be split between Greenland and Denmark. The first 500 million DKK must be divided fifty-fifty, as in all minerals finds, while no agreement exists on how to split the rest. This is related to the fact that Greenland does not hold the property rights to the subsoil. This right, though, is vital in relation to a desire for more self-reliance and independence from Denmark. At the end of 2002, the two Greenlandic representatives in the Danish parliament therefore made a proposal by which the Danish government would hand over all property rights to the subsoil to the Greenland Home Rule.

The strive for property rights and the hope for oil and mineral finds has an international perspective with the renewed interest in the North Pole and the resources of the Polar Sea. Russia has already submitted a rights claim to the UN Sea Rights Commission while Denmark does not expect to sign the UN Sea Rights Convention until 2003. The Danish government though, has set aside several million DKK for investigation of the Greenlandic continental shelf over the coming years.

Trade and industry

Although the Home Rule places great expectations on oil and minerals, 75 % of the grants for developing business and industry go to hunting, fishing and farming. According to the Greenlandic Council of Business and Trade, this distorts the structure of the industries and maintains the society dependent upon the fishing industry.

Development of other businesses is increasingly needed in times of escalating crisis in the fishing industry. The shrimp fishery, which is far the most important industry in Greenland, is facing the worst crisis ever due to a global overload of the world market, resulting in low prices. To improve the economy and profitability of the fishing industry, a reduction in the number of vessels in the coastal fishery was therefore started during the spring.

The large fishing company, Royal Greenland A/S, which is vital for the Greenlandic economy has, as have Home Rule companies in general, often been criticised of having leaders without the abilities to lead a business. This was also the case at the beginning of 2002, when Royal Greenland A/S's new board took over, comprising only members from the Home Rule's own ranks.

Another example is the scandal of the Home Rule's corporation Puisi A/S. The corporation should have produced seal sausages and seal oil pills for the Chinese market but faced significant financial problems after only two weeks of production. The Greenlandic parliament wanted to find who was to blame and consequently a Danish firm of solicitors was appointed to advise the Parliament. The final report concluded that most of the company's senior executives and the accountant had acted irresponsibly. The trial will start in early 2003.

Infrastructure

During 2002, a debate on the closure or downgrading of some of the smaller and more costly airports took place. Air Greenland has to replace its worn out Dash 7 planes with smaller planes in line with the low number of passengers and in order to reduce operation costs.

In addition, overseas flights were discussed as the Scandinavian company SAS stopped flying to Greenland in 2002. Another topic was the possible closure of the oversea airport, Narsarsuaq, in southern Greenland, and the plans to build a new regional airport in Qaqortoq (also in southern Greenland). Many municipalities have protested and Narsaq and Nanortalik had a report carried out by the Danish professor, Gorm Winther. This concludes that the closure of Narsarsuaq and the building of an airport in Qaqortoq would cost Greenlandic society at least 292 million DKK (US$ 45 million). Furthermore, the Home Rule's plans do not account for the expenses of moving the 112 households in Narsarsuaq who rely entirely on income generated by the airport. Neither do they take into account the economic consequences when passengers from southern Greenland have to be carried by plane to overseas connections in Kangerlussuaq on the west Coast. The airports continue to await the decisions of the new Home Rule Government.

Living resources

On 1 January 2002, new and more restrictive regulations concerning bird hunting came into force and prolonged the closed season for seabird hunting. This caused discussions and disagreement among hunters, biologists and managers. The hunters' dissatisfaction caused the fishermen's and hunters' organisation (KNAPK) to complain to the ombudsman that the Home Rule had not presented the regulations to the Hunting Council, which is to be heard in cases of living resource management.

The ombudsman, however, could not say whether this was enough to claim the regulations invalid. According to the environment department, all parts represented in the Hunting Council were heard, including the hunters, even if the council had not formally been convened. Anyway, the Home Rule Government decided to comply with the demands from KNAPK and ease the regulations.

The former Home Rule Government decided to begin intensive educational work on the sustainable use of living resources and to involve the population to a larger extent in the management debate. At the same time, the Home Rule Government wanted to produce an action plan on how to solve the existing management problems in order to counter the growing criticism from animal welfare organisations and the media abroad. The strategy is still awaiting a decision from the new Home Rule Government. ❑

SÁPMI - NORWAY

S ince the Alta issue and the subsequent processes leading to the establishment of the Saami parliament, Norway's role as defender of indigenous peoples' rights has been undisputed. The well-known hydroelectric power plant issue in the late 70s and early 80s led to a complete shift in Norwegian policy towards the Saami people, and a series of acknowledgements of cultural and political rights emerged. A brief recapitulation of events during the 80s and 90s should demonstrate the positive progress made over the last couple of decades:

1980 - Saami Rights Commission (SRC) established
1981 - The Guovdageaidnu agreement
1984 - SRC first report
1987 - The Saami Act
1988 - Constitutional amendment §100a
1989 - Saami Parliament established
1990 - Norway first country to ratify ILO Convention169
1990 - The language amendment to the Saami Act
1997 – SRC second report

In addition, several reports have been produced as amendments to the official SRC reports, following pressure from the Saami parliament.

Critical land rights test about to fail?

In 1997, a report on the relationship between the suggested new land management models and international law was published, along with, in 2001, an additional report covering traditional land-use and legal systems.

The Saami parliament and all relevant parties embarked on a lengthy round of commenting on the management models proposed in the 1997 report. On the basis of those comments, the Government was supposed to draft a new management model for the so-called 'state-owned' land in Finnmark County. Core elements in the report were the legitimacy of state ownership over traditional Saami ownership, and different management models for a new system of landownership.

On 4 April 2003, the Norwegian government presented the long awaited bill for new land rights management legislation. Surprisingly to all, the Government chose to present a completely new proposal without any basis in the SRC proposals. According to the Minister of Justice, the bill is supposed to bridge the gap between the conflicting parties in the region, securing peace and preventing an increased number of court cases.

Although the bill, in its presentation, was wrapped in the rhetoric of conflict resolution and heralded as a preventive measure with which to stop a flood of new court cases, the end result may be just that. The new act seems to be introducing a range of problematic principles, at least according to contemporary interpretation of international legal instruments. I will endeavour to point out some issues that are clearly problematic, and also to give a description of the political thinking behind those issues.

No prior consent to the proposed act

The principle of free, prior and informed consent in all new measures affecting indigenous peoples is a principle that is not only expressed by indigenous peoples as a basic principle but is also clearly enshrined, for example, in article 6 of ILO Convention169 as a clear requirement. This may not be in the very same wording but it is definitely with the very same philosophy. If Norway had followed its exercise with the SRC through to a final bill, following the report's recommendations and the ensuing political process, they would have been in a strong position to argue that they had complied with the requirements of ILO 169. Now that the government has chosen to pull a completely new proposal out of its pocket, even stressing the fact that it is not based on any of the previous proposals, it is hard to see that the procedural part of this issue is in compliance with the ILO convention.

The Saami Parliament is, of course, free to support the proposed bill now, after the government has made its proposal but, at the moment, the possibility of this seems very remote.

The Minister for Local Government and Regional Development, Ms Erna Solberg, explained why the government came up with this solution in relation to presentation of the bill:

> But with the position taken by some Saami interested parties on what they want to achieve through this, I understand that they are disappointed, but that wasn't a position that anyone could support, because it would have been wrong considering the Norwegian population in Finnmark.

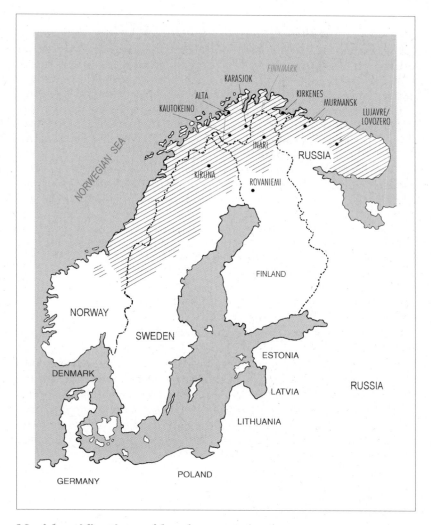

No identification of land as required

ILO 169 divides land rights into categories, whereby a distinction is made between areas where indigenous peoples have the right to "ownership and possession", and areas that have traditionally been shared with others and where they will have protected access to use those areas. Steps must be taken to identify these areas in order to guarantee effective protection of their rights to ownership and possession.

Norway is failing to comply with this requirement, and the only argument used to support this is that the government does not want to distinguish between Saami and non-Saami in Finnmark County. For the record, it should be noted that inner Finnmark is totally dominated by Saami (90%) and that the SRC sub-report on the relationship between the proposed legislation and international law indicated that recognition of Saami ownership and possession in inner Finnmark was a basic requirement, and that this may probably also affect other parts of some coastal areas. The call for identification is thus a logical consequence.

The political reason for neglecting these requirements may be found in a statement by the State Secretary to the Ministry of Justice, Mr. Jørn Holme, during the presentation, when he stated that:

> But more important is to stress that Finnmark, and especially inner-Finnmark, with its fantastic natural resources, is for everyone. With this bill we have given everyone in Finnmark special rights.

No recognition of Saami land rights

The Norwegian government has introduced an act that fails to address the fundamental recognition of the existence of Saami rights to land and waters within Saami territory. The main purpose of the act seems to be to protect non-Saami interests from Saami recognition claims. The act is supposed to transfer the so-called "state-owned" property in Finnmark to a new ownership, via the proposed "Finnmark property" Land Rights Management body. At the same time, the government has explicitly stated that land can be expropriated for public purposes without compensation, when necessary.

As a consequence, government control over Saami territory is not only safeguarded but, to a large extent, strengthened and recognition of Saami traditional ownership and possession seems to be far beyond the ambitions of this government.

This is probably also best expressed in Minister Solberg's own words, when she states that:

> We have not given away the state ownership forever. We have made a managing construction to which the management and responsibility is transferred, thus also the ownership, but we haven't given it away so that private ownership rights can block the state from taking it back.

Still time to overturn the decision?

The bill is now up for approval in the Norwegian Parliament. The Parliament will take it up for decision in Autumn 2003. One could hope for rejection of the bill and a revised process to get the issue back on track but I would be surprised if that were to happen. ❏

SÁPMI - SWEDEN

Toward a Saami convention

T he work to establish a Saami convention has been ongoing for quite some time. The Saami are one people living in four countries: the Russian Federation, Finland, Sweden and Norway. In 2002, the Swedish Minister responsible for Saami issues signed an agreement with colleagues from Finland and Norway, in order to start preparing a joint Nordic Saami convention.

Through the Nordic Saami convention, the various legislation concerning Saami issues in Finland, Sweden and Norway will be adjusted in order to make the conditions in the three countries more similar. It will also be based on the lowest level of ILO Convention 169. Today, various laws and courts in Sweden are reducing the rights of the Saami people, or the possibilities for the Saami to use the land and waters in a traditional way.

It should also be noted that none of the mentioned Nordic ministers is of Saami origin, nor have they been elected by the Saami people. Yet they claim to be Saami ministers. It should also be noted that Sweden, together with the Saami parliament in Sweden, has agreed not to include a large part of Sápmi, i.e. the Sápmi part in the Russian Federation, in an attempt to ease the process. Thus the Saami in one country will not be included in the negotiations on a Saami Convention that is valid for all Saami.

The Saami people's land rights

2002 held good prospects for the reindeer owners. Spring was early and the weather stayed fine during May which, for the reindeer calves, is a sensitive time of year.

However, the uncertainty about reindeer herding areas remained, and resulted in 7 cases brought to the civil court by private landowners, be they companies or individuals.

After the first case had gone to court, the companies withdrew but the individual landowners continued the process, and started new ones in similar ways. The first case generated a further 6 court cases with support from the landowners' organisations that had supported the first case.

The longest ongoing case was one in southern Sápmi and the decision of the appeal court was that the Saami did not have the right to use land for winter pasture herding outside land that is used for all-year-round pasture.

Now the Saami lawyers are trying to bring the case to the High Court. The reason given by the private landowners for bringing this case to court was the uncertainty about where the rights of Saami reindeer herders can be exercised in Sweden. It is also quite significant that it is possible to hold such trials in Sweden, a country that has been promoting human rights in other countries all over the world. Where should national legislation allow the Saami to express their cultural and traditional knowledge if not in Sápmi? What will the consequences be for the Saami people as one people in four countries, if legislation in one country offers the option of manoeuvring out of the practical possibilities for exercising traditional Saami rights? In this situation it would be rather inappropriate to discuss the "Nordic Saami convention".

The Saami in Sweden face a lack of protection in state legislation and the division between the Saami and the majority population is increasing rapidly.

ILO Convention 169

The Government's minor attempts at initiating an investigation into the consequences of a possible Swedish ratification of ILO Convention 169 have been met with wide protests from the majority groups and their political representatives. Their voices have been really loud and their arguments based on the lowest possible common denominator. They have proposed finding local solutions, at the level of the municipalities, where Saami villages usually find it very hard to make their voices heard.

The basic principles of ILO Convention 169 are respect and participation, but such issues have never been considered in the debate, either by the farmer, hunter and landowner organisations or by the government.

On 24 January 2002, the Swedish government instigated a one-man commission to define the areas for reindeer herding. The commission will make a proposal for the borders between traditional Saami-owned lands and the land shared with others, as ILO Convention 169 states.

The prime focus of the commission will be to base its report on existing documentation in government archives. The directive to this commission mentions particularly that the Kingdom of Sweden has been criticised on various occasions for violating the Saami people's human rights. The last time was in the Committee on the Elimination of Racial Discrimination (CERD) on 10-11 August 2000.

NGO co-operation within the Barents Euro-Arctic Region

The Saami Council was among the signatories of the Kirkenes Declaration in 1993, which formally established the Barents Euro-Arctic Council but, since then, it has not been very active within the Barents co-operation. The Kirkenes Declaration states:

> *The Council will serve as a forum for considering bilateral and multilateral cooperation in the fields of economy, trade, science and technology, tourism, the environment, infrastructure, educational and cultural exchange, as well as projects particularly aimed at improving the situation of indigenous peoples in the North.*

In June 2002, the president of the Saami Council, Anne Nuorgam, sent an application to the ministries of foreign affairs of Finland and Sweden for funding for the International Saami Cultural Centre, Chum,[1] located in Lujavre/Lovozero, Murmansk oblast, in the Russian Federation.

This Centre will, among other things, house the office of the local Saami association, and the studios of Kola Saami Radio. Kola Saami Radio is another project with 18 funders in 5 different countries.

The total amount applied for from each foreign ministry was 133,500 Euro and the total budget was 400,000 Euro. The project was already in the pipeline when the Kirkenes Declaration was signed 10 years ago, so the process towards its implementation has been extremely slow. The Norwegian Foreign Ministry was the first to pay its part of the budget to the Karasjok community and the rehabilitation of the Chum started in autumn 2002.

The situation, however, became critical when the project ran out of money at the onset of the long winter. Finally, on 12 December 2002, the Government of Sweden decided to support the Saami Council's application and transfer 133,500 Euro to the "Chum project". Everybody is, of course, very grateful that the Swedish Government acknowledges the importance of the Kirkenes Declaration and we hope and believe that other responsible governments will also show the same commitment. ❏

Note

1 *Chum* is a traditional Saami tent, made of reindeer skin (ed.note).

SÁPMI - FINLAND

Land rights

The question of land rights in Saami areas of Finland has not made any progress over the last two years. There have been several bodies researching this matter, as noted in *The Indigenous World 2000-2001*. These included a committee to investigate the possibilities for ratifying ILO Convention 169, a board for the administration of state land in northern Lapland, which was opposed by the Finnish Saami parliament, and a one-man committee comprised of Judge Juhani Wirilander. The Saami parliament itself set up a committee to look into the Saami's right to forest lands, protected areas and water areas.

More recently, the Finnish Ministry of Justice ordered research from the Universities of Oulu and Lapland into land rights in Lapland. Their task is to undertake an extensive study into settlement and population history, land use and land ownership from the middle of the 18th century to the beginning of the 20th century. The research is expected to take three years.

Law on Saami language

In Finland, a Saami language law has been in force since 1992. According to this law, a Saami-speaking person has the right to use the Saami language in their contact with the authorities. In practice, the law has not functioned very well. The Saami parliament therefore appointed a working group, which suggested several improvements: the Finnish and Saami languages should be declared as having equal status in the Saami area; civil servants who want to learn Saami should be able to do so during their working hours; the three Saami languages spoken in Finland should be noted in the law, and 11 new jobs as Saami language translators and interpreters should be made available. The Ministry of Justice, however, opposes many of these suggestions.

Minority group ombudsman

The position of a Minority Group Ombudsman was created on September 1, 2001 and the first ombudsman, Mikko Puumalainen, began work on January 1, 2002. The tasks of the ombudsman are:

* to promote good ethnic relations
* to promote the status and rights of people belonging to ethnic minorities
* to monitor equal opportunities
* to supervise the prohibition of discrimination due to ethnic origin
* to provide information and prepare reports

The ombudsman has his office in Helsinki. He has spent his first year gathering information about the Saami, travelling to Sápmi and becoming acquainted with Saami culture. The ombudsman has particularly emphasized the role of the Saami language in revitalizing Saami culture. Without a Saami language, one can hardly talk about a Saami culture.

Reindeer herding project

The Saami Vocational Centre in Inari has started a reindeer herding project for the period 2002-2005, together with the Arctic Council and Northern Forum. The Centre is organizing courses for indigenous reindeer herders, veterinarians and butchers from Russia. The aim is to teach European standards for slaughter and improve the quality of reindeer meat.

Saami Parliament, Saami encyclopaedia

The number of employees of the Saami parliament has increased in recent years from 12 to 14 persons. The Parliament is working to get its own building, which would be a cultural centre for the Finnish Saami. There is some hope that the centre will be ready by 2007. The University of Helsinki is working on a Saami encyclopaedia, the first of its kind for the Saami population.

By way of conclusion

Every year, more and more laws are passed in Finland that mention the Saami. In the 1970s, five such laws existed, in the 1990s 30 and in 2002, 60. So developments are, generally speaking, a little better than in previous years. Yet there is still very much to do in order to improve the position of Saami culture, society and livelihoods. ❏

RUSSIA

The numerically small indigenous peoples of Russia were also faced with serious problems in 2002. The fight for land rights of the 40 peoples, numbering only about 200,000 individuals, continues to be extremely difficult, as federal legislation on territories of traditional land use is ignored by the authorities in the regions, where bureaucracy and endless discussions on how to apply for fishing and hunting quota prevent the indigenous peoples from leading their traditional way of life. The oil industry, the timber industry and the fishing industry represent a threat to the environment and indigenous peoples locally. Moreover, reports from the regions indicate that the indigenous peoples are actually dying out in some regions – and alcoholism, smoking, drug abuse, unemployment, suicide, tuberculosis, HIV, racial discrimination and harassment now constitute a threat

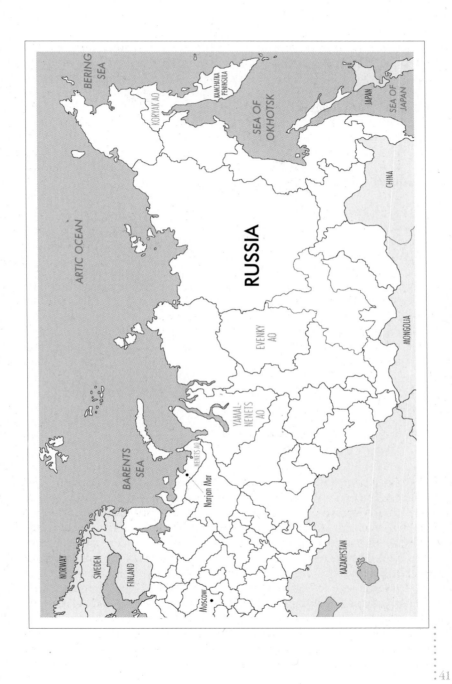

to the future existence of the peoples of the north, Siberia and the far east. It is, however, not easy to get a complete picture of the situation as Russian methods of gathering statistics vary from region to region. A long-awaited census of the total population of Russia took place in the autumn but it was carried out unprofessionally and the final results have only been partially published. However, the situation is undoubtedly very different from one region to another.

Federal legal developments

The Administration of the Russian President has established a Presidential Commission for the development of legal drafts, defining the sharing of responsibilities and power between the federal government, regional administration in the Russian provinces and local authorities. This Commission's task is to study the existing legislation of the Russian Federation and to develop relevant amendments and additions.

The Russian laws on the rights of indigenous peoples are on the list of laws subject to changes. To start with, the law 'On the guarantees of the rights of indigenous peoples of the Russian Federation' fell victim to the Commission's decision to withdraw all indigenous peoples' rights that the Commission deemed to be 'declarative', including the right to play a role in controlling the use of natural resources on indigenous territories, and rights to preferential and free access to traditional natural resources. Related laws on the use and protection of natural resources also ensure these indigenous rights. Hence, such laws are also subject to revision.

In November and December 2002, the Commission sent its proposals to the Government of the Russian Federation. The Government will submit all proposals to the Duma. Following the timetable suggested by the Government, this will take place in the last quarter of 2003.

The Russian Association of Indigenous Peoples of the North (RAIPON) has taken part in the process of legal revision since February 2002. Thanks to its firm position, the decisions of the Commission were reversed and basic indigenous rights were retained.

In November, RAIPON wrote a letter to the Russian Prime Minister, M.M. Kasyanov, asking him to include representatives of RAIPON in the working groups developing amendments and new laws.

The first session of the Governmental Council on problems of the northern and Arctic regions, took place in Salekhard, in late December 2002. RAIPON's President, Sergey Haruchi, presented the demands of the indigenous peoples, and M.M. Kasyanov, who was present, promised to undertake a comprehensive study of these demands.

At the same time, regional indigenous organizations used their rights to participate in environmental monitoring. For example, due to the strong stand of the indigenous organizations "Yamal to Descendants" (Yamal-Nenets Autonomous Okrug) and RAIPON, Gazprom agreed to carry out an ethnological assessment of its gas and oil prospecting in the area of the Obskaya and Tazovskaya bays.

The right to free use of natural resources has been deleted from the law 'On territories of traditional natural resource use of indigenous peoples of the north, Siberia and the far east' because the new Land Code of the Russian Federation envisages only the right to own and to rent land. As a result of this legal revision, federal and regional authorities have begun to reject demands by indigenous communities to establish territories of traditional land use and other demands to exercise their rights, on the grounds that corresponding legal norms on how to establish territories of traditional land use have not yet been developed, and that the laws on territories of traditional land use have to be revised. These refusals are illegal. A law is in force until it is repealed and government authorities must abide by these laws.

Regional issues

The Nenets

In the *Nenets Autonomous Okrug*, a province bordering on the Barents Sea in the European part of the Russian North, about 6,500 Nenets live as a minority among 50,000 inhabitants. The Nenets are represented by one member (out of eight) in the local Duma (parliament). The Nenets' indigenous organization, Yasavey, has the right to bring legislative initiatives.

The oil industry is expanding in this Okrug, drilling towers and pipelines characterize large parts of the landscape, and the industry's violations of environmental legislation lead only to symbolic fines. Yasavey is working on a legislative initiative that would increase the fines to a level that would make it profitable for the industry to respect environmental regulations. The movement has been able to monitor developments to a certain extent and report back on the situation both to the authorities and the industry directly. The industry, which consists of several different companies of varying sizes, is interested in a good relationship with the indigenous movement, as the public in general is skeptical about the costs of oil exploitation. A dialogue between the indigenous movement on the one hand, and the oil industry and local government on the other was formally established in 2001 and continued throughout 2002. Yasavey has gained more authority, establishing an independent office through project co-operation with Russian and foreign partners, a step that has made it possible for the movement to strengthen its position, both in relation to the industry and the authorities and in the eyes of the public.

The problems of the indigenous peoples in the region are manifold. Many of the smaller communities in the area are being closed or were abandoned as a result of the breakdown in the planned economy. A few indigenous representatives have since started working in family communities, going back to traditional subsistence methods as fishermen, hunters and reindeer herders. Others have successfully established workshops and other businesses related to their traditional way of life. Many more people, however, are not able to adapt to the new conditions and end up in the capital of Naryan-Mar as social losers.

The indigenous peoples have few possibilities for cultural development, although the Nenets, as one of the big peoples (totaling about 30,000 in Russia as a whole), should have a chance to preserve their language and culture. Attempts at a Nenets TV and radio have so far not succeeded but some theater and other performance activities do take place, even though on a very limited scale.

Still, the relatively stable social situation in the area – also characterizing the neighboring province Yamal-Nenets Autonomous Okrug – does mean that the total Nenets population is not declining: there even seems to be a small increase underway.

The peoples of Evenkia

Reports from the *Evenk Autonomous Okrug* in central Siberia give alarming figures reflecting a disastrous situation for the small peoples of the area. The indigenous population has fallen from 5,180 individuals in 1995 to 3,312 in 2002 according to official statistics (the total population being 18,029). The majority of the indigenous people are reported to live below the official poverty line and 60% are not involved in any kind of employment. Only 10% consider their own health situation as 'good'.

A general problem is the diminishing reindeer herds. In 1992, there were 20,000 reindeer whereas the number in 2002 was about 2,000. In

1992, the area had a production of about 3,000 silver foxes, now the figure is 117. The bad economic situation of the area also means that public institutions, transport etc., do not function as before. Even though the main community of the indigenous Ket, Sulomaj, which was washed away by floods in 2001, has been partly reconstructed, the Ket now number as few as 141 in the entire province. At a rough estimate, there are now less than ten people who know the Ket language.

As in the rest of Russia, the average life expectancy of the numerically small peoples is about 45-48 years for women and 41-42 for men, which is about 20 years less than for the Russian population in general. Tuberculosis is one of the main killers, along with other infections and alcohol-related deaths.

The indigenous peoples of Evenkia face great challenges in the competition with the oil and gas industry, which is dominated by one company, Yukos. Hunting and fishing quotas, distributed by the authorities, are insufficient for traditional use. The indigenous movement of the area is weak, although a minor improvement could be noted last year as the administration and even the Yukos Company have become more involved with the regional indigenous organization and have even provided it with some funding for its activities. Still, the risk of becoming dependent upon this funding should be taken seriously in the coming years. The indigenous peoples have no formal representation in the political system of the province.

Kamchatka

In the far east of Russia, the situation is particularly serious in the *Koryak Autonomous Okrug* on the northern part of the peninsula of Kamchatka. Although the province has an indigenous population of about 30%, the indigenous peoples have a dramatically high unemployment rate, tuberculosis is widespread and the first case of HIV was registered in 2002. At a conference held by the indigenous movement in the autumn it was decided, "to open a discussion at citizens' assemblies regarding the question of prohibiting the import and consumption of alcoholic beverages on the territories of traditional habitation of the indigenous numerically small peoples".

Public awareness actions regarding the problem of pollution in the settlements as a consequence of the lack of appropriate waste dumps have also been high on the agenda as an example of something the average person could be involved in to improve the health situation. In contrast, it still seems difficult for the indigenous peoples to prevent

Kamchatka from being exploited by the mining and fishing industry, and by poachers. The indigenous peoples are only formally involved in decision-making, with a few representatives on advisory bodies in which nothing is being done to efficiently address the problems of the peoples. A cause for slight optimism is the growing ability of the indigenous movement to use the press and work through international projects, although the involvement of indigenous peoples in big development projects in Kamchatka carried out by UNDP, IUCN, GEF and others has not so far been successful.

The rejection of a claim by the Council for the Revival of the Itelmen in Kamchatka resulted in a court appeal. The case of the territory of traditional land use surrounding the Itelmen community of Kovran – a model area that was formally established by the former governor of the Koryak Autonomous Okrug and then abolished by the next governor – went all through the court system of Russia in 2002. On 3 December 2002, the Moscow Presnensk Court refused to take up the case under federal legislation. This case was meant to be a model case for other regions of Russia where it has only been possible to get territories 'defined' at local level, not legally recognized and registered for the free use of the inhabiting people.

Looming crisis

The indigenous movement of Russia is perhaps moving towards a bigger crisis than many of its supporters realize. The opposition to acknowledging specific rights for the numerically small peoples is still strong, and the will to do something about their problems is still weak. Federal programs on numerically small indigenous peoples are not financed and implemented; legislation is being ignored by civil servants, the industry and the majority population. Part of the problem can be explained by the general crisis in Russia, old routines and ways of thinking. Although some stability has been gained in Russia over the last couple of years, the situation of indigenous peoples does not yet seem to have improved, and no matter how optimistic the progress of RAIPON's work makes one feel, there is still a long way to go and, for some of the peoples of the north – it is already too late. ❑

Sources

RAIPON's Web site: www.raipon.org
RAIPON's newsletter *Indigenous Peoples' World 'Living Arctic'*:
    www.raipon.net/yasavey/

ALASKA

Words may describe the land: tundra; forests; grasslands; glaciers; rivers, lakes and fjords; mountains and volcanoes - majesty everywhere - but words fail to communicate the different feelings one experiences by being in the land. The sense of the land itself, ancient and vast, is enthralling. Sixteen percent of the people living in this land are indigenous: Inuit (Yupik and Inupiaq, Aleut, Sugpiaq) communities are located on the coast or along major rivers, Athabascan communities in the interior, Tlingit, Haida and Tsimshian along the south-eastern coast. The population is growing slowly, somewhat faster among indigenous people in rural and remote villages. And with growth come issues. The rights of the peoples with respect to the land, and their right to determine their own future as a people are primary among these issues.

Scientists say indigenous peoples came to Alaska between 12,000 and 14,000 years ago. They used the land and governed themselves. Over the last 150 years, however, their rights to land and self-governance have been modified by events such as the purchase of the occupation rights to Alaska from Russia by the United States and Alaska's subsequent status as a territory and later (since 1959) as a state. These rights have been redefined several times in law, latest by the Alaska Native Claims Settlement Act (ANCSA 1971), which ceded 44 million acres (11% of Alaska's land mass) and US$ 962.5 million to Alaska Natives to settle their land claims (about three dollars per acre for lands lost). ANCSA also provided for the division of the state into twelve geographic regions and for the creation of regional Native corporations to administer the settlement in ways that provide for economic development and for the well-being of shareholders and their families. This is a living document that has been subject to continuing interpretation and amendment.

Economic development, but at a cost

Newly-elected Alaska governor Frank Murkowski (November 2002) has expressed a commitment to close the state's fiscal gap by means of projects that aggressively develop Alaska's natural resources in oil and gas, forests and fisheries, trade and tourism, and mineral extraction. The proposed development of the Donlin Creek gold mine is one example. This project, which intends to tap one of the largest undeveloped gold resources in the world, is located in western Alaska, far from any power source and without the infrastructure that would provide access to electricity or fuel in order to power the operation. It is estimated that the project will cost US$ 600 million but that the payoff will be calculated in hundreds of jobs and millions of dollars each year for thirty years or more for residents of the region. One approach to the power generation problem is to barge the 20 million gallons of diesel fuel needed annually up the Kuskokwim River to a plant that would be built near the mine site. Another is to locate the plant in Bethel, the regional hub, and transmit electricity over 150 miles of high-voltage power lines that would be built. This latter solution might bring the additional benefit of significantly lowering power costs for all regional residents.

The Donlin Creek mine could produce 1 million ounces of gold each year. At US$ 300 an ounce for thirty years, the resulting US$ 9 billion would be the most significant economic development in the history of the region. However, it would not be an unmitigated good. The impact of development—of barges on fish, of electric lines on wildlife, of new roads laid across land utilized for a subsistence-based lifestyle—will likely be as significant to the environment as to the economy. Economic development is desired as a means to a better life. But it is a necessity that those most impacted, in this case the Native people of the region, play central roles in determining the nature and character and extent of the development.

Wellness efforts from Alaska's indigenous leaders

The Alaska Federation of Natives (AFN) and its affiliated Native regional and tribal organizations are beginning to see 20 years of efforts to gain self-determination in their fight against alcoholism and drug abuse come to fruition. Through support from Alaska's Senator Ted Stevens, AFN will receive US$ 15 million a year for three years to begin finding grassroots solutions to the indigenous peoples' battle with alcohol. Concurrent with AFN's efforts, the Alaska Daily News profiled the plight in "A People in Peril," a Pulitzer Prize winning series published in the late 1980s. At an AFN convention, Native elders called for the leadership to begin looking into the consequences of rampant alcoholism and drug abuse in Native society. A Blue-Ribbon Committee was formed, which determined that there was a need to establish a Sobriety Council and a movement to begin combating alcoholism on a state-wide scale.

ALASKA

By 1994, the Alaska Natives Commission Report, prepared at US Congress' request, outlined the extent of the effects of alcoholism on Native peoples. The overarching principles outlined in the report focused on the self-reliance, self-determination and integrity of Native cultures. These principles assert the need to recognize indigenous cultures, customs and values, especially in the area of subsistence hunting and fishing as well as the need of Alaska Natives themselves to be self-reliant even though they have a special relationship with the Federal Government. It is self-determination, however, that governs the quality of that recognition and relationship.

The new approach to fighting alcoholism among Alaska's Native population is a paradigm shift in government thinking. Essentially, tribes working in concert with their regional Native non-profit organizations have, for the first time, framed the age-old problem for themselves and can now implement their own solutions. And the solutions are as varied as the villages themselves.

With AFN's leadership, community-based wellness models are beginning to emerge state-wide. Some village leaders are holding sobriety meetings, seminars and workshops. For many, it is the first time a community has come together to address the myriad of problems associated with alcohol and drug abuse such as bootlegging, illness and suicide, accidents and domestic violence, and enforce-ment of local option laws.[1]

Some communities are also returning to culture-based wellness models, long dormant within Alaska's indigenous societies. One such model is built around the traditional healer or traditional doctor and represents a reawakening of the positive aspects of the holistic prac-tice of healing not only the body but the mind and spirit as well.

Rita Blumenstein, doctor, healer

In June 2002, tribal doctor and traditional native healer Rita Blumen-stein was given the "Woman of Distinction" award by Soroptimists International of Cook Inlet (SICI). SICI is an international voluntary service organization of women in business, management and other professions, committed to advancing human rights and the status of women. This award is given to a woman who exhibits outstanding leadership and character in promoting the overall status of women on a global scale. Dr. Blumenstein speaks on behalf of women and people in general, passing on her knowledge of healing traditions and practices as well as cultural knowledge.

Blumenstein, a Yup'ik, was born in the south-western Alaska village of Tununak in the 1930s and was raised during a time when outside influences were causing great changes among the Yup'ik people. Native people were prohibited from practicing what was regarded as 'shamanism'. Raised by her mother and grandmother, Blumenstein lived a traditional subsistence lifestyle, living intima-tely with the land and learning the magical healing abilities of medicinal plants. It was not until the 1990s that her special gift of healing came to the attention of Southcentral Foundation, an Alaska Native healthcare organization. The process to certify Blumenstein as a Tribal Doctor and recognize her as a healer was a long drawn out one. However, the staff at Southcentral Foundation persisted and she was finally certified in 1999.

In addition to her work as a doctor, Blumenstein has spoken to many regional, state-wide, national and international gatherings. She shares her knowledge, experiences and talent with whoever needs it, but always reaffirming that her gift of healing comes through her from the power of the Creator.

Inuit Studies Conference

Self-determination and pride in cultural heritage was evident as indigenous peoples in Alaska and the University of Alaska Rural Development students and staff planned and hosted the 13th Inuit Studies Conference. In August 2000, an Alaska delegation, which included Rural Development graduate students and faculty members from the University of Alaska Fairbanks, attended the 12th Inuit Studies Conference in Aberdeen, Scotland. As a result of their participation, faculty and students were asked to host the 13th Inuit Studies Conference, which was held in Anchorage, Alaska in August 2002. Over 200 people from Alaska, Greenland, Russia, Japan, Europe and other states of the U.S. attended. The next Inuit Studies Conference is scheduled to be held in Calgary, Alberta, Canada in 2004. ❑

Note and sources

1   The local option laws regulate or prohibit the sale of alcohol.

Alaska Federation of Natives: www.nativefederation.org
Calista Corporation: www.calistacorp.com
Alaskool: www.alaskool.org

NUNAVUT

The territory of Nunavut covers 2.1 million square kilometers of Canada's Central and Eastern Arctic, and was created in 1999 as a result of a land claims agreement signed between the Inuit of the region and the State in 1993. The government of Nunavut (GN) is a public government, elected by, representing and delivering programs and services to all residents of the territory. All residents of Nunavut (Inuit and non-Inuit) vote for the Members of Nunavut's Legislative Assembly (MLAs). The rights and responsibilities accorded to the Inuit by the Nunavut Land Claims Agreement are managed by an Inuit representative organization called Nunavut Tunngavik Incorporated (NTI), whose leadership is elected solely by Inuit.

News from the Government of Nunavut

In 2002, the GN encountered its first major headaches. Coincidentally, both involved fossil fuels.

All fuel that enters the territory is purchased by the GN, shipped by boat to the various communities, stored in 'tank farms' and then resold to companies and individuals as the year progresses. The size of the territory and the small population (29,000) and economy result in the state playing a role that the private sector plays in most other jurisdictions. This can prove to be a very big problem when, as happened in 2002, it turns out that the gas the GN purchased was bad – it was missing some additives it was supposed to have, and it contained some things it should not have. This resulted in snowmobiles' engines becoming fouled, machines breaking down, hunters sometimes being stranded on the land and expensive repair bills for people who often could not afford them. The GN ended up paying out millions of dollars in compensation, seeking redress from the company it had purchased the fuel from, and instituting new fuel testing procedures. The good news, as the weekly newspaper *Nunatsiaq News* noted, was that, "Nunavut residents saw their government recognize a serious error and take responsibility for it.".

The second headache was political. After Jack Anawak's public criticism of the cabinet's decision (of which he was a member) to create the Qulliq Energy Corporation and locate its headquarters at Baker Lake, he was removed from cabinet by a vote of the MLAs. He had broken the principle of "cabinet solidarity", which requires cabinet members to support all decisions taken by the cabinet even if they do not personally agree with them. Anawak's response to being stripped of his cabinet portfolio was to state that the people of Nunavut had wanted a government that was "new" and "different" and that currently, that just was not the case.

Another expression of the frustration of the MLAs, which *Nunatsiaq News* calls "traditionalist" came when the government introduced a *Human Rights Act* that would bring Nunavut into line with federal legislation banning discrimination on the basis of ethnicity, gender, age, disability, religion or sexual orientation. MLA Enoki Irqittuq said that it would be "absolute unfathomable" for Nunavut to treat gays and lesbians the same as heterosexuals. "In the South, people are free to do as they wish. For Inuit, I would outright refuse such a provision in the Human Rights Act. It's not in our lifestyle." Gays and lesbians in Nunavut – both Inuit and non-Inuit – have so far kept a low profile, but Premier Okalik pointed out that the rights of gays and lesbians are already protected under federal law – so whether or not territorial legislation fully conforms with federal legislation, "It's just an issue for people that want to raise a fuss, that want to score cheap political points." It is, after all, an election year...

Other events of the year

Nunavut's first major piece of home-grown legislation, a revised *Education Act*, was rejected by the MLAs. They felt it failed to recognize the importance of strengthening Inuktitut as a language of instruction in the classroom and took powers away from elected community education authorities, giving them to the Department of Education. Education remains a huge issue in a jurisdiction where unemployment levels are high, where levels of formal education remain well below the national average, and where the median age is just 22.1 years (compared to 37.6 years for Canada as a whole). 60% of the population is under 25 years of age, and the population is growing at twice the national rate.

A proposed new *Wildlife Act* was received much more positively, especially its attempt to incorporate many guiding principles and concepts of *Inuit qaujimajatuqangut* (Inuit traditional knowledge).[1]

Federal Indian and Northern Affairs Minister Robert Nault said that Nunavut is "not ready" to handle a share of the royalties from non-renewable resource development or handle the administration of mining, and of oil and gas drillings. This comment drew sharp criticism from Premier Okalik, who heads a government that is deprived of both resource revenues and the ability to make decisions concerning resource development in the territory.

Premier Okalik joined the two other territorial Premiers (of Yukon Territory and Northwest Territories) in demanding increased funding from the federal government for the delivery of health care programs and services. The lobbying effort received considerable support from across the country, and Ottawa eventually came through with an additional C$60 million for the three territories.

The first 10-year funding period of the Implementation Contract for the Nunavut Land Claims Agreement (NLCA) ends in July 2003, and little agreement has been reached on the contract for the second 10-year period. The contract defines the amount that the federal government will give the territorial government, the Inuit representative organizations (such as NTI) and the institutions of public government (such as the Nunavut Wildlife Management Board) in order to meet their obligations under the NLCA. The Government of Nunavut and NTI are insisting that considerable amounts of money will be required if the territorial government is to achieve a "representative" (85%) level of Inuit employment at all levels of the bureaucracy as required by Article 23 of the NLCA. The level of Inuit employment in the GN was once as high as 45% but has now fallen to 40%. (Only a third of the employees in federal government offices in Nunavut are Inuit, while more than 85% of the employees of the municipal governments are Inuit.) The GN maintains that many of its other key goals, such as making Inuktitut the working language of government, can only be achieved if the government's work force truly reflects the population it serves.

While progress continues to be made in many ways, social and economic conditions in Nunavut remain well below those of Canada as a whole and the challenges facing the GN are enormous. Unemployment among Inuit remains high, health indicators reveal a population that is significantly less 'well' than the nation as a whole, social housing remains woefully inadequate, and there are serious deficiencies in municipal and transportation infrastructure. And while giving students in Nunavut a test in what, for many, is their second language may lower their scores somewhat, Nunavummiut were nonetheless startled when the national School Achievement Indicators Program revealed that only 8% of 13-year-olds in Nunavut met the national minimum skill levels in mathematics. ❏

Note

1 For more information, see www.nunavutwildlifeact.ca

NUNAVIK

N unavik is the northernmost region of the Quebec province of
Canada. Some 10,000 Inuit live in 14 coastal communities near
the Ungava Bay, the Hudson Strait and Hudson Bay. Even though
clearly living a modern life where wages do represent the majority of
monetary income, hunting, fishing and berry picking and the like are
customary activities that continue to contribute an important part of
the diet, and are a central focus of contemporary identity.

Persisting resource problems

Beluga whale hunting is one such activity, which was at the centre
of a profound disagreement throughout 2002. According to government officials, the Eastern Hudson Bay beluga population could dis-
appear within 15 years if hunters kill belugas at their current rate. As
a consequence, the federal government cut the 2002 beluga quotas to
15 whales per community, and banned beluga hunting in the Ungava
Bay and in the Eastern Hudson Bay areas. Disappointed hunters that
could no longer practice their activity were offered money to subsidize
additional travel costs incurred by the new harvesting rules and the
importation of beluga *muktuk* (skin fat of the whale – a delicacy) from
Nunavut, the neighbouring Canadian territory, has been contem-
plated.

An inventory of abandoned mining exploration sites was completed and published in 2002. Researchers who interviewed hunters
in all the villages discovered close to 600 sites in Nunavik where
mining exploration equipment, such as fuel drums, heavy machinery
and, in a few cases, toxic chemical compounds, had been left behind
by exploration companies between 1945 and 1978. Based on this
evidence, the regional government will now try to convince the central
provincial or federal governments to support a clean-up effort that
could last for years.

Social problems, political solutions?

Social issues have continued to be at the centre of many concerns. The
number of assaults is still growing, from 525 in 2000 to 723 in 2001.
According to the Kativik[1] Regional Police Forces, this rate is increas-

ing in line with drug and alcohol consumption. Moreover, a study revealed that 80 % of Nunavik adolescents smoke, and that 30% of adolescents begin smoking when they are less than 10 years old. This is especially alarming when it is considered that respiratory-related diseases are the main cause of hospitalisation in Nunavik, according to official statistics recorded in the Métrinord databank.[2]

Could a solution be found in the political arena? Some think that way, and efforts are still ongoing toward the creation of a truly autonomous government for Nunavik. Official discussions between the three parties are continuing and a breakthrough is expected sometime next year. In the meantime, Quebec province government and Nunavik representatives concluded a 360 million Canadian dollar deal that will last for the next 25 years. This agreement does cover a lot of issues within the existing political and administrative bodies and is expected to improve their economic situation, the regional capacity to take appropriate decisions and administrative efficiency.

The Inuit Circumpolar Conference General Assembly

Nunavik was at the heart of the Inuit world in August when the Ninth General Assembly of the Inuit Circumpolar Conference was hosted in Kuujjuak, the administrative capital of the region. The 2,000-inhabitant village was flooded by delegations from around the Arctic Circle. The conference ended with a resolution pressing the United Nations to ratify the draft Declaration on Indigenous Rights. ❑

Notes

1 Kativik is the name of the regional government of Nunavik.
2 Banque Métrinord is a statistical database on the social situation of northern populations.

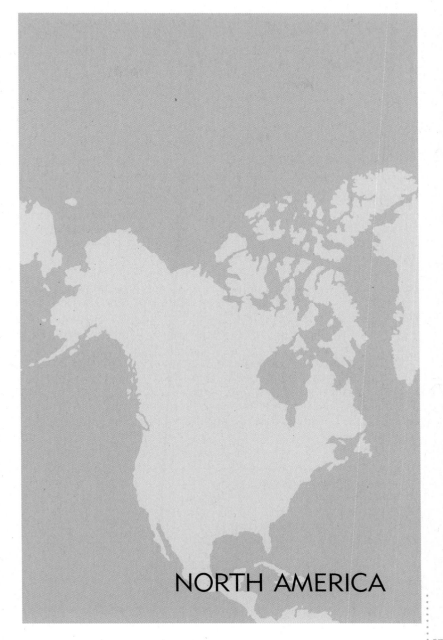

NORTH AMERICA

CANADA

I f it is, indeed, helpful to speak of a *Zeitgeist* (the spirit of a period, ed.n.) in trying to understand political currents, then the Zeitgeist of the present moment, at least here in North America, is characterized largely by xenophobia. This phenomenon is, of course, not at all new. Nor has it, historically, been more characteristic of North America than of Europe or of many other parts of the world.

Xenophobia and First Nations relations

In this article, I want to consider the significance of xenophobia in the shaping of *First Nations relations* in Canada and, particularly, its influence on Canadian federal Indian policy.[1] (I use the term "First Nations relations" to describe a set of relationships that deserve to be discussed in much the same way as Canadians talk about "federal-provincial relations" or "foreign relations." I use the term "Indian policy" to refer to policies handed down in ministerial statements and that have typically been devoid of elements of mutuality or dialogue.)

If xenophobia has always been a major factor underlying Canadian and American Indian policy, then what is the news value that justifies discussing it in this Yearbook? First, it points to the close relationship between First Nations relations as they are currently practiced, i.e., "Indian policy", and international relations or foreign policy. The passage by the U.S. House of Representatives in April 2002 of a bill to open the Arctic National Wildlife Refuge in Alaska to oil drilling cannot be separated from the general energy policy, and hence the foreign policy, of the Bush regime.[2] This refuge on the Arctic Ocean side of Alaska has special significance for the Dene communities of the Yukon, who depend upon the caribou herds that migrate through their lands every year shortly after they finish calving. Although there has been a great deal of talk expended about Canadian independence and American indignation when Canada did not join the attack on Iraq, there has been nothing said by the Canadian government in objection to the threat posed by George Bush to the survival of the Dene economy. There is no indication of a divergence of policy on this attack.

The FNGI hearings

The legislative package – the First Nations Governance Initiative (FNGI) – presented by Robert Nault, the Minister of Indian Affairs and Northern Development, was a suite of three bills: one about First Nations Governance, a second on land claims and a third on First Nations financial institutions (see *The Indigenous World 2001-2002*). Since the three bills were, by the Minister's own admission, part of a single comprehensive program, any serious legislative review would have studied them as package. Instead, the government chose, in the fall of 2002, to ensure that the bills were studied separately, often without any assurance that the same MPs would participate in either the hearings or the report writing on all three bills.

The First Nations Governance bill was sent to a Commons Committee shortly before Parliament adjourned for the summer in 2002. Since the bill was sent to committee before its second reading, i.e., approval in principle, the committee could have conducted wide ranging hearings and brought in a comprehensive report rather than a narrow, technical report aimed only at approving a bill already approved in principle by the House of Commons. Instead, the Committee Chair chose to postpone hearings until late in the fall, when the bill had been re-introduced at the start of a new parliamentary session.

Very hasty hearings at which First Nations had to demand to be heard were held on the other two bills, in the winter of 2002-2003, only after they had been approved in principle. When the Committee traveled across Canada holding hearings on the Governance Act, discussion of the two companion measures was not part of its mandate.

This conduct by the chair and the Liberal majority would have been appalling enough under any circumstances. Those of us whose own memory or historical studies make us familiar with the work of the Commons Indian Affairs Committee in the 1970s and early 80s, when Members of Parliament (MPs) sought to engage in a genuine dialogue with First Nations leaders and, during a study of First Nations self-government, had *ex officio* Members representing the Assembly of First Nations, the Native Council of Canada and the Native Women's Association join the Committee with all the rights of an MP other than voting.

The willingness of this present committee to abandon any effort at genuine dialogue and, instead, to become the willing handmaiden of the Minister reflects the rising tide of xenophobia that characterizes almost all facets of political thought in North America today. Questions from Liberal and Alliance MPs demonstrated the kind of ignorance that can be achieved only by careful cultivation. There was no more interest in the historical record of the committee's own predecessors than there was in the rich and complex political and legal systems of the First Nations.

Liberal MPs appeared determined to support the Minister regardless of what he set before them. Reform MPs continued their long-standing line about the Indian Act and, hence, the current legislation amending the Indian Act as "race-based legislation." (In fact, no First Nation's own citizenship laws have been "race-based." The Canadian *Indian Act*, like most colonial legislation, has long used racial criteria, always to the disadvantage of First Nations.)

This, however, may prove to be the government's undoing. One of the few grounds on which the appointed Senate becomes willing to interfere with legislation sent up to it from the House of Commons is if the other House has either failed to hear witnesses or failed to consider their testimony. Another key reason for Senate intervention is if a bill violates the fundamental rights of citizens. In this instance, it may also be possible to appeal to a recent report of a Senate Committee that strongly favored genuine self-government legislation drafted with the cooperation of First Nations.

As recently as three years ago, the Senate Committee on Aboriginal Peoples issued a study on implementing the Report of the Royal

Commission on Aboriginal Peoples called *Forging New Relationships*. In contrast, this Commons Committee, far from wanting to forge new relationships, gave all the signs of returning to the xenophobic attitudes characterising the *Act for the Gradual Civilization of the Indians*.

This attitude was further reflected in their decision to hold separate and very abbreviated hearings on the bills on land claims and financial institutions. When the Minister began his campaign, in 2001, he said that it was his job to create the ideal institutions for First Nations Governance. Now he has persuaded the Commons Committee to treat the First Nations' land base and First Nations' financial institutions (including powers and methods of taxation) *separate and apart from institutions of governance*.

Thirdly, it might have been at least a little bit more difficult to sell such a legislative package either to Parliament or to the Canadian public if the general North American political atmosphere were closer to the *Zeitgeist* of the early 1980s when the Commons Committee on First Nations Self-Government produced a report that was widely acclaimed for speaking about First Nations political issues in the same language that First Nations leaders spoke about their concerns. It is no coincidence that this legislative package was first introduced following the events of September 11 and reintroduced as the United States was gearing up for its attack on Iraq.

Increasing "homeland security"

A certain amount of "antipathy to foreigners" was perhaps to be expected following such an horrendous event. The decision to ride this wave of xenophobia by promoting a variety of measures pretending to increase "homeland security" is already well-known.

Less well–known, and much in need of discussion, are the variety of ways in which these measures and the attitudes that have made them possible have worked to throw First Nations relations back to the dark days when an Indian could be convicted of a criminal offense for exercising ordinary human rights.

Nault's threats to destabilize the elected leadership of First Nations that were unwilling to fall in line with his program took on new dimensions over the past year: First Nations communities in Ontario and Manitoba which had refused to follow departmental directions on non-financial matters were put under third-party receivership, a process intended only for communities verging on bankruptcy. M'chigeeng, an Anishnabek community on Manitoulin Island, for example, was put under third-party receivership when it adopted a traditional mode of government. The Minister, ostensibly attempting to implement a Supreme Court order, demanded that M'chigeeng have mail-in ballots for band members who live off-reserve.[3] Pikangikum First Nation, in North Western Ontario, won a court order setting aside Nault's dictatorial order because it violated fundamental rights of due process.

Some of the earliest video footage from American planes over Afghanistan carried the voices of pilots and crew members describing their new enemy territory as "Indian country", much as could be heard in similar footage from U.S. planes over Vietnam. Few of these successors to the U.S. Cavalry will know that "Indian Country" was the territory to which the "Five Civilized Tribes" were driven by Andrew Jackson's order in what is still known as "The Trail of Tears".

Even more bizarre was the photo in a Toronto newspaper of the crew members of a U.S. Tank Corps preparing for battle in Iraq by doing what they described as "a Seminole War Dance". Apart from any issue of authenticity, there appears to be a need both to appropriate the customs and rituals of those these warriors claim to have conquered and then, in each new battle, to re-enact an imagined proto-battle. Perhaps this is why the American media so strongly adopted the curious phrase they took from Saddam Hussein, in 1990, of "The Mother of all Battles".

This atmosphere has come to permeate First Nations relations in Canada in a number of ways. The hostility of the Alliance Party to Aboriginal and treaty rights is a part of the ideology that they have imported from the right wing of the U.S. Republican Party. It is unlikely that the present Liberal government would resist a move by the Bush administration to develop the Alaska North Slope at the expense the caribou herd on which the Dene in the northern Yukon depend. Historically, policies of assimilation and termination of Aboriginal and treaty rights in Canada have been adaptations of U.S. measures such as the 1887 *Indian Allotment Act*.

The media have sent all their most energetic reporters overseas. Any attempt to gain serious media for a First Nations issue has always been in danger of falling on deaf ears. Now it is most likely that nobody will answer the phone.

Anyone planning serious public demonstrations of the kind that have commonly been necessary to gain public attention for First Nations issues in Canada is likely to give very careful consideration to any such decision. The supposed anti-terrorist legislation will allow leaders of such demonstrations to be detained indefinitely without trial.

A significant number of First Nations people from Canada are serving in the U.S. military in Iraq. This has long been a route by which people who have a recognized right to cross the border into the United States have been able to solve the poverty issues arising from their loss of land and to meet a variety of other needs.

Doug Cuthand, a well-known Cree journalist from Saskatchewan, wrote a commentary about his compatriots who carried on a warrior tradition in this way. He lamented the American decision to enter the war but concluded, on balance, that regardless of one's political views, it was essential to support the troops because of the high rate of enlistment of First Nations people from both Canada and the U.S. It would appear disloyal to suggest that this analysis plays into the hands of the political movements that want to suspend all political discourse until the Axis of Evil has been conquered.

When Nault's train gets far enough down the track that we can all regain some perspective, it will become apparent that the First Nations are all still here. Nobody will have gone away. Neo-colonialism will have generated enough resistance to blunt many of its intended effects. Nault's ideal institutions will have done nothing to improve daily life in First Nations communities. Meanwhile, the more determined and dedicated First Nations people will continue to renew and re-create their own institutions of self-government. ❏

Notes and references

1   Some readers may be familiar with the 1969 "White Paper" introduced by Canada's present Prime Minister when he was the Minister of Indian Affairs. The formal title of that "White Paper" was Jean Chrétien, *Statement of the Government of Canada on Indian Policy*, 1969, Ottawa, Queen's Printer.
2   "Bill to open wildlife refuge for drilling", *Toronto Globe and Mail*, April 12, 2002.
3   Given the legendary level of reliability of the Canadian Post Office, nobody outside of the Indian Affairs Department would suggest that a mail-in ballot was a reasonable way in which to conduct an election in Canada.

THE UNITED STATES

A s in the past, numerous concerns face the Native peoples of the United States. With war looming, a sagging economy and local fears of terrorism, however, little federal policy has addressed issues facing Native Americans. Fortunately, a number of elected officials, in collaboration with Native leaders and various interests groups, have continued to strive for the rights of Native peoples. In order to illustrate the uphill battle faced by these individuals, this chapter addresses controversies surrounding sacred sites, the Bureau of Indian Affairs' oversight of Indian trust monies and sovereignty issues.

Sacred sites

Weatherman Draw, also known as the Valley of the Chiefs, contains numerous petroglyphs and is considered sacred to at least ten Native nations. Last year, the Bureau of Land Management, an agency under the Interior Department, leased the region to Anschutz Exploration Corporation. Philip E. Anschutz had been a major donor to the Bush campaign. Twelve days after President Bush's election, executive protection given to the site by outgoing President Clinton was overturned. The Sierra Club, National Trust Foundation and numerous Native communities fought the corporation's right to drill in the region. Local politicians from Montana also added their voices to the issue. Once Anschutz became aware of the significance of this region to Native peoples, the corporation donated their leases to the National Trust for Historic Preservation. In addition, the Bureau of Land Management promised not to issue new leases in the future.

This outcome will probably not occur in a number of other situations, however. An incredibly critical site, located at Indian Pass, California, is in imminent danger of being destroyed due to gold mining. After President Bush revoked Clinton's order protecting the site, Glamis Gold, a Canadian Mining Company was given permission to start open pit mining in the area. The region's dream trails are used by the Quechan community for visions and spiritual travel. Glamis gold intends to excavate an 88-story pit and use cyanide to remove gold from the rock. According to the company's prospectus, for every 280 tons of rock removed, Glamis will receive 10 ounces of gold. If Glamis prevails, then the site will be destroyed, disrupting the cosmological balance of the Quechan.

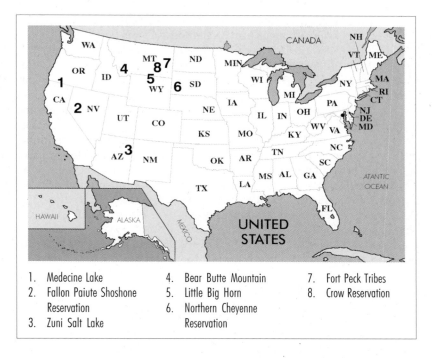

1. Medecine Lake
2. Fallon Paiute Shoshone Reservation
3. Zuni Salt Lake
4. Bear Butte Mountain
5. Little Big Horn
6. Northern Cheyenne Reservation
7. Fort Peck Tribes
8. Crow Reservation

Another endangered sacred place involves Salt Lake, located approximately 60 miles south of Zuni Pueblo in New Mexico. During the summer months, the Zuni, Navajo, Acoma and Laguna harvest salt from the lake's shoreline. Salt taken from the shores symbolizes the flesh of Salt Woman. Her gift provides blessings, medicine and nourishment to the indigenous peoples of the region. Pilgrimage paths to the area are considered sacred trails that are protected by shrines. In addition, these roads lead to numerous other sacred sites.

Salt River Project, the United State's third largest public utility, wants to strip mine at Fence Lake, 10 miles from the Zuni Salt Lake. In order to engage in this project, 85 gallons of water a minute will be pumped from the lake to settle coal dust. It will be operated for 40 years. Native peoples fear the pumping will take water from the spring that feeds Salt Lake. A federally sponsored study of the underground water systems, which is still incomplete, states that this pumping will not adversely affect Salt Lake. A number of non-profit water specialists claim, however, that the underground aquifers are linked, and that pumping by the Salt River Project will drain the shallow Salt Lake. Besides the potential damage to Salt Lake, there is the imminent destruction of numerous important sites near Fence Lake. So far, over 550 burial and archeological sites have been located in the region. The Zuni, Navajo, Acoma and Laguna had managed to convince President Clinton to protect the region. Unfortunately, after Bush's inauguration, the Salt River Project received a permit to begin mining.

Medicine Lake, located in the volcanic areas east of Mount Shasta, California is also in imminent danger of destruction. Water from the lake is used for healing and training spiritual leaders belonging to the Modoc Nation as well as leaders from other communities in northeast California. President Clinton had protected the region. Upon Bush's election, however, the Bureau of Land Management and the Forest Service granted the Calpine Corporation the right to develop a $120 million, 48-megawatt geothermal power plant to drill wells one acre from the lake.

Bear Butte Mountain on the border with South Dakota and Wyoming is another sacred place in imminent danger. Private investors have bought land four miles from the place in order to open a vast shooting range and sports complex. Representatives from the Cheyenne, Lakota, Arapaho, Kiowa, Crow, Mandan, Hidatsa and Arikira are attempting to block the development of the project. According to their view, Bear Butte is holy and critical for visions and other religious activities. The land has never witnessed violent behavior except for when soldiers from the United States cavalry entered the area. According to these Native Nations, the noise of the guns at the fire range will disturb the land's sacredness. Because town leaders from Strugis, South Dakota are fighting for the development of this project, it will be difficult for Native peoples to block construction.

A number of national leaders have been involved in assisting Native peoples' efforts to protect sacred sites. Congressmen Nick Rahall and Dale Kildee, both Democrats, are attempting to strengthen President Clinton's 1997 Executive Order mandating consultation with tribes prior to development of sacred areas. In addition, they are trying to add teeth to Clinton's Executive Order that federal projects may not negatively impact on sacred lands. The passage of this legislation currently looks unlikely. Federal agencies are advocating self-sufficiency in terms of energy sources. Prime drilling areas have been identified in regions considered sacred to Native peoples.

Unfortunately, it has been difficult to protect indigenous sites. It is estimated that 75% of tribal sacred land is unavailable to Native peoples. This is due to the fact that 90 million acres were taken from Native peoples between 1887 and 1934. Most the land base that was lost entered into private, state or federal hands. During the current political climate, sacred sites will remain in danger of being destroyed. It is estimated that at least 10% of untapped energy sources are on Indian lands.

Indian Trust Accounts

In 1996, Eloise Cobell and four other Native peoples filed a class action suit against the United States Department of the Interior. The Department of the Interior oversees trust lands for indigenous peoples in the United States. This relationship dates from the 1887 allotment act, when nearly 11 million acres were placed in federal trust. The Bureau of Indian Affairs, a sub-agency of the Department of the Interior, leases Native lands for the extraction of resources. Native owners of these lands were to receive income on the leasing of their property for oil development, mineral extraction, timber and grazing. As Cobell and other Native peoples learned, however, the government did not keep accurate records of monies owed to the landowners. Accounts dating back to the 1800s have been misplaced, never filed or destroyed. Receipts from 1906 to 1990 are stored in 120 different locations. Some are written on napkins or other scraps of paper. The United States Congress wants to place a cap on the accounting cost of finding all this missing information. Consequently, they only want to apportion 500 million dollars to the project and limit its search to between 1985 and 2000. Native peoples, on the other hand, want a full accounting of all trust monies determined. It is estimated that they are owed at least 10 billion in back payments.

Because of the stonewalling of federal officials in the face of this lawsuit, nearly 40 former or current senior managers, attorneys and employees, along with the Department of the Interior, Bureau of Indian Affairs, Solicitor's Office and Department of Justice are under contempt. In addition, two Secretary of Interiors and two Assistant Secretaries of Indian Affairs, as well as the Secretary of Treasury, are facing contempt charges. The case will more than likely be capped at 500 million dollars and only date back to 1985.

State issues

Senator Tom Daschle of South Dakota has established a panel of reconciliation with Native peoples of the region. In the past, the state's legislature has passed laws considered racist by many Native peoples. Most recently, the legislature outlawed hanging items from the rearview mirrors of cars. Many Native peoples dangle dream catchers, feathers and other items of power from their rearview mirrors as protection. In addition, the state legislature instituted the use of county numbers on car license plates. According to Native peoples, this identifies them as members of a reservation community, which in turn leads to police harassment. Senator Daschle is hoping to defuse some of the problems through his reconciliation panel.

On June 25, 2003, the 127th anniversary of Little Big Horn, Native peoples are dedicating a memorial to those soldiers who fought Custer. Currently there is a memorial to Custer and numerous headstones to the fallen soldiers. This new monument will commemorate the Lakota, Cheyenne and Arapaho warriors.

Over 100 Native firefighters from the Fort Peck Tribes, Northern Cheyenne Reservation and the Crow Reservation have been involved in the search for pieces of the shuttle that crashed in East Texas. Local law enforcement officials, as well as NASA, have frequently noted their contributions.

Tribal sovereignty

In the past, each federally recognized tribe maintained an internal court system for a wide array of situations. Various federal laws - the list continually grows - are under the jurisdiction of federal agencies, however. Recently, a situation at the Fallon Paiute-Shoshone reservation has suggested a further erosion of tribal law. In this case, state officials entered tribal lands to execute a search warrant against a tribal member. When the case went to the Supreme Court, the court ruled that federal law, "neither prescribes nor suggests that state officers cannot enter a reservation to investigate or prosecute such violations." Native peoples interpret this ruling to mean that tribes have no legal rights unless granted by the federal government. ❏

MEXICO,
CENTRAL AMERICA AND
THE CIRCUMCARIBBEAN

MEXICO

T he position of the indigenous peoples in Mexico experienced a backwards slide over the last year. The Supreme Court of Justice of the Nation judged the constitutional disputes presented on 14 August 2001 as inadmissible. Chiapas became immersed in a "low intensity conflict", in which indigenous communities suffered harassment at the hands of the army and paramilitary forces virtually on a daily basis. To this must be added the events that took place in Zacatecas and Oaxaca, caused by agrarian conflicts, and in Guerrero, where the indigenous peoples of the Montaña, Costa Chica and Central regions of the state have had to confront security forces and the Mexican army.

Constitutional disputes

As will be recalled, between July and October 2001, municipalities in the states of Oaxaca, Chiapas, Guerrero, Morelos, Veracruz, Michoacán, Jalisco, Puebla, Tabasco, Hidalgo and Tlaxcala submitted 330 constitutional disputes against reforms of articles 1, 2, 4, 18 and 115 of the federal Constitution – known as the *Ley Indígena* (see *The Indigenous World 2001-2002*). On 6 September 2002, the Supreme Court of Justice of the Nation declared inadmissible 322 of the 330 constitutional disputes presented against the congressional procedure to approve constitutional reforms to indigenous rights and culture, published on 14 August 2001. This highest court decided by a majority of eight votes to three to declare itself incompetent to consider these demands. Subsequently, indigenous and human rights organisations, intellectuals, federal and state authorities etc., declared themselves opposed to the Supreme Court's resolution.

Agrarian conflict in Zacatecas and Durango

On 21 February 2002, around 350 Tepehuano community members from Durango, armed with machetes and - allegedly - guns, removed more than 200 *ejido*[1] members from the Zacatecas communities of Pajaritos and Bernalejo de la Sierra, and made as if to forcibly remove another 180 inhabitants. The indigenous Tepehuano were demanding the provision of 5,465 has of forest that had been disputed for 40 years in the border area between Zacatecas and Durango.

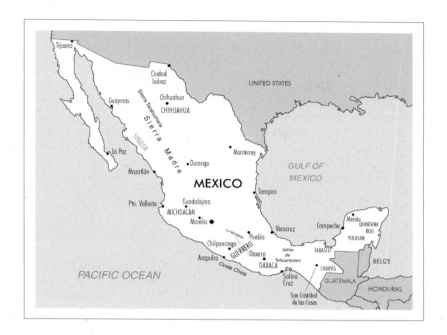

A number of previous points must be recalled. Firstly that, by Presidential Resolution of 19 August 1936, an area of 421,139 had been returned to the Santa María Ocotán community, the owner of paramount titles protecting their territory.[2] Implementation of this decision was only partly carried out up to 20 September 1975, "by virtue of the judicial protection granted to individuals; through material impossibility, and because 5,465 has were allocated to the Bernalejo *ejido*."[3]

In 1956, by means of a Presidential Resolution, an area of 5,465 has had been granted to Bernalejo as a land allocation.[4] It was after this that the Zacateca farmers began to exercise their rights over the lands which, in the end, became the focus of a dispute. These lands were disputed for many years, until President Zedillo decreed their expropriation in June 1997 from the Bernalejo *ejido*, in return for a sum of 4,645,250 pesos compensation, in favour of the community of Santa María Ocotán and Xoconostle, municipality of Mezquital, Durango.[5] The *ejido* did not agree with the decision and, on 19 February 2003, the Unitary Agrarian Court (TUA) of district 1 declared the expropriation decree null and void.

Following the occupation of February 2002, further tense days arrived, exactly one year on, in February and March 2003. Resisting the TUA's decision, the indigenous surrounded the Zacatecas communities of Bernalejo and Pajaritos, annexed to the Bernalejo *ejido*. This incursion of approximately 2,000 indigenous Tepehuano to forcibly evict 260 *ejido* members who were settled on the lands at dispute was supported by indigenous Huichol from Jalisco. Some days later, due to the siege imposed on them by the indigenous Tepehuano, around 200 people, including at least 30 minors, left the Pajaritos settlement heading for the municipal centre of Valparaíso, Zacateca.

Then the situation intensified with the arrival of around 500 members of the Preventive Federal Police, 200 soldiers and 100 members of the state police. To prevent the passage of the *ejido* members,[6] the Tepehuano again blocked the entry road to Pajaritos for 12 days, until, with no further setbacks, elements of the Preventive Federal Police entered the settlement.

Finally, the Bernalejo *ejido* members decided to sell their lands for 52 million pesos, but the problem is that the lands are not certified, in addition to the fact that, at the moment, they have no *ejido* committee, as the previous one ended its term of office last year and no elections have been called to appoint a new one.

Massacre in Agua Fría, Oaxaca

One of the bloodiest events of the year for indigenous communities was the Agua Fría massacre in Oaxaca.

Land has been one of - if not the - main trigger of many of the conflicts that have occurred within indigenous populations. In the case of Oaxaca, there are 656 agrarian conflicts, 96% of which are over boundaries. Of the boundary conflicts, 370 (57%) involve indigenous communities and the remaining 286 non-indigenous communities. Of the indigenous communities with conflicts, 130 are among the Zapoteco people, 92 Mixteco, 49 Chinanteco, 39 Mixe and 30 Chatino, there being less than 12 conflicts among the Mazateco, Cuicateco, Huave and Náhuatl. The total number of hectares involved is 400,500.[7]

This strong agrarian factor was one of the causes of the massacre on 31 May 2002, in which 26 indigenous Zapoteco were murdered in an ambush on the inhabitants of Santiago Xochiltepec, a mountain community south of the city of Oaxaca, allegedly by members of the Las Huertas community (part of the municipality of Santo Domingo Teojomulco). The authorities hypothesise that the causes of the massacre were inter-community conflicts, problems with tree felling, drugs trafficking or border conflicts. Some people suggest the motive may have been "personal revenge", and even that the ambush could have been "a mere robbery".[8]

The victims were travelling in a dump truck when they were intercepted by a group of armed men. They forced the driver to get out of the van. Immediately, the rest were killed by bursts of high power gunfire, leaving the bodies in the van. The driver was then ordered to remove the bodies from the van, leaving them piled up, and they were immediately stripped of their possessions. The driver, Antonio Pérez López, was unhurt, and two people survived the massacre, one of whom later died. Following these events, the police arrived in Santo Domingo Teojomulco to arrest people from the community but, in the action, committed excesses such as searching houses without producing a warrant.

The governor of Oaxaca, José Murat, blamed the massacre on the marginalisation in which the indigenous communities live, while the Ministers for the Environment and for Agrarian Reform each gave their own reasons: the first stated that the problem was a dispute over 4,622 has of land and the second that the violence broke out over the issuing of a permit for logging to the Santa María Zaniza community.[9] Both soon attempted to deny any responsibility. The State Attorney-General arrested 17 people allegedly responsible for the Agua Fría massacre, 15 of whom were taken to the Santa María Ixcotel state prison and two, being minors, placed at the disposal of the Guardianship Council and later freed. Paramilitary group involvement in the massacre cannot be ruled out, as noted by indigenous and human rights organisations. Towards the end of May 2003, the third Collegiate Court of the thirteenth circuit, cancelled the arrest warrants for three inhabitants of Santo Domingo Teojomulco accused of being responsible for the murders, and issued arrest warrants for another seven people allegedly involved in the massacre.

In its report on the case, the National Commission for Human Rights states that the events "were due to issues related to border conflicts between communities, revolving around old resentments concerning violent acts between both communities, in the face of the impunity created by the lack of clarification of crimes committed, within the context of constitutional resolutions and trials recently resolved that led to a heightened climate of tension; additionally, forest exploitation of the natural resources in territories or areas in dispute strained the atmosphere in the zone, aspects which [...] even led to groups made up of alliances between communities in conflict."[10]

Chiapas: the violence continues

In Chiapas 2002 began with the visit of Cardinal Roger Etchegaray – President Emeritus of the Pontifical Councils of Justice and Peace, and the Pope's Emissary – who stated that "the problem in Chiapas is a real one, a serious one, and also a symbolic one, in the sense that these social problems are to be found in all areas of Mexico. That is, problems of poverty, respect for the dignity of man, every man." He also said that the "nervous peace" in Chiapas was of concern to the Pope. This "nervous peace" was more "nervous" than he thought, as the military presence in Chiapas during 2002 had consequences for the indigenous populations. Various newspaper articles demonstrated that the army was one of the indigenous peoples' main aggressors. There were patrols, overflights in areas of Zapatista support and autonomous municipalities, arbitrary detentions[11] and interrogations, the persistence of police posts, armed manoeuvres, troop and arms mobilisations within the territory, the offering of sweets and money to children to provide reports on the EZLN, harassment of women, the continuation of "social works", etc.

The areas in Chiapas where military presence is noted are also at the forefront of the autonomous municipalities, including: "El Trabajo", "17 de Noviembre", and "Primero de Enero",[12] in addition to established municipalities such as Palenque, Tila, Polo, Francisco Gómez, Jolnixtié, Huitiupán, Sabanilla, Benemérito de las Américas, Marqués de Comillas and Ocosingo.

The paramilitary groups operating in Chiapas have been involved in various ways: harassment of human rights defenders, kidnappings, death threats, community aggression, evictions, illegal detentions and, most serious of all, murders, most of which go unpunished, although last year members of the "Peace and Justice" paramilitary group were arrested.[13]

At the time of writing this article, the situation in Montes Azules, Chiapas is tense. There is the possibility of eviction of communities settled on those lands. The army presence continues in Chiapas and the capture of alleged members of paramilitary groups has not put a stop to the harassment of the communities. In addition to this, the underlying problems of fighting poverty and achieving justice have not been resolved.[14]

The situation in Guerrero

Faced with the inefficiency, corruption and discrimination of the state's justice system, a project of the Regional Coordinating Body of Community Authorities of Costa-Montaña (*Coordinadora Regional de*

Autoridades Comunitarias de la Costa-Montaña), known popularly as Community Police, has taken a *de facto* decision to form its own system of law and justice administration. This decision has elicited a violent reaction from the state authorities, which have fabricated crimes against the communal authorities, such as an abuse of authority, usurping of responsibilities and illegal deprivation of liberty, in order to arrest and prosecute them.

In February 2002, at the *Palacio de Gobierno* (the seat of state government), and in the presence of the military authorities and the Solicitor-General of the Republic, the state security department warned the indigenous authorities in threatening tones that if they continued with their Public Security project then the full force of the state would be implemented against them in order to disarm the Community Police, arrest the chiefs of police and dismantle their autonomous movement.

The response of the indigenous peoples was overwhelming: in a huge march to the administrative centre of San Luis Acatlán, in which more than 4,000 people participated, the Mixteco and Tlapaneco peoples, with the support of social and civil organisations, reaffirmed their decision – before state and society – to consolidate and extend their system of indigenous law and justice administration.

Two distressing events that caused outrage among the people of Guerrero were the cases of rapes committed by members of the Mexican army against two Tlapaneco women from the communities of Barranca Bejuco, municipality of Acatepec, and Barranca Tecuani, municipality of Ayutla. These despicable acts were reported to the civil authorities but, in an attempt to cover up for those authorities responsible, they have declared them to be outside their sphere of competence, and have handed both cases over to the Office of Military Justice (*Procuraduría de Justicia Militar*), thus leaving the two Tlapaneco women, who are suffering derision and persecution, defenceless. These cases have demonstrated a clear subordination of civil authority to military authority.

One reality that has marked the indigenous peoples is their condition of migrant agricultural day labourers. In Montaña, Central region and Costa Chica, 60% of male heads of household go to work in the Sinaloa fields in degrading conditions. Gradually, they have begun to organise in the fields of the country's north, demanding medical care and better wages. In March 2002, around 200 indigenous people went to the *Palacio de Gobierno*, in Culiacán, the capital of Sinaloa state, to demand an audience with the government and to request recognition of their agricultural day labourers' union. The authorities' response was to call upon the anti-riot squad to violently evict them, beating up and arresting their leaders. The Guerrero state government at no time made any statement against this discriminatory and abusive treatment: the state's Secretary for Indigenous Affairs showed neither the will nor the capacity to defend, either legally or politically, those indigenous migrants who were the victims of state repression.

At a community assembly in the administrative centre of Xochistlahuaca, situated in Costa Chica, the Amuzgo suggested electing their own municipal authorities in accordance with Amuzgo traditional law. Their bitter history of tyranny, violence, misery and discrimination has gradually created a movement of organised resistance and struggle to take on the responsibility of community government in place of the caciques, the political parties and the State Electoral Council. So the chiefs (the elders) of the Amuzgo people appointed their traditional authorities and, since 1 December, the indigenous authorities have been occupying the municipal buildings in Xochistlahuaca in order to revitalise their own path as an indigenous people. Beyond recognition and a subsidy from the state authorities, what the Amuzgo want is respect for their decisions and their self-determination. ❑

Notes and references

1   Ejido – in Mexico, a communal or cooperative-run farm – trans. note.
2   *Diario Oficial de la Federación*, organ of the Constitutional Government of the United States of Mexico,   22 September 1936, p. 6.
3   Minister for Agrarian Reform, Press Release SRA/006, 22 February 2003.
4   *Diario Oficial de la Federación*, 9 April 1956.
5   *Diario Oficial de la Federación*, 25 June 1997, p. 73.
6   Information based on newspaper reports taken from *La Jornada*, *Reforma* and *Imagen* in Zacatecas.
7   National Indigenist Institute, *La problemática de los Pueblos Indígenas en el Estado de Oaxaca*, México, 11 June 2002.
8   Sergio Santibáñez, Attorney-General for the State of Oaxaca, was the person who maintained this. See *La Jornada*, 2 June 2002.
9   See *La Jornada*, 4 June 2002.
10 National Commission for Human Rights, *Informe Especial: Caso Agua Fría*, Mexico, 2002.
11 See Fray Bartolomé de las Casas Human Rights Centre. "Detenciones arbitrarias, práctica recurrente en Chiapas". Press Release, 5 November 2002.

12 The other autonomous municipalities are "Ernesto Che Guevara", "Miguel Hidalgo", "Lucio Cabañas", "Vicente Guerrero", "17 de Noviembre", "Olga Isabel", "Ricardo Flores Magón", "San Juan de La Libertad", "San Manuel", "San Pedro de Michoacán", "Tierra y Libertad" (south of the Lacandon rainforest), and "Francisco Gómez."

13 For more information: www.laneta.apc.org/cdhbcasas/

14 This section of the country report is part of a research on violence in indigenous communities under the responsibility of Dr. Rudolfo Stavenhagen, Colegio de México. I am grateful to Alvaro Bello for his comments.

GUATEMALA 2002

The trend towards a low public profile continued throughout the year, both in terms of the Maya Movement and ethnic issues as a whole. This was due to a number of factors: the slowdown in the FRG (*Frente Republicano Guatemalteco*/Guatemalan Republican Front[1]) government's commitment to the peace process, a lack of interest in and insensitivity towards anything associated with the country's multicultural makeup on the part of Guatemala's non-indigenous society, and a lack of coordination between the different expressions of organised indigenous people, still expectant and dedicated to reflection. Violence and impunity persist.

The political environment continues to be characterised by ungovernability and government corruption, which is increasingly leading to political and social polarisation. The erosion of the figure of the President and the party has meant that, despite being halfway through the legislative term, positions have already begun to be taken in relation to the general elections planned for the end of 2003. A great deal of effort has been expended in the race for places and votes within the political world, increasing the atmosphere of tension and violence. While lynching of and uprisings against municipal officials have continued, the violence has been showing increasingly clear signs of political warning. A large number of events were clearly "signed", demonstrating the intention to maintain the pressure on certain political players. This atmosphere has influenced the behaviour of the organised sectors, including the indigenous, and reports from organisations such as MINUGUA and Amnesty International have repeatedly denounced this climate.

A protest that began halfway through the year gives a good illustration of this atmosphere. The notorious Civil Self Defence Patrols (*Patrullas de Autodefensa Civil* – PAC) were created during the period of heaviest state violence as a military strategy to involve the peasant farming population – mostly indigenous – in the counter-insurgency. One of the most emphasised points of the Peace Accords was precisely that this militarisation of the civilian population should be brought to an end, but none of this whole parallel power system has yet been dismantled. This was seen when, from June onwards, they began to demonstrate – sometimes violently – demanding economic compensation of some US$2,500 each for "services rendered" during the armed conflict. In contrast with the passivity shown to peasant and indigenous demands, the government immediately agreed to find the necessary funds to provide them with some compensation which, whilst not amounting to the above figure, would require money that the government did not and still does not have. The reorganisation and public appearance of these militarily-controlled structures shows the power of mobilisation of FRG members, as was demonstrated in January 2003, when a mass meeting of ex-patrol members was organised in support of President Portillo.

The actions of these parallel powers have directly affected the more organised elements of the indigenous population, through a series of outrages, threats and assassinations. In February, the Nebaj community centre was burned down; in July, Guillermo Ovalle, from the Fundación Rigoberta Menchú was murdered. And in December, various murders took place of members of the Maya political movement: Diego Velasco Brito, a well-known ex-deputy of the Christian Democracy party (*Democracia Cristiana*) in the department of Quiché and three Mayan priests in Baja Verapaz, Huehuetenango and El Quiché. But it was the kidnapping and subsequent death in Cobán of Antonio Pop Caal that had the most impact. He was a recognised forerunner of Mayan thought. One of his finest and most critical articles, written in 1974, was published in *Utopía y Revolución* (Utopia and Revolution), the classic book in which Guillermo Bonfil Batalla gathered together indigenous voices from throughout America, and he was the husband of another important activist, Dominga Tecún.

In spite of this oppressive environment, certain indigenous initiatives for action and demands can be identified. The first is the efforts of various Maya to gain a foothold in the state and party political system. There has been no lack of public figures in government bodies, trying to develop programmes and policies for the indigenous population. Another is the resumption of the discussion on and various

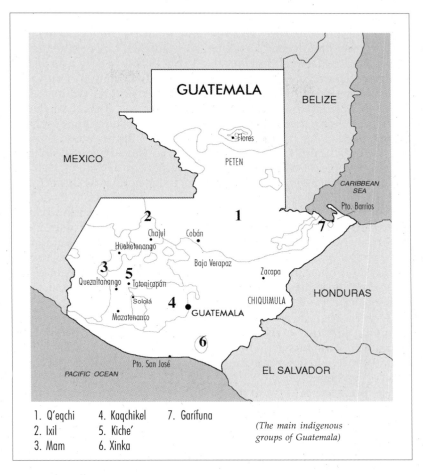

1. Q'eqchi 4. Kaqchikel 7. Garífuna
2. Ixil 5. Kiche'
3. Mam 6. Xinka

(The main indigenous groups of Guatemala)

complaints of racism and discrimination, which have led to certain reactions on the part of the indigenous movement and even the state. Lastly, the development, more autonomous and less well-known, of the population at local and regional levels must be noted, which is expressed in very different and often contradictory ways.

Mayan action in the state

Since the failure of the 1999 referendum and the end of unified expression through COPMAGUA (*Coordinadora de Organizaciones del Pueblo*

Maya de Guatemala – the Coordinating Body of Maya Organisations in Guatemala) in 2000, the Maya movement has not managed to come up with any half decent coordination strategies. It was thus unable to respond collectively when an oil concession in Lago de Izabal threatened the area's ecology and the living environment of the Q'eqchi communities of the region, leaving other sectors and bodies to form an opposition. In addition, the spaces for coordination and discussion that began to form in 2001 have not moved beyond isolated efforts, such as the presentation of a "Maya Political Agenda" on 30 May by the Committee for the Decade of the Maya People (*Comité del Decenio del Pueblo Maya*); or the submission of a "Bill of Law on Indigenous Nationalities" by the National Indigenous and Peasant Coordinating Body (*Coordinadora Nacional Indígena y Campesina* – CONIC) on 21 November. There were some sectoral events of note that formed important spaces for discussion, such as the 3rd Meeting of the Latin American Network of Legal Anthropology (*Red Latinoamericana de Antropología Jurídica*), which took place in Quetzaltenango in August and, again in that same month, the 3rd National Congress of Maya Education, organised by the National Council of Maya Education (*Consejo Nacional de Educación Maya –CNEM*) in Huehuetenango.

A desire to participate in state bodies and define public policy is becoming an increasingly generalised trend. The aim is to promote an equitable coexistence with the rest of society but this has also led to acquiescence when participating in government, in state bodies or in "power" in general.

The presence of Maya in the government apparatus has thus continued and expanded. Perhaps the most significant is the continuing presence of the Vice-Minister for Education, Dr. Demetrio Cojtí, and his team of Maya professionals in the General Directorate for Bilingual Education (*Dirección General de Educación Bilingüe* – DIGEBI), involved in implementing educational reform policies; and that of the Minister of Culture, Ms. Otilia Lux, together with her two Maya Vice-Ministers. Over the course of the year, the presence of the K'iche' José Us was added to this list, first as Vice-Minister for the Environment and subsequently as Vice-Minister for Agriculture.

One example of how demanding this participation is for the Maya, and the heavy political costs it entails in relation to the very population they want to represent, is given by the case of the Q'eqchi' Raymundo Caz. He is one of the most experienced and charismatic leaders and, in March, he was appointed judge of the Supreme Electoral Court, a key political post in this pre-election period. He worked arduously in the renewal of mass sponsorship programmes, the formation of polling stations and the registration of candidates. All this seems to have been viewed as an obstacle to the followers of General Ríos Montt, who – despite the unconstitutionality this presents – are seeking to present him as a presidential candidate and, unexpectedly, in October, Caz handed in his resignation, apparently because he had received strong pressure and threats against himself and his family. He subsequently withdrew his resignation after being offered substantial support from his colleagues in the Supreme Electoral Court. The political parties form the other privileged space for participation, and the proximity of the elections has meant that moves have begun, both on the part of organisations and of individual leaders, to form alliances with parties that have a possibility of winning seats. The alternative of creating their own Maya representation does not yet appear to have taken shape. The most successful path has been demonstrated by the experience of the *Xel-ju'* civic committee in the Quetzaltenango municipal government. The mayor, Rigoberto Quemé, a person who enjoys wide support from the Maya and other political and social sectors, has encouraged promotion of his presidential candidacy through a small political party: the Social Action Centre (*Centro de Acción Social –CASA*), via which he is ready to enter into negotiations with other parties.

The debate on racism and some institutional progress

In June, something took place that led to a whole chain of events around the problem of discrimination: an elegant bar banned the academic, Irma Alicia Velásquez, from entering because she was dressed in her traditional Maya clothes. The company was forced to apologise to Ms Velásquez, who refused to accept their apology, causing a public debate on structural racism in Guatemala, until then a taboo issue. As a consequence, a National Committee against Racism was formed, made up of a number of important figures, both indigenous and non-indigenous.

In September, following the visit of the UN Special Rapporteur on Indigenous Rights, Rodolfo Stavenhagen, the Law against Discrimination and Racism was urgently and unanimously approved, criticised by the Maya because they were not consulted and because it did not specify the ethnic issue with sufficient strength. At the end of the month, the first session of the Racism and Discrimination Court took place publicly, at which various acts of racism were denounced, and whose officiants included Rigoberta Menchú and Arturo Willemsem.

This initiative enjoyed the presence of Maya from almost all tendencies (with the exception of those closest to the former revolutionary Left), along with many non-indigenous, achieving a consensus that had not been seen in years. With his customary opportunism, President Portillo created a Presidential Committee against Discrimination and Racism against Indigenous Peoples, which some leaders who questioned the Law approved in September have joined.

In addition, the government has continually produced new initiatives that are supposedly favourable to the indigenous population, such as the Municipal Code and the Law on Development Councils, which should encourage decentralisation and forms of local organisation. But, as the French analyst Hugo Cayzac notes, the discourse and rhetoric of multicultural recognition may be employed but there is a reluctance to make this concrete in the actual content of specific policies and regulations. The situation of state bankruptcy and the persistent lack of political will regarding the ethnic problem means that these and other bodies, initiatives and programmes – such as the Academy of Mayan Languages, the Indigenous Fund or the Indigenous Women's Ombudsman – remain deprived of development possibilities.

Other paths

The peasant farmer organisations have continued along their own path and within their own logic, outside - although close to - the Maya movement. As Guatemala falls into deep economic crisis due to the drop in coffee prices, with the massive unemployment of thousands of day labourers and the consequent situation of famine in the countryside, peasant farmer organisations have continued to draw attention to the situation, occupying estates, holding marches and proposing measures. In the National Coordinating Body of Peasant Farmer Organisations (*Coordinadora Nacional de Organizaciones Campesinas – CNOC*), the peasant farmers have publicly taken to considering the consequences of the Plan Puebla-Panamá, becoming involved in international networks and themselves raising the indigenous flag where necessary.

In this context of uncertainty, some groups of Maya youths and/or women are taking the opportunity to follow their own path, finding out about their own identities and demonstrating their skills in creating a rapprochement with other non-Maya social sectors. It seems that the sign of the times, with growing urbanisation, migratory dispersion and relative access to education, is an indigenous presence in spheres hitherto unknown to them due to ideology and the practice

of exclusion. This is something that may enable unforeseen indigenous expressions and demands to develop.   ❑

Note

1   The FRG is a nationalist, populist and authoritarian party led by General
    Ríos Montt, the "protagonist" of the genocide/ethnocide of the early
    1980s. Throughout the period of this government, since 2000, it has
    presided over Congress.

NICARAGUA

The regional process of autonomy

A majority of indigenous and multi-ethnic populations continue
to advocate the approval of regulations governing the Statute of
Autonomy of the Autonomous Regions of the Atlantic Coast of Nicaragua as a key factor in establishing and consolidating a relationship
of coexistence and real integration between Nicaragua's Caribbean
and Pacific coasts. Other sectors linked to the leadership of one faction
of the indigenous party, Yapti Tasba Masraka Nanih Asla Taranka
(YATAMA), are demanding a reform of the Law on Autonomy. In turn,
the Council of Elders of Indigenous Peoples (*Consejo de Ancianos de los
Pueblos Indígenas*) represents a more radical position on the part of
sectors of indigenous Miskito who support, as an extreme measure, the
secession of the indigenous territories as the most viable solution to the
constant abandonment experienced by Nicaragua's Caribbean Coast
since 1894. This Council is of the opinion that the current Statute of
Autonomy has represented a step backwards on the part of the indigenous and ethnic peoples and it is therefore in favour of a total reform
or, in its place, the promulgation of a new Law on Autonomy.[1]

Some political analysts believe that strong business interests are
putting pressure on National Assembly deputies to block the approval of regulations governing the Statute of Autonomy. According
to this interpretation, the regulations are being delayed in order to
prevent the regional authorities from gaining greater influence over

decisions on natural resource exploitation, given the clear interest of central government and national and foreign businessmen to maintain their control over the management and exploitation of all natural resources of the Nicaraguan Caribbean Coast.

Regional elections of March 2002

As reported in *The Indigenous World 2001-2002*, a great indifference and frustration was observed among the indigenous and multi-ethnic population from the very start of the electoral campaign. The situation became even worse when a long and heated debate took place between the Supreme Electoral Court (CSE) and the main organisations participating in the elections in the North Atlantic Autonomous Region (*Región Autónoma Atlántico Norte* - RAAN).

The fourth regional elections, held on 2 March 2002, were branded as the most disorganised and controversial of the country's Caribbean Coast, due to the injustices, partialities and ineptitudes of the CSE. Subsequently, the crisis within the CSE grew when the four Liberal judges came into conflict with the three Sandinista ones over the swearing in of those elected and the election of the regional government coordinators and the Governing Board of the respective autonomous regional councils.

The growing disinterest in regional elections is illustrated by the following abstention figures: 1990, 22%; 1994: 26%; 1998: 58%; and 2002: 63%. It should be noted, however, that abstention rates are significantly higher among the *mestizo* population than among the ethnic Miskito, Sumu-mayangna, Rama and Garífunay Creole (Afro-Caribbean) minorities. It is clear that the minority ethnic groups identify on a significantly greater level with the process of autonomy.[2]

With an eye to the future, the Institute for Development and Democracy (*Instituto para el Desarrollo y la Democracia* - IPADE), the Centre for the Human Rights of Citizens and Autonomies (*Centro de Derechos Humanos de los Ciudadanos y Autonómicos* - CEDEHCA) and other similar organisations are agreed that it would be useful to hold municipal elections at the same time as regional ones, to avoid people wearying of having to vote year after year. These organisations believe that one of the main causes of abstention in the regional elections of March 2002 was the successive elections of the last three years (municipal (November 2000), presidential and legislative (November 2001) and regional elections (March 2002).

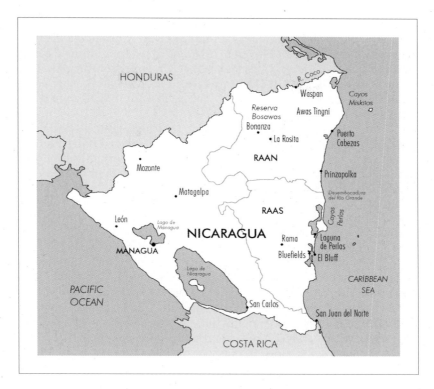

Regional authorities and political power

On 4 May 2002, the date the new regional authorities in the Nicaraguan Caribbean were to be sworn in, there was a volatile national political environment, in which the following two elements could be noted: a) the anti-corruption campaign of Enrique Bolaños Geyer, new President of the Republic since January 2002, directed particularly at Dr. Arnoldo Alemán Lacayo, President of the Republic from January 1997 to January 2002 and, at that moment, President of the National Assembly; and b) a repressed struggle between these two same people for control of the Constitutionalist Liberal Party (*Partido Liberal Constitucionalista* - PLC), the dominant party in the Liberal Alliance that was victorious in the presidential elections of November 2001.

Within this excitable political context, although the PLC gained a greater number of votes in the regional elections, supporters of Dr. Alemán were under pressure in both autonomous regions. Thus, for example, although they have 21 councillors in the RAAN, the Liberals lost their hegemony in the region, being displaced by an alliance made up of the Sandinista National Liberation Front (*Frente Sandinista de Liberación Nacional* - FSLN), YATAMA and the Multi-ethnic Coastal Party (*Partido Multiétnico Costeño* - PAMUC), which jointly gained 27 council seats. As a result of this alliance, YATAMA took over Coordination of the Regional Government, whilst the FSLN gained the Presidency of the Regional Council.

In the middle of dramatic episodes that highlighted once more how the political conflicts of the Pacific are displaced onto the Caribbean, the struggle between the PLC judges (supporters of ex-President Alemán) and the FSLN judges affected the legitimacy of the regional bodies. In the case of the RAAN, the crisis created by attitudes of - and contradictions between - the electoral court judges lasted from 4 May to 24 June 2002, when defence of the application of the Law on Autonomy was victoriously imposed.

The situation in the RAAS was marked by greater conflict throughout the whole year. As of February 2003, the situation in this autonomous region had still not been satisfactorily resolved. In this case, the Liberal majority of the faction supporting Dr. Alemán, was displaced by an alliance made up of the FSLN, YATAMA and the "ethnic group", made up of dissident Liberals. However, this alliance has not been able to consolidate itself, with instability and recurrent spurious elections occurring within the Regional Council throughout the first year of its legislature.

Indigenous and ethnic human rights

With the aim of extending its geographic coverage in the face of the persistent and systematic violation of the most basic human rights of the Nicaraguan Caribbean Coast's population, the Human Rights Ombudsman (*Procuraduría para la Defensa de los Derechos Humanos* - PDDH) has, since March 2002, had offices in the RAAN and the RAAS. With a paltry state budget for the autonomous regions of approximately US$40,000, this public institution is becoming embroiled in a difficult context in which delays in justice, insecurity of citizens, domestic violence and land conflicts between indigenous communities and settler farmers, landowners and international consortia who have taken over large areas claimed as communal lands prevail.

The other event that had a high impact on human rights during the period in question was the fact that a group of lawyers and indigenous Miskito ex-combatants were preparing a multi-million lawsuit against the national state. The main cause of this proposed action is the 1982 forced displacement, caused by the Sandinista government, of more than 8,500 indigenous Miskito living along the banks of the Río Coco, who were relocated to the Tasba Pri settlements while around 4,000 were moved to various settlements in Jinotega department. Another 15,000 Miskito chose to flee to Honduras, forming the greatest indigenous exodus from Nicaragua of the 20th century. The Organisation of American States (OAS) is awaiting this possible lawsuit against the Nicaraguan government.

Land conflicts

In addition to the various important conflicts that have arisen in previous years, and which are still the subject of legal dispute, in November 2002 a new land conflict occurred, this time in the RAAN, and which has acquired media fame. The Sumu-mayangna community of Wasakin and Mr. Kemal Jerab Benn, originally from Tunisia but of Nicaraguan nationality, are involved in the conflict. The Wasakin community is denouncing the misappropriation of 4,250 hectares of communal lands in the municipality of Rosita, while the person in question argues that he holds five agrarian titles received from people who sold the 4,250 hectares of land, in addition to having a public land deed registered in the Public Property Register of Bluefields.

Members of the community's Council of Elders have communicated their decision to resort to arms to remove Mr Jerab if the national and regional authorities do not resolve this conflict. Given the Awas Tingni precedent, they are also considering the possibility of submitting their case to the Inter-American Commission on Human Rights (IACHR).

Awas Tingni: Nicaraguan government fails to comply

Faced with the Nicaraguan government's delay in implementing the Inter-American Court of Human Right's decision, the Sumu-mayangna community of Awas Tingni submitted a complaint for violation of constitutional rights to the Bilwi Appeals Court in Puerto Cabezas in December 2002, in order to force central government to comply fully with the IACHR's decision. In these legal proceedings, the community alleged that the period established for fulfilment of the decision (15 months) had already passed and that the government had not only not finished defining, demarcating and titling the communal lands of Awas Tingni but had not yet even undertaken the required studies that form the first stage in this process.

In the middle of February 2003, and with funding from the World Bank through the Property Regularisation Project (PRODEP), the Nicaraguan government was considering bids from two consultancy firms to undertake an assessment of the use and tenure of land in Awas Tingni.

Indigenous communities of the centre and north of Nicaragua

The Regional Forum of Indigenous Peoples of the North of Nicaragua (*Foro Regional de los Pueblos Indígenas del Norte de Nicaragua*) was held in 2002 with the involvement of the governing boards of the communities of Mozonte, San Lucas and Cusmapa, located in Las Segovias. The aim of this event was to strengthen alliances and achieve a consensus around proposed solutions to their problems, and to publicise the progress achieved in institutional strengthening, self-management and sustainable production. Representatives from PRODEP, the UN Population Fund and NGOs ActionAid and the Institute for Human Promotion all attended. Through this action, the communities were able to highlight once more their high level of organisation in comparison with others of the centre and north of the country, and even in comparison with some from the Pacific.

Also worthy of mention are the continuous demonstrations on the part of the indigenous community of Jinotega, which is protesting against a possible privatisation of the state electricity company and the Apanás reservoir, the main source of water for hydro-electrical energy generation in Nicaragua.

Process of legalisation of indigenous communal lands

In September 2002, following numerous negotiations on the part of those involved, President Bolaños included a draft law on the legalisation of communal lands as one of the priority laws to be considered by the National Assembly.

With a bill of law that had been on ice for more than four years, and in a situation in which the FSLN deputies and supporters of President Bolaños had already approved half a dozen laws during the first half of December 2002, the indigenous peoples and ethnic communities of the Caribbean celebrated the historic approval of Law No. 445, "The Law on the System of Communal Property of the Indigenous Peoples and Ethnic Communities of the Atlantic Coast of Nica-

Photo: Diana Vinding, 2002

ragua, and of the rivers Bocay, Coco, Indio and Maíz" on 13 December 2002. It entered into force on 23 January 2003. The Law was approved by only 48 deputies: 38 votes from the FSLN, 8 from the *Azul y Blanco* group (supporters of President Bolaños), and two votes from the PLC.

This Law, which merits a chapter apart, determines the context of action and procedures for the defining, demarcation and titling of communal lands, in addition to establishing a number of guidelines on the exploitation of renewable natural resources. To protect communal property, the Law obliges the regional authorities to review the property titles in the hands of nationals and foreigners who obtained their properties after 1987. In this respect, article 35 of the new Law literally states that, "the property rights and historic occupation of the indigenous and ethnic communities will prevail over titles issued in favour of third parties who never owned them and who, from 1987 onwards, claimed to occupy them".

Law No. 445 may not have a notable effect in the short to medium term on the resolution of the autonomous regions' structural problems, such as economic backwardness, high levels of unemployment, extreme poverty, etc. However, the Law will have positive effects in terms of resolving other problems of indigenous peoples and ethnic communities, such as the misappropriation of communal indigenous lands, citizen insecurity, the irrational exploitation of natural resources, the predatory advance of the agricultural frontier and the invasion of protected areas. The general expectation is that the Law will greatly contribute to a fuller exercise of the right to the use and enjoyment of communal lands, waters and forests, as established in the Political Constitution of Nicaragua and the Statute of Autonomy. ❑

Notes and references

1 The point of view of the Council of Elders of Indigenous Peoples can be found in a document entitled "*Preceptos y Normas Supremas de la Nación Comunitaria Moskitia*", approved during the Tenth General Assembly of the Indigenous Nations and Ethnic Communities and the Second Moskitia Convention held in Bilwi on 25 October 2001.

2 **Chávez, Harry. 2002.** "La participación electoral en la Costa Caribe" in *Wani,* No. 29, April-June 2002: 28-37.

Mattern, Jochen. 2003 "Las Regiones Autónomas: Un Desafío para el Proceso de Descentralización en Nicaragua" in *Wani,* No. 32, January-March 2003:19-35.

La Gaceta, Diario Oficial, No. 16, 23 January 2003.

La Prensa, 3 March, 7 May, 10 June, 19 November and 7 December 2002

Nuevo Diario, 31 January 2003

COSTA RICA

A s part of the 9th National Census of the Population, which was held in June 2000, the National Institute for Statistics and Census (*Instituto Nacional de Estadística y Censos* - INEC) took specific actions to obtain statistical information on the country's indigenous population. This resulted in valuable information about the indigenous territories.

Precise clarification of the number of indigenous people living in Costa Rica was obtained. According to data from the census, there are 63,876 indigenous people, distributed as follows:

Province	Total population	Indigenous population	Percentage indigenous
San José	1,245,750	9,220	0.7
Alajuela	716,286	3,469	0.5
Cartago	432,395	4,261	1.0
Heredia	254,732	2,213	0.9
Guanacaste	264,238	4,663	1.8
Puntarenas	357,483	15,034	4.2
Limón	339,295	25,016	7.4
Total Costa Rica	3,810,179	63,876	1.7

According to INEC, only 27,032 (42.31%) of these live in their respective territories. 31% live in areas around the territories and the remaining 27% live scattered throughout the rest of the country, mainly in the capital.

This data is a substantial increase on previous figures (39,264), which is a positive sign. However, the fact that only 27,032 live within their territories means that the Costa Rican state is going to reduce considerably its contributions in terms of infrastructure, education and the like. Such a reduction will be sorely felt, particularly given that state contributions are already derisory.

Relations State - indigenous peoples

The indigenous peoples – as has been the case for decades – lack a state body to coordinate joint lines of action for the public sector in terms of managing and technically directing.

The National Commission for Indigenous Affairs (*Comisión Nacional de Asuntos Indígenas* - CONAI) - a governmental organisation - has not fulfilled its role in terms of coordinating programme strategies and defending the interests of indigenous communities. Its governing board has not changed for more than 10 years and, by exploiting various legal mechanisms, they have managed to develop and transform CONAI into a political and powerful body, creating divisions between the indigenous populations and curbing their development.

National Indigenous Development Plan

For several years now, the indigenous communities have been formulating their own National Indigenous Development Plan, which sets out general guidelines as to who, how, where and when development programmes will be implemented in native communities.

Perhaps inspired by direct negotiations with the government, it was hoped that the broad outlines of their proposal would be supported without having to be included within national governmental plans. Unfortunately, this was not to be the case, and the indigenous organisations and leaders have not actively participated in the inclusion of their proposals into the governmental development plan. This effectively means they have had no involvement in these initiatives whatsoever.

With a few exceptions the communities were unaware of this situation, for they are either not generally informed promptly or they are unaware of the participation mechanisms. In spite of this exclusion, of little interest to the upper echelons of the Ministry of Planning (MIDEPLAN), many mid-level technicians have shown concern and are making great efforts to ensure that, at the last moment, indigenous proposals are taken into account in the planning for 2004.

Boruca Hydroelectric Project

In the south of Costa Rica, in the Buenos Aires canton, important actions are being taken for the potential construction of the Boruca Hydroelectric Project (PHB), a large-scale dam (250 square kilometres) that would flood the indigenous territory of Rey Curré (Brunca) and indirectly affect the territories of China Kicha and Ujarrás (Cabécar), Salitre and Cabagra (Bribri), Térraba (Teribe), Coto Brus (Guaymí) and Boruca (Brunca).

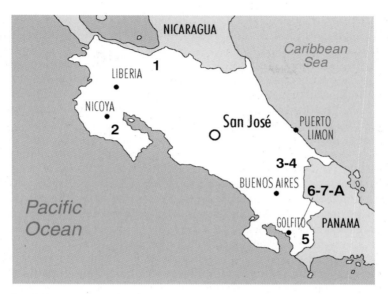

1. Huétar	3. Bri-bri	5. Guaymí	7. Brunca
2. Maleku	4. Cabécar	6. Teribe	A. Proyecto Hidroeléctrico Boruca

(Approx. locations of the indigenous peoples of Costa Rica)

Murals in Rey Curré. Photo: Diana Vinding

This mammoth venture is being promoted by the Costa Rican Electricity Institute (*Instituto Costarricense de Electricidad* - ICE), a state body that is still talking of "potential construction" even though this is now at the feasibility stage.

Although clearly nothing can be done until the environmental impact study is complete, indigenous representatives and various environmental organisations consider this to be a mere formality as the project has the backing of the country's two largest political groups, which alternate in power. Moreover, the project is part of other similar regional initiatives included in the Plan Puebla Panamá.

The population of Rey Curré is leading the fight against PHB construction. However, they have achieved little in their three years of confrontation. Perhaps the most significant achievement is that they have maintained direct dialogue with senior figures from the PHB's executive management. Measuring this dialogue by verifiable results or concrete actions, however, is impossible because they quite simply do not exist.

As a community, Rey Curré has made great efforts to endure this dialogue process, given the huge technical and economic differences between themselves and the ICE. The mere fact of attending a meeting means paying out money for transport, food and accommodation, funds the indigenous people just do not have.

Considering that this is a process of dialogue, and there are great difficulties in continuing it, we can but imagine the colossal task of a negotiation process, all the more so if they were to take the initiative of direct confrontation to prevent the project.

Transfer of territories

During conversations with the ICE, the Association for the Development of the Indigenous Territory of Rey Curré (*Asociación de Desarrollo del Territorio Indígena de Rey Curré*) realised that one of its weaknesses was that it was not the legal owner of its territory.

In 1977, Indigenous Law 6172 was promulgated, article 9 of which states, "Lands belonging to the Institute of Lands and Colonisation (Instituto de Tierras y Colonización - ITCO), included in the demarcation of Indigenous Reserves and the Boruca y Térraba Reserves must be handed over by this institution to the indigenous communities." In spite of this, twenty-four years after being instructed by law, the Institute for Agrarian Development (*Instituto de Desarrollo Agrario* - IDA) (successor to the ITCO) has not ceded property titles to the indigenous communities for lands belonging to them.

They therefore presented an appeal for legal protection to the Constitutional Court of the Supreme Court of Justice, which passed judgement in favour of the indigenous in September 2002, requiring that the IDA "immediately initiate the necessary steps to undertake the required topographical data gathering to transfer (via registry) the lands belonging to the Boruca and Térraba Reserves to the corresponding indigenous communities. These plans must be concluded no later than six months following notification of this decision."

Given that more than six months have now passed without this decision being fulfilled, various indigenous organisations are exerting pressure for its immediate application. This includes the Costa Rican Ombudsman (*Defensoría de los Habitantes*), who supports the indigenous demands. The transfer of their territories would give the inhabitants of Boruca, Térraba and Rey Curré a valuable weapon with which to face up to the "potential construction of the Boruca Hydroelectric Project."

Indigenous organisations

The current situation of indigenous organisations can be analysed from two different perspectives.

One, quite negative, refers to the effects of large-scale funding. The well-intentioned contributions of many international cooperation agencies are finite and, when they come to an end, the enormous overheads of the huge and monstrous structures they have created cannot be supported. This has weakened the way in which regional and national level indigenous bodies are run.

Dependency has created devastating effects on these organisations. This predictable situation, frequently discussed with the organisations was, however, approached with a lack of planning and future vision on the part of the indigenous leaders who, at the time, did not appreciate the need to commence a transition during times of economic boom. Some of the organisations are now trying to make this transition towards business systems that will make them self-sufficient but, lacking in economic resources, this is very difficult.

The second perspective, far more positive, refers to the collaboration of a number of cooperation agencies (few, admittedly) that channel their economic funding directly to the different grassroots organisations and through them. Thus we have such bodies as the Small Projects Fund (*Programa de Pequeñas Donaciones*) of the United Nations Development Programme (UNDP), which funds almost a dozen projects to the total tune of around US$200,000. Similarly, the Canadian

Fund for Local Initiatives invests its economic resources in local organisations, in contrast to the traditional norms of external cooperation whereby funding tends to go to supporting large multi-million
projects with few visible and verifiable results.

Indigenous women

Women's organisations from different indigenous cultures are working hard on agricultural, handicraft and marketing projects, and are
heavily involved in indigenous demands, for example, heading actions
against the potential construction of the Boruca Hydro-electric project.

Although within their organisations women fight fierce power
struggles, it is interesting and important to recognise the degree of
organisational progress that has been achieved. This enables them to
participate on a certain level of equality with indigenous men in
community development, contributing their ideas in the search for
solutions to the problems afflicting them.

It should be clarified that these women's initiatives are undertaken
within the indigenous communities. Unfortunately, the women do
not have a working mechanism at regional level, far less at national
level. This fragmentation of efforts is exploited by some organisations
that have access to information on international initiatives in order to
claim representation of Costa Rican indigenous women within different fora, congresses, workshops or meetings around the world.

However, with knowledge of the facts, we can affirm that in Costa
Rica there is no single *representative* organisation or organisation
facilitating the development of indigenous women. For this reason, we
hope that in the short to medium term, Costa Rican indigenous women will be able to take on and assume wider initiatives.   ❏

PANAMA

The indigenous peoples of Panama have generally made more
progress in gaining their rights and territories than other indigenous peoples in Central America, progress that has been more obvious in terms of legal issues. There are currently five legally constituted

comarcas or Indigenous Territories representing a little over 10% of the national population and which are located in the provinces of Chiriquí, Bocas del Toro, Veraguas, Darién and in Kuna Yala (see map). Of these, the largest in numerical terms is that of the Ngöbe.

Bills of law to legalise two new territories are currently being discussed by the Indigenous Affairs Committee of the Panamanian Legislative Assembly: the Naso Teribe Comarca (also known as Naso Tjër Di) on the Costa Rican border and the territory of the *Tierras Colectivas* or 'Collective Lands' (which would legalise the communities that the 1983 law left out of the Emberá-Wounaan Comarca).

There are proposed laws, not yet presented but which exist in draft form, for the creation of the Kuna de Takarkunyala Comarca (in Darién province, on the border with Colombia) and the Bri-Bri Comarca on the border with Costa Rica. Both of these fall within the boundaries of protected areas, that of Bri-Bri within La Amistad International Park (PILA) crossing Panama and Costa Rica, and that of Takarkunyala in the Darién National Park. This therefore warrants greater discussion and negotiation with the national government, although the indigenous people were there long before the creation of these parks.

The Law on the *Tierras Colectivas*

In 2002, this law led to a great deal of discussion among the non-indigenous population of Darién province, particularly settlers who have emigrated from other parts of the country and Colombians who have become naturalised or who have fled the continuing war in their country.

The case of the *Tierras Colectivas* relates to approximately 50 Emberá and Wounaan communities that were left out of the comarca in 1983 because the demarcation did not manage to include them. 99% of these communities currently hold no property title because their access to land is family-based and they live collectively in groups of 10 to 15 families. According to the Ngöbe lawyer, José Mendoza, advisor in the office of Indigenist Policy of the Ministry of Government and Justice, "This led to the lands being defined under the special comarca system, whereby private property title is secondary. In other words, the concept of the comarca is one of collective property, and this forms part of the State structure."

Given this situation, one of the people that opposes the creation of the *Tierras Colectivas* is the National Deputy (Honourable Legislator in Panama) Haydé Milanés de Lay, and this is because, "The Emberá-Wounaan Comarca and that of the Wargandí (Kuna) were created behind the backs of the governors and the non-indigenous people of Darién, (...) This situation came about by creating comarcas without consultation." According to her, the Emberá-Wounaan population holds a "world record for square kilometres of land ownership per inhabitant. In addition to this, out of what they left us in Darién, they now want tierras colectivas (collective lands), after having created a comarca without any consultation."

In Panama, it is well-known that this deputy has always been opposed to indigenous demands, in spite of the fact that she gained office through the votes of the indigenous peoples of Darién. In addition to this, given that this province has the greatest areas of virgin forest in the whole country, a great deal of interest has been shown by timber dealers and traders, who see the indigenous presence in the area as an obstacle. For this reason, they are trying to exert influence at all levels of national government to prevent the indigenous from gaining another comarca.

However, indigenous resistance and lobbying have meant that the majority of the Panamanian population is in favour of creating these *Tierras Colectivas*, and so legalisation of these lands will very soon be a fact because the other national deputies will vote positively in the Legislative Assembly to approve it.

Proposal for the creation of the Naso Teribe Comarca

Not so long ago, little was known about the Naso people, also known as the "Teribe", due to their location on the river Teribe. Many studies of indigenous issues have come to the conclusion that this is one of the continent's few indigenous peoples to be governed by a monarchy, in which the supreme ruler is the "King".

The territory currently inhabited by the Naso people forms part of their historic territory, which extends from the river Teribe basin, Changuinola, Sixaola to the islands of Bocas del Toro. It is a territory of great biological diversity and natural beauty, which means that it is constantly under threat from landowners, traders and tour operators along the border with Costa Rica. These threats affect both the Naso people and their territory as well as the PILA protected areas in the Atlantic sector.

Current law establishes a legal framework for establishment of the comarca, within the territory that has been occupied by the Naso people since before the European conquest and which is fundamental to recognition of their rights, with the aim of achieving their economic, cultural, social and political development in accordance with the Political Constitution and agreements adopted by the Panamanian

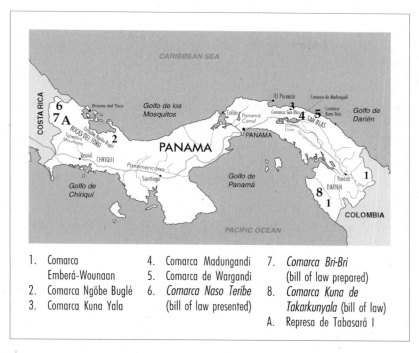

1.	Comarca Emberá-Wounaan	4.	Comarca Madungandi	7.	*Comarca Bri-Bri* (bill of law prepared)
2.	Comarca Ngöbe Buglé	5.	Comarca de Wargandi	8.	*Comarca Kuna de Takarkunyala* (bill of law)
3.	Comarca Kuna Yala	6.	*Comarca Naso Teribe* (bill of law presented)	A.	Represa de Tabasará I

state. Everything indicates that, for the moment, the legal creation of this indigenous territory will raise no significant obstacles.

New dams in indigenous areas

The construction of two new dams in the western part of Panama, particularly within the Ngöbe-Buglé territory, will affect the peasant farmer and indigenous communities of the provinces of Veraguas and Chiriquí. In recent years, there have been national level demonstrations (see *The Indigenous World 2001-2002*) but there was a setback this year when the Supreme Court of Justice ruled in favour of the Tabasará Consortium for the construction of a hydro-electric power station in the area.

According to one of the legal advisors to the affected parties, this ruling means that the Tabasará Consortium's business promoters now have the "green light" to build Tabasará II. The indigenous and peasant farmer families of the Ngöbe Buglé Comarca are now defenceless in the face of the magistrate's refusal to overrule the National Environmental Authority (ANAM), the government body that approved the Environmental Impact Study for the Tabasará II project. This has meant that indigenous and peasant protests have been resumed with renewed force, leading to closure of the Pan-American Highway and marches to the different government offices involved in the issue.

Consortium will reform the Mining Code

Panama has a Mining Code that was established in the early 1960s and which has led to many injustices being committed when granting licences to transnational companies, particularly in indigenous communities. There is also nervousness on the part of businesspeople because, given that there are no legal guarantees in Panama that protect and defend their interests, indigenous communities have always been opposed to mining operations. For this very reason, it is now these same indigenous peoples who are waiting to see what the new Mining Code will offer. The national government therefore put out a tender, which was won by a Consortium made up of the University of Montana (USA) and Clifton Associates Ltd. from Saskatchewan (Canada), to reform the Panama Mining Code. This suggests it will be a main topic of interest for 2003.

Convention 169: statement by the Solicitor-General

In spite of the large number of indigenous lands legalised, governments of the past ten years have been opposed to ratification of ILO Convention 169, despite unusual actions such as including entire articles from Convention 169 that refer to indigenous land into Law 44 of 1998 of the General Environmental Law.

Indigenous demands have always fallen on deaf ears as far as the government is concerned, for which reason National Deputy, Enrique Garrido, of Kuna origin and President of the Indigenous Affairs Committee, once more requested the opinion of the Solicitor-General as to whether the Legislative Assembly (National Congress) could ratify international agreements should the corresponding ministers (Foreign Affairs and Labour) refuse to present them to the plenary Assembly.

In this respect, the Solicitor-General, Alma Montenegro de Fletcher, in a note to Deputy Garrido of 18 December 2002, stated that:

For ... constitutional and legal reasons..., this office is of the opinion that ILO Convention 169 must be submitted to the plenum of the

*Legislative Assembly for its consideration, being the competent au-
thority to examine the legal interpretations and observations that
may be made in relation to Convention No.169, in accordance with
article 153, numeral 3, of the Political Constitution and, lastly, it is
suggested that international instruments should be evaluated in the
light of current national legislation.*

This opinion of the Solicitor-General is very important as it is the first
time a senior magistrate of the Republic has made a statement in this
regard, and it will result in indigenous legislators presenting Convention 169 to the plenary Legislative Assembly for ratification.

Massacre in Paya and Pucuro

The complaints that have long been made regarding the fact that
irregular Colombian groups (be they guerrillas, army or paramilitary)
operate freely along the border areas of Panama without the national
authorities dealing with them came to a head with tragic consequences on 18 January 2003.

The Kuna communities of Paya and Pucuro, located within the
proposed Kuna de Takarkunyala Comarca, mentioned above, were
attacked and their traditional Kuna authorities (*saylas*) cruelly assas-
sinated by a contingent of Colombian paramilitaries from the Urabá
Peasant Self-Defence Units (AUCU).

Showing great disrespect for the traditional culture and ceremonies of the Kuna, the murderers burst into the village and, having
eaten and drunk with them, abducted their leaders, later brutally
killing them. Those killed were all leaders or *sayla* from the community
of Paya. Before returning to Colombia, the paramilitaries blew up the
outskirts of and roads into the community in order to terrorise the
communities even more and to prevent them from fleeing elsewhere.

Following this violent and bloody raid, it was painful to observe,
via the media, the great displacement of entire peoples in search of
security, children lost in the forest with their mothers, things Panama
never imagined could happen in its own backyard. The whole country shed tears for Paya and Pucuro and united the Panamanians in
defence of their brothers and national sovereignty.

This incursion also demonstrated the Panamanian National Police force's inability to protect its citizens and frontiers, something
that may be used as an excuse to request the presence of foreign forces
in "defence" of national borders. ❏

THE CIRCUMCARIBBEAN

A ny reference to indigenous peoples within the Caribbean region is often not taken seriously, as the myth of extinction still prevails even among people living within the sub-region. To counter this myth, indigenous peoples are vigorously reclaiming their heritage and demanding participation in the international indigenous peoples' movement. This overview does not include the entire Caribbean region, which in our definition includes both the archipelago as well as the coasts of the surrounding mainland countries from Mexico to the Guyanas. It spotlights indigenous peoples within four mainland countries and on one island: Belize in Central America; Trinidad and Tobago; and Guyana, Suriname, and French Guiana in north-eastern South America.[1]

BELIZE

W ithin the Caribbean region, Belize is the country where two great traditions of Aboriginal America meet. They are the Meso-American, represented by the Maya and the Amazonian, represented by the Garifuna. The Garifuna and Maya make up almost 18% of the national population, one of the highest proportions of indigenous peoples within the region.

Belize lies within the south-west Meso-American culture area, which extends from the Yucatan Peninsula west into Chiapas and Guatemala and further south into northern Honduras and El Salvador. The Maya inhabited this region from as early as four thousand years ago up to the current time period. Today there are three Maya nations in Belize, together forming almost 11% of the national population of 233,000: the K'ekchi (12,366), the Mopan (8,980) and the Yucatec (3,155). The Maya are predominantly (90%) rural and are scattered in over fifty villages, mainly within the southern one-third of the country.[2]

The great Amazonian tradition is found among the Garifuna, who were formerly known in literature as Black Carib. They number 14,061, or 6% of the national population. They originated in north-eastern South America and migrated during Pre-Columbian times as Carib

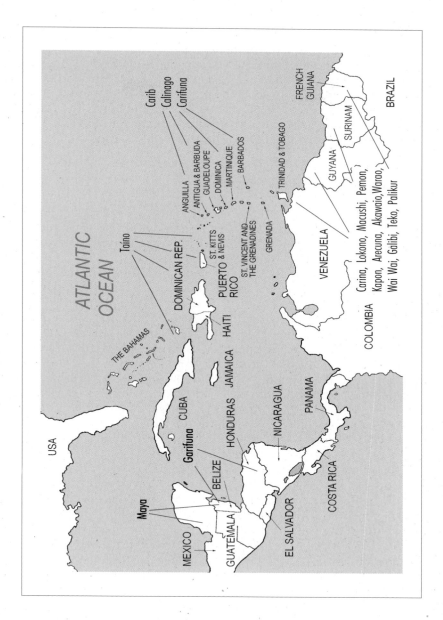

The Circumcaribbean with main indigenous groups. Source: Maximilian C. Forte

and Arawak peoples into the Lesser Antilles. There they mixed with escaped African slaves and gradually took over the larger part of the island of St. Vincent. From St. Vincent, the British exiled them to Central America in 1797. While being truly pan-Caribbean in heritage, they are today found along the north-east coast of Central America in their hundreds of thousands. Unlike the Maya, the Belize Garifuna are predominantly urban, being found mainly in Belize City and the southern towns of Dangriga and Punta Gorda.

Political and legislative context

As is the case of other Caribbean countries, there is still no legislative recognition given to the indigenous peoples within the constitution of Belize. An effort to introduce such a provision during a 1994 exercise on constitutional reform was not successful.

On the other hand, senior level government ministers, including the Prime Minister, have engaged in serious dialogue with leaders of indigenous peoples' organizations. Two prime examples are the Memoranda of Understanding (MOU) signed in 1998 and 2002 between, in the first instance, the Prime Minister and the National Garifuna Council (NGC), the main body representing the Garifuna people, and between the Prime Minister and leaders of the Maya organizations, including the Toledo Maya Cultural Council (TMCC), the K'ekchi Council of Belize, the Toledo Alcaldes' Association, the Toledo Maya Women's Council and the Toledo Village Councils' Association. The MOUs specify the government's obligation to acknowledge the respective organizations as representatives of their peoples, and to assist them in cultural preservation and the sustainable use of land and water resources.

The Memorandum of Understanding with the Maya was thorough and focused. It exacted commitment from the government towards a comprehensive development programme to take place within their sub-region in the aftermath of a large-scale road-building project. This commitment came after the Inter-American Commission on Human Rights (IACHR) had agreed to accept the petition of the Maya against the government of Belize for their 202,350-hectare homeland claim. It is a point that we will pursue further below. It is necessary to ascertain here that the IACHR will play a significant role in bringing to the attention of the rest of the region and the world as a whole the government's glaring deficiencies in overlooking the rights of indigenous peoples, both Maya and Garifuna.

Specific policies and projects

The previous discussion on MOUs indicates the willingness of the government to engage in development projects with indigenous peoples. So far, most of these have been of a generic nature mirroring the need of the sub-region in which most indigenous peoples are found to catch up with the rest of the country in terms of roads, education, health and social welfare. It has also been in response to studies that have repeatedly shown that indigenous peoples lag behind the rest of their Belizean counterparts in all basic services. The next step is for the government to engage the indigenous peoples themselves in programmes in which they will have full voice in planning and implementation.

The impetus toward this phase comes from the Toledo Development Corporation (TDC), a statutory body invoked by the government in 2002 to implement ameliorative measures that consultants and communities had identified for the surfacing of the Southern Highway in order to link the indigenous peoples' heartland with the rest of the country. The TDC is currently laying the groundwork for this undertaking. The renewed thrust on development - which this time would be transparent, accountable and participatory - is in keeping with the spirit of an agreement that the government signed with the Inter-American Development Bank (IDB), which had helped with feasibility studies for the Southern Highway. The Southern Highway is one of the largest development programmes the government has undertaken over the past decade. In passing through the traditional lands of indigenous peoples, it has drawn new lines of engagement between the government and indigenous peoples.

On the other hand, indigenous peoples are questioning the level of the government's sincerity as it continues to grant logging concessions within their traditional lands. Furthermore, non-indigenous peoples continue to buy large tracts of lands with no restrictions. These are the kinds of deleterious post-highway construction impacts that the indigenous people identified in their negotiations with the government.

Indigenous peoples' movements

The inevitable slippages in MOUs, the need to pursue the struggle for their rights through the IACHR and other means, the conspicuous underdevelopment of their heartland in relation to the rest of the country, the unrelenting neo-liberal policy of the government towards privatisation of water, electricity, telephone and other public services

– all these have strengthened the resolve of indigenous peoples to work within their organizations for effective representation. For the Garifuna, this is the National Garifuna Council and for the Maya the Toledo Maya Cultural Council and K'ekchi Council of Belize. Through these organizations, they hold high hopes of reclaiming their identity, peoplehood and natural resources. The organizations themselves receive substantial technical and financial assistance from agencies linked to the global indigenous peoples' movement. The dilemma remains as to how much these agencies should do to retain a focus on overwhelming problems while building capacity among the indigenous peoples themselves. ❏

TRINIDAD & TOBAGO

Amerindian peoples have existed in Trinidad for as long as 6,000 years before the arrival of Columbus, and numbered at least 40,000 at the time of Spanish settlement in 1592. The population consisted of almost a dozen different tribal groupings, many from the nearby mainland. The first Catholic Missions were established in the 1600s, in an effort to 'reduce' and 'pacify' those tribes that remained on the island. In 1785, the Mission of Arima was formed, and the Carib tribes who had been pressed to live there eventually converted to Catholicism. They later came under the leadership of a Titular Queen of the Carib, responsible for overseeing communal preparations for the annual Santa Rosa Festival, a Catholic feast day that continues to play a special role in bringing together Arima's Amerindian descendants.

Loss of lands

In the mid-1880s, the Amerindians of Arima were disenfranchised of 1,320 acres of land. These holdings had been granted to them as inalienable property by the Spanish colonial authorities, and were initially respected by the British under the terms of a formal international treaty of cession signed with Spain in 1802. However, the

British reneged on these agreements and put measures in place to alienate those lands and offer them for commercial sale. Attempts by the Roman Catholic Church, lasting until the 1880s, to retain portions of this land for the Amerindians were dismissed by the largely Anglican political elites in power. As a result, dozens of families were forced to migrate from Arima and find means of supporting themselves as squatters and hired hands on cocoa estates. But while the literature of the time, written by local colonial elites and foreign travellers, cast the Carib as having become extinct, or nearly so, the Carib who remained in Arima maintained themselves as a visible and cohesive entity, in large part through their involvement with the Church in the annual Santa Rosa celebrations. In addition, given the geographic proximity of Venezuela, only seven miles away, their numbers were reinforced by Venezuelan immigrants of Amerindian descent, who shared many of the same traditional practices.

Cultural survival and revival

Today, at least 12,000 people in north-east Trinidad are of Amerindian descent, according to rough estimates. However, the Santa Rosa Carib Community (SRCC) is the only formally organized group of people identifying with an Amerindian identity. Its membership consists of several related families of indigenous ancestry.

Since its formal reorganization in the early 1970s, under the leadership of Ricardo Bharath Hernandez, the SRCC has been engaged in a concerted effort to maintain those Amerindian traditions that had been retained (such as weaving, cassava growing, traditional medicines), as well as reviving traditional practices that had been lost (religious rituals, language). It has been actively engaged in researching its history. In addition, it has pursued a determined policy of establishing durable linkages with other Amerindian communities in Guyana, St. Vincent, Dominica, Belize and North America. Since the early 1990s, it has been a member of the Caribbean Organization of Indigenous Peoples and has hosted three international gatherings of indigenous peoples in Arima. Amongst its goals have been the achievement of formal recognition by the national government, financial support and the granting of state land in order to build an Amerindian village, where they would cultivate cassava, utilize local resources for craftwork and provide an independent means of earning revenue and creating employment.

National recognition and reparations

Following several decades of living on the margins of national con-
sciousness, the revamped SRCC began to attract considerable attention in the nationalist press of the 1970s, and from the government of
Dr. Eric Williams, Trinidad and Tobago's independence leader and
first Prime Minister. The SRCC received the financial assistance of the
Community Development Division of the Office of the Prime Minister
to build its first headquarters in Arima, and the titular head of state,
the President, attended the SRCC's annual Santa Rosa festivities. On
the other hand, the government also oversaw the incorporation of the
SRCC as a limited liability company, purportedly to formalize the
process of granting them profit-earning lands. This organizational
form has long acted as a straight jacket on the SRCC, and induced a
degree of previously unsought formalization and state surveillance.
Even so, in the last few years, national governments have begun to
speak explicitly in terms of "paying reparations" to the Carib, ironically in compensation for the actions of the British.

Today, the SRCC is recognized by the government as, "representative of the indigenous Amerindians of Trinidad and Tobago", and it
receives an annual grant of $30,000 TTD (approximately $5,000 US).
An Amerindian Projects Committee was established by the government in the early 1990s. The SRCC also receives financial support
from the Arima Borough Council. In 1996, the government assisted
by providing funds and labour for the reconstruction of a large, new
SRCC Community Centre. In 2000, a national commemorative day,
Amerindian Heritage Day, was officially instituted as a national day
of recognition to be observed every 14 October. Subsequently, the
SRCC also obtained funds for the building of a new Resource Centre.

New lands granted

The SRCC is about to embark on a major new phase of development
and self-transformation. Since November 2002, the national government has, after 26 years of applications from the SRCC, decided to
grant the SRCC a portion of state land in a prime eco-tourist location
on the island's north coast. Details concerning the size and boundaries of the land grant are still being discussed. Various state agencies,
including the Lands and Surveys Division and Town and Country
Planning, are still debating the extent of the land and the purposes for
which it is to be used. Although the stated sentiments of the state are those

of equity and justice, the formal process itself seems to have been appropriated by state bureaucrats operating on conventional assumptions, rather than those of compensating a marginalized minority. While at this stage some supportive pressure is needed to ensure that Carib interests remain central to this process, the SRCC is still looking forward to achieving financial independence and the land base needed for cultural survival. For its part, the Roman Catholic Church donated the lands on which the current SRCC Centre is based, as well as homes for some of the member families. To date, their tenure has yet to be fully regularized, however.[3] ❏

THE GUYANAS

While Suriname, Guyana and French Guiana, collectively known as the Guyanas, are on the north-east coast of South America, for demographic reasons they are included within the Caribbean. Indeed, Suriname and Guyana are both active members of CARICOM.[4] French Guiana is an overseas department of France and therefore part of the European Union. All three form part of the Amazon Basin. Indigenous peoples in Guyana number approximately 60 – 70,000 persons comprising nine peoples. In Suriname, there are at least four indigenous peoples comprising 20,000 persons and some 60,000 maroons, tribal peoples, constituting six different nations.[5] In French Guiana, there are 6 indigenous peoples (15,000 persons) and approximately 25,000 maroons. While the situation varies in each of the three countries, indigenous and tribal peoples are all facing substantial threats to their rights, environments and cultural integrity.

Suriname

Suriname is the only country in the Western hemisphere where indigenous peoples are found that does not recognize that indigenous peoples have some form of rights to own and enjoy their ancestral lands and territories. Even the most rudimentary rights are not protected under Surinamese law. This problem is further compounded by the fact that Suriname has granted numerous, and is presently in the process of granting further, logging and mining concessions to multinational corporations, many of whom have dubious environmental and human rights records. These concessions presently affect over 60 percent of the indigenous and maroon communities and were granted without any form of consultation or agreement. In some cases, the communities find themselves in the middle of mining operations and in others they have been forced off their lands or are threatened with forcible relocation. Logging concessions have also caused severe environmental and social problems.

Indigenous peoples and maroons have begun to take legal action to address this situation. The Saramaka maroon people, for instance, filed a complaint with the Inter-American Commission on Human Rights. The complaint seeks the Commission's assistance to bring about legal recognition of their territorial and other rights. In August 2002, the Saramaka were informed that the Commission had issued precautionary measures requesting that Suriname "take appropriate measures to suspend all concessions, including permits and licenses for logging and mine exploration and other natural resource development activity on lands used and occupied by the 12 Saramaka clans until the Commission has had the opportunity to investigate the substantive claims raised in the case."[6] To date, Suriname has failed to comply. Indigenous communities are also now using the Surinamese courts to challenge the failure of the state to recognize territorial rights and active violation of those rights due to logging and mining concessions and the establishment of nature reserves.

Guyana

In Guyana, indigenous peoples are in the midst of a major revision of the Amerindian Act of 1951, an example of highly paternalistic and discriminatory colonial legislation reminiscent of Brazil's1973 Indian Statute. The agreement to revise the Act is a major victory for, and a long-standing demand of, indigenous peoples in Guyana. They are currently organizing to ensure that the revised Act is consistent with their rights and interests. On the negative side, small-scale mining continues to wreak havoc with the indigenous peoples' environment, subsistence resources and social well-being. While a major judicial decision was issued in 2002, upholding sections of the Mining Act that prohibit small-scale mining on lands occupied and used by indigenous peoples, this precedent has not affected government policy and concessions continue to be issued. In some cases, miners are using river dredges and digging into the villages themselves. Mercury contamination has never been adequately assessed and is expected to be considerable.

With regard to land rights, while 74 villages today hold title to approximately 7 percent of Guyana, the majority of these are seeking recognition of rights over additional areas. Some 30 villages lack any form of title. A precedent-setting aboriginal title suit was filed by the Akawaio and Arecuna villages of the Upper Mazaruni River basin in 1998 but, thus far, no trial date has been set. Government action has been equally inconclusive, insisting that demarcation of existing titles must be undertaken before any discussion of additional lands or title for those communities without land can take place. In the meantime, the state continues to issue large-scale mining permits and has come to agreements with conservation groups to convert massive areas of traditional indigenous lands into national parks and nature reserves.

French Guiana

In French Guiana, indigenous peoples are first and foremost seeking recognition of their status as "indigenous peoples" with rights additional to those enjoyed by all French citizens. The major blockage is Article 2 of the French Constitution, which has been interpreted to require that no distinction be made among citizens. This may change, as French Guiana is in the midst of a protracted renegotiation of its departmental status, which came about largely due to calls from the Creole elite for greater autonomy. Indigenous peoples are using the opportunity to assert and insist upon greater recognition of their rights within the French legal system.

At present, indigenous and maroon peoples may only acquire title to their lands under a 1987 Decree that applies to all "traditional forest-dependent communities". This has enabled some communities to obtain title but only if they incorporate as an association, a requirement vigorously opposed by most communities as a violation of their right to maintain their traditional forms of organization. Mining is also a serious problem, especially along the border with Suriname, and a number of multinationals have been granted permits to operate on indigenous and maroon lands. ❑

Notes

1 The authors make full apology for not covering other Caribbean territories and are not implying that the peoples they are discussing are
representative of the wide spread of indigenous peoples in the region.
For further information, see the Caribbean Amerindian Centrelink
www.centrelink.org and the Journal of Caribbean Amerindian History
and Anthropology www.kacike.org .
2 These figures derive from the 2001 national census in which respondents were asked to self-identify.
3 For further information on the SRCC and its activities see:
www.kacike.org/srcc/index.html.
4 CARICOM: The Caribbean Community and Common Market.
5 Maroons are the descendants of escaped African slaves, whose freedom
from slavery and rights to territorial and political autonomy were
recognized by treaties concluded with the Dutch in the 18th and 19th
centuries.
6 Letter of Ariel Dultisky, head of the Executive Secretariat, Inter-American Commission on Human Rights, 8 August 2002.

SOUTH AMERICA

COLOMBIA

In the past, most of the indigenous territories, along with those of the black communities and, to a large extent, the settler areas in the Orinoco, Amazon and Pacific regions, were marginalised from the dynamics of economic development and national life. But, over the last two decades, they have become strategic territories for multinational companies. Strategic territories, too, for the war, as they play host to the worst fighting, massacres and violations of human rights and infringements of international humanitarian law on the part of all armed players: guerrillas, paramilitaries and even the state's armed forces. This change is due, among other things, to the geography of the indigenous territories, conducive to hiding armed groups, growing illicit crops and arms trafficking, and also due to the growing presence of multinational companies and large mining, oil, water and road projects, along with other trading, cattle and logging interests.

Backdrop to war

The Colombian countryside has become the stage for the most important capital accumulation strategy in Colombia. Hence it has also become the main arena of war.

Since the breakdown in peace negotiations between the government and the Revolutionary Armed Forces of Colombia (*Fuerzas Armadas Revolucionarias de Colombia* – FARC) on 20 February 2002, this situation has become unbearable for all social sectors living in rural Colombia. This is due to the increased massacres, the selective assassinations and disappearances of leaders, and the threats and strong pressure exerted on our organisations and authorities to commit ourselves to a war that is devoid of alternative organic projects. In addition to this, it is a war in which we, along with the Afro-Colombian and peasant populations, are the main victims.

Faced with such a situation, it is the state's responsibility to protect people and communities from the armed conflict and to provide care for the displaced population. There are international agreements,[1] and a national policy expressed in law 387 and regulatory decrees, that establish the state's commitments in this regard. The Political Constitution of Colombia recognises the Colombian nation as multi-ethnic and pluricultural. Hence the state must take responsibility for "guaranteeing in particular" the preservation and ethnic integrity of

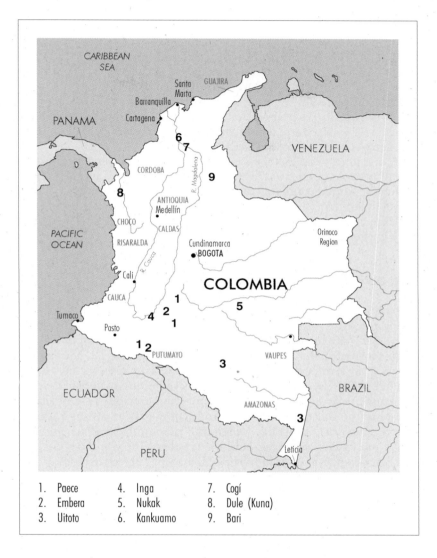

1. Paece
2. Embera
3. Uitoto
4. Inga
5. Nukak
6. Kankuamo
7. Cogí
8. Dule (Kuna)
9. Bari

indigenous peoples, black communities and other ethnic groups, all now seriously threatened by the armed conflict.

And yet the state has not identified with these internationally recognised legal standards, let alone addressed constitutional principles such as the defence of the nation's cultural diversity. What is more, there are many national and international complaints accusing the Colombian state, particularly its Armed Forces, of failing to act in a timely and effective manner in the case of such publicised massacres as that of Alto Río Naya, in which around a hundred indigenous Paece, Afro-Colombians and settlers were murdered by paramilitaries; that of Bojayá, in which 127 Afro-Colombians, seeking refuge in the church, were killed by a cylinder bomb thrown by FARC guerrillas; or the massacres perpetrated by paramilitary groups in the Sierra Nevada de Santa Marta where, during 2002, more than one hundred indigenous Kankuamo and Cogí were killed.

Indigenous peoples are particularly vulnerable to such aggression from the armed players. This has been demonstrated by the way in which the armed conflict is undermining their ethnic integrity, their rights to territory, autonomy and cultural identity, endangering not only the lives of individuals, families and communities but also their very existence as peoples.

The policy of "democratic security"

In May 2002, a majority of the Colombian people elected their new President, Álvaro Uribe Vélez, whose electoral campaign had focused around the slogan "firm hand, warm heart", in order to put an end to the violence in the country. Once invested as president, he vaunted a policy of 'democratic security' with which to resolve the armed conflict. Quite clearly, a large section of Colombian society is desperate for security. Systematic violations of human rights, a worsening economy the destruction of the production system through globalisation, the crisis in justice, spreading paramilitarism, armed confrontation extending throughout the whole country and the despair that has taken hold of millions of Colombians, all led them to opt for the authoritarian alternative, with an accompanying limitation of democracy and restriction of spaces for popular participation.

During the first six months of Álvaro Uribe Vélez' government, and in order to implement the policy of "democratic security", "rehabilitation zones" of total military control were established, taxes to fund military operations were implemented and the participation of civilians (as informants) in the conflict encouraged, among other measures.

Perhaps of most concern with regard to these measures is that they have not produced results in terms of reducing the violence. On the contrary, they have merely exacerbated the intentions of guerrilla groups, leading to acts of terror, such as the car bomb that destroyed eleven floors of the exclusive "El Nogal" club in Bogota, with a death toll of 43 and more than 100 wounded, and the "house-bomb" in the town of Neiva, aimed at bringing down the presidential plane but which took the lives of more than 20 people, most of them from poor backgrounds. Currently, and in the face of the murder of one US soldier and the kidnapping of another three by the FARC, the United States has increased its military presence and there is significant US troop infrastructure and military advisors beginning to appear on Colombian soil. For many, President Uribe's requests to the United Nations to send UN peacekeeping forces and his request to President Bush to commit himself to military intervention in Colombia and in the Caribbean to eradicate drugs trafficking and terrorism hark back to the early days of the Vietnam war.

The Free Trade Agreement

This escalation in violence is taking place against an economic and political backdrop that is not favourable to the interests of the popular sectors, given that the successive economic crises caused by the last ten years of neoliberal policies have destroyed the production system.[2] The last three governments in Colombia have implemented policies that have tended to dismantle many of the standards and requirements of our legal system in relation to protecting the indigenous territories, the collective territories of black communities, the environment and biodiversity, standards that prevented the implementation of economic mega-projects that were not environmentally, socially and culturally viable. In this way, they have been smoothing the path towards implementing a Free Trade Agreement for the Americas (FTAA), an economic strategy of neo-colonial integration that seeks the free circulation of goods and services throughout the whole continent. It is an economic strategy defined and governed by the interests of the United States, the most powerful country on the planet in economic, political and military terms. The most worrying thing is that the FTAA will open the path to the plundering of Colombia's strategic natural resources, ending up with the country's agriculture in ruins and a consequent loss of food security.

The biggest problem is that the FTAA is accompanied by a "military component", such as the *Plan Colombia*, which encourages a violation of the human rights of indigenous people and other rural communities leading, among other things, to further displacements of communities from their territories when mega-projects or the exploitation of natural resources is planned.

Fuelling the violence

But while ten years of neoliberal policies have led to increased poverty among wide sectors of Colombian society, it is the countryside that has been hit the hardest. Recent studies show that 82% of the rural population now live below the poverty line. This poverty, together with the cultivation of illicit crops (coca and poppy), is what primarily "fuels" the violence, given that the armed players' main source of funding is illicit drugs trafficking and the most important source of recruitment of young people into the war is to be found in economically and socially depressed rural regions. Three decades of drugs trafficking have created a so-called "drugs culture".

The impact of this "drugs culture" which, in a neoliberal context, has led to rent-seeking, corruption and social breakdown, is another phenomenon that has contributed to the spread of the country's economic and social crisis and to the delegitimisation of the political parties and their ruling class.

Guerrilla totalitarianism

In the same way that the government's authoritarianism has ignored our independence and our demands, the rebel forces that are fighting against it enjoy neither credibility nor legitimacy among wide sectors of the population, due to the authoritarianism of the main guerrilla force in the country, the FARC, whose arrogance and intimidating weaponry have led them to ignore and even attack the most deeply held democratic feelings and to deny the indigenous peoples and organisations spaces for their expression, autonomy and government. The FARC, but also other rebel forces, are not only threatening those communities and organisations that do not yield to their demands but murdering distinguished indigenous leaders in Cauca, Antioquia, Chocó and Valle.

With these actions, the FARC has not only abandoned the political path once and for all but it has crossed the path of social organisations (such as those of the indigenous) that had managed to achieve spaces for their own government. In this way, they are placing themselves on the same side as those who also threaten us by preventing social change and our political progress.

Facing up to the armed conflict

To safeguard the communities from the armed conflict, the regional and national indigenous organisations have been undertaking many actions. However, concrete results have been few, for talks with the armed groups have not put a stop to the murder, kidnapping and disappearance of indigenous leaders. Neither have they prevented the forced displacement of communities. The complaints we have made, the requests for state protection of our communities and the declarations made by our organisations stating that our people identify with none of the aggressors, have merely exacerbated the warring intentions of all groups and increased the threats. The solidarity and support we have received from friendly national and international organisations, while mitigating the hardship, has been powerless to protect our lives.

For the indigenous communities, the organisations are their main support against the armed conflict. However, the repression they have suffered in recent years has weakened them and created barriers, not only within the indigenous movement but within the Colombian popular movement as a whole. Whereas town councils used to be the main network of solidarity and support in defence of our territories and resources, they now often have "closed attitudes", with policies focused on the defence of their own immediate interests - understandable in the current situation, as they want to preserve the standard of living they have managed to achieve - but unfavourable in terms of making joint progress to defend ourselves from the war.

Nonetheless, it is for the town councils and organisations to continue to guide the future of their communities and peoples. And it is they who must lead the processes of resistance to the war.

Similarly, the indigenous authorities are what unite and draw together the indigenous peoples. It is they that guide, govern and represent the peoples and communities. In united communities, with strong authorities accepted by all members, it is more difficult for the armed groups to impose their will. This explains why many indigenous leaders have been murdered, both by the paramilitaries and by the guerrilla groups.

But in communities where organisation is weak, and where there are no authorities capable of intervening in community affairs or resolving internal conflicts, far less of mobilising their peoples in defence of their territory, it is more likely that powers (more often than not armed) will be able to supplant or co-opt those authorities.

Resistance

In the many meetings, congresses and other events held by the indigenous peoples over the last 2 years, the indigenous organisations have reaffirmed their will to resist the violence and to prevent their people from being stripped of their belongings and territories. We have also decided to consolidate our fight to emerge from the marginalisation into which we have been forced by an exclusive economic system that favours the private interests of small power groups who spare no violence to achieve their selfish aims.

But while we have decided to resist our violent exclusion from economic and social development, we have also been resisting our inclusion, also violent, in this armed conflict.

Our territorial roots, our community cohesion around traditional authorities, our organisational strength and tradition of struggle as a social movement, along with the fact that we have ended up the victims of all armed players, are the reasons why we indigenous have opted for a strategy of peaceful resistance, within our territories, to all players in the war: state, rebels and paramilitaries.[3]

Although forced displacements of indigenous populations are less marked because the indigenous usually avoid displacing to urban areas, preferring to do so within their territories, or towards other communities, the number of displaced indigenous now stands at around 10,000.

This resistance to displacement, and their deep roots in the land, mean that a contrasting problem to that of displacement is being caused: many communities are virtually "held hostage" by the armed players, for they cannot leave or freely cross their own territories.

Indigenous uprising

In the social, political and economic environment described above, the indigenous peoples and organisations have decided to unite all our forces to begin 2003 with a series of actions and protests that we have called an *uprising*.

An *uprising* in all areas of our cultural, social, political and economic life.

This *uprising* will be a gamble we are taking on life in order to survive as peoples.

An *uprising* to rescue our spirituality and regain the dignity of our peoples. To trust more in ourselves and shake off our fear.

An *uprising* to contribute to ending the war and its humanitarian degradation, to put an end to the barbarity to which we indigenous, black and peasant peoples are subjected by the armed players. To rescue the indigenous who have been recruited into the war. It is an *uprising* that actively seeks peace.

It is fundamentally an *uprising* to strengthen us from within, to revitalize our cultures, reaffirm our governments and develop our own justice, because only then can we control our territories and strengthen our resistance.

An *uprising* to return the displaced to their territories.

An *uprising* for mutual support, to continue developing our life plans, albeit in the most adverse circumstances of this war.

An *uprising* to meet once more, with our peoples firstly, and then with all the excluded and oppressed of Colombia.

An *uprising* to show the country that indigenous peoples are an organic and active part of the Colombian nation and that, as such, we are not going to wait forever for a lazy state to resolve our problems.❏

Notes

1   ILO *"Convention 169"*, ratified by Colombia by means of law 21 of 1991; *"UN Resolution 217 of 1948 on the rights of man"*; *"Convention for the prevention and punishment of the crime of genocide"*, approved by Colombia by means of law 28 of 1959; *"American Convention on Human Rights"*, now law 16 of 1972; *"International Convention on the Elimination of all forms of racial discrimination"*, now law 22 of 1981; *"Convention against torture"*, now law 70 of 1986, among other legal regulations.

2   The 1999 crisis, the most serious in the last 20 years, left 2 million people living in absolute poverty. Along with another 2 million displaced by the violence, they have lost their jobs and homes, and now drift hopelessly on the margins of society.

3   Unfortunately, some communication media – along with senior government officials and military spokespeople – have tried perversely to show that indigenous resistance is opposed only to the guerrilla forces and supportive of the state. The magazine *CAMBIO*, for example, entitled an article on indigenous resistance to its people taking up arms as "Popular Counter Insurgency". Similar treatment has been given by the daily *EL TIEMPO* to this position of the indigenous peoples.

VENEZUELA

To understand the situation of indigenous peoples in Venezuela at such a polemic and eventful time (never before witnessed in the country), it is helpful to have some knowledge of the country's history since independence, when Simón Bolívar decreed the aboriginal nature of our peoples and their right to self-determination. Almost two centuries were then to pass before a chapter on the rights of the indigenous peoples would be included in the Bolivarian Constitution of Venezuela, following a turbulent constituent process.

This historic event has initiated an irreversible process of participation on the part of traditionally excluded social sectors and has had the consequence of a series of events that are defining the bases of the government system that is enshrined in the Constitution. The social groups that have governed Venezuela since its birth as a Republic are obviously not too happy about this.

The economic interests of national and international businesses and the aspirations of the Venezuelan people to establish a truly inclusive, participatory and consequential democratic system are currently in conflict.

Progress and political crisis

With regard to our rights as indigenous peoples, the following must be noted:

1. In 2002, after long years of waiting, the Bolivarian Republic of Venezuela ratified ILO Convention 169, thus converting it into national law.
2. The Bolivarian Constitution of Venezuela recognises the indigenous as peoples, in the sense given to this term by ILO Convention 169.
3. Decrees, laws and regulations have been approved that guarantee our right to the collective ownership of our territory, to the protection of our traditional knowledge, to the application of justice and to our own education. Among these can be mentioned the Law of Demarcation of the Territories and Habitat of Indigenous Peoples and the creation – by Presidential Decree – of a National Commission and various regional commissions[1] for the process of demarcation of Indigenous Territories. This latter is of bipartite composition (representatives from the indigenous peoples and from the

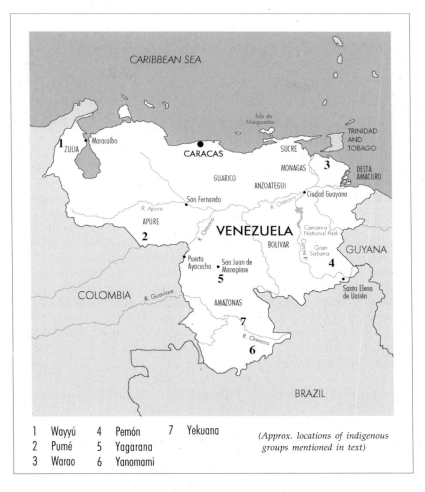

1	Wayyú	4	Pemón	7	Yekuana
2	Pumé	5	Yagarana		
3	Warao	6	Yanomami		

(Approx. locations of indigenous groups mentioned in text)

government), even though it is chaired by the Minister for the Environment and Natural Resources.[2]

It should also be noted that the Organic Law of Indigenous Peoples and Communities (LOPCI) was approved by the National Assembly at its first reading, the driving force and content of which were the original initiative - and have involved the direct participation of - all regional indigenous organisations, in addition to the National Indian Council of Venezuela (*Consejo Nacional Indio de Venezuela* - CONIVE). It is hoped that it will be approved and will enter into force later this year.

4. Our authorities and organisations have been legitimised as players in the development process being discussed in the country.
5. Our right to political participation has been guaranteed, enabling us to have direct representation in the country's legislative and executive powers. In this respect, we have a governor[3] in Amazonas State and various mayors[4] nationally.

In Amazonas State specifically, there are two indigenous representatives on the Regional Legislative Council. Indigenous peoples continue to be represented in the National Assembly in the form of three deputies. The Vice-Presidency of this Assembly is currently held by one of our deputies, Mrs. Nohelí Pocaterra.

And yet, despite these achievements, weaknesses can be observed at a political level. For this reason, we are undertaking a study[5] with the aim of identifying the critical implementation points in these regional and local governments, from a perspective of having authorities which – whilst set within the national and international legal and political reality – are in line with and respect traditional forms of public administration.

Whilst progress in terms of rights has been significant due to the constituent process, it is also the case that the country's political situation is undergoing a serious crisis, which became apparent with the coup of April 2002. This coup endangered the rights established and the political spaces won by Venezuela's indigenous peoples. In addition to the death threats received by indigenous leaders at that time, it must be recalled that the Presidential Decree issued by businessman Pedro Carmona Estanga (self-declared President during the days of the coup) cancelled all the public authorities elected during the government of President Hugo Rafael Chávez Frías. To give you some idea, the indigenous movement in Amazonas lost one governor and three mayors. The Bolivarian Constitution of Venezuela was also ignored, thus riding roughshod over rights that had taken years to be recognised.

Feelings of sympathy or not for the current President of the Republic aside, what was proposed during April 2002 and then from December of that year on (with the so-called National Strike)[6] was fully sanctioned by the indigenous movement. Any change proposed in terms of policies or at the level of government representatives must take place within the framework of the Constitution. The violent actions of the opposition during those three days were sufficient[7] for the indigenous movement to come out against them. This was made known to the Secretary of the Organisation of American States, César Gaviria, in a meeting held in January 2003.

In terms of our immediate reality

This said, it would seem appropriate to mention that, in spite of the fact that the policies proposed by the National Executive are aimed at a more democratic society, with a more equitable distribution of wealth, their application is still not without its difficulties. In this regard, according to a report of the Pan-American Health Organisation (PAHO), social spending has increased as a percentage of total public expenditure. The national budget increased from 8.6% in 1995 to 11.6% in 2000. The priorities of the portfolio of projects that receive co-funding from the Inter-American Development Bank (IADB)[8] have also been completely reversed. Whilst traditionally this expenditure was aimed at large works or projects linked to policies of a macro-economic nature, now the portfolio of IADB projects for Venezuela includes a significant number of social investment projects.

Nonetheless, and beyond statistical data, the following agreements and disagreements between formally recognised rights, established policies and the well-being of our communities should be noted.

With regard to the process of land demarcation, the Regional Organisation of Indigenous Peoples of Venezuela (*Organización Regional de los Pueblos Indígenas de Venezuela* - ORPIA) has commenced and almost finished the process of self-demarcation of its lands.[9] Even though the Constitution notes that it is the National Executive's responsibility to undertake this process, it is clear that more than two years after the entry into force of the Law of Demarcation of the Territory and Habitats of Indigenous Peoples, the National Demarcation Commission – for various reasons, including a lack of financial resources – has been unable to do this. In the last quarter of 2002, conversations began between the Ministry for the Environment and Natural Resources and ORPIA in order to move forward together in the process. Even though ORPIA has now almost finished the self-demarcation of lands, the next phases, relating to the digitalisation of maps and the production of files for the discussion on collective property titles, will be undertaken in joint coordination. For this, resources will be available from the National Executive, through this Ministry.

With regard to the right of indigenous peoples to "….maintain and develop their ethnic and cultural identity, world view, values, spirituality..." and the relationship with the Laws on Environmental Protection, the indigenous peoples of Amazonas State are the victims of violations of this right on the part of various authorities involved in environmental protection, who ignore their right to certain uses and customs. A few examples will serve to illustrate this. The National Guard tend to confiscate fish or hunted animals from indigenous inhabitants, arguing a prohibition on fishing or hunting in certain areas. However, needless to say, the basic foodstuffs of our peoples come from fishing and hunting. Similarly, they are denied permits to obtain various palms for building their traditional houses.

In this respect, ORPIA and the Ombudsman of Amazonas State are making efforts to reconcile both interests which, from our point of view, need not be in contradiction. In our opinion, a negotiation process with a clearly established agenda, along with a process of mutual awareness raising, would lead to a consequent harmony between the parties.

In terms of health, despite the budgets allocated and the policies proposed, this continues to be an issue of great concern for the indigenous peoples and communities of Amazonas State. The communities state their problems in terms of three areas: 1) Insufficient frequency of visits from medical staff, 2) Lack of appropriate training and motivation on the part of medical staff to work in indigenous communities. 3) Lack of adequate means of transport with which to move patients in emergencies. This is in line with what was expressed by the Pan-American Health Organisation in its "Preliminary Analysis of Health in Venezuela", in which it indicates that "72.8% of rural health centres in indigenous populations have no doctor." The main illnesses these populations suffer from, according to the incomplete data, are tuberculosis, malaria, parasitosis, malnutrition, diarrhoea-based and respiratory illnesses.

Sadly, communities can recount the tragedies of deaths of family members who were not treated in time for lack of a doctor or through the impossibility of transferring the patient to a hospital. It must be recalled that the geographic conditions of the Amazon require river or air transportation and there are currently no public services of this kind. Patients are required to pay amounts that are beyond their reach in order to travel.

Similarly, we are concerned at the training received by doctors in the universities, who are trained only to treat patients from the city. To begin with, they have to communicate with many people who do not speak Spanish and, what is more, they have ways of understanding health and illness that are radically different from our own.

The misunderstandings between the traditional uses of the indigenous peoples and the services linked to health care must also be noted. For example, they do not tend to consider the foods traditionally used by the indigenous people, a basic aspect in curing any patient.

With regard to the issue of intercultural education, recent preliminary data obtained by ORPIA within the context of a Youth Network Training Project,[10] indicates that young people feel that intercultural schooling is more bilingual than intercultural. The methods and infrastructure used for teaching traditional knowledge have no similarities with the traditional methods of knowledge transmission. The teaching of knowledge from the "Western" world is frequently imparted by people from the communities who have only recently obtained their baccalaureate, and who have an insufficient conceptual understanding of the issues they are teaching, with little or no pedagogic training and reflection. It is serious to note that this has the consequence of making it impossible to continue to develop our lives in ancestral ways whilst, at the same time, we are prevented from enjoying a fitting relationship, with our own identity, with the rest of national and international society.

In conclusion

We at the Regional Organisation of Indigenous Peoples of Venezuela believe that it is impossible that rights so recently established can become a reality in such a short space of time. Similarly, we believe that this is a responsibility that has to be shared by government and the organised communities.

Now we have our rights recognised but we do not have sufficient trained leaders to take forward the process of planning and negotiation that will enable the government to make the policies proposed more effective. We have the government's political goodwill, and we ourselves must actively contribute to putting the proposed policies into practice. It is also the government's responsibility to encourage among its representatives an understanding of the different realities and the democratic intent expressed in the Constitution.

These arguments enable us to tell the world that, despite difficulties in effectively achieving our well-being, we are fighting in Venezuela to build a country from the vision of the excluded majority, who are only demanding greater participation, better resource distribution, that justice is administered ethically and responsibly. From our perspective, we believe we are moving down a path that goes against the principles that govern world economic policy, but we are convinced that it may be the only way of applying a development plan that is not in contradiction with the principles of nature, of the dignity of humankind. We believe that the contribution of indigenous peoples to this process is enabling a way of life to be take into account that is based on integrated development with a collective vision and our own identity, and which will enable us to make great efforts to humanise the principles that govern the current economy, to radically recapture social equity and promote life in a more ethical dimension, bearing in mind all elements that make it possible and that will enable this planet to survive the process of destruction to which it is being subjected with this current development model. ❑

Notes

1 In those federal entities with indigenous population.

2 This is in line with the provisions of the Constitution, article 119 of which indicates that, "It is for the National Executive, with the participation of indigenous peoples, to define and guarantee the right to the collective ownership of their lands, which will be inalienable, non-seizable and non-transferable...."

3 Highest authority of the states. Venezuela is divided politically and geographically into states. The states, in turn, are divided politically and geographically into municipalities.

4 Highest authority of the municipalities.

5 As part of an international IWGIA/European Union project.

6 It should be noted that the impression we have in ORPIA is that the strike did not occur until the opposition decreed the Oil Stoppage which, because of its strategic significance, forced the paralysis of many activities, with the consequent financial imbalance. We noted that at the start of the so-called National Strike, on the part of the Coordinating Body of the opposition known as the Democratic Coordination, shops located in the upper middle class areas of the country's largest towns stopped functioning. The centre of these towns and other neighbourhoods continued operating as normal, a situation that the media did not broadcast. This was also the case in Amazonas State, where the strike never took place apart from the paralysis of two or three shops.

7 One only has to recall the invasion of the Cuban Embassy with the involvement of various players from the political opposition, who threatened to evict all those inside. They shut off the water and electricity, with men, women and children inside, including the Ambassador's wife.

8 It must be recalled that the priorities established for IADB investments are laid down by the National Executive.

9 With the support of IWGIA, the GAIA Foundation in Colombia and the Human Rights Office of the Apostolic Vicariate of Puerto Ayacucho.

10 With UNICEF support.

ECUADOR

E cuador is going through an historical process in which the indigenous peoples and nationalities have become a powerful social
player in the country's political, social and cultural routine.

Over the last 20 years, Ecuador's indigenous peoples have embarked on incessant struggles aimed at achieving their recognition as
collective entities and their individual rights. In this regard, the deep
questions raised by the indigenous regarding the construction of
nation states that have adopted systems in which societies are not
considered to be diverse and culturally heterogeneous have rung out
loud and clear.

But the indigenous peoples of Ecuador, through one of the most
representative organisations, the Confederation of Indigenous Nationalities of Ecuador (*Confederación de Nacionalidades Indígenas de Ecuador* - CONAIE), have embarked on an incessant struggle to achieve their
recognition as peoples and nationalities. The country's legal code has
changed qualitatively in terms of recognising indigenous rights. And,
more importantly, the indigenous peoples have become legal subjects
with rights and new social actors in the political electoral scene.

The political participation of indigenous peoples

Out of a need to exercise their political rights, the indigenous peoples
and nations, in particular CONAIE through its political wing, the
Pachakutik Movement, have made incursions into the country's political arena, radically modifying the electoral scene. Both at national
and provincial level, indigenous representatives took up the challenge of participating in the public authorities, with the aim of infil-
trating the state's power and attempting to resolve the serious problems of exclusion and marginalisation experienced throughout Ecuador's history.

In 1996, the Pachakutik Movement participated with their own
candidates in the presidential, national and provincial elections, as
well as in the elections for local mayors and councillors, winning a
number of important political positions. Two years later, indigenous
leaders participated in the Constituent National Assembly, in which
they achieved the introduction of constitutional reforms that were
very favourable to the indigenous peoples. In the 2002 presidential
elections, an alliance was formed between the indigenous and sectors

of the military (the *Partido Sociedad Patriótica* – Party for Patriotic Society and the Pachakutik Movement) that gained an overwhelming majority in the second round of elections.

Colonel Lucio Gutiérrez was appointed President of the Republic and 11 deputies from the Pachakutik Movement were elected, plus a significant number of provincial councillors. As part of the Alliance, many indigenous people gained positions in state departments. Of the indigenous representatives within the new government, we can mention Dr. Nina Pacari Vega, Minister for Foreign Affairs, Luis Macas, Minister of Agriculture and Livestock and Dr. Lourdes Tibán as Under-Secretary in the Ministry of Social Welfare.

The new Minister for Foreign Affairs stated that, "In a globalised world, there is recognition of the identities being built in Ecuador and of a political project that includes this diversity and seeks to promote the participation of social sectors that have historically been pushed aside and discriminated against."

Moreover, she stated that Ecuador would maintain a policy of non-intervention in the Colombian conflict and would promote a peaceful solution, supporting the reinstatement of peace talks between the Colombian government and the guerrillas.

No sooner had she been appointed Foreign Secretary than Pacari criticised the entry into force of the Free Trade Area for the Americas (FTAA) without relationships being modified between the countries forming a part of it and the weaknesses and specific character of each country being taken into account.

In the current conditions, it would be suicide for Ecuador to enter the FTAA. It would not even provide guarantees for national big business.

But internal differences within the national government are putting the alliance at risk due to positions taken on the Iraq conflict, Colombia and economic policy. At the Congress of the Confederation of Peoples of Kichwa Nationality (*Congreso de la Confederación de Pueblos de las Nacionalidad Kichwa*) in April 2003, a demand was made for the "immediate resignation of the economic team of Lucio Gutiérrez's government, headed by Mauricio Pozo. And a demand that the new economic team refocus the measures and economic policies to benefit the poorest sectors of the country. If we are not listened to, we will demand that the Pachatkutik Movement breaks its alliance with this government." A possible breakdown in the alliance would represent a significant step backwards along the path being forged by the indigenous movement in Ecuador.

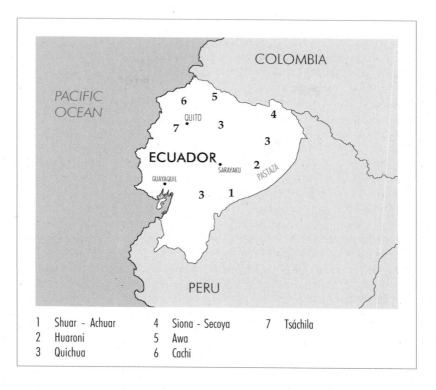

1	Shuar - Achuar	4	Siona - Secoya	7	Tsáchila
2	Huaroni	5	Awa		
3	Quichua	6	Cachi		

In the Ecuadorian Amazon

Meanwhile, the Amazonian peoples continue to face serious conflicts with oil companies, such as the case of the Kichwa community of Sarayaku de Pastaza, which is opposed to oil exploitation on its territories.

On 26 January this year, military troops attacked the "Tiutihualli" camp, set up by the inhabitants of Sarayacu the day previously to defend themselves from the constant harassment of the CGC/ChevronTexaco oil company, which was trying to forcibly carry out seismic explorations on the Sarayacu territory.

In the commotion, four people from Sarayacu were captured by the soldiers. They were blindfolded and bound hand and foot and left on the ground with no water. They were then taken by helicopter to the CGC/ChevronTexaco operations centre in Chontoa. They were again mistreated by people they could not see for their blindfolds but, according to conversations they overheard, they identified them as being "engineers" from the company.

For its part, the Sarayacu community managed to detain four soldiers, who they immediately proceeded to set free.

That same night, they managed to negotiate an agreement with the soldiers in which the four indigenous people held captive were freed, the people from Sarayacu were allowed free passage across the river Bobonaza and the two hundred soldiers in the Sarayacu region were immediately withdrawn.

On the basis of these events, on 5 May 2003, after hearing the request and arguments of the Amazonian indigenous people from the community of Sarayacu, the Inter-American Commission on Human Rights, IACHR, stipulated that the Ecuadorian government should take precautionary measures in relation to the conflict with the CGC oil company:

1. Adopt all measures considered necessary to guarantee the lives and physical, psychological and moral integrity of all members of the Sarayacu Indigenous Community...who may form the object of threats or terrorisation on the part of the army or civilians from outside the community.
2. Investigate the events that took place on 26 January 2003 in the Campo de Paz and Vida Tiutihualli in the Sarayacu community and their consequences, prosecute and punish those responsible.
3. Adopt those measures necessary to protect the special relationship of the Sarayacu community with their territory.

The Centre for Economic and Social Rights (*Centro de Derechos Economicos y Sociales* - CDES) and the Centre for Justice and International Law (*Centro por la Justicia y el Derecho Internacional* - CEJIL), organisations providing the community of Sarayacu with legal representation, announced that they would continue to put pressure on the Ecuadorian government to implement the IACHR's resolutions.

In addition, the IACHR required the Ecuadorian state to implement the precautionary measures in direct consultation with the Sarayacu community, through the Inter-American system, granting a period of six months for this purpose.

José Serrano, CDES lawyer, noted that this important resolution is an urgent legal mandate obliging the Ecuadorian state to directly intervene to protect the indigenous leaders, facilitate a process of investigation and take express and immediate measures to protect the community's environmental and cultural relations with its territory.❑

PERU

Over the past twelve months, the indigenous world in Peru has been characterized by a weakening of the state's institutions for indigenous peoples. Pro-indigenous rhetoric has remained at the level of declarations and has not been accompanied by decisions demonstrating the government's political will.

As of March 2003, the National Commission for Andean, Amazonian and Afro-Peruvian Peoples (*Comisión Nacional de Pueblos Andinos, Amazónicos y Afroperuanos* - CONAPA), created by Supreme Decree 111-2001-PCM in November 2001, had held only three ordinary sessions, the decisions of which were politically insignificant and its agreements nil. This situation has been in part caused by its unclear design from the start. Chaired by the wife of the President of the Republic, Eliane Karp de Toledo, CONAPA has never been more than a space for dialogue between indigenous leaders and some representatives of various public sectors. It has had no greater implementing powers, a low level of representation of the state sector, no public budget allocated to it and comprises all *ad honore* members.

CONAPA has been languishing in improvisation and ineffectiveness while the media has increased its criticism of a lack of transparency in the First Lady's management who, apart from her official office, chairs CONAPA and a private foundation with its headquarters in Panama, known as "*Pacha para el Cambio*". The Supervisory Commission of the Congress of the Republic has commenced investigations into requests for financial resources made in France, Spain and other countries on behalf of indigenous peoples, using her position as wife of the President, and which may have been channelled to her private institution. Similarly, questions are being raised as to the many high-salaried staff she has in her service, paid by the state and, in part, the Development Project for Indigenous and Afro-Peruvian Peoples (*Proyecto de Desarrollo para los Pueblos Indígenas y Afroperuanos* - PDPIA), a pilot project financed by the World Bank and whose overall funding totals US$5 million.

Institutionalisation frustrated

While various indigenous spokespeople have, since the government came to office in July 2001, insisted on the need to define the institutionalisation of the state, on 13 February the government issued Supreme Decree 013-2003-PCM by means of which it dissolved the

Technical Secretariat of Indigenous Affairs (*Secretaría Técnica de Asuntos Indígenas* - SETAI), the only public institution addressing indigenous peoples' issues. The argument was that there was an overlap of roles with CONAPA, despite the fact that this latter is not an implementing agency but a coordinating body of the state and indigenous peoples. In replacing SETAI, the appointment of an Executive Secretariat within CONAPA was agreed. In other words, after twenty months in government, the only institution with an implementing role in terms of addressing indigenous peoples' concerns is the Executive Secretariat of a coordinating body with poor performance and an erratic direction.

In addition, the stated provision decrees a timescale of 120 days within which to hold "free and democratic elections" for indigenous representation within CONAPA, elections that will be supervised by the National Office for Electoral Processes (*Oficina Nacional de Procesos Electorales* - ONPE). This decision took the indigenous members of CONAPA by surprise who, whilst being in agreement with using legitimate mechanisms to elect indigenous representatives, did not wish to have a public body supervising them in such an imperative manner. The Ombudsman has issued an opinion in this regard, stating that ONPE lacks the authority to organise or supervise elections within civil society bodies.

The election of a new PDPIA Project Coordinator and the need to implement the project before losing it once and for all through institutional incapacity and an inability to spend the money means that the government will need to establish at least one executing agency over the coming months. Meanwhile, the indigenous movement has included the need to create a decentralised public body, at the level of Ministry, within its constitutional proposal, a body that would have legal status, technical, administrative, economic and financial autonomy and the authority to regulate, manage and implement development policies, plans and programmes for indigenous peoples.

Campaigning for inclusiveness

One of the most important actions of Peruvian indigenous organisations has been their campaign for the inclusion of the rights of indigenous peoples and communities in the process of constitutional reform. The campaign is the responsibility of the Coordinating Body of Indigenous Peoples and Communities (*Coordinadora de Pueblos Indígenas y Comunidades*), a coalition made up primarily of organisations

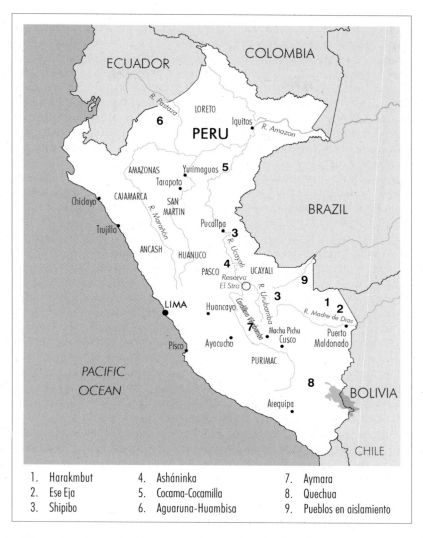

1.	Harakmbut	4.	Asháninka	7.	Aymara
2.	Ese Eja	5.	Cocama-Cocamilla	8.	Quechua
3.	Shipibo	6.	Aguaruna-Huambisa	9.	Pueblos en aislamiento

affiliated to the Permanent Coordinating Body of Indigenous Peoples of Peru (*Coordinadora Permanente de Pueblos Indígenas del Perú* - COP-PIP) and other non-members such as the Agro-forestry Coordinating Body of Indigenous and Peasant Farmers of Peru (*Coordinadora Agro-forestal Indígena y Campesina del Perú* - COICAP) and the Confederation of Amazonian Nationalities of Peru (*Confederación de Nacionalidades Amazónicas del Perú* - CONAP). The initiative for the campaign came from the Inter-ethnic Association for the Development of the Peruvian Rainforest (*Asociación Interétnica de Desarrollo de la Selva Peruana - AIDESEP*).

The Coordinating Body has managed to postpone the debate on the section on indigenous peoples, which was due to be held in March, in order to hold a prior day of consultation and has participatively drawn up a joint proposal to include the rights of indigenous peoples in the planned constitutional reform. On 12 and 13 April 2003, an Indigenous Consultation was held with delegates from indigenous organisations from all of the country's regions along with an Indigenous Forum in the Legislative Chamber, at which a proposal for formulation of the reform and its justification was submitted.

The reform process will continue with a discussion of the draft until July, after which Congress will submit the approved text to a referendum for its approval or rejection. The indigenous organisations are confident of promoting a strong campaign over the coming months in order to mobilise public awareness and the political forces within Congress to achieve acceptance of their proposals. For a start, an article on the definition of the state has already been approved, which expressly recognises Peruvian society as "pluricultural, multilingual and pluriethnic".

Among other innovations in the indigenous proposals is their own definition of indigenous:

The indigenous peoples, peasant communities and native communities exist in law and have legal status. Indigenous or ancestral peoples predate the state and have their own social, economic, cultural and political institutions, their territory and they identify themselves as such.

The indigenous peoples are social organisations of public law, autonomous in their organisation and in the use and administration of their territories and natural resources. They include the peasant and native communities, whatever their legal position, and their organisations.

Similarly, protection of the right of peoples in situations of isolation or initial contact to voluntarily maintain or change their situation is proposed, guaranteeing them the rights of possession and ownership of their territories.

The proposal demands the inalienable, nonseizable, imprescriptible and inexpropriable nature of indigenous territories and understands the consultation process as being one of providing full information and of giving one's consent or opposition, freely expressed with full knowledge of the facts.

People from Madre de Dios protest against loggers' depredation of their forests.
Photo: Claus Kjærby/IBIS Denmark

The indigenous proposal demands ownership and autonomy in the control, use and management of the natural resources existing within their territory, along with the direct or associated exploitation of their land, sea and subsoil resources.

The indigenous organisations undoubtedly have a hard battle on their hands to achieve their inclusion as indigenous peoples, given that to date the various Political Constitutions have only recognised the communities, whose rights have been reduced by the questionable 1993 Constitution promulgated by Alberto Fujimori's regime and other unconstitutional laws such as the Law on Mining Access, promulgated under its aegis.

Unity of indigenous organisations

Another noteworthy event is the process of convergence that is taking place between the main Peruvian indigenous organisations of the Andes and the Amazon which, in October 2002, decided to formally establish the Permanent Coordinating Body of Indigenous Peoples of Peru (*Coordinadora Permanente de los Pueblos Indígenas del Perú* – COPPIP), a national umbrella organisation of Peruvian indigenous organisations.

The process of unity began in 1998 with the First Congress of Human Rights and Indigenous Peoples, held in Cusco, at which it was agreed to establish a Permanent Conference of Indigenous Peoples. Following several years of exchange of experience, rapprochement on various issues but also disagreement on others, AIDESEP, the National Coordinating Body of Communities Affected by Mining (*Coordinadora Nacional de Comunidades Afectadas por la Minería* - CONACAMI), the Permanent Workshop of Indigenous and Amazonian Women (*Taller Permanente de Mujeres Indígenas y Amazónicas*) and the Association for the Defence and Development of the Andean Communities of Peru (*Asociación de Defensa y Desarrollo de las Comunidades Andinas del Perú* - ADECAP), among others, decided to take a step towards unity and turn the Conference into a Coordinating Body. COPIP now has duly constituted legal status and plays an important role as a promoter and catalyst in processes of indigenous convergence such as the campaign for constitutional reform.

Decentralisation: a new challenge

Regional and municipal elections were held in November 2002, thus initiating a new attempt to decentralise the country and to rebuild regional government after so many years. This time, the region has not been defined on the basis of geographic, socio-economic or historic/cultural criteria but a political/administrative criterion has been maintained in which each department is also a region.

For the elections, Congress issued a law on quotas such that the lists of candidates in constituencies with an indigenous presence had to comprise a minimum of 15% indigenous representatives. This law has caused a great deal of confusion and division because indigenous individuals from the same people or organisation have to participate on the different parties' lists and compete against each other.

As demonstrated by a workshop in the central forest (January 2003) on indigenous relations with the state, the decentralisation process is viewed very critically by the indigenous organisations because it is a top-down process, one that reproduces the centralism in which a political and administrative criterion predominates, ignoring social, historical and cultural criteria.

Whilst regionalisation opens up the possibility of influencing the formulation of regional policies that have an intercultural focus, there will be a need for other civic participation mechanisms as neither the regions nor the municipalities recognise the pluriculturality of the spaces for social representation and there are no mechanisms ensuring the true participation of civil society.

It should also be noted that regional government is an attempt to gradually transfer resources and power, and that the municipalities in areas with indigenous population have little income as they cannot generate their own funding like the urban municipalities. Moreover, transport in the forest is very difficult and expensive, increasing the cost of public works.

In the future, indigenous peoples will have an opportunity to enforce their right to participate at the level of the regions, and provincial and district municipalities, and to turn them into something positive but only provided that the indigenous organisations gain greater information, knowledge and undertake training actions in all regions.

Main battles of the Amazonian movement

The peoples in isolation

There are at least 14 recorded peoples in Peru who are in isolation or in a situation of initial or sporadic contact. They live nomadically in forested areas with difficult access. Their main subsistence activities are hunting and gathering.

Their absence of any contact with national society is due to a fear of suffering further traumatic experiences similar to those experienced in the past, the consequences of which were death and illness, which decimated their population. In some cases, they are groups consisting of only a few dozen people, such as the Isconahua or Ikobakebu, from the Pano ethno-linguistic family, living in the Lower Ucayali (headwaters of the Shesha and Abujao). Others relate to somewhat larger peoples, such as the Kugapakori, Nanti or Kirineri, settled in the Cusco forests, within the sphere of the Camisea project, and whose population is calculated at over a thousand people.

The number one enemy of uncontacted peoples or peoples living in isolation are the fossil fuel companies and loggers, who have no qualms about entering the areas inhabited by these indigenous populations. Warnings that their entry could lead to epidemics or that the changing of their habitat could endanger their basic subsistence needs fall on deaf ears.

One example is Block 88 of the Camisea Gas Project, which is super-imposed on the Nahua-Kugapakori Reserve, established by the state in 1990 to protect the indigenous Nahua and Kugapakori groups (also known as the Nanti) from the dangers of contact with national society and to avoid violating their right to isolation.[1]

The only effective defenders of these uncontacted peoples are indigenous organisations such as FENAMAD and AIDESEP, who stand up to the state's lethargy and the voracity of predatory companies.

Another sign of this is the attempt to approve the bill of law known as the Salhuana Law, the intention of which is to increase the period of time allowed for transporting timber extracted from an area in which uncontacted peoples are present in the Amazonian department of Madre de Dios. At the time of writing this report, indigenous and environmental organisations and INRENA itself are trying to convince Congress and the President of the Republic not to begin to process the said regulation, which casts doubt on the model of agreed concessions established in the new Forestry Law, in which reserved areas and procedures were also defined.

In addition, AIDESEP is continuing its pressure to improve its participation in the management of protected natural areas, specifically in the Indigenous Participation in Protected Natural Areas Project (*Participación Indígena en Áreas Naturales Protegidas* - PIMA) being monitored by the World Bank with the aim of ensuring effective joint implementation along criteria of equity and with an intercultural approach. One of the specific demands is that the land regularisation of Amazonian communities should be supported in order to avoid the superimposition of protected areas onto indigenous territories.

Vilcabamba mountain range: important achievement

On 15 January 2003, Supreme Decree No. 003-2003-AG was published, which officially declares the Categorisation of the Apurímac Reserved Zone, known as the Vilcabamba mountain range, over an area of 709,347.06 has in the departments of Junín and Pasco, and which establishes the following permanent protected natural areas: the Asháninka Communal Reserve (184,468.38 has), the Machiguenga Communal Reserve (218,905.63 has) and the Otishi National Park (305,973.05 has), included within both reserves.

Main battles of the Andean movement

The mining problem

Mineral exploitation has become the main problem affecting Peru's indigenous communities in the Andes and along the coast, and there is a long history of abuses that have gone unpunished. The state's power to exclusively exploit minerals and fossil fuels means, in practice, an infringement of rights such as the right to life and to communal property. The state permits the purchase of lands for mining at an unrealistic value, causing displacement of the people, who lose everything: their land, their customs, their economic subsistence activities and their cultural roots. These people, who only have experience of agricultural and livestock activities, find it difficult to take up other activities. The mining projects promise to generate new jobs but this is not the case as the demand is for highly qualified workers.

Peru is one of the largest producers of gold, silver, zinc and other metals in Latin America and directs its policy of promoting private investment at the mining industry, giving this priority over agriculture, industry and fishing. The mining industry enjoys a favourable regulatory framework offering access to land, cheap labour, flexible environmental regulations and tax benefits. This framework creates socio-environmental and territorial problems and conflicts for more than 3,000 indigenous communities and local populations who, without proper consultation, are forced to live alongside the mining industry and suffer its impacts.

The greatest impacts are on the hydro-graphic basins, in which liquid and solid effluents are deposited. In addition, river courses are changed for mining activity, and lakes dry up. Another macro-impact is the atmospheric contamination in towns such as Oroya, Moquegua and Callao.

Mining activity in areas of poverty also distorts local economic indicators, creates enormous social divisions locally, and promotes activities that alter local customs and economies.

CONACAMI maintains that mining in Peru is environmentally, socially and economically unsustainable in its current form. The mining industry is experiencing a crisis in economic, but also environmental and social, profitability. The government maintains that the economy is improving through mining activity. However, mining has yet to demonstrate a capacity to substantially improve the quality of life of those communities in mining areas.

The March for Life and frustrated dialogue

From 1 to 10 July 2002, a Great National March for Life, Land, Water and Farming took place in Lima, attended by approximately three thousand community members from 13 of the country's departments affected by mining. President Alejandro Toledo refused to receive a delegation from the march but, through his representative, signed a commitment to form a high-level tripartite Dialogue Commission within 45 days, made up of representatives from government, the companies and the communities.

This commitment was signed by presidential advisor César Rodríguez Rabanal and three government ministers holding portfolios in Energy and Mining, Agriculture and Health. Nonetheless, as of March 2003, the government had not issued the supreme decree creating this Commission, frustrating the communities hopes for dialogue.

Peruvian state denounced before the IACHR

Due to this frustrated dialogue, on 28 February 2003, CONACAMI presented a petition to the Inter-American Commission on Human Rights (IACHR) of the Organisation of American States (OAS) in Washington on behalf of the members of the communities affected by mining activity in Peru and against the state for violation of the fundamental rights enshrined in the American Convention on Human Rights.

Among the main rights violated can be noted the right to life, property, personal integrity, equality, non-discrimination and free association, along with the right to freedom to work, legal protection and the gradual development of economic, social and cultural rights.

The complaint states that, from 1990 to the present day, the state has promoted private sector involvement in mining and fossil fuel extraction by means of regulations that contradict the rights of people belonging to these communities, creating an inequality in application to the detriment of the indigenous peoples.

Among the pro-investment regulations are Law 26505 (1995), which places land ownership in a position of legal uncertainty, and Law 26570, the "Law on Mining Rights", which serves to put pressure on and break up the communities. It should be noted that the majority of peasant farmer communities in Peru are of indigenous origin, and thus protected by ILO Convention 169. The lawsuit comprises more than 600 pages and demonstrates how the Peruvian state has favoured the mining companies, affecting the local communities and populations.

The damage caused by mining activities continues without the Peruvian state dealing with the issue, and there are no public bodies to effectively monitor protection of the rights of the indigenous peoples and peasant and native communities that suffer its bitter consequences.   ❑

Note

1   More information on this reserve and its peoples can be found on the web at: www.serjali.org and www.onr.com/cabeceras

BOLIVIA

2002 will go down in the country's history as that of the "democratic rebellion of 'illegal' Bolivia". The general elections held on 30 June led the indigenous Aymara, Evo Morales, leader of the coca growers of El Chapare and of the Movement to Socialism (*Movimiento Al Socialismo* - MAS) to the doors of the Presidency of the Republic, having won the second vote. Alongside him, around 30 indigenous and peasant representatives entered parliament as deputies and senators.

Background

The general elections were preceded not only by multiple conflicts that led to various social demonstrations but also by a chain of decisions on the part of those in power that engendered the people's reaction.

Different analysts[1] highlight the emergence of parallel but independent social movements, in the wake of the "water war" of April 2000 in Cochabamba. Marches on the part of indigenous and peasant farmers from the Oriente, road blocks in El Chapare and the La Paz *altiplano*, teachers' and truckers' protests and the violence against peasant farmers over access to agrarian property, have all been a constant factor of the last two years. Aware that the progress made by their demonstrations was not resolving their problems or changing the situation of exclusion they found themselves in, the social sectors - primarily rural – started to move on from sectoral demands to making demands for structural changes in the development model and political system.

Over the same period, strong disagreements were also arising between the parties of the past governing coalition, which led to the intervention of the Catholic Church to broker a Memorandum of Under-standing to guarantee relative political stability.

In this context, the ruling class made a series of erratic decisions that led to the electoral results of 30 June. The first of these was that of excluding the coca growers' leader, Evo Morales, from parliament, accusing him of being the author of clashes between coca growers and police that left several dead on both sides in early 2002. This decision, instead of gaining the approval of urban sectors opposed to the roadblocks, only broadened the sympathy for the excluded leader. Evo Morales' exit was sealed with his threat to return to parliament once more, only this time accompanied by a further 20 elected members. His threat has been fulfilled and more. Then came the news of the approval of a Constitutional Reform bill. The Memo-randum of Understanding signed months previously between the traditional parties, at the request of the Catholic Church, included a commitment to promote reforms to widen civic participation, in-cluding the possibility of establishing a Constituent Assembly as a mechanism for constitutional reform. But instead of opening up the political system, the announced reform put it once more above legal and social control, paying only lip service to democratic opening up.

The news of the reform, together with the first reading of a bill of law that exclusively favoured the logging sector and the news of other measures that would affect the decimated agrarian rights of indig-enous and peasant farmers yet further, were the reasons behind the "March for Popular Sovereignty, Territory and Natural Resources", which took place in May with the involvement of organisations from the Bolivian Oriente.

This march, together with a new disagreement between the pro-government parties caused by the Electoral Court's decision to dis-qualify the leader of one of these parties from running for president, buried the draft reform once and for all. But the occasion served for members of parliament to approve, in secret sitting, lucrative lifelong and inherited allowances for the presidents of both legislative cham-bers and other members of parliament. There was uproar and the decision had to be overturned only days later, while the march con-tinued to gain support for a Constituent Assembly.

1	Weenhayek	4	Chiquitano	7	Itonama	10	Yuqui
2	Ayoreo	5	Guarayo	8	Tacana	11	Aymara
3	Guaraní	6	Sirionó	9	Ese Eja	12	Quechua

During May, in the most important towns in the country, debates were held between the presidential candidates. The participation of the coca growers' leader in the first debate was so well received that he was excluded from subsequent debates organised by business groups. This exclusion also had an impact on the electorate and the candidate benefited from this.

One last event relates to the declarations issued by the US Embassy warning the government that it would withdraw its support to Bolivia should the coca sector return to parliament. Although the electoral growth of the MAS was already a fact, the Ambassador's declarations had the effect of giving it its final recognition.

But, in general, the utter discontent with government policies and corruption, which led to a growing social awareness around the need for an opening up of the political system and structural change, is what led a large part of the Bolivian population to opt for the inclusion of the excluded in the elections.

The results of the elections of 30 June 2002 favoured not only the social sectors linked to the coca leader but also the indigenous trend within the peasant farmer movement of the *altiplano*, the Indigenist Pachakuti Movement (*Movimiento Indigenista Pachakuti* - MIP), led by Felipe Quispe, also an Aymara. Adding together the votes obtained by both movements, it can be seen that the excluded social sectors were the winners of the electoral debate, gaining more than 27% of the total votes cast in the country. In contrast, the traditional political parties (MNR, MIR, ADN, UCS and MBL) recorded a clear fall in electoral favouritism, together achieving only 48% of the vote. Three of them (ADN, UCS and MBL) virtually disappeared from the national electoral scene.

The 2002 March[2]

Despite the failure of the draft constitutional reform, the March for Popular Sovereignty, Territory and Natural Resources that began in May continued, with many social sectors linked to the countryside joining forces behind it, identifying with the demands for a participatory Constituent Assembly and a break with the monopoly of the political parties. In addition to this, the march demanded the final filing of the draft Law on Sustainable Development and made land demands. Other social organisations of an urban nature, civil society institutions and democratic personalities publicly announced their support of the demonstration's demands and the natives of the highlands undertook their own marches from Chuquisaca and Potosí under the same banner, led by the Council of Ayllus and Markas of Quyasuyo (*Consejo de Ayllus y Markas del Quyasuyo* -CONAMAQ).

The march became a real influencing factor not only on the government but also on the political parties, who were strongly challenged. Various spokespeople from the ruling class spread the idea that the march was a politico-electoral strategy on the part of the MAS and others argued that its aim was to boycott the general elections of 30 June. But, contrary to the first statement, the march was at that time

On their way to La Paz - 2002. Photo: APCOB, Bolivia

condemned by this (then) minority party. In spite of many points of agreement in terms of the exclusion to which they were victim, the coca growers' sector chose the electoral path instead of joining the demonstration. Whether for or against the demonstration or their electoral proposal, what is clear is that for them there were more than enough reasons to concentrate on gaining the vote of excluded sectors, as it was a question of reversing the arrogant expulsion of their leader from parliament via the ballot box.

After more than 20 days on the road, the march that started in Santa Cruz reached Cochabamba where it stayed several days, and during which time there was an attempt to reach an agreement with the government on land demands and on organising a political summit to analyse the issue of constitutional reform. When this attempt failed, the march moved on from Cochabamba but a faction of the Landless Movement (*Movimiento de los Sin Tierra* - MST), headed by its then top leader, signed a sectoral agreement and went to La Paz, where the announced summit of political parties with this movement and with pro-government indigenous leaders was held.

The march that started in Santa Cruz met up with those from the *Altiplano* and together they arrived at the seat of government 10 days before the elections. By this time, the leaders that had participated in the summit had signed an agreement with the majority parties by which they accepted the constitutional reform without including anything relating to a Constituent Assembly.

The organisations involved in the march signed a new agreement requiring that a constitutional reform should include a participatory National Constituent Assembly and that the draft law should be agreed by a joint commission of parties, government and organisations.

This mobilisation certainly made some achievements, notably the filing of the draft law in support of sustainable development and the delegitimization of the measures announced by the government, known as the "agrarian package". In addition, they managed to get the issue of constitutional reform into the national debate, an issue considered until then as an issue for experts only, and forced the political parties to publicly state their positions, placing the issue on the agenda for political and social discussion.

But most important was the fact that the march became a reference point for the social movement, due to the fact that it managed to coordinate different sectors that had traditionally been seen as contradictory, not only due to their regional and cultural differences and even their ideological outlook but also due to their different levels of coordination with the current political system. The fact that peasant farmers, indigenous and natives of the high and lowlands, came together to fight for common goals shows that not only is it a country in which differences remain possible but that there is an awareness that brings people together in the search for structural change.

The Constitutional Reform

Although damaged by the electoral results, the dominant parties soon reacted in the face of the new scenario imposed by the ballot box and, once free from the pressure exerted by the march and the electoral debate, got down to the task of gaining a consensus for a coalition government with the Constitutional Reform bill.

Even before he was elected president, and despite the fact that the elections of 30 June sent an explicit message that future government should be based on an agreement between the state and civil society, Gonzalo Sánchez de Lozada managed to force through approval of a reform bill that did not encompass the demands of the people. On the contrary, the reforms closed the circle of power within the "partidocratic" system yet more and included regulations on natural resource management that were in open contradiction with the repeated demand of indigenous and peasant farmers for greater national control over these and other strategic sectors of the economy.

But most reprehensible was the fact that the reform bill provided that decisions over the exercise of public powers and other issues of great national significance would be approved by a simple majority of members of the legislative chambers. With this, the government coalition, which has this majority, would guarantee the exclusion of the recently elected indigenous-peasant farmer group and of the other members of the opposition, showing their determination to remain in political control of the country.

This reform has yet to be ratified, precisely because the government coalition does not have the two-thirds of votes required for its final approval.

New government and old exclusions[3]

Once in office, President Sánchez de Lozada called for a "social truce" of 90 days in which to present his anti-crisis programme, a deadline that was respected by the social organisations and opposition parties. But even before the expiry of this period, economic shock measures, anti-popular and devastating to the national economy, began to emerge, a number of which had to be reversed due to the fierce reaction they provoked.

To deactivate the discontent, the government announced a pause in the coca crop eradication, pending the results of a new study on legal consumption of the leaves. The announcement was rapidly retracted, because the US was not in agreement.

Once the period of "social truce" had expired, the social sectors began to demand measures that were not forthcoming. The coca growers demanded a pause in the eradication and together defined the conditions for the production of a study on legal consumption. Agribusiness was demanding measures for the revival of their sector, including legal security of land tenure. For their part, the indigenous and peasant farmers were demanding fulfilment of numerous agreements to provide land to their communities, signed by previous governments.

Violence over land

The complaints over serious irregularities in the agrarian process, which is producing such poor results, and the constant demand for land on the part of peasant farmers, caused the conflicts to resurface in November.

According to a communiqué from the indigenous and peasant farmer organisations of Santa Cruz, on 14 November the ex sub-prefect of the Sara Province (Santa Cruz), who is disputing the lands of the Nueva Jerusalem farming settlement, ordered the destruction and burning of houses and crops, which was carried out with police support. The peasants, who had withdrawn to a neighbouring community, held four of the policemen who participated in the action in order to pressure for the arrival of the authorities. Because of this action, the peasants were detained and kidnapped, while the ex-authority prepared to appropriate their lands.

At daybreak on Monday 18 November, en Yapacaní, an owner also in conflict over the land of a peasant union, organised and mobilised hooded and armed people to evict the farmers. During the action, they killed Luciano Jaldín, a peasant farmer from a neighbouring community, and other farmers were reported disappeared. The event sparked off a tense situation in the area, in which the state was unable to intervene, leaving it virtually open to the rule of the strongest. After only two weeks, 4 people had been murdered, among them peasant farmers and estate workers. A delegation led by the Ombudsman that visited the area verified the presence of camps of armed persons and the use of instruments of torture.

The Mojeño indigenous territory

The violence then moved on to the Mojos plains, in the Department of Beni. During the night of 24 November, a cattle rancher affected by the process of titling of the Multi-ethnic Indigenous Territory (TIM) physically assaulted the communicator from the Peasant Research and Promotion Centre (*Centro de Investigación y Promoción del Campesino* - CIPCA), an indigenous support institution, and the parish priest of San Ignacio de Mojos, Enrique Jordá.

This action was preceded by the visit of a Multi-sectoral Commission to San Ignacio de Mojos to verify complaints made by the indigenous regarding irregularities in the process of titling of their lands, partiality on the part of the agrarian, administrative and judicial authorities in favour of the cattle ranchers, and the involvement of armed individuals in field inspections, terrifying and threatening community members and leaders. The last straw for the indigenous communities, and that which led them to make complaints to the seat of government, was the decision of an agrarian judge who, at the request of a cattle rancher, ordered the eviction of the Mercedes del Apere community, which had been settled in the Mojeño indigenous territory for more than 60 years.

In the days following the commission's visit, the press and television published special reports on the situation in Mojos. This unleashed the fury of the cattle ranchers, who decided to ask the authorities for the expulsion of CIPCA, giving them 72 hours to leave the building, and commencing legal action against the journalists. Then came the physical assault on the Mojos parish priest and CIPCA worker and, in the following days, intimidation of other employees of this organisation.[4]

The processes of titling the territories claimed by the indigenous peoples in the region are extremely delayed. The Mult-ethnic Indigenous Territory was recognised in 1990, covering an area of 352,000 has, and the Mojeño Ignaciano Indigenous Territory (TIMI) was requested by the communities in 1998, covering an area of 98,388 has. To date, the processes for the regularisation and consolidation of these indigenous territories have made no progress. In both processes, INRA irregularities and pressure from the cattle ranchers have been a constant and, in response to complaints, death threats have been made against various community leaders and members.

The Monte Verde indigenous territory

The process of titling the Monte Verde territory, suspended for almost two years awaiting decisions of the National Agrarian Court and the Constitutional Court, commenced once more in March 2002. INRA was to rectify errors made in the implementation of previous stages and publicise the results of the process in relation to the plots claimed by third parties. Days prior to the date on which INRA was to publish these results, this action was unilaterally suspended by the National Director of this institution, on the pretext that the farmers and stockbreeders had requested this of the government.

During the same period of time, the Federation of Cattle Ranchers of Santa Cruz (*Federación de Ganaderos de Santa Cruz* - FEGASACRUZ) carried out a symbolic closure of INRA, demanding that the process of regularisation of agrarian rights over indigenous lands should be suspended once and for all, arguing that the time given in law for titling had expired.

By then, the clashes in Yapacaní had become public knowledge, and the government announced the Land Plan with reforms of the current regulations, which would eliminate work as a requirement to acquire or maintain agrarian property, increase the animal load and implement other measures favouring illegal settlers, cattle ranchers and estate owners who were disputing indigenous lands. It was then that the suspension of the Monte Verde process took place with the aim of awaiting the adoption of the announced reforms, which would change the situation of more than 70 supposed cattle ranchers who should have been evicted from this territory.

The organisations' protests and the land conflict scandal, widely publicised in the media, resulted in INRA's decision being reversed and the results of the process were presented in the municipality of Concepción on Sunday 24 November, amid great tension and rumours of the presence of armed groups. In spite of the fact that the communities requested the protection of the government authorities, none were present.

The above, however, is no guarantee for the titling of this indigenous territory, as the issuing of the final resolutions, and the subsequent intervention of the National Agrarian Court, where appropriate, is still required. But its titling is not only dependent upon legal procedures. One illegal property has become the greatest threat not only for the titling of the territory but also for the life and integrity of indigenous leaders and their support professionals.

The La Unidad cooperative, a fraudulently obtained property of 15,000 has, has been the focus of the fiercest conflicts over the last two years, during which it has illegally cleared around 800 has of forest in the Monte Verde territory. To avoid the continuing destruction of the forest and violation of their territory, the communities re-established community controls over access to third parties and it was then that the violent actions began in September 2001, including the kidnapping and attempted murder of the lawyer advising the communities. At the time these events took place, officials of the Forestry Superintendence who were attempting to inspect illegal levelling were threatened at gun point to leave the area.

In December, the communities again denounced the presence of armed individuals and, recalling the cases of Pananti and Yapacaní, demanded that the authorities establish measures to avoid bloodshed on their territory. But, to date, nothing has been done. A recent report from the Agrarian Superintendence, responsible for monitoring land use, verifies the presence of armed men preventing access on the part of its officials to the land claimed by the La Unidad cooperative.

Meeting for Land and Territory

The land conflicts have affected virtually all indigenous territories, particularly those in which the claimant organisations are exerting greater control over the process being implemented by INRA. During 2002, 439,000 has were titled to three Native Community Lands (*Tierras Comunitarias de Origen* - TCO) in the Department of Beni, which brings the total amount of lands titled to indigenous peoples to 2,500,000 has. But it must be noted that, as on other occasions, areas claimed by the indigenous continue to be unjustifiably reduced. In the case of the Movima people, for example, less than 6,000 has were titled to them.

With regard to peasant farmers, those most affected by the violence, the first communal property was finally titled in 2002, covering an area of 268 has for 36 families in the Department of Santa Cruz.

In the first days of December 2002, the peasant, indigenous, women, settlers and landless peasant organisations and the *ayllus* of the *Altiplano* held a Meeting for Land and Territory. At this event, they analysed the government's "Land Plan" in relation to the problems of their communities, observing that it was aimed at benefiting unproductive estates and lands fraudulently acquired, and at continuing to grant forestry concessions over lands the government had for several years been promising would be given to indigenous and peasant farmers.

In a manifesto published at the end of the event, the organisations expressed their opposition to the regulatory amendments anticipated by the government and demanded the approval of a "Law on Land and Territory" to replace the current Law on the National Agrarian Reform Service. They repeated their demand to re-institutionalise INRA, beginning with the dismissal of its National Director through lack of legitimacy and credibility, and also asking for the restructuring of the Agrarian Judiciary. In relation to the violence, they demanded that the state dismantle the armed groups that were acting on behalf of the landowners in various parts of the country and announced that they would maintain their coordination to initiate new methods of pressure.

2003: more clashes and violence[5]

In the early days of the year, the coca growing sector and peasant farmer organisations, headed by Deputy Morales, announced a plat-form of demands to the government which, in addition to issues of coca and land, included national issues such as the sale of gas, integration of Bolivia in the Free Trade Area of the Americas (FTAA), measures for economic reactivation and the national budget. The government refused to dialogue, considering that the spokespeople were not representative to deal with the issues proposed, and a road-block began on 13 January 2003.

The response was the militarization of the country with combined police and army forces, mobilising more than 22,000 people (almost 50% of the country's troops). After 13 deaths, 60 people wounded and around 200 arrests, the government agreed to dialogue by means of seven thematic committees which, to date, have produced no results.

Before the blockades commenced, the government launched an-other measure, this time aimed at the 'dedollarisation' of the economy, but beginning with the income received by retired people. These eld-erly people began a demonstration to demand a reversal of the gov-ernment measure but the response they received was initially also one of repression of their peaceful protest. The demonstrators were vio-lently forced onto buses to return to their places of origin. One of the buses, contracted from a friend of the Minister of the Presidency, had technical faults and caused a road traffic accident in which 7 of the elderly people being forcibly transported were killed. The scandal forced the government to allow the march to reach La Paz and, once there, to initiate a dialogue to resolve their demands.

But still with no resolution of these conflicts, which had left 20 dead, the President announced the application of an income tax of 12.5 % from a level of 880 BOB. (US$ 116.40) arguing the need to reduce the fiscal deficit.

The reaction from all social and economic sectors was immediate, as this measure would affect the already fragile economy of the workers and would deepen the country's economic crisis.

The injustice of the measure became all the more clear when the Minister for Sustainable Development himself admitted, in front of all the media, that the ministers and vice-ministers would continue to receive their lucrative emoluments, increased by an extra tax exemption, paid to them out of a "secret expenditure" account.

The Bolivian Workers Union (*Central Obrera Boliviana*) called a protest march on 12 February in La Paz and the police decided to mutiny nationally against the "*impuestazo*" or tax hike, in turn renewing an old demand for salary increases.

The government ordered the suppression of the police mutiny by army personnel, unleashing a clash between uniformed groups right in the middle of the Plaza Murillo and virtually at the doors of the government buildings. The result was 16 dead and 125 wounded, including police, soldiers and civilians, and a popular reaction that was now out of control. The population took to the streets and various public administration buildings were burnt. The headquarters of the political parties in the current government coalition suffered the same fate, along with that of the main party of the previous government. Shopping centres, banks, tollbooths, patrol posts and some businesses (the Cervecería Boliviana Nacional and Aguas del Illimani) were also looted.

The city of La Paz was militarized. The air force flew low overhead, tanks and armoured cars patrolled the streets and avenues and took the Plaza Murillo, repeating scenes from dictatorial times. Dozens of snipers posted at strategic points fired at close range.

On Thursday 13 February, mass rallies took place in all of the country's towns. In La Paz, El Alto, Cochabamba, Oruro and Santa Cruz, the burning and looting of buildings, warehouses and political party headquarters continued. The balance of the second day was 17 dead and 48 wounded.

In all these demonstrations (roadblocks, march of the elderly and the police mutiny), the government publicly maintained that it would not negotiate under pressure. But the reality is that it only dialogues under pressure and after many deaths. Just one example of this is that the national budget, which established the income tax, was one of the issues to be discussed by the Dialogue Committees formed with the social sectors who mobilised in January. Whilst the Committee 'dialogued', the government presented the draft budget to parliament for its approval by the group of coalition parties, leaving the dialogue as no more than a demagogic exercise. ❑

Notes

1   See *Revista Artículo Primero*, No. 11. CEJIS, Santa Cruz, September 2002.
2   **Romero B., Carlos y Betancur, Ana Cecilia. 2002.** "Movimiento Social, Régimen Político y Reformas a la Constitución. Retrospectiva sobre el estado de cosas". In *Revista Artículo Primero,* No. 11. CEJIS, Santa Cruz, September 2002.
3   **CEJIS. 2003. "Bolivia – Realidad y Trasfondo de los Conflictos".** In *Revista Artículo Primero* No. 12. CEJIS, Santa Cruz, March 2003.
4   Information obtained from unpublished document "Ayuda memoria sobre la situación en Mojos". CIPCA, November 2002.
5   **CEJIS. 2003.** (*op.cit.*).

BRAZIL

2002 was a noteworthy year for Brazil in terms of the presidential elections. On 27 October, the union leader, Luís Inácio Lula da Silva, from the Workers' Party, was elected President of the Republic by a huge majority. The new president, of humble origin, has a long history of defending sectors excluded from Brazilian society and his election offers new prospects for progress in Brazil's social achievements, including for indigenous peoples.

The Coordinating Body of Indigenous Organisations of the Brazilian Amazon, COIAB, the most active indigenous organisation in the country, provided input into the elections, the transition period and the establishment of the new government. Their actions signify a strengthening of indigenous participation in the Brazilian political process, based on the observation that government actions at municipal, state and federal level have an impact on indigenous interests, and they are also a way of making indigenous desires known to the political parties and Brazilian society as a whole.

In the pre-electoral phase, COIAB presented a document with its proposals to the presidential candidates, highlighting the importance of protecting the country's socio-cultural diversity. The document was presented to Lula on 23 August, in Manaus. In summary, indigenous peoples were demanding the approval of a new Statute for Indigenous Peoples, the demarcation of indigenous lands, their indigenous control and the withdrawal of non-indigenous inhabitants. They also wanted special public policies in areas of education, health and sustainable economic development, protection of biodiversity resources and traditional knowledge, the participation of indigenous people in bodies dealing with their rights and interests, and particular care in the protection of the rights of indigenous women.

On receiving COIAB's proposals, Lula commented that they already formed part of his government programme and he made a commitment to implement them in order to advance the rights of indigenous peoples in Brazil. President Lula took office in January 2003 and reiterated his commitment to address the demands of indigenous peoples.

Lula will need to fulfil his political programme presented during the electoral campaign and maintain direct dialogue with the indigenous communities in order to guarantee them protection of their rights and interests. Considering that the new government has only recently taken office, it is not yet possible to evaluate its policies.

In addition to involvement in the electoral process, COIAB continued with all its other areas of work. Seminars and courses were held on institutional strengthening for itself and its grassroots organisations. In this respect, COIAB gave priority to concluding the process of administrative restructuring, including the hiring of technicians and advisors to support its activities.

COIAB also carried out activities aimed at intercultural school education and special attention to indigenous health. It also supported projects aimed at the sustainable economic development of indigenous communities, seeking to guarantee them a better quality of life, along with protection of their lands, environment and culture.

In addition, the following activities can be mentioned:

Meeting of indigenous women

The First Meeting of Indigenous Women of the Amazon was held from 27 to 29 June with the support of COIAB and the Norwegian Development Cooperation Agency, NORAD. More than 70 leaders took part, representing 20 organisations of the Apalai, Apurinã, Arapasso, Bakairí, Baniwa, Baré, Dessana, Gavião, Guajajara, Guarani, Karajá, Macuxi, Mayoruna, Mura, Poyanawa, Pira-Tapuia, Tariano, Terena, Tirió-Kaxuyana, Ticuna, Tukano, Sateré Mawé, Wanano, Waiana, Waiãpi, Wapichana, Xavante, Xerente and Xocleng peoples.

The aim of the meeting was to discuss the situation of indigenous women in their communities, their special rights, the relevance of their involvement in the indigenous movement and the creation of COIAB's Indigenous Women's Department. The participants elected Rosimere Maria Vieira Teles, from the Harapazo people, and Débora Tanhuare, from the Bakairí people, to run the new Department.

The military and indigenous lands

The Brazilian Constitution guarantees indigenous peoples the right to ownership and use of the lands traditionally occupied by them. This right applies to any area of Brazil where the traditional occupation of indigenous peoples can be established.

The Constitution also establishes that border areas will be devoted to national territorial defence. As the Federal Constitution permits no internal conflict between its regulations and considers that its principles are in harmony with each other, the border strip envisages the traditional occu-

1. Cinta larga   3. Macuxi   5. Guaraní   7. Guajajara
2. Yanomami   4. Xavante   6. Ticuna

pation of indigenous peoples and also serves for the country's defence. The Federation of Indigenous Organisations of Río Negro, FOIRN, acting together with various indigenous communities affected by the presence of barracks on their lands, requested the intervention of the National Council for Combating Discrimination, the CNDC, to resolve the conflicts between Indians and soldiers. FOIRN feels there is a need to create a specific instrument to govern relations between indigenous and the military in lands located in the border area.

Together with FOIRN and COIAB, the CNDC initiated a discussion process between indigenous peoples and the military in order to resolve the conflicts. Various meetings were held, which included other indigenous organisations working in the border regions.

On 17 and 18 February 2003, a meeting was held in COIAB's offices with the participation of FOIRN, CIVAJA[1], CGTT[2], CIR[3], APIRR[4], FOC-CIT[5], CUNPIR[6] and APIO[7], the Amazonian Military Command and the CNDC, along with other government institutions and NGOs. The indigenous organisations presented a document entitled, "Bases for dialogue and new relations between the indigenous peoples and the Brazilian Armed Forces", in which they demanded:

1. Recognition of Brazil as a multi-ethnic and pluricultural country and respect for the particular rights of indigenous peoples.
2. Relations with indigenous peoples based on dialogue, within a new concept of protection of the border area and promotion of indigenous peoples as historically important in the protection of sovereignty and the national territory.
3. Support to actions for the protection of indigenous lands and their natural resources and biodiversity, provided this is requested by the communities and public bodies responsible for protecting indigenous rights (Ministry of Justice, National Foundation for Indians, Federal Police, Ministry of the Environment, etc.).
4. The inclusion of specific courses on human rights and the history of the rights of indigenous peoples in the training programme for soldiers directly working in indigenous lands.
5. Specific selection and preparation of officers who will be working directly with indigenous communities.
6. Repeal of Decree 4412 of 7 October 2002, which governs the actions of the Armed Forces and Federal Police on indigenous lands.
7. Creation of a Permanent Inter-institutional Forum to evaluate, deliberate and propose measures and criteria to regulate the presence of the military in indigenous lands located in the border area.

Among other things, the organisations declared themselves against the establishment of military barracks on indigenous lands, relations between soldiers and indigenous women, impunity in cases of human rights violations in indigenous communities committed by members of the armed forces and the construction of a military base in the hamlet of Uiramuta, located in the Raposa de Sol territory in Roraima.

At the end of the meeting, the National Secretary for Human Rights agreed to submit a proposal to President Lula for the creation of an inter-ministerial Working Group, made up of representatives of the Armed Forces, indigenous organisations and support institutions.

Raposa Serra do Sol

The Indigenous Raposa Serra do Sol Land, located in Roraima state and inhabited by Makuxi, Ingarikó, Wapichana, Taurepang and Patomana peoples, has an estimated population of 15,000 indigenous, divided into 157 communities.

The process of demarcation of these lands should have been concluded in 1998 but this was not possible due to a failure on the part of the federal government. The delay in concluding the demarcation process has been causing various human rights violations in indigenous communities.

The report of the Indigenous Council of Roraima, CIR, on crimes against indigenous peoples during the period 1981 to 1999 notes 20 murders, 21 attempted murders, 51 cases of physical aggression and 54 death threats against indigenous people.

The communities continue to face serious conflicts, such as the establishment of the Municipality of Uiramuta in January 1996, within the community of the same name. The municipality, which arose on the basis of a *garimpeiro* (prospectors') population, was formed with the support of the state government and, since then, conflicts have intensified between indigenous and non-indigenous people.

In 2001, the Ministry of Defence established a border squad in this same community, creating further conflict between indigenous and the military.

In this context of violence against indigenous communities, the indigenous Macuxi, Aldo da Silva Mota, was murdered in the first week of January 2003. According to the CIR, the event took place in the Retiro Estate, occupied by a land invader known as Chico Tripa, a councillor from the Municipality of Uiramuta.

The indigenous communities are infuriated at all these events and demand that the federal government conclude the process of demarcation of Raposa Serra do Sol as it only requires the signing of the decree ratifying it on the part of the President of the Republic.

Cinta-larga People

The indigenous Cinta-larga people live on the lands of the Aripuanã Park, Serra Morena and Aripuanã, in Rondônia and Mato Grosso states, covering a total area of approximately 2.7 million has. The total Cinta-larga population is 1,200 people, grouped into 33 hamlets.

The Cinta-larga had their first contact with national society during the 1960s and since then, numerous invasions of their lands have taken place on the part of loggers and *garimpeiros* (golddiggers).

From 2000 onwards, *garimpeiro* invasions onto Cinta-larga lands intensified as a consequence of the discovery of a high value diamond deposit. There is strong evidence of a large-scale international trade in and smuggling of diamonds originating from the Cinta-larga lands, involving countries such as Israel, Belgium and Canada.

The health situation of the Cinta-larga is an important indicator of the gravity of the diamond extraction system. The Cinta-larga are currently the only indigenous people whose population is decreasing in demographic terms. Due to the impact of the invasions on indigenous health, in 2002 approximately 3.5% of the Cinta-larga population were quite simply decimated. This is a figure that clearly indicates the likely future for this indigenous people.

The Cinta-larga, together with other indigenous peoples of Rondonia state, and with the support of the Federal Police and FUNAI, achieved the removal of the *garimpeiros* from their lands. But there is still a need for the public authorities to provide permanent programmes for the protection of these lands and to carry out special actions to improve the health and quality of life of the indigenous people.□

Notes and sources

1 *Conselho Indígena do Vale do Javari*
2 *Conselho Geral da Tribo Ticuna*
3 *Conselho Indígena de Roraima*
4 *Associação dos Povos Indígenas de Roraima*
5 *Federação das Organizações e dos Caciques e Comunidades Indígenas da Tribo Ticuna*
6 *Coordenação da União das Nações e Povos Indígenas de Rondônia*
7 *Associação dos Povos Indígenas do Oiapoque*

"Pueblos Indígenas en Brasil: violaciones a la Convención Americana sobre Derechos Humanos da OEA. " Document presented by Brazilian indigenous leaders to the Inter-American Commission on Human Rights of the OAS, February 2003.

Web pages
Coordenação das Organizações Indígenas da Amazônia brasileira:
www.coiab.com.br
Conselho Indígena de Roraima – CIR: www.cir.org.br
Instituto Socioambiental: www.socioambiental.org

PARAGUAY

2002 resulted in a negative balance yet again in terms of the enjoyment of fundamental rights for the country's indigenous population, due primarily to the institutional vacuum left by the government's failure to redesign public policies aimed at the sector on the basis of the accompanying neoliberal agenda. In 2001, it was noted that the initiative to reform Law No. 904/81, published by the Reform Department of the Presidency of the Republic, was merely a continuation of the national indigenist policy of the last three years: one of denying indigenous peoples their rights by giving them as little attention as possible in terms of funding and policies.

Right to life and health

Various epidemics occurred during the first months of 2002, devastating indigenous communities, mainly in the Chaco, and causing fifteen fatalities in early January through sickness and diarrhoea caused by lack of clean water.[1] In the Eastern region, various outbreaks of malaria were recorded, affecting 90% of the indigenous Mbya people in the department of Caazapá and infecting 495 people on just one occasion.

According to current data, tuberculosis continues to be an illness that is almost exclusive to the indigenous population. Whilst the national average is 38/100,000, it is 587/100,000 in Boquerón department, 189/100,000 in Presidente Hayes department, and 238/100,000 in Alto Paraguay. In addition, parasitosis, Chagas disease, respiratory illnesses and other illnesses associated with malnutrition continue to permanently affect the country's indigenous population, particularly the children and elderly.

With regard to pulmonary illnesses, 50% of those treated in the specialist Instituto Juan Max Boettner are indigenous. Official measures to alleviate this situation remain largely absent or else ineffective. Such is the case of the Indigenous Roque González Hospital in Santa Cruz which, according to official data, treats an average of 3,000 indigenous people per year, but which acts more like a halfway house. In general, people who go there are already in a serious state, and yet the hospital lacks infrastructure (radiography, ecography, surgical equipment), and it has only two doctors – no paediatricians or other specialists – and so most patients are referred to other health centres such as the Instituto Max Boettner, mentioned above.

In terms of treating epidemics, in addition to the lack of hospitals or health centres, particularly in the Chaco, medical aid arrives late or in insufficient quantities. In the case of the La Patria community, the medical team arrived five days after symptoms had been reported and, when it moved on, it left only one nurse to care for the 14 hamlets of the area, with no resources and few medicines.

During the last months of the year, the extreme drought caused by lack of rain exacerbated the situation of the indigenous people of the Chaco, causing new health problems in the vast majority of communities through dehydration and gastro-intestinal complications, with the result that 20 indigenous people died.[2]

It should lastly be noted in this section that, despite these serious health problems and risks to the lives of the country's indigenous population, the rampant corruption in local government, as in Presidente Hayes and Alto Paraguay, has meant that significant resources that could have helped indigenous communities were misappropriated in those departments. In the case of the President Hayes government, the Comptroller General of the Republic and the Court of Auditors detected embezzlement of 1,900 million guaraníes (approx. US$ 292,300)[3] intended for the indigenous population and which, to date, has not been recovered. In fact, the Chamber of Deputies prevented the government's intervention to clarify events, for political reasons. To this we must add that what little assistance was provided led to complaints from the communities that bad milk had been distributed, causing yet further illness. Faced with these complaints, the response of the governor of this department, Eugenio Escobar Cattebeke, was that "the indigenous create many problems." Complaints of clientilism and backhanders were also made, indicating that Escobar Cattebeke visits some communities merely for the purposes of propaganda.

For its part, the government of Alto Paraguay spent the sum of 550 million guaraníes for education without having built a single classroom or even a toilet in the area, according to complaints from teachers. What is more, an audit of this government revealed that, over the last three years, approximately 30,000 million guaraníes of public funds have been misappropriated.

Finally, of the many murders depriving the indigenous of their right to life during the year, the assassination of four indigenous people in mysterious circumstances in October, allegedly at the hands of a Satanic sect, has taken on particular relevance, in the context of a wave of attacks against the communities of Uej Lhavos (Nivaclé people – three dead) and Laguna Negra (Guaraní people – one dead), both situated in the area of Filadelfia, Boquerón department, Chaco. Reports

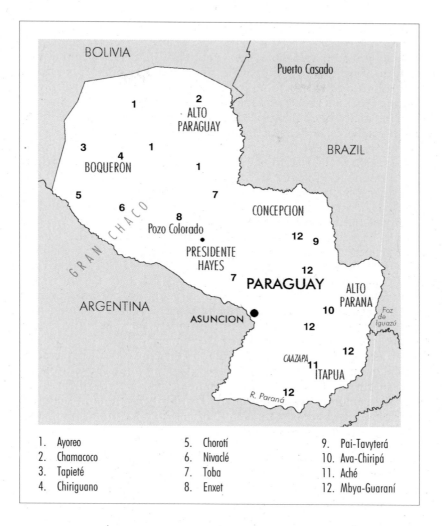

1. Ayoreo	5. Chorotí	9. Pai-Tavyterá
2. Chamacoco	6. Nivaclé	10. Ava-Chiripá
3. Tapieté	7. Toba	11. Aché
4. Chiriguano	8. Enxet	12. Mbya-Guaraní

note that, following a lengthy and suspicious lack of action on the part of the police, the two communities went as far as to form armed defence groups which, after seven days of investigations, apprehended two suspects. The departmental police inaction led to the dismissal of the police chief and a complete change of staff, together with the allocation of a special brigade to protect the indigenous communities.

Right to property

Closely linked to validity of the right to life, food, health and education are indigenous rights to ownership and possession of their lands.

According to a recent study presented by CEJIL and Tierraviva during the 116th Period of Sessions of the Inter-American Commission on Human Rights (Villagra, 2002), the lands guaranteed for the indigenous in the Eastern region total some 66,356 has and in the Western region some 972,256 has, and do not even cover the minimum established by Law No. 904/81 of 20 and 100 has per family for each region (an amount in itself out of line with and paltry in relation to that recognised by the National Constitution and Law No. 234/93).

To cover this minimum, and bearing in mind the estimates of the National Indigenous Census 2002, which is still being processed, it would be necessary to provide around 240,000 has in the Eastern region and 1,200,000 has in the Western region. This report also indicates that there are pending claims – grounded in legality – dating from 6, 10 and 20 years ago for restitution of 60,400 has in the Eastern region and around 828,088 has in the Chaco. In addition, official data from INDI for the current year notes that 60% of the country's indigenous communities are without land or in the process of trying to acquire it.

According to data provided by INDI in early January of this year, this body owed a total of 20,000 million guaraníes by way of payment for the purchase of lands for indigenous communities bought in previous years and not yet settled. In spite of this, and the threat to the security of indigenous rights that a failure to pay for the lands acquired represents, the budget allocated to the Institute for the whole year is scarcely 3,600 million guaraníes.

Faced with this situation, INDI submitted a request for additional funding of 30,000 million guaraníes from the legislature so that it could cover not only payments for land it had already agreed to buy but also for lands that need to be returned to the communities, the reparation of whose rights the state has committed itself to before the IACHR, namely Yakye Axa, Sawhoyamaxa and Xakmok Kásek (Enxet people). Unfortunately, this and other measures taken by INDI have been rejected by the legislature, in whose hands primary responsibility for this year's denial of the property rights of various indigenous communities lies.

In fact, due to the lack of allocation of resources on the part of the legislature for payment of indigenous lands, along with its now customary rejection of the expropriations, some 90 communities throughout the whole country, claiming a total of 888,400 has, have had the possibility of a return of their property rights frustrated (Villagra, 2002).

As an example of one of the pending cases mentioned above, the Xa-kmok Kásek community, comprising 55 families and located in the Salazar Estate (Km 340, Transchaco Road) on a plot of less than four hectares, only needed funding to be allocated for purchase of their ancestral lands in order to resolve their claim, given that the owner of the property was willing to sell to INDI in order to transfer it to the community. However, they were frustrated by the refusal of the members of parliament to grant the sum required.

In a more conflictual case – in which INDI had to use the path of expropriation, given the refusal of the owners of the indigenous ancestral lands to release them by direct sale – parliament, or more precisely the Senate, refused reparation of the rights of the Yakye Axa community in the middle of the year, despite the fact that this measure formed an international commitment on the part of the state before the IACHR.

State corruption in the purchase of overvalued or unclaimed lands is another determining in this situation of denial of the indigenous population's right to property. Thus, to date, not one guaraní of the millions embezzled from INDI during Valentín Gamarra's administration have been returned. Quite the contrary, the said Institute has been forced to face a demand for 419,000,000 guaraníes on the part of owners with whom Gamarra agreed the purchase of their lands. Similarly, INDI is facing judicial action from Nery Páez Mauro for damages, due to the failure to pay for lands that are currently considered by the Institute as overvalued and which were acquired during Lenny Pane de Pérez Maricevich's administration.

Lastly, there is the plundering of the habitat of a number of communities who have already had their lands allocated, primarily for illegal exploitation of the forests[4] such as the indiscriminate hunting of forest species[5], largely in the Chaco, and also on the part of drugs mafias. Similarly, new conflicts have been noted between third parties invading indigenous lands with the sole aim of logging, in many cases creating the forced migration of indigenous people to urban centres.

Organisational and political rights

Finally, one aspect must be noted which, in part, represents the nucleus of hope at this current historical time and which could well change the direction of events: the emergence and consolidation of the indigenous peoples' own organisations in the process of affirming their rights both at national and international level, such as the Commission for the Self-Determination of Indigenous Peoples (*Comisión por la Autodeter-*

minación de los Pueblos Indígenas - CAPI), a body made up of community leaders and representatives of indigenous organisations from both regions of Paraguay, demanding the right to consultation and participation in the reform of Law No. 904/81.[6] This is something that we should certainly be proud of, for it skilfully demonstrates the hypothesis that, in these times, the problems and debate around the indigenous issue have been decisively transferred into the orbit of these people, communities and leaders, within the context of a new universal legal awareness that recognises their participation in forming a new model of social, legal and political relations in their own right, on an equal footing with the societies with whom they live alongside, within the borders of nation states.

During the year, CAPI continued with its meetings and task of formulating a basic document for the legislative reform proposed by the executive, highlighting as central aspects those relating to ethnic identity and the defence of rights already acquired through the legislative advances of the last two decades.

At the moment, in spite of the fact that the indigenous organisations are facing a tacit abandonment of the consultation process on the part of the state, the CAPI authorities have decided to continue with the consultation of the country's leaders, communities and organisations until the end of the process, as had been initially proposed: through the holding of an Indigenous National Congress and approval of the final version of the proposed indigenous law to replace Law No. 904/81.

This and other organisational aspects have been evaluated by the country's indigenous leaders, together with their counterparts from the rest of the continent, during international seminars held to exchange experience and legal expertise on issues such as discrimination, and the current situation of debate in universal and regional fora on indigenous issues, to name but two issues. The most recent of these was held in the capital from 1 to 3 April, organized by Tierraviva and ONIC from Colombia, with IWGIA's support, and entitled "Workshop Seminar on the Permanent Forum on Indigenous Issues and the Draft Declaration on the Rights of Indigenous Peoples".   ❑

Notes

1   This situation was most severe in the La Patria community, comprising 14 hamlets and approximately 390 families (*ABC Color*, 19 Jan.2002).

2   According to approximate figures from the radio station AM Paí Pukú (Irala Fernández district, Chaco).
3   On the basis of an exchange rate of 1 US$ = 6.500 guaranies, current at 25 October 2002.
4   The report from the area of Carmelo Peralta, Chaco, indicates that they tried to conceal the palo santo timber extraction taking place within the territory of the Ayoreo people by causing fires (*ABC Color*, 24/09/02). This trafficking provides an annual profit of 3,000 million guaraníes to the traffickers (*Última Hora*, 3 July2002).
5   The report refers to the seizure, in Fuerte Olimpo, Chaco, of more than 1,600 alligator hides, 200 from capibaras and 307 boa skins (*ABC Color*, 24 September 2002).
6   A process that took place during the first half of this year.

ARGENTINA

O ver the past year, Argentina has had a visible presence in the international press. The institutional violence exercised by the police against demonstrators and activists demanding economic, social and cultural rights, along with the deaths of children from malnutrition, are the extremes of a social situation that continues to astonish Argentinians and foreigners alike.

As a consequence of 25 years of neoliberalism, 60% of the country's population now lives below the poverty line, 30% of whom live in absolute poverty.[1] In some provinces, the figures are as high as 78% and 40% respectively. Since the start of the economic recession in 1998, unemployment has increased by 74.2%, poverty by 67% and absolute poverty by 180%. General unemployment is now over 24%, with figures as high as 50% and even 70% in some regions. Successive economic adjustment plans, deregulation and privatisations implemented by a ruling class who prefer to 'make easy money' through corruption have been the main causes of this disaster, a disaster that is not only economic in nature but also moral. Argentina possesses enormous wealth in terms of energy and food resources, enough to enable all those living within its borders to live comfortably. However, in a context of economic opening, the product of this wealth has been transferred abroad, whilst dealing a fatal blow to national production. Such a situation would not have been possible without the growing debt that arrived with the military dictatorship in 1976 and has been with us ever since. In the 1990s, Argentina pegged its national currency to the US dollar.

This strategy collapsed in 2001, leading to a massive devaluation, the appropriation of private savings on the part of the state and, finally, the fall of the democratically elected government. In 2002, the Ministry for the Economy was forced to admit to international creditors that the country had "virtually" suspended repayments. Almost all year, the debate revolved around negotiations with the International Monetary Fund. The successiv e technical "missions" on the part of the Fund were with the sole aim of implementing new economic adjustments.

This crisis of representation has led to deep political scepticism on the part of the people. Some groups are demanding a Constituent Assembly to discuss a new model for the country and a new form of government that will serve the interests of society and not those of the international banking sector and its internal economic Establishment 'cronies'. Others –more moderate – demand an end to electoral mandates and new general elections. But the government's response has been to organise presidential elections for 27 April 2003, to sign a weak and confusing agreement with the IMF and to leave pressing social demands to the new government.

Criminalization of social protest

The deteriorating living conditions of poorer sectors have led to many children dying from malnutrition, and to increasing numbers of entire families walking the streets by day looking for paper and cardboard as a means of survival. The state's answer to social mobilisation has been the criminalization of protest and repression via persecution of, and threats against, activists and human rights defenders. These regular occurrences at the hands of security forces, aimed at aborting possible social organisation and creating terror among the population, revolved around a number of violent epicentres during the year. The worst of these took place on 26 June when, during a peaceful demonstration of unemployed workers, the Federal Police pursued and shot two demonstrators at point-blank range. Luckily, the press were covering the event and filmed what took place, so there could be no doubt as to what happened and who was to blame.

Social assistance and solidarity

Exclusion from the state system, a denial of social rights and vulnerability in the face of police harassment were the defining factors of a

1.	Ona	6.	Huarpe	11.	Chulupí
2.	Tehuelche	7.	Diaguita-Calchaquí	12.	Toba
3.	Mapuche	8.	Rankulche	13.	Chorote
4.	Mocoví	9.	Kolla	14.	Qom
5	Mbya-Guaraní	10.	Wichí	15.	Pilagá

bleak outlook in terms of social conflict. Faced with this, and in an attempt to ward off famine, the federal government implemented a plan of economic aid for unemployed heads of households. This plan, with the financial backing of the World Bank, consists of a monthly payment of approximately US$50, paid in a state bond known as and individuals have set up local canteens providing free meals to the most needy. Other grassroots initiatives such as bartering, popular in previous years, have now been monopolised by opportunists. The international community has also demonstrated its awareness of the needs of poor Argentinians, sending donations in food and medicines.

Setbacks in indigenist policy

2002 has been a paradoxical year. On the one hand, the state's financial bankruptcy and questions as to the institutional system's legitimacy curbed the application of effective measures for the recognition of indigenous rights. Budgetary limitations prevented the National Institute for Indigenous Affairs (*Instituto Nacional de Asuntos Indígenas* - INAI) from paying grants to students, without which it was difficult to study. No programmes or plans designed by the communities were negotiated. No lands or territories were recognised or demarcated. Travel to the communities on the part of state employees and technicians was restricted. With no indigenous representation in terms of the way it is run, the Institute continues to plan its activities unilaterally, prioritising social assistance above all other issues (Heads of Household Plan). On the other hand, two indigenous development programmes continued with support from the international community: the Inter-American Development Bank's Indigenous People's Welfare Component (*Componente de Atención a la Población Indígena* - CAPI) and the European Union's Indigenous Development Programme in Ramón Lista (*Programa de Desarrollo Indígena en Ramón Lista* - DIRLI). At the same time, the World Bank's Community Development Programme (*Programa de Desarrollo Comunitario*) was launched in the Mapuche community of Pulmarí (Neuquén), in the Kolla communities of the ex-Santiago estate (Salta) and in the India Quilmes community (Tucumán).

Legal status: help or hindrance?

Legal status is a useful instrument both in the titling of lands and in community project management. The National Constitution recognises the legal status of indigenous communities, requiring only their registration. And yet although this would seem to be a simple administrative procedure, political practice has turned it into an instrument of control with which to neutralise the power of 'certain' organisations. INAI created the National Registry of Indigenous Communities (RENACI) but some provinces, jealous of the power that control of this register might imply, have used internal regulations to justify the creation, in turn, of provincial registries.[2]

This apparent lack of inter-state coordination is not a mere oversight but a deliberate strategy to control the possible empowerment of indigenous organisations. Salta province is putting pressure on the member communities of Lhaka Honhat to obtain their own individual legal status. In June 2002, the heads of each of the 37 communities making up this organisation received a note from the Controller of the Provincial Institute of Indigenous Peoples of Salta (*Instituto Provincial de Pueblos Indígenas de Salta*), Decree 768 and a model statute to which they had to adapt as a prior requirement to the election of representatives to this Institute. Whilst this initial attempt to fragment the organisation was a failure, provincial civil servants continue to visit the communities to convince their leaders of the 'benefits' of gaining provincial legal status.

Despite the fact that INAI has signed an agreement with Jujuy province that recognises RENACI during implementation of the National Plan for Land Regularisation (*Plan Nacional de Regularización de Tierras*), the provincial Solicitor-General's Office (*Fiscalía de Estado*) is issuing absurd resolutions demanding various requirements of the communities in order to avoid approving their legal status, thus denying them their right to land titling. Similarly, in June 2002, the Neuquén provincial government passed decree 1184 regulating the communities' legal status. It is quite clear that the Mapuches' passionate defence of their rights disturbs the local power base. All the more so when there are conflicts pending resolution in which powerful economic interests are involved (Kaxipayiñ, Paynemil/Repsol-YPF, Chapelco tourist complex). In addition to its overwhelming and controversial requirements, this decree establishes that field work will be undertaken "with each and every community", without specifying who, how or for whom it will be done. Finally, it adds that "any other data or additional documentation" may be required at any moment.

The indigenous movement

This scenario of conditionalities and opportunities is not being assessed by the indigenous movement. Although some accept the contribution of the Heads of Household Plans, the impact of these plans on a movement still under construction is not known. Nor is the movement taking advantage of considerable international support to focused groups in a context of more poverty and less state intervention. For the moment, struggles are being taken forward in local contexts and in quite isolated situations. There are no supra-local self-organisation bodies nor strategic alliances or coordinations to obtain common goals. The federal state is incapable of fulfilling its responsibility in terms of implementing effective constitutional rights and provincial governments make headway with their practices of co-option and clientelism. Faced with these institutional conflicts, the indigenous movement does not seem to have developed its own agenda.[3]

Cases of violations of rights

Theft of ancestral lands

In 1912, the President of the Nation reserved lands for the communities of the Qom people of the Chaco. This settlement is an historic place for the communities because, in 1924, it was here that the Napalpí massacre took place, the victims of which included men, women and children. Through its revised 1994 constitution, the province is obliged to title the existing reserves. In 1996, 20,000 has were titled, of which almost 4,000 were occupied by non-indigenous people. At that moment, 2,500 has were excluded from the reserve for two non-indigenous producers, their occupation prevailing over ancestral rights. The community presented a complaint for theft of their lands. But in 2002, the provincial Supreme Court of Justice validated the theft, rejecting the indigenous claim. The community have since appealed.[4]

Police repression and violence

On 16 August, the Toba community of Nam Qom in Formosa was attacked by 100 police officers. With no court order, they entered the community in search of indigenous persons accused of the murder of a police officer. They beat and mistreated children, women and men. A number of women were subjected to threats and humiliation. Two girls aged 6 and 3 and a three-month-old baby were left abandoned in their house when the police arrested their parents. An elderly man of 74 was forced to undress and remain standing for two hours, suffering humiliation and physical and moral exhaustion. One woman saw the police submerge her husband in a well and bury her father-in-law's head in mud. Once at the police stations, threats and violence were used to force them to sign their statements. Finally, 8 men were held in prison, accused of murder and resisting arrest. They were held incommunicado and tortured. Some were hooded with oilcloth, such that it covered their head and made it difficult for them to breath while they were being interrogated, forcing them to make statements and to give information on their families under threat of death. One man recounted how they insulted him saying, "You Indian shit, we're going to hang you, we're going to make you pay. It was an Indian shit that killed our colleague, so an Indian is going to pay!" Another suffered serious injury to his eardrum. A child of 10 was held in a cell and brutally treated by a group of police officers.

Terrorised by such violence, the community's reaction was a delayed one but, finally, together with lawyers, they all debated the measures to be taken. A criminal report was filed and, amongst other things, a demonstration was held in Buenos Aires to draw the attention of the general public to the provincial police, who report to the governor. Whilst the legal process continues, some people remain in prison.[5]

New threats: gold in Esquel

This year important gold deposits were discovered near the town of Esquel (Chubut). Eager to make some money, the local government has already distributed 180,000 has in concessions for exploration and exploitation, affecting three Mapuche communities and the area as a whole. The Canadian company, Meridian Gold, owner of the El Desquite mine, will use some six tonnes of cyanide every day. A confidential report notes that the exploitation will take place by dynamiting thirty thousand tonnes of stone every day, and denounces the fact that the company could not explain how it would deal with cyanide and heavy metal residues and acid drainage. The inhabitants of the area, Mapuche and non-Mapuche, have joined forces to decide via a referendum whether the community is in agreement with the gold mining or not. The Huisca Antieco community submitted an appeal for legal protection in defence of its right of participation and consultation, guaranteed by ILO Convention 169, in force in Argentina since 2001.

Visit of the IACHR due to violation of indigenous rights

In August, the IACHR (Inter-American Commission on Human Rights) travelled to Salta province to participate in a working meeting between the parties in the case of Lhaka Honhat against the Argentinian state.[6] At this meeting, it was agreed that the process of a friendly agreement would be continued once more, in order to consider the handover of the lands of State plots 33 and 14 in Salta province to the communities, under the permanent supervision of the IACHR. Within the context of a friendly agreement, Lhaka Honhat submitted to the officials their work of self-identification of land use undertaken by indigenous surveyors in each community.

A visit was also made to the area of the Mapuche communities of Painemil and Kaxipayiñ (Neuquén), affected by hydrocarbon contamination from Repsol-YPF's Loma de la Lata deposit (see *The Indigenous World 2001-2002*).[7] In the meeting between the parties, it was agreed that Repsol would provide drinking water in bulk to the communities until the waterworks is up and running. This is the first time that the Commission has been involved in protecting indigenous rights in Argentina and creates an interesting precedent for the future.

❏

Notes

1. Official data from the National Institute of Statistics and Census as of May 2002: people below the poverty line 18,219,000 (51.4%); people in absolute poverty: 7,777,000 (21.9%); children and youths living in poverty 8,319,000 (66%). According to the same source, as of February 2003, the rate of poverty had reached 62% (Corrientes, Formosa, Chaco, Gran Buenos Aires).
2. For more information on legal status, see: tpfalaschi@arnet.com.ar ; ricardoaltabe@ciudad.com.ar
3. On indigenous peoples in Argentina: www.pueblosindigenas.net
4. For more information on land theft: julmirs@ciudad.com.ar
5. For more information on the repression in Nam Qom: ricardoaltabe@ciudad.com.ar
6. On the IACHR's visit: mcarrasc@filo.uba.ar ; desc@cels.org.ar
7. For more information on hydrocarbon contamination: wajmapu@neunet.com.ar; www.ecoportal.net/articulos/lomalata.htm

CHILE

A s in other countries, the belligerent foreign policy of US President George W. Bush has also put a strain on national politics and, alongside this, has diverted the state and Chilean society's attention away from the situation of indigenous peoples.

The commencement of Chilean/US negotiations around a free trade agreement, postponed for several years, "coincided" with North American support for the country's non-permanent membership of the UN Security Council, which some analysts have interpreted as a trade-off by which Chile has, in part, committed its support to Bush's foreign policy. Also in the domestic sphere, the Lagos government has had to face up to a profoundly adverse political environment following a series of corruption allegations in which senior civil servants and parliamentary members from the current administration were implicated.

The Population and Housing Census held in April 2002, the results of which were published in March 2003, produced new figures on the indigenous population. It was the second time that a question on the country's indigenous population was included in the national census. However, it came as a surprise to find that the 2002 census figure was lower than that of 1992. In the 1992 census, the indigenous population had totalled 928,385 people, whereas in the 2002 census the total came to only 692,192. Some sectors have been quick to take this figure as indicative of a fall in the indigenous population. However, specialists consider that the most recent figure is more accurate given that the question in the 1992 census was badly formulated, leading to non-indigenous people defining themselves as indigenous. Some indigenous organisations feel that the figures have been manipulated in order to reduce their importance in the national context. Whatever the case, it is difficult to come to premature conclusions without further analysis.

Worsening human rights situation

Such apparently dissimilar events as the mass arrest of Mapuche community and organisation leaders within the context of the new criminal procedural system, a multi-million development project in indigenous communities financed by international organisations, the signing of an Association Agreement between the European

Union and Chile in actual fact all seem to be linked or, at least, this may well be the case. Several years on from the start of the so-called "Mapuche conflict", the Chilean government seems to have finally decided to resolve the "indigenous problem": by applying all the force of the law against those fighting for their just demands and claims, and this in a context in which the government needs to demonstrate to US and European governments and investors that it is capable of controlling the Mapuche and protecting future investments.

Since the beginning of 2002, and with the backing of the right-wing newspaper *El Mercurio* and right-wing parties, an escalation of arrests has begun to take place, primarily of community leaders from Traiguén commune, and including a number of *Lonkos* (traditional leaders) and, since the middle of the year, leaders of the Arauko-Malleco Coordinating Body (*Coordinadora Arauko-Malleco*). All have been subjected to irregular trials, both in form and in content.[1] In August 2002, a number of these Mapuche prisoners went on hunger strike until the end of September.

The speed and efficiency of the courts in expediting trials against the Mapuche is in stark contrast to the apathy and disinterest of the authorities to resolve their main demands, such as constitutional recognition, ratification of ILO Convention 169 or the problem of land conflicts with forestry companies.

The situation of Chile's indigenous peoples during 2002, particularly the Mapuche, thus deteriorated to previously unseen levels. A number of events, in addition to those already mentioned, combined to form what would seem to be a discouraging and worrying outlook. The Senate's rejection, on 3 July, of the government's constitutional reform bill aimed at recognising the country's indigenous population was connected to a debate organised two days previously by right-wing sectors and even parliamentary members of the government's own coalition, in which Mapuche demands were criminalized once more, characterising the organisations as violent or as terrorists. A number of "victims of Mapuche violence" attended the session, and provided information on the situation they had allegedly experienced. Without denying that violence is clearly an important element of the current relationship dynamic between some Mapuche communities, the police and the large forestry consortia (the main owners of the land demanded by the Mapuche in Malleco Province), the stigmatisation of Mapuche demands as something "beyond the law" seems to be a constant in the press and among sectors opposed to Chile's indigenous peoples, with the apparent aim of delegitimising their

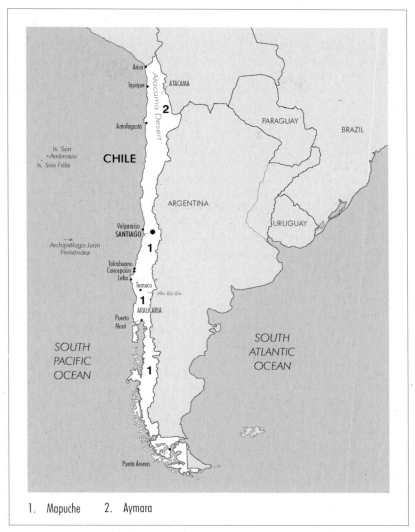

1. Mapuche   2. Aymara

aspirations. Such was the case of a report that appeared in the *El Mercurio* newspaper in December 2002, entitled "Internet Terrorism", and which attempted to denounce a number of web pages and sites promoting the Mapuche cause as terrorist. The aim of the article was to raise an "information barrier" around the Mapuche conflict, seeking a reaction from the authorities that would close down or censor the only medium that is giving a different version of events.

The extreme point to which the Mapuche conflict has gone became clear with the death of Alex Lemún, 17 years of age, shot in a clash with the police during the "taking" of an estate. This was the first victim recorded within the context of the Mapuche conflict and for this reason it unleashed a wave of protests and declarations, both from the Mapuche organisations themselves and from politicians, important figures and national and international organisations.

To the conflicts between forestry companies and Mapuche communities must be added a series of other conflicts resulting from implementation of large projects on Mapuche lands, some already mentioned in *The Indigenous World 2001-2002*. The establishment of municipal rubbish tips adjacent to Mapuche communities and lands, the construction of the coastal highway and the already long conflict between Ralco and the ENDESA-España company must all be mentioned, this latter being a case in which the human rights of indigenous peoples and a number of the standards contained in the 1993 Indigenous Law have been systematically violated. This led to a complaint being submitted to the Inter-American Commission on Human Rights against the Chilean state by members of the Ralco Lepoy community from Alto Bío-Bío.

The critical situation of the rights of Chile's indigenous peoples was reflected in a series of human rights reports produced by various national and international bodies. In the Indigenous Rights Programme's report (October 2002) from the Institute for Indigenous Studies of the La Frontera de Temuco University (Chile), the negative implications of the criminal procedural reform on the Mapuche people was one of many issues noted, despite the creation of a Mapuche Criminal Defence Office. The Report notes that since the reform was implemented in the region, there have been more than ninety people from organisations and communities prosecuted or imprisoned, and it also denounced many situations in which the police were used against Mapuche communities and people, including minors and the elderly, who were demanding land they believe is rightfully theirs.

Another report was that of the International Federation for Human Rights (FIDH, March 2003). This report notes the many causes at the origin of the conflicts with forestry companies and the environmental destruction of Mapuche territory, and it analyses the situation of the Pewenche in relation to construction of the Ralco dam. The Report highlights with concern the acute situation of police repression of Mapuche communities and organisations. Despite the fact that they are presumed to be conflicts between individuals, the police and government have clearly sided with the forestry companies, as they previously did with ENDESA. The report also highlights the way the conflict has been handled by the press which, as noted in last year's *The Indigenous World*, attempts to link the indigenous organisations to armed groups in other countries. Lastly, the FIDH report notes that, during the current government of President Lagos, repression of the Mapuche has intensified, along with the application of a number of laws intended to leave those accused with few legal options. In addition to this, they have lost their legitimate right to defence, given that there has been alleged monitoring of telephone calls between defence lawyers and imprisoned indigenous leaders.[2]

Concern among the different national and international sectors with regard the situation of Chile's indigenous people was demonstrated in varying ways: in November, the Chilean Episcopal Conference issued an important document on the historic and current situation of the Mapuche,[3] noting in one part, "We must stress that the joint effort to build social justice in our southern region implies a will to compensate for the historical damage inflicted on the native peo-

Source: Coordinadora de Comunidades Mapuches Kollipuli

ples, the effects of which are still being felt. This will is being diminished with the denial and criminalization of the legitimate demands for recognition of the rights of the Mapuche people".

The 'Origins' Programme

In terms of government action, the 'Origins' Programme was launched in 2002, a project financed by the Chilean state, with a major share of the funding coming from the Inter-American Development Bank. This programme aims to introduce new public intervention practices for indigenous community development. 'Origins' prioritises civic and community participation and includes an innovative system of promoters, who form the link between the programme and the communities involved. Another new aspect is that the specialist technical consultants are elected by the communities themselves. As of December 2002, the 'Origins' programme had invested a total of 3,400 million pesos (around 4.5 million dollars) in projects of community and public institution strengthening, production development, education and cultural and intercultural health in regions I, II, VIII, IX and X. The Araucanía region, in which the highest percentage of rural Mapuche live, has received the greatest amount of project funding: 315 out of a total of 641 initiatives financed. Implementation of the 'Origins' programme has not been free from controversy, however, due to its delayed commencement and accusations of a lack of transparency in the election of the professionals, advisors and technicians hired for its implementation.

Xenophobic acts against Peruvians

Other events of increasing concern, although not directly linked to the situation of the country's indigenous peoples but which does involve indigenous people of Peruvian nationality, are the growing acts of xenophobia, discrimination and violence against immigrants from this neighbouring country. The arrival en-masse of Peruvian immigrants to Chile in recent years, more than 50,000 by some accounts, has become a new focus of intercultural conflict. The Peruvians are constantly harassed by the police and ordinary civilians who, in a context of economic crisis and almost 10% unemployment, according to official figures, see them as a threat to Chilean jobs. The problem is more serious if we consider that, in spite of having signed agreements and conventions on discrimination, intolerance and xenophobia and in spite of having received repeated recommendations from the respective UN commissions, the country has taken no legal initiatives to control or punish actions of this kind, which affect not only foreigners but a whole group of sectors of Chilean society. ❑

Notes and sources

1 **International Federation for Human Rights (FIDH). 2003.** *Pueblo mapuche: entre el olvido y la exclusión.* Informe Misión Internacional de Investigación, nº 358/3, March 2003.
2 A further two reports of importance were published during the same period: one by the Public Interest and Human Rights Programme of the Diego Portales University in Santiago, another by an Amnesty International mission. Both come to conclusions similar to those already mentioned but through lack of space we will not go into their detail here.
3 **Obispos del Sur. 2002.** *Al servicio de un nuevo trato.* Working document instigated by the National Commission for Indigenous Pastoral Care of the Chilean Episcopal Conference (Comisión Nacional de Pastoral Indígena de la Conferencia Episcopal de Chile).

Web pages
www.mideplan.cl
www.diarioelgong.cl
www.origenes.cl
www.mapuexpress.net

AUSTRALIA AND THE PACIFIC

AUSTRALIA

Australia – and the 'un-Australian' other

On February 22, 2003, the *Good Weekend* magazine in *The Age,* Melbourne, and the *Sydney Morning Herald* newspapers devoted its cover story,[1] to exorcising the term "un-Australian" from political and popular usage. It has become an all-purpose form of political abuse in an increasingly xenophobic era encouraged by the Howard government's indigenous, immigration, "border protection", "anti-terror" and other social and cultural policies, a throwback to Senator McCarthy's 1950s "Un-American activities" scaremongering and scapegoating. The amusing article reminds us that even Aborigines have been deemed "un-Australian" at various times.

New research has demonstrated that "what can only be bluntly described as the white vote" and its rejection of "a social justice and global agenda" has provided Prime Minister John Howard with his government's winning electoral edge.[2] Howard's Aboriginal policies have been central to this approach since the 1996 election first brought him to power. He has expanded his *repertoire* in recent years. For example, Australia was the only country apart from Britain to commit itself to war in Iraq from the beginning of George W. Bush's campaign, with Howard often talking more aggressively than Bush himself. A major background factor has been the October 12, 2002, Bali (Indonesia) bombing of low-cost tourist nightclubs where nearly half of the *c.* 190 killed were Australian tourists. This has been treated by news media and federal as well as state governments as a *de facto* September 11 attack on Australia as a whole, even before it was found that the alleged bombers were Islamic extremists. In the government-manipulated climate of fear and anger centred on the *Tampa* incident and remote prison camps for boat people fleeing Iraq and Afghanistan (see *The Indigenous World 2001-2002)*, general xenophobia and specific anti-Islamic feelings have made life difficult for visible minorities. Now we are fighting to save Iraqis in their homeland, we are told, having hitherto been locking them up or watching them drown!

A sort of policy

From early 1996, Howard fought many indigenous issues noisily – native title, child removal, international human rights scrutiny, etc. –

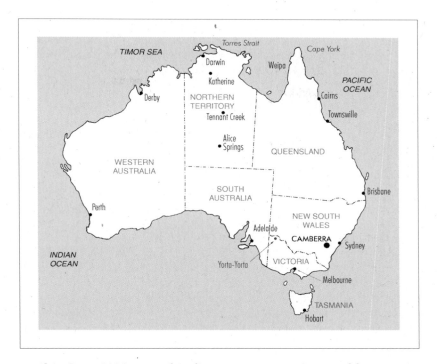

until in June 2001 several indigenous community notables, unwittingly, and the sensation-hungry press, greedily, made black on black violence and family/community dysfunction the sole acceptable indigenous issue of interest. Nevertheless, Howard has made one major recent foray into indigenous policy with an intriguing interview in *The Australian*.[3] Most of the interview dealt with wider issues, *The Australian* eager to present Howard as newly enthusiastic about its own multi-culturalist agenda, while they daily give him increasingly shrill and shallow support for his war, economic, anti-Labor, and other sentiments. Howard is probably less comfortable with social and cultural diversity than anyone else in high office in Australia, so *The Australian's* campaign is quixotic, to say the least. In his indigenous reconciliation interview we learn:

> The anger in the dialogue between the Government and Aboriginal leaders has disappeared, raising fresh hope for progress towards reconciliation, John Howard believes...'A year or 18 months ago, people said we were going nowhere on Aboriginal policy,' Mr. Howard said. 'Paradoxically, I think we are going somewhere on it now.'

However, he said the state of Aboriginal communities remained disgraceful and the experience of indigenous people compared poorly with the nation's success in absorbing migrants. 'I think it is still one of the hardest things we have. There are plenty of Aborigines, indigenous Australians, who are fully integrated. But there are still quite a lot who aren't,' Mr. Howard said.

He said part of the problem was that many Aborigines were physically separated from the rest of society. 'One of the accepted cornerstones of our immigration policy has always been that you shouldn't allow ghettoes or enclaves to develop. You never call them ghettoes or enclaves because they are Aboriginal communities – but in a way that is exactly what has happened and it is one of the difficulties we have."

Mr. Howard said the heat had gone out of the debate. 'I hesitate to say it, but the anger in the previous dialogue has disappeared. It's not that I'm suggesting that my critics are embracing me on it, but I think there has been quite a change,' he said. 'I hope it means we are inching towards a more sensible and harmonious outcome.'

Whether Howard believes this or is simply trying to rile his critics, these views are nonsense. His studied deafness to all but his own populist one-liners has made public debate futile; he must simply be removed, replaced, or bulldozed to one side before any progress on indigenous or other socio-cultural issues is possible. And this is not the only time he has made intransigent aliens of the original inhabitants of the continent.

Deep dispute

The basic dispute in Aboriginal and Islander affairs in recent years has been just this: the government, ably supported by sections of the news media, wishes to see indigenous problems as a widespread black failure of will to rise above the lowest national ranks of squalor and social violence, a situation to which whites can contribute little or nothing but Victorian chastisement and exhortation; while a better informed minority, together with most indigenous leaders, see that historical displacement or worse, legal marginalisation, and a politico-constitutional vacuum are an integral part of today's problems and integral to their solution.

Nowhere is this clearer than in the social histories of Queensland by historian Rosalind Kidd, *The Way We Civilise* (1997) and *Black Lives,*

Government Lies (2000). In an attempt to re-start intelligent discussion, journalist Rosemary Neill has written *White Out: How politics is killing black Australia* (2002). Particularly useful is her chapter retelling the furious debate, especially since 1997, on Australia's 20th century policies of removing children (the Stolen Children). However she also unwittingly reveals the deeper issue in her final chapter, on the Northern Territory (NT). The NT is undigested frontier, where larger or smaller indigenous home territories -with their unique languages and cultures - are threaded together by one main road, along which are four main largely white centres – Alice Springs, Tennant Creek, Katherine and Darwin. There is no regional "Australian" society able or willing to embrace this NT reality and work with it; rather, it is effectively "unorganised territory" dominated until 2001 by an anti-indigenous populist demagogic government (whose crypto-racist electoral policies were adopted from the mid/late 1990s by the Howard government, together with their NT personnel!). The new Labor government since 2001 has so many other urgent messes that the speed of any move into basic politico-constitutional issues, despite its good intentions, may be questioned.

Unless and until there is a negotiated political settlement between indigenous NT residents and other Australians – the throughput of transients being so great and fast that it is hard to talk of non-indigenous permanent residents – it will be impossible to have political and administrative arrangements workable for or satisfactory to either community.[4]

Setbacks

The most significant setback of the past year was the High Court's decision in the Yorta Yorta land claim, December 2002, making the requirements for native title claims much more difficult for indigenous people to fulfil. The national ombudsman for indigenous rights, Dr Bill Jonas, addresses these issues fully in his *Native Title Report, 2002,*[5] and calls on Australia to live up to its international rights commitments. Releasing the report on March 19, 2003, he said,

> *What has emerged from the High Court is a concept of recognition as not simply the law providing a vehicle for Indigenous people to enjoy their culture and property rights... Rather the law becomes a barrier to their enjoyment and protection... The implications of these decisions are being felt by indigenous people and a re-evaluation of the*

law needs to occur at the political level... Human rights principles should be at the forefront of such a process.

In April 2003, the Howard government renewed its push to diminish further the elected federal Aboriginal and Torres Strait Islander Commission (ATSIC) leadership's power and autonomy, using intensely reported (and quite defensible) discretionary actions of the Chairman, and well publicised legal problems in other matters of Chairman and Vice-Chairman, to imply that it was "out of control", squandering tax dollars and run by crooks. Aboriginal and non-Aboriginal realists had foreseen such opportunism by Howard before the 2002 ATSIC elections and urged both men to stand aside for the greater credibility of the organisation. ATSIC is also much targeted by both federal and state governments and news media for continued failures in indigenous socio-economic, health and court/jail statistics, although state governments are primarily responsible for these. With such levels of intellectual dishonesty and scapegoating of blacks among the highest levels of the white community, and few senior politicians (other than retiring Brisbane mayor Jim Soorley) willing to articulate moral and intellectual leadership, prospects remain bleak.

Signs of life

Research, publishing and the arts are vigorous areas of indigenous self-determination. Indigenous works such as the book, *Rabbit Proof Fence* by Doris Pilkington, now an international film, or the interviews with young indigenous women in *Black Chicks Talking* edited by Leah Purcell, or performance and graphic arts, are booming and reaching new audiences at home. Academic or joint academic-indigenous studies are flourishing despite tight times in publishing. *Indigenous Peoples and Governance Structures* (2002), by Nettheim, Myers and Craig draws heavily on Nordic and North American comparative studies to face Australian needs squarely; while Deborah Bird Rose and her collaborators in *Country of the Heart* (2002) clearly and accessibly explore the meanings of territory and culture for Aboriginal people near Darwin; and Nonie Sharp bridges the gap in white-black perception of coastal environment and culture in *Saltwater People* (2002), drawing on Aboriginal peoples and Torres Strait Islanders across the Tropical north of the continent. Useful inquiries of interest include a Queensland state parliament inquiry into indigenous political representation.

The Senate in Canberra is conducting an Inquiry into (the lack of) Progress Towards National Reconciliation by Federal Government because the proposals put forward so dramatically and publicly in mid-2000 at the conclusion of the 10-year work of the Council for Aboriginal Reconciliation seem to have been forgotten. As Sydney-based constitutional and treaty experts George Williams and Sean Brennan told the Inquiry:

> Despite a strong and continuing grassroots commitment, reconciliation has gone off the boil as a federal political issue. In part this is due to the Howard Government pursuing 'practical reconciliation' to the exclusion of any 'rights agenda' for indigenous people. ... Practical reconciliation and the rights agenda are not mutually exclusive. Steps to improve service delivery and government performance are necessary and important, but... Indigenous people have been excluded from our constitution for more than a century... In 1901 we cast indigenous people as outsiders to the nation. In 1967 these discriminatory references were deleted from the constitution by referendum. However, the change left the constitution, including its preamble, devoid of any reference to indigenous people. The system moved from explicit discrimination to silence, rather than to inclusion and acknowledgement.
> ...
> The Government should also establish a process to negotiate with indigenous people on the possibilities for treaties or other models for acknowledging indigenous rights and interests. This could lay a platform for the recognition of specific indigenous rights and for the building of economic and other partnerships through a national instrument that brings a formal close to the reconciliation process.[6]

Meanwhile, the 77% whose support was revealed in polls for Howard's supporters in the Tampa fiasco and other xenophobic and tough measures against "foreigners," among whom Howard himself seems to categorise many or most Aborigines, and the 23% who support an inclusive liberal cosmopolitan society, seem to have stopped speaking to each other. Careful research, such as *Dark Victory* by David Marr and Marian Wilkinson (2003) on Howard's 2001 (mis)-use of the *Tampa* and other boat people would sink a North Atlantic government but has had no apparent impact on the 77%. We 23-Percenters write articles for each other and attend each other's book launches, while the 77% presumably support cutting back funds which might flow to institutions (universities, public schools) where we are found. The 77% are represented or hijacked by a shrill dozen or so writers, especially in the Murdoch newspapers such as *The Australian,* which seem more interested in shouting down or abusing 23-Percenters than seriously arguing about ideas. Public debate has shrunk audible Australia down to a size Howard can handle, the sort of mid-20th century Anglo-society and attitudes that were mocked and, some of us thought, gone forever in the whimsy of Monty Python send-ups. Of course, the silence of so many is not consent. ❏

Notes and references

1 "Aussie Rules". Mark Dapin, *Good Weekend,* 22 February 2002: 16-22.
2 "White fringe fury feeds Labor's fall". M. Millett, *Sydney Morning Herald,* 28 December 2002.
3 "PM's reconciliation hopes". G. Megalogenis, *The Australian, 6 May 2002.*
4 See "Reconciliation Constitutions: Canadian & Australian Northern Territories". P. Jull, www.eprint.uq.edu.au/archive/00000322/.
5 The report can be accessed at:
   www.humanrights.gov.au/social_justice/ntreport_02/index.html
6 See *Sydney Morning Herald,* 8 April 2003.

THE PACIFIC REGION

The Pacific Islands region is home to 6 million people, both of indigenous and other ethnic groupings, occupying the 6,000 islands in the region defined for this purpose as the Pacific. Altogether there are 50 island nations, of which 20 have regained their political independence, while the remaining colonial occupied territories continue to be the subject of discussion for human rights, self determination and sovereignty at national, regional and global fora.

The region has had many achievements, including some of the more reasonable living standards in the developing world. However, it is also true that the issues of "under development" and "poverty of opportunity" remain to be addressed. It has had its share of disappointments and lost opportunities and many of the current trends are not very positive.

Regional concerns and threats

Some of the major threats that stand out in the Pacific region are an erosion of cultural values systems, corruption, the effects of global warming and the effects of economic globalisation.

The Secretariat of the Pacific Islands Forum[1] has highlighted other current concerns, which include: environmental degradation and resource depletion; poor economic performance; high population growth rates; socio-economic inequalities; health problems; political instability; poor governance; trans-national crime; climate variability and sea level rise; and transportation of nuclear radioactive materials.

There is continuing destruction and pollution of the environment and a rapid depletion of the natural resources. The majority of Pacific Islands suffer from many social problems and are trying to make ends meet in a rapidly changing social, political and economic environment, either because of limited skills and capacity or because the existing conditions do not provide them with opportunities.

The Pacific region receives the highest per capita aid but, according to the Forum Secretariat, this does not translate into higher sustainable economic growth or political stability. The Pacific continues to face corruption, crime, money laundering, drug trafficking and people smuggling nationally, regionally and internationally.

The Pacific is also experiencing rapid population growth in parts of our region, putting further pressure on our limited and shrinking resources.

Small islands continue to feel enormous pressure from the forces of globalisation, many of which, while creating new opportunities, are also creating new problems. The main negative impact of globalisation is increasing levels of poverty and a growing gap between rich and poor.

This is the new challenge for the region's governments and the Forum Secretariat. While it has succeeded in meeting its original goals, it must now adapt to the new challenges facing the Pacific region.

Corruption

Termed as "a crime against future generations" the head of the 16-member country inter-governmental South Pacific Applied Geoscience Commission (SOPAC), Mr. Simpson, told the 2002 annual meeting of the organisation that corruption was wreaking havoc on the Pacific's environment and leading to serious civil and political instability.

Pacific countries have an average marine environment that forms approximately 98 percent of their national jurisdiction but, until October 2002, not one had any coordinated ocean policy in place.

Government authorities have been prepared to accept unsustainable development on land and overexploitation of forests and marine resources, "as long as someone gets their thirty pieces of silver".

Mr. Simpson said security was not just merely the defence of national boundaries and jurisdiction. There was also security of life and communities, such as land tenure, traditional rights, natural resources, food security, human security and natural and anthropogenic disasters.

All these provide ingredients for instability, unrest and insecurity. Exploitation of both terrestrial and marine resources proceeds without any understanding of its sustainability. To assume that fair compensation is acceptable is indeed a crime against future generations and against every guideline for sustainable development.

Good governance

The issue of what constitutes "good governance" in the Pacific context is open to many interpretations, especially when most Pacific states have their own indigenous systems of governance versus Westminster-style parliamentary democracy. Even though the colonial pow-

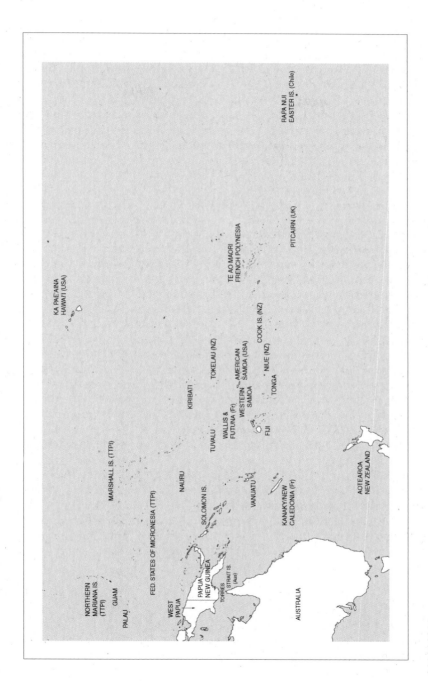

ers dismantled indigenous power structures, countries such as Tonga, Samoa, Fiji, Kiribati, Vanuatu and Tokelau have institutionalised aspects of their indigenous governance within their national constitutions.

However, in reality, when there is conflict in the application of these two systems, introduced governance and laws undermine indigenous value systems and overrule respect for the indigenous sacredness of the issue. Some of the worst conflicts that have led to violence in the Pacific region relate to a Western legal dominance that neither respects indigenous laws nor has the capacity to deal with indigenous land tenure systems.

To measure the results of good governance on Pacific community livelihoods we must have indicators. Indicators that are produced by international agencies are debatable in the Pacific since they do not reflect the strong links with indigenous cultures that still exist. However, the United Nations Development Programme's *Human Development Report 2002*, which ranks 173 countries by a composite measure of life expectancy, education and per capita income, ranked Fiji top in the Pacific at 72, followed by Samoa 101, Vanuatu 131 and Papua New Guinea 133.

Apart from ranking countries according to their level of human development and well-being, the report also covers a range of ideas on human development. For 2002, the principal one highlighted was the role of politics in human development. The report states that, "the big lesson of this period is never to ignore the critical role of politics in allowing people to shape their own lives. Political development is the forgotten dimension of human development."

And political development must lead to good governance which, according to the report, means "not only ridding societies of corruption, but also giving the people the opportunity, the right, the means and the capacity to participate in the decisions that affect their lives, and to hold their governments accountable for what they do."

Visionary leaders, leaders with genuine integrity, leaders who can navigate through both the indigenous system and introduced forms of governance, leaders that make use of the resources at hand - this is the challenge for Pacific communities.

Effects of global warming

The heads of governments from Small Islands States warmly welcomed the acceptance of the Kyoto Protocol by Japan and approval of the Protocol by the European Community. They called for urgent action to reduce greenhouse gas emissions and for further commitments in the future by all major emitters. They also emphasised the need for all nations to commit to global efforts to reduce gas emissions and the adverse impacts of climate change, taking into account the special circumstances of the small island developing states that face serious threats to their survival if the sea level rises. They further expressed disappointment at the decision of the United States to reject the Kyoto Protocol and agreed that the only truly effective way to address the issue of climate change globally was through full commitment by all the signatories of the UN Framework Convention of Climate Change (UNFCCC) to the objectives of the Convention.

Regional developments and achievements

On the positive side, the year 2002 witnessed the consolidation of Pacific peoples into a stronger, more cohesive community, able to face challenges together. The year 2002 also highlighted new visions for indigenous identity among the 6 million people. In the official arena, the Secretary-General of the Forum Secretariat reflected this commitment in his statement to the 33rd Pacific Islands Forum Leaders Summit in 2002.

Protecting traditional knowledge and culture

Twenty-two Pacific island countries endorsed the framework legislation to protect Pacific intellectual property rights during 2002, calling it the "root of our identity." The aim of the framework is to ensure that cultural and traditional intellectual property is recognised at the highest level and protected against looting.

The framework document was designed to be adapted and amended to suit the needs of each particular country and covers a very broad range of traditional knowledge and culture. It identifies common elements of cultural heritage and complements any existing intellectual property legislation.

The main breakthrough is the creation of a new set of rights, which are community rights. This means protecting indigenous communities and the knowledge that belongs to the entire community.

The framework also protects designs, dances, performances and traditional music, even those that have never been written down. It also protects traditional music that has been used for thousands of years by indigenous communities, but is sometimes appropriated by those recording albums without the permission of the rightful owners.

Pacific Partnership Agreement with the EU

In preparation for the negotiations on new trading arrangements with the European Union, the commitment within the Pacific nations was to "build a solidarity among themselves and develop efficient, home-grown - and region-wide – industries that can hold their ground by 2008 and beyond."

When Pacific ACP[2] Trade Ministers met in August 2002, they agreed to adopt a two-phase approach: the ACP-wide issues being dealt with first by the ACP collectively, followed by a Pacific phase when a Regional Economic Partnership Agreement (EPA) would be negotiated. The Ministers also adopted a five-year Regional Action Plan 2002 - 2007 to guide the Pacific ACP states in their negotiations.

The Pacific states felt that this two-phase approach would maximise ACP solidarity while ensuring flexibility with regard to the special needs of Pacific ACP states in the economic partnership agreements. It would also take into account the differing levels of development in the member states and their capacity to adapt to liberalisation. Noting that the goals of the Cotonou Agreement were to reduce poverty, promote sustainable development and progressively integrate the ACP countries into the global economy, Pacific governments' stand on the EPA was clear. The EPA should not be a conventional trade treaty but rather a development agreement that also acknowledged the need for special and differential treatment of the island nations - especially the Least Developed Countries.

Clear in their collective decision, when the ACP – EU Summit was held in Nadi, Fiji in August 2002, it was an opportunity to find common cause with other developing countries around the world and face the challenges ahead as a group. However, the Pacific was aware that there was no such thing as "open and tariff free access" to EU markets without giving the EU even greater market penetration into the Pacific. After significantly winding down fishing in European waters, it seemed the EU was particularly interested in Pacific fish stocks in return.

The EU/ACP accepted the Pacific proposal for a two-phase approach. The first phase of negotiations 2002 – 2004 will only deal with issues of common interest to the ACP groups, such as fisheries, tourism, investment and trade facilities, safeguards, dispute settlement and rules of origin. Market access issues will be dealt with in the second phase of negotiation 2004 – 2007 for an economic partnership.

PICTA and PACER

Despite the many questions raised by various advocacy groups on the benefits of PICTA and PACER, a number of Pacific governments ratified the two free trade agreements in 2002, enabling the PACER (Pacific Agreement on Closer Economic Relations) to come into force in October 2002. The Pacific Island Countries Trade Agreement (PICTA) came into force in April 2003.

Hailed as major new regional trade initiatives in the Pacific Islands, parties to the agreements believe these agreements will facilitate the integration of small economies into the global trade arena. The Regional Trade Facilitation Programme will help the Forum Island Countries to access the market opportunities provided by the PICTA.

It is assumed that Forum Island countries will only benefit from globalisation, and regional trade integration, if they can improve their trade performance with each other, and their developed country partners.

The Forum emphasised that trade facilitation was not just an issue of meeting the import standards of our trading partners. It also means improving our ability to safeguard against the "dumping" of unsafe or undesirable imports onto domestic markets.

The Forum Secretariat is required to develop a comprehensive programme of trade facilitation activities within one year of entry into force of the PACER.

The Pacific communities will be able to assess the benefits of the PICTA and PACER when they come into force.

United Pacific voice

There is recognition that, over the years, the Forum has emerged as a united voice of the Pacific Islands and in regional development achievements, such as in the following:

- The setting up of the Pacific Forum Shipping Line, which is now a major operator in sea transport in the region;

- The establishment of the Forum Fisheries, now playing a crucial role in the management of one of the Pacific's most valuable commercial sets, tuna;
- The banning of drift-net fishing;
- SPARTECA, under which preferential access is given to Pacific Islands goods into Australia and New Zealand;
- The continuing commitment from donor partners to provide substantial development assistance to the Pacific Islands;
- The clear opposition to nuclear testing in the region;
- The Cotonou Agreement, which now includes all Pacific Islands in a trade and aid arrangement with the European Union;
- The setting up of a Forum trade office in Beijing in addition to Auckland, Sydney and Tokyo.

There are also Forum agencies, such as:

- The South Pacific Geo-Science Commission (SOPAC)
- The South Pacific Tourism Organisation (SPTO)
- The South Pacific Regional Environment Programme (SPREP)
- The University of the South Pacific (USP)

Other official regional development initiatives undertaken by the Pacific Islands Forum during 2002 include:

- The institutional arrangements for the implementation of the Basic Education Action Plan
- The establishment of the Pacific Eminent Persons Group
- The Election Observer Mission
- The Forum's Pacific Anti-Terrorist Strategy, including new measures against illegal immigration and trans-national crime
- The Forum Secretariat's Policy on Engagement with Non-State Actors

NGOs' Memorandum of Understanding

Eleven major regional non-governmental organisations signed a Memorandum of Understanding on the Capacity Building Framework in November. This also enabled the NGO community to provide collective input to the Forum Secretariat Policy on Engagement with Non-State Actors, which was approved in November.

Pacific Churches' response

The Pacific Churches have switched from condemning HIV / AIDS to supporting an awareness of it. This was a landmark change, since the churches have the advantage of having a huge following in the Pacific. Journalists have also been urged to break the stigma on AIDS.

The Pacific Conference of Churches and the World Council of Churches - Pacific Desk coordinated a process that led to a publication known as 'Island of Hope – Pacific Churches Response to Globalisation'.

COUNTRY REPORTS

A s a region, the Pacific collectively continued to face the legacy of colonialism, militarism, Christianisation, neo-colonialism, the prominence of foreign systems, education, laws and institutions that alienate us from indigenous spiritual links with the land, the sea and our own cultural value systems.

OCCUPIED NATIONS

Colonial occupied territories fall into two categories. The first category consists of those whose colonial administrators have listed them on the United Nations list of Non-Self-Governing Territories with the intention of eventually phasing them out to run their own affairs. This category includes American Samoa, Guam, Tokelau and Pitcairn.

The second category is made up of countries that have been struggling for their sovereign rights and independence against colonial administering powers for centuries. Only one, Kanaky (New Caledonia) has been listed as a Non-Self-Governing Territory. Five others, West Papua, Te Ao Maohi (French Polynesia), Ka Pae'aina (Hawai'i), Bougainville and Rapa Nui (Easter Island) continue to be refused their fundamental right to independence. Indigenous peoples of these countries pay the price of freedom with their own lives.

The first Pacific Regional Seminar on Decolonisation to mark the beginning of the UN-declared Second Decade to Eradicate Colonialism (2001 – 2010), convened in Fiji, called on the administering powers and territories to dialogue and identify the forms of self-determination processes and options applicable to them.

GUAHAN (GUAM)

As America Fish and Wildlife officials unveiled their plan to designate 28,800 acres on Guam as critical habitat for three endangered species, they were met with frustrations and strong anger from Chamorro families waiting for the return of their seized land. The United States federal government controls 19,800 acres of the land area proposed, under the jurisdiction of the US Air Force, Navy and Fish and Wildlife. The government of Guam holds 2,800 acres and 2,100 acres are privately owned. (The Fish and Wildlife plan also calls for 6,000 acres on Rota, just north of Guam, in the southern part of the Commonwealth of the Northern Mariana Islands (CNMI) to be designated for the same purpose. In that area, 500 acres are privately owned and the rest is the property of the local government.) Termed as the "Battle of Guam: Indigenous versus the Environment", indigenous land owners stated, "Give us back our land, we are Chamorros, we will stand strong, we will fight. We are the endangered species."

WEST PAPUA

West Papua was this year again dominated by gross human rights violations, ranging from random killing, raping, looting and burning by the Indonesian military to the denial of justice in the long-awaited trial of high-ranking military officials involved in the murder of Papuan leader Theys Eluay. But the tragedy that undoubtedly brought West Papua to world attention this year was the killings in August 2002 of three teachers - 1 Indonesian and 2 Americans - employed by the Freeport-Rio Tinto mining company.

The "Freeport killings" sparked international outrage not so much because they occurred once again in Indonesian-occupied West Papua but because they claimed the lives of two Americans. Foreign powers, including those known to have longstanding relations with the military regime in Jakarta, did not hesitate to condemn the killings and to call for independent investigations into the circumstances surrounding the Freeport events. Such immediate reaction was unheard of in the years of Indonesian military occupation and mass killings in West Papua, East Timor, Maluku, Aceh and other occupied territories.

Pursuing its campaign to discredit the Papuan movement for independence from Indonesia, Jakarta issued statements claiming that the Papuan guerrillas, namely *Operasi Papua Merdeka (OPM)*, were involved in the shootings. However the results of two independent investigations carried out separately by the Institute of Human Rights Study and Advocacy for West Papua (ELSHAM) and the US Federal Bureau of Investigation (FBI) both confirm the involvement of the Indonesian military in the "Freeport killings".

The "Freeport killings" should serve as an eye-opener for the international community to finally acknowledge the longstanding power exerted by the military within the state apparatus in Jakarta. The "Freeport killings" are but the tip of the iceberg in a series of human rights violations instigated by the Indonesian military in their campaign to discredit Papuan efforts to establish dialogue with the new government of President Megawati Soekarnoputri.

Peaceful campaign towards independence

Amidst the all too familiar cases of human rights violations instigated by the Indonesian military, Papuans have intensified lobbying on the diplomatic front to rally international support for their peaceful campaign towards independence. At regional level, a joint statement prepared by all major factions was submitted to the Pacific Islands Forum at the Fiji Summit in August 2002. Two months later, Papuan leaders made the same appeal for peace at the Third Conference of the International Solidarity Network for West Papua in London.

But, for Jakarta, a peaceful dialogue with the Papuans is still a threat to the "integrity" of the state. Foreign Affairs officials immediately embarked on a charming offensive to persuade Pacific leaders of the alleged threats to security and stability in the region should West Papua gain independence. Banking on the support of its allies, most of whom are major power players and aid donors in the region, Indonesia sought good-will relations with Pacific governments and was accepted as a post-forum dialogue partner. Less than six months later, Indonesia opened its first diplomatic mission in Fiji in an effort to "foster greater trade relations" with neighbouring countries.

Meanwhile, the Papuan leadership consolidated its regional network among sympathetic governments and, after numerous attempts again derailed by Indonesia's interference, finally opened the West Papuan People's Representative Office in Vanuatu in March 2003.

Constitutional Developments

Following the entering into force of the Special Autonomy Law, passed in January 2002 but rejected by Papuans, President Megawati Soekarnoputri issued Decree No. 1/2003 dividing West Papua into three provinces – Papua, Central Irian Jaya and West Irian Jaya provinces.

The decision, endorsed by the House of Representatives, to divide West Papua into 3 smaller provinces sparked strong protests from both the Papuan authorities and religious leaders (a joint statement was issued by Catholic, Protestant and Islamic leaders), who stated that it was in contradiction of Law No. 21/2001 on Papua special autonomy. This law stipulates that the formation of new provinces should gain approval from the Papuan consultative assembly, which is yet to be established.

The division of West Papua caused greater instability and led to people fleeing the threat of tighter control and imminent crackdown by the Indonesian military. The number of refugees fleeing into Papua New Guinea has dramatically increased, prompting the PNG government to issue a directive for the repatriation of the border crossers, starting on March 13.

KANAKY (NEW CALEDONIA)

L and disputes between Kanaks and Wallisian squatters on the outskirts of the capital Noumea and the near-abortion of a multi-billion dollar mining project in the south made headlines in yet another controversial year for the Noumea Accord, which saw the New Caledonia government toppled by its own partners in the Noumea Accord.

Ethnic clash over land

Following clashes between the indigenous Kanak landowners of Saint Louis village and a Wallisian settlement south of Noumea in January 2002, representatives of both communities have agreed to a peaceful solution to the 11-month violent conflict that has already claimed three lives. At the heart of the conflict is a piece of land made available in the early days to the Catholic Church to establish the Catholic Mission of La Conception. Some thirty years ago, a small group of immigrants from the neighbouring French Territory of Wallis and Futuna settled within the vicinity of the Catholic mission. Outgrowing the space made available, the Wallisians are now squatting on customary land on the periphery of the urban village of St Louis thus ignoring the customary boundaries and indigenous protocols of Kanak villages.

Snap elections

After months of protest and dissension among the local partners of the Noumea Accord, *Union Calédonienne* (UC), one of the major components of the pro-independence coalition triggered the downfall of the local government in November 2002 when it announced the "collective" resignation of not only its sole member in government, Gérald Cortot, but of all of his co-lists.

Under the Noumea Accord and the organic law that stemmed from it, for the sake of balance and power-sharing between parties, if a government member resigns and cannot be replaced by one of their co-lists, then the whole government is deemed to resign. The move made it impossible for a reshuffle to take place under an organic law that institutionalised the territorial government for the first time in 1999 within an autonomy-loaded Noumea Accord. But, in a legal twist, the Accord also unexpectedly allowed the UC's resignation to topple the whole executive.

However, two weeks later, the members of the previous government were almost all re-elected, bar one, as the Territorial Congress had in the meantime endorsed a motion to downsize the new government to 10 members.

Three main political groups submitted their lists of candidates for what was the French territory's third local government since it was set up in 1999. RPCR and FCCI had submitted a list that included most of the outgoing executive: President Pierre Frogier and most of the incumbent government members. As a result of the proportional vote in the 54-seat Congress, Frogier remains President and the RPCR/FCCI coalition gains seven seats out of ten in the cabinet.

Due to the reduction in size of the executive, a former RPCR government member was dumped. Pro-independence coalition FLNKS (National Kanak Socialist Liberation Front) had included in its list former party President Roch Wamytan, and the other FLNKS seat is now held by incumbent Kanak woman leader Déwé Gorodey (who remains Vice-President of the executive).

Meanwhile, the French presidential election returned the right-wing government of Chirac to power with 80.42% of the vote, followed by Le Pen with 19.58%. Voter turnout: only 50.56%. A result that prompted the FLNKS to express concerns for future implementation of the Noumea Accord.

Constitutional developments

In March 2003, the French Congress, a special gathering of both the National Assembly (Parliament) and Senate, opened its special session in Versailles (near Paris) to amend the French Constitution along the general lines of decentralisation.

Under the principle of decentralisation, three of the ten proposed amendments are of direct interest to French Overseas departments and territories, including those three in the Pacific (New Caledonia, Wallis and Futuna, French Polynesia). For these overseas countries and territories, the "decentralisation of powers" relates to articles 13, 34 and 74 of the French Constitution. Article 13 refers to "representatives of the (French) government in overseas territories", which would be re-phrased "overseas collectivities". Article 34 would change the term "local collectivities" into "territorial collectivities", and article 74 is supposed to define a new status for overseas collectivities.

The French Congress meets on an *ad hoc* basis and is the only institution empowered to amend the Constitution. Earlier plans to change the term "overseas territory" into "overseas countries" were apparently dropped.

Furthermore, the French council of ministers has passed legislation aimed at implementing commitments by President Jacques Chirac to improve economic development in overseas departments and territories. Overseas Minister Brigitte Girardin presented the legislation, which covers a 15-year period and has provisions linked to several main points. These include job creation, boosting private investment and strengthening territorial continuity, which covers cheaper travel and transport between the territories and France.

New head of Customary Senate elected

Kanak high chief, Pierre Zeoula, was appointed head of the Customary Senate at the annual congress attended by 150 customary chiefs from throughout Kanaky. The customary senate was set up in 1999 as a result of the signing of the Noumea Accord, which for the first time stressed the importance of the Kanak identity.

According to the Noumea Accord, the Customary Senate must be consulted on all matters pertaining to Kanak traditional identity and related symbols, traditional land tenure or customary civil status. The Senate is elected for a term of six years, and consists of 16 members, all high chiefs from their respected jurisdiction. At their 2002 Congress, they were briefed on the ethnic conflict in Saint Louis between Kanaks and the Wallisian community.

They were also informed about the importance of preserving the environment, the coral reef and their natural resources - with a focus on the sensitive issue of the Canadian-owned Goro-Nickel Plant. They decided to focus on designing an indigenous land development fund as well as a mediation system that will resolve land matters in line with traditional practices and Western-style law.

However, with regard to the coral reef, a delegation of the Customary Senate failed to move French authorities in February 2003 to re-launch an earlier bid to have the French territory's coral reef listed on UNESCO's World Heritage List. The application faced strong opposition from local right-wing, anti-independence movements that claimed "interference" in local affairs and claimed such a move by traditional leaders was "politically motivated". The bid was supported by the Northern and Loyalty Island provinces but strongly opposed by the affluent Southern province. Supporters of the project argued that if the reef obtained the World Heritage label, the French territory could capitalise on it to boost an ailing tourism industry.

Kanaks march for environmental protection

Meanwhile, an estimated 5,000 protesters in Noumea demanded better environmental protection from local and French authorities and voiced their concerns about the country's coral reef and the granting of nickel mining rights to Canadian mining giant Inco to exploit a mining site in the south that surrounds a fragile ecosystem endemic only to the area.

After preliminary studies undertaken in 2001, Inco announced that it would suspend work and review its operations costs, which could rise with 15% over initial estimates and delay production to the first half of 2005.

I n January 2002, a conference organised by the Centre of Documentation and Research on Peace and Conflict (CDRPC) and *Moruroa e Tatou* at the French Senate submitted a number of requests to the French government:

a) A list of all former workers on the test sites of Moruroa and Fangataufa,
b) Access to military files of test site workers,
c) Presumption of the origin of radiation illnesses,
d) Establishment of a nuclear test follow-up commission and the
e) Creation of a fund for the families of nuclear test victims.

Although two months later the full disclosure of medical history to patients was authorised by law, nuclear veterans still have difficulties accessing their medical files and only receive a statement of dosimetry zero from the Army Radiological Protection Service.

In July 2002, *Moruroa e Tatou*, the association of over a thousand former workers of Morurua and Fangataufa, held its First Annual General Assembly. The Assembly was also a follow-up to the meeting that was held in the French Senate in Paris in early 2002, linking the French Association of Nuclear Veterans (AVEN) and *Moruroa e Tatou* with nuclear veterans of other countries. Invitations to the *Moruroa e Tatou* assembly had therefore been extended to its network of veterans in Fiji, Australia, New Zealand, France, Britain and the United States.

Meanwhile, a bill was submitted to the French National Assembly to investigate any link between nuclear testing and health problems, in particular "genetic damage".

BOUGAINVILLE

T he Papua New Guinea parliament passed the Bougainville autonomy bill in March 2002 paving the way to peace on the island and a transitional period of 15 years to decide its destiny. Traditional chiefs, church leaders, women leaders and the communities had made extensive efforts to gain this level of reconciliation and reconstruction.

Under it autonomous government, Bougainville will have its own constitution, court and banking system, police, immigration, aviation, shipping and fishing rights, post and telecommunication network and other national functions transferred under a complex legal arrangement.

Yet this can only happen once the UN is satisfied that stage 2 of the weapons disposal program is complete.

Weapons disposal programme

Completing the "Strategic Plan 2002-2004" for the Weapons Disposal Programme in Bougainville depends much on the goodwill of ex-combatants and on technical and financial assistance from governments and international agencies to implement the plan. By March 2002, it was reported that 720 weapons (137 of which high-powered) had been handed in by the Bougainville Resistance Forces (BRF) and Bougainville Revolutionary Army (BRA).

Ex-combatants also called for pardon and amnesty to be issued prior to the conclusion of the weapons disposal program and the final establishment of the autonomous government.

After several delays in releasing funds, a budget of PGK 86 million (US$ 24.8 million) has been approved for the Bougainville Interim Provincial Government for peace restoration. PGK 58 million (US$ 16.7 million) was provided by donor countries (Australia, New Zealand, European Union) and PGK 28 million (US$ 8.1 million) by the PNG government.

As of February 2003, it was estimated that ex-combatants had surrendered 87% of weapons. However UN envoy Noel Sinclair says the containment of weapons may not be completed by the end of June despite the fact that the UN Peace Monitoring Team is scheduled to withdraw from the island on June 30.

Class action suit

Bougainvillean landowners maintained their legal action against giant Rio Tinto for genocide and environmental damage in operating the giant Panguna copper mine. The judge hearing the class action suit in California dismissed the case after hearing from the US State Department that the case might adversely affect US foreign policy interests. She made her dismissal conditional upon the landowners' ability to continue their action in a Papua New Guinea court, which is contrary to PNG Law.

NORTHERN MARIANA ISLANDS (CNMI)

C hamorro people of the Commonwealth of Northern Mariana Is lands (CNMI) confirmed their opposition in a survey to any attempts to change the constitutional provision restricting land ownership to the indigenous people of Northern Mariana. Article 1 of the islands' Constitution dictates that individuals of non-CNMI descent can only lease private lands for 55 years and public lands for 40 years. The result of the survey conducted by a private firm for the CNMI's Strategic Economic Development Council showed that 87 percent of local people believe protected land rights are crucial for preserving local culture, traditions and lifestyles.

Indefinite moratorium

The Public Lands Authority in Northern Mariana has imposed an indefinite moratorium on accepting and processing homestead village applications on Saipan and Rota, due to a shortage of public land. The moratorium took effect as of September and gave the Authority the opportunity to thoroughly screen up to 4, 000 applicants and plan more practical ways to equally distribute the remaining public property for homestead purposes.

INDEPENDENT COUNTRIES

T wenty independent Pacific countries collectively face specific issues associated with the absence of a coordinated development vision for peaceful co-existence, Western democratic system, good governance, economic justice, market access, free trade agreements, media freedom, HIV / AIDS tragedy, sea level rise, regional security and sustainable human security.

FIJI

I n Fiji, the *Blueprint*, which is the government policy document
attempting to support indigenous Fijian development and to prevent a repeat of the 1987 and 2000 coups, has been labelled as racist
by the former Prime Minister, who is of Indian ethnic origin.

Government calls for the teaching of culture and tradition

Ro Teimumu Kepa, a high chief and deputy Prime Minister responsible
for education admitted that Western influence was taking a hold among
Fijians, causing emerging identity crises, and which resulted in the
events surrounding the 2000 coup. Western societies have poisoned the
minds of the once simple, peaceful people who began to believe they
should change the status quo – often outside of the law. She called on
parents to instil and enforce in their children the importance of their
culture and tradition as a source of unity in our society. She also called
on the provincial councils to draw up policies to strengthen the family
unit so that it could carry out responsibilities as the foundation of society.
She said that disrespect for traditional authority and the breakdown in
family and village life all emanated from the advice given by those who
are confused between traditional Fijian life and modernisation.

Other developments

The sugar industry suffered from political instability and an expiry
of land leases. Until the land lease issue is resolved and the confidence of farmers (in majority of Indian ethnic background) restored,
crop size will not return to their expected levels.

The country began harvesting one of the world's last great stands of
mahogany trees, often referred to as the real reason behind the 2000 coup.

KIRIBATI

K iribati elections were held in November for the 40-seat *Maneaba*
ni Maungatabu (or parliament) amidst strong competition between President Teburoro Tito and the opposition leader Harry Tong.

22,000 election pamphlets belonging to Harry Tong were seized after President Tito declared the pamphlets illegal because they displayed the national flag on campaign material.

According to the President, the law forbids the use of the national emblem on anything without the permission of the President acting in accordance with advice from the Cabinet. The opposition spokesman said that the law only prohibits the use of the national flag for commercial purposes or to mislead people.

Tito won his parliamentary seat as well as the presidential election with a narrower margin. By April 2003, there was still no government in place as election petitions and the battle for a majority continued.

MARSHALL ISLANDS AND FEDERATED STATES OF MICRONESIA

The Marshall Islands and the Federated States of Micronesia (FSM) signed a new funding deal with the United States totalling US$ 3 billion with "reservations"'. This replaced the first one that came to an end guaranteeing long-term funding under the Compact of Free Association. In the *Nitijela*, the Marshall Islands legislature, the President criticized American attempts to 're-write history' in order to avoid commitments.

Utirik

Marshall Islands nuclear test veterans continued to seek a multi-million dollar compensation settlement for cleaning up residual radiation on Utirik and for hardships suffered as a result of 67 nuclear bomb tests by the United States from 1946 – 1958. Utirik is 250 miles downwind from where the tests occurred.

PAPUA NEW GUINEA

National elections in Papua New Guinea were marred by violence, forcing the electoral commissioner to declare six seats in the

Southern Highlands region null and void. Women candidates in the Chimbu province condemned the elections as the worst and "darkest" since independence. Despite this, parliament convened in August and elected Sir Michael Somare as Prime Minister. Sir Michael was the first prime minister when PNG became an independent nation in 1975.

Policy change

A change in policy saw the suspension of the privatisation policy and abolition of vice-ministerial positions to concentrate on the parliamentary committee systems and reinforce parliamentary democracy in order to ensure that ministers, ordinary members of parliament and government bureaucrats are made accountable for their decisions and actions.

Economy

The government stated that the PNG economy was down but not out. The Prime Minister rejected what was termed as World Bank 'blackmail' and warned the World Bank of changes in policy. When warned by the Governor of the PNG Reserve Bank of a government financial deficit of 210 million Kina (or US$ 59,500,000), the Prime Minister assured the country of the new government's commitment to restoring stability and dealing with the issue.

Corruption

There have been major breakthroughs in uncovering many of the corrupt practices that have been investigated. Six outstanding cases highlighted by the Community Coalition Against Corruption were: the Cairns Conservatory; the National Provident Fund saga; the Malagan House Report; the Passport Scam Report and the Defence Force Retirement Benefits.

Law on HIV/AIDS

A new law to tackle discrimination and protect the rights of people living with HIV / AIDS, including those looking for employment, was in its final stage at the end of 2002 for presentation to parliament. Work on the piece of legislation began in 1999 and the draft was presented at a workshop conducted by the National Aids Council in October 2001, seeking the opinions of a wider community sector and incorporating their opinions into the final draft.

SOLOMON ISLANDS

In the Solomon Islands, the government was accused of bias in police action against Guadalcanal Liberation Front Leader, Harold Keke, as attempts to arrest him failed. In the process, more casualties were encountered. While the country returned to normalcy, the peace and security situation still remained very fragile.

TONGA

Elections to the 30-seat legislative assembly were held in 2002. The Kingdom's 33 nobles, who acquire their title by descent, gathered around the traditional *kava* bowl and nominated their 9 representatives. King Taufa'ahau Tupou IV appointed 12 members of his Cabinet for life and the estimated 58,000 eligible voters from the population of 140,000 elected their 9 commoner representatives from a total of 48 candidates.

The 12-member cabinet appointed by the king for life is headed by HRH Prince 'Ulukalala-Ata, as Prime Minister.

Supporters of the Human Rights and Democracy Movement in Tonga won 7 out of the 9 commoners' seats. Their focus during this term in parliament is to propose an alternative structure comprising an upper house to be known as the House of Nobles, and a House of Representatives that will consist of 21 members directly elected by the people and open to all Tongans: commoners, nobles or members of the royal family.

"Terrorist" accusations

The government of Tonga labelled the Human Rights and Democracy Movement in Tonga as "terrorist". This label came as the Tonga legislative assembly passed an amendment to the Criminal Offences Act defining terrorism as an indictable offence carrying a fifteen-year imprisonment term. The Human Rights and Democracy Movement described the law as an attempt to seriously destabilise or destroy the fundamental political, constitutional, economic and social structure of the country.

VANUATU

Vanuatu elections saw the return of Prime Minister Edward Natapei heading a coalition government of the Vanuaaku Pati and the Union of Moderate Parties.

Law on Kava

Parliament passed a new law in December that regulates the ownership and protection of the Vanuatu *kava* industry. Although kava and its related products are banned from major buyer countries, Vanuatu kava finds its biggest market inside the country. While scientific studies were continuing, the results of which could counter claims made by the European pharmaceutical companies, Vanuatu decided to clean up and regulate its kava industry first before looking to conquer overseas markets.

Melanesia m Arts Festival 2002

"Preserving Peace through Sharing of Cultures" was the theme of the 2002 Second Melanesian Arts Festival hosted by Vanuatu. Its purpose was to preserve and develop Melanesia indigenous cultures.   ❑

Notes

1   Pacific Islands Forum is a regional intergovernmental cooperation body with 16 member countries (ed.note).
2   APC: African, Caribbean and Pacific Group of States (ed.note).

EAST AND
SOUTHEAST ASIA

JAPAN

In memory of Masaharu Konaka,
a friend and brother to the Ainu and Burakumin people in Japan,
who passed away on 25 November 2002.

J apan is often regarded as a homogenous nation. However, the country has a number of both larger and smaller groups of indigenous peoples. The larger groups are the Okinawan, the Burakumin and the Ainu. This article deals with the Ainu people of Hokkaido in northern Japan, who number about 500,000 of the country's 117 million population. It is somewhat impossible to attempt to summarise the activities of an entire group of people over a year. The following is merely a glimpse of Ainu activities in 2002-2003.

The Ainu Nation

Discussing the Ainu as one people is really to apply an alien concept to their identity. It does not take account of the numerous differences that have always existed, manifested nowadays in a variety of ways. In recent times, there have been more frequent displays of the Ainu flag, designed by artist Bikky Sunazawa, at gatherings and events. Perhaps this can be seen as one sign of a greater sense of an 'Ainu Nation' amongst a growing number of active Ainu.

Legal matters

In March 2002, a lawsuit against the Hokkaido government by 24 Ainu, seeking the full disclosure of records for assets taken away and managed for them by successive Hokkaido governors, was dismissed in court. The only records that have been released so far by the government reveal major gaps, with complete logs for only the six years up to 1980.

Also at issue is the return of 1.47 million yen (US$12,250) of their assets seized from them in the 19th century. Whilst the Hokkaido government has agreed to return this, the Ainu plaintiffs argue that it does not account for inflation and is ridiculously insufficient. At the time the assets were seized, the governor assigned to manage the assets had an annual salary of about 6,500 yen. Today, it is some 2,500 times that amount (16.25 million yen).

Whilst no concrete figure has been set, some suggest it should be at least 1,000 times the proposed amount. There has been a tentative

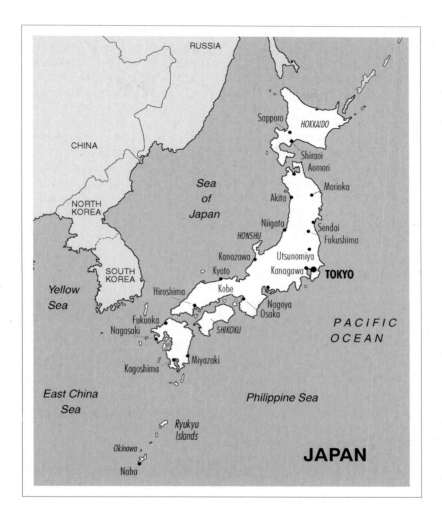

agreement to use this to initiate a fund for educating young Ainu or caring for the elderly. The group is now in the process of appealing against the decision.

Cultural activities

Following the enactment of the Ainu Culture Promotion Act (CPA) in 1997, there seems to have been a veritable explosion of Ainu cultural activity. The danger is that those who hold the purse strings (i.e. the government and their bureaucrat lapdogs) now have more power to decide what is acceptable as Ainu culture and what is not. Musician Oki Kano strongly criticised the CPA at the United Nations Working Group on Indigenous Populations (WGIP) for not providing, "an opportunity for us to decide, for ourselves, in what manner we will promote our own culture. It is a law for the Japanese government to co-opt, limit and control Ainu culture."

Of course a great deal continues, as always, outside the officially sanctioned system. Much of it is perhaps not considered 'cultural' enough, such as hunting, fishing and gathering plants for preparing foods and medicines, or perhaps it might lead to thorny issues of land rights and ownership. As Ainu counsellor Ryoko Tahara put it, "Ainu culture is not limited to language or ceremonies or dance. It is Ainu life itself. Whatever happens every day within the household is Ainu culture."

At the 35th Ainu crafts competitive exhibition in February 2003, held annually in Sapporo, the high quality of embroidery and carving on display, together with the large volume of entries, attested to the appeal and vitality of traditional Ainu art forms in the 21st century.

From April - September 2002, an exhibition of Ainu artefacts collected by the Scottish physician Neil Munro was held in Sapporo and Kanagawa. As part of a novel collaboration, it had first involved seven Ainu craftsmen and women who visited Edinburgh, Scotland in order to make replicas of selected pieces. The replicas were brought to Sapporo and Kanagawa along with the originals and displayed together. After the end of the exhibitions, the replicas remained 'at home'. In this way, the loss of a large number of Ainu artefacts to overseas collections can be partly alleviated and Ainu are now able to see and enjoy them.

A report submitted by the Ainu Association of Hokkaido (AAH) to the WGIP in 1991 clarifies their position regarding such collections: "Furthermore, cultural relics of the Ainu have not remained in Japan but lie scattered in museums in America and Europe, having been taken there by missionaries and scholars. We request that this cultural property be returned, and we are studying ways to develop this campaign."

Special Rapporteur's visit

In November 2002, as part of his official duties as United Nations Special Rapporteur on the situation of human rights and fundamental freedoms of indigenous people, Rodolfo Stavenhagen made a three-day visit to Hokkaido. He spoke with Ainu people in Sapporo, Shiraoi and Nibutani to learn more about their situation, and met with senior officials from the AAH and the Foundation for Research and Promotion of Ainu Culture (FRPAC). At the FRPAC, he asked whether positions were specially set aside for Ainu who were learning about their culture, similar to 'affirmative action' programmes. He was told that whilst study scholarships are given to young Ainu, they can apply for positions like everyone else, with no special preference given.

A central issue of the Rapporteur's visit was the issue of land rights and *Ioru*, traditional living spaces for the free practice and transmission of Ainu traditions. Concern was expressed about the difficulty in overcoming the various legal regulations concerning government land, fishing and hunting etc. that would relegate the concept to the hollow provision of more research centres and museums on Ainu culture. Also discussed were Ainu Land Rights claims to the Northern Territories island chain off Hokkaido and the representation of Ainu history and culture in school textbooks.[1]

Ainu globalisation

In addition to the many festivals, ceremonies and cultural events that took place throughout the year there were also a number of exchanges with native peoples from all over the world.

This growing trend in international exchanges with other indigenous peoples not only provides mutual inspiration and encouragement but also enables Ainu people to globalise their local struggle. According to Tessa Morris Suzuki, at the Australian National University, Ainu participation in, "an emerging worldwide movement of indigenous people has enabled (the Ainu) to re-interpret their own past and traditions in new ways, and to see new connections between their history and the history of indigenous societies in other parts of the world."

In addition to official AAH delegations to the WGIP in Geneva, Switzerland and other indigenous fora, Ainu representatives attended the 3rd World Water Forum, held in Kyoto in March 2003, to provide an Ainu perspective.

New music

This year also saw the release of an exciting album of contemporary Ainu music by OKI and his Far East Band, entitled "No One's Land".

It includes eclectic collaborations with a Chukchi shamaness, an Ethiopian singer and a poet from Timor Lorosa'e. Whilst receiving much attention overseas,[2] it has been practically ignored 'at home' in Japan.

Perhaps one day, belated official recognition of the Ainu as indigenous by the Japanese government may help to remedy a virtual ignorance of Ainu people and culture by their fellow Japanese neighbors.❑

Notes and references

1   The Special Rapporteur's report for 2003 on the situation of human rights and fundamental freedoms of indigenous people, including this visit, is available at: www.193.194.138.190/huridocda/huridoca.nsf/ (Symbol)/E.CN.4.2003.90.En?Opendocument
2   See: www.bbc.co.uk/radio3/world/guidejapan2.shtml

TIBET

After more than 50 years of Chinese occupation, Tibetans are still being denied their fundamental right to self-determination. As inhabitants of an occupied country that is increasingly being colonized by China and in which the number of Chinese settlers continues to grow, the Tibetans share many characteristics with indigenous peoples the world over. Regarding themselves as an occupied nation, most Tibetans want the return of their former independence.

Human rights in Tibet

The year 2002 began with good news from Tibet. The Chinese authorities released exiled Tibetan music researcher Ngawang Choephel in January, after 6 years in prison. He had originally been sentenced to 18 years for "espionage". Although he was released on "medical grounds", there is no doubt that the international pressure on the Chinese government to reconsider his case played a role in his being released at this relatively early stage in his imprisonment. During

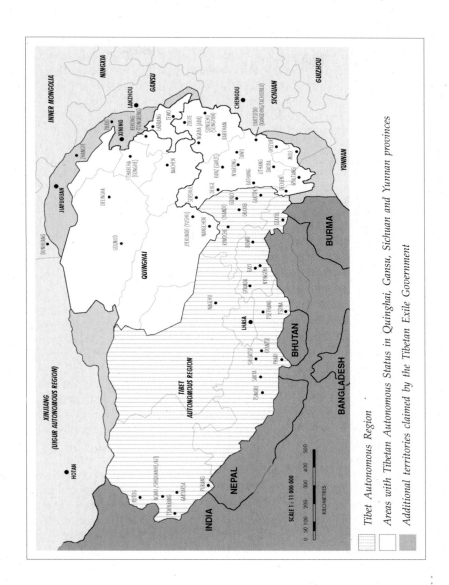

Tibet Autonomous Region

Areas with Tibetan Autonomous Status in Quinghai, Gansu, Sichuan and Yunnan provinces

Additional territories claimed by the Tibetan Exile Government

2002, a number of other prominent Tibetan political prisoners were freed, including the nun Ngawang Sangdrol, who was first arrested at the age of 13. The international community has frequently requested her release. Another nun, Ngawang Choezom, who was only 22 when she was first arrested, was released 9 months before the end of her 11-year-long sentence and Tibet's "oldest" political prisoner, the 77-year-old Takna Jigme Zangpo, who has spent more than 40 years in prison altogether, was released and chose to go into exile.

Although a positive development, the release of these and other political prisoners should not make the world forget that there are still a large number of political prisoners in Chinese prisons in Tibet and that there is a good chance that any Tibetan who is openly critical of the Chinese government and China's dominance over Tibet will be arrested.

There has been no change for the better for those who want a free Tibet but there are some indications that the Chinese government has become more open towards international appeals. The expectations of Beijing hosting the Olympic Games in 2008 may be one reason for this. However, this positive development was suddenly interrupted in December when two Tibetans, Tenzin Deleg Rinpoche and Lob-sang Dhondrup, were condemned to death for their alleged participation in a bombing incident in eastern Tibet in April. International organisations were worried that the two Tibetans did not receive a fair trial. According to the Chinese authorities, the trial was closed to the public because it related to "state secrets". International observers were puzzled by the severity of the trials. There is reason to believe that they were as much a consequence of China's participation in USA's war against terrorism as of its strict control over Tibet. As a consequence, Chinese law has been modified so that everybody who does not agree with the regime may be accused of terrorism. The punishments for "terrorist" crimes have also become more severe.

The issue of Tibetan refugees continues to draw the attention of human rights organisations, such as the United Nations Commission on Human Rights (UNCHR) and the Tibet Justice Centre, which published a report in 2002 entitled, "Tibet's Stateless Nationals - Tibetan Refugees in Nepal". The situation of Tibetans trying to flee from Tibet to Nepal has continued to deteriorate, partly because the Chinese authorities have strengthened their control of the Tibetan borders with Nepal, and partly because of the worsening situation in Nepal. Chinese pressure on Nepal continues to grow but the most serious problem is that Nepal does not recognize the Tibetans' status as refugees and that, in recent years, it seems to have forgotten its "gentlemen's agreement" with the UN High Commissioner for Refugees (UNHCR) on Tibetan refugees. On several occasions over the past year, Tibetans have been arrested or forced to pay large penalties for being in Nepal without a valid visa and it is common for border police to send back Tibetan refugees to Chinese-occupied Tibet. The Tibetan refugees in Nepal are not allowed to own property or shops and they cannot move freely in Nepal. Those refugees who arrived in Nepal after 1989 have no legal status. In reality, many Tibetan refugees are stateless and as the possibility of their return to Tibet in the near future is remote, they are in a difficult situation.

A step towards dialogue?

An incident which may have important consequences for Tibet's future was the visit of an exiled Tibetan delegation to China and Tibet in September. During the visit, the two special envoys of the Dalai Lama had, for the first time in twenty years, the opportunity to meet Chinese and Tibetan government officials with whom they had what they themselves afterwards called "cordial and open discussions". The visit was interpreted in many different ways but only time will tell whether the visit has brought Tibet and China closer to a solution.

Worsening living conditions in Tibet

The living conditions of the Tibetan population in Tibet have not improved and the pressure on the Tibetans and their traditional way of life continues to grow. They are suffering from marginalisation and pressure as a consequence of China's development of Lhasa and other towns, the intensified development of what China calls its "western regions" and China's participation in the USA's "war against terrorism".

Reports published in 2002 show that the Tibetans are lagging way behind the majority of Chinese in terms of access to health services and education and that the gap is widening. With few exceptions, the Tibetans have not benefited from the economic growth in Tibet, the exploitation of Tibet's resources, the fast growing tourism industry or the development of the towns and infrastructure. A report "Delivery and Deficiency. Health and Health care in Tibet" published by the London-based organisation Tibetan Information Network (TIN) documents the fact that affordable and adequate health care is still not available to the majority of Tibetans. Many diseases that have been endemic to the Tibetan plateau for centuries are still not under control, and emergency health care is virtually non-existent. During the 1990s, there was a reduction in the Chinese state funding for health care, and whatever funding there is mostly benefits the predominantly Chinese population in urban areas. There is little focus on health, education and other "soft" aspects in China's current development policies for Tibet. The international organisation Médecins sans Frontières (MSF) decided to stop most of their activities in Tibet at the end of the year. MSF had been under pressure from the Chinese authorities for quite some time.

Exploitation of mineral resources

Another TIN report "Mining in Tibet" shows that the current model of development in Tibet enhances disparities between rich and poor and between Tibetans and Chinese. Tibetans generally remain on the margins of the industry that threatens their traditional livelihoods but presents little in terms of long-term alternatives. Mining projects often threaten their religious and economic relationship with the land. China prioritises the exploitation of Tibet's important mineral resources in its effort to meet growing domestic demands. There has been little foreign investment in the mining industry in Tibet yet international companies and agencies and Western scientists are looking for possibilities in China's "Western regions" and the Chinese government is on the look out for more foreign investment. The exploitation of Tibet's mineral resources can be expected to grow and to be extended into hitherto isolated areas as a consequence of China's focus on improving the transport infrastructure, especially the railway between Lhasa and Golmud, which is already under construction.

Tibet in the world

In 2002, the World Summit for Sustainable Development was held in Johannesburg in South Africa. Although the Chinese authorities succeeded in excluding two important Tibetan organisations, the Tibet Justice Centre and the International Campaign for Tibet, other organisations accredited for the summit allowed a Tibetan delegation to participate as their members. Tibet's serious environmental and developmental problems played only a minor role at the World Summit but it was nevertheless important that Tibet was represented. In September, the annual Asia-Europe Meeting (ASEM) meeting was held in Copenhagen in connection with Denmark's presidency of the EU. China participated as one of the ASEM countries and some organisations in Denmark, including the Tibet Support Committee, focused on Tibet in a seminar at the parallel NGO Forum. In December, the European Parliament held an international conference on Tibet with the participation of representatives from European national parliaments, Tibet organisations and other interested parties. At the end of the conference, the participants agreed on a resolution in which they once again urged the European countries to put more pressure on China and the EU to appoint a special representative for Tibet similar to the special coordinator for Tibet in the USA. ❑

TAIWAN

Taiwan's indigenous peoples constitute 1.7% of the country's total population. They are divided into 10 tribal groups, each with its own language. Most of these live in the eastern and central mountain region of the country.

The Tao and nuclear waste

Orchid Island, or *Poso no Tao* ("Island of Human" in the language of the local indigenous people), is located off the coast of south-eastern Taiwan. The island is home to the Tao people, an indigenous community comprising 3,500 members.

In 1982, the Taiwan government started construction on the island, saying it planned to build a fish-canning factory to promote the local economy. In fact, the factory was a storage facility for nuclear waste, accepting regularly delivered waste from nuclear power plants in Taiwan.

The blatant deceit with which the storage facility was imposed on the Tao and the severe impact that nuclear waste could have on such a small community immediately ignited a sharp response from both indigenous and non-indigenous intellectuals. Activists from indigenous and non-indigenous communities supported the large-scale protests organized by the Tao people. In 1994, international attention was focused on the Tao nuclear issue when a representative of the Taiwan indigenous community made a statement to the UN Working Group on Indigenous Peoples (UNWGIP). Faced with such domestic and international pressure, the Taiwan government stopped delivering nuclear waste in the mid-1990s and promised to remove all waste from the island by the end of 2002. Nevertheless, by the beginning of 2003, the government had still not identified a permanent storage site.

Since the beginning of 2002, the Tao people have tried every possible way to express their determination and to force the government to honor its obligations. Examples include an elementary school student trying to hand a plea to President Chen during a school field trip; a Tao assistant of an indigenous parliamentary member successfully urging his boss to lobby related administrative offices on the timetable of the removal; and emails pleading the cause filling up people's email accounts. Government officials, from the President to related cabinet members, including the Chief Executive Officer of Taipower Company, visited the island. Some of them went there to give further assurances, but some went there looking for the possibility of renewing the storage contract.

No contract was renewed, but neither the government nor Taipower followed through on their obligations to remove the waste from the island. Without any effective lease to the land, the nuclear waste remains in place while the "compensation" formerly paid by Taipower is no longer being paid. The 'compensation' had amounted to 3 billion NT$ (approx. US$ 8,5 million), before the resentment of the indigenous communities boiled over and the Tao refused to be paid for being cheated. The fact that the Tao people had at one point accepted payment became a curse on them. They were condemned as immoral because their demonstrations were asking for nothing but money. Some non-indigenous parliamentary members even outrageously proposed that the Taiwan government should "buy up" the island by giving every resident 1 million NT$ to keep them quiet forever.

After protesting for years, the island and the Tao people are left with the Nuclear Waste Storage Facility and two committees set up by the government, a "Community Rebuilding Committee" and a "Storage Removal Committee", without any serious plans for removal of the waste. Resentment and despair is widespread on the

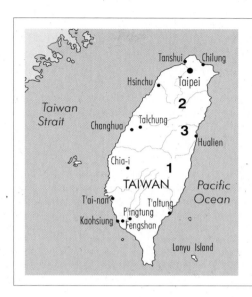

1. Yu-shan National Park

2. Shei-pa National Park

3. Taroko National Park

island, and it is likely that 2003 will see concrete measures by the Tao to force the government and Taipower to honor their obligations.

By the end of 2002, the Tao people had managed to organize a "Tao People's Counsel" to represent them in negotiations with the government. At the very beginning of 2003, the counsel called for a campaign to protest against Taipower for failing to remove all nuclear waste before the end of 2002. The Tao struggle continues.

Objectifying indigenous identity through "eco-tourism"

The 2002 International Year of Eco-tourism planned by the Taiwan government was intended to encourage travel in indigenous areas. As with other commercial activities in indigenous areas, local indigenous peoples are usually not the greatest beneficiaries of such activities. They are, on the contrary, very likely to become those who have to deal with all the accompanying unpleasant by-products of tourism.

The eastern part of Taiwan is home to the largest indigenous community, known as the Pangcah. Its population is widely scattered and the tradition is for each village to hold its annual ceremonies in summer. The local county governments have long turned these ceremonies into the biggest attraction during the peak tourist season, and the local tourist offices have tried to ensure that the dates of the different village ceremonies do not coincide, so that tourists can visit them one by one, thereby maximizing the possible profit. In 2001, these offices organized different activities and issued a tourist passport as a marketing strategy. They also provided the famous villages with some subsidies for the ceremonies, and printed the date of their ceremonies in the passport. Villages that have experience of dealing with such arrangements gave the dates of the less important rituals to avoid interruptions caused by large crowds of tourists.

In 2002, however, the local tourist offices did even more. They sent people to the villages a few days before the ceremony to carry out "sanitary examinations", telling people to sweep the floor, pick up trash and even asking the young villagers not to dye their hair. Humiliated and angry, villagers in Cepolan forced the tourist official to leave, making sure he understood that the villagers did all the necessary preparations for the sake of their ancestors and not for the paltry subsidy.

What happened in Cepolan is not the only example of the government's attitude towards using indigenous ceremonies as a way of increasing GNP without paying a minimum of respect. The local county governments' held a "Miss Pangcah" contest to help promote tourism, ignoring all controversy around beauty contests. In Chiayi, the county where the Cou community is located, the local government followed this pattern and held a contest for "Cou warrior and beauty". Sponsored by non-indigenous businessmen involved in tourism, the contest offered an incredibly high prize (600,000 NT$ in an area where 800NT$ is plenty for weekly expenses) for winners, making participation in the contest all but irresistible for individual Cou members.

It seems that, in promoting "eco-tourism", there has been an objectification of indigenous peoples to meet the greed for novelties. First, indigenous traditional artistic patterns and graphics were adopted by cheap souvenir producers. Now, indigenous human images have become the next prisoner of the capitalist tourist market

Struggling for self-government: the Maqaw case

The proposal to set up a new national park in the Maqaw area first came about in 1998, when environmentalists found that a government department was allowing an ancient natural cypress forest to be logged. In response, they campaigned for the establishment of a new national park, in order to keep the loggers from cutting down more precious wood. The local indigenous community was against such a proposal, as a result of the always uneasy relationship between the national park office and indigenous communities. Three of the six existing national parks (Yu-shan, Shei-pa, Taroko) in Taiwan are located on indigenous ancestral land, and the indigenous inhabitants in the national park areas are prohibited from maintaining their subsistence economy. All hunting and gathering activities are taken as criminal offenses. Opposition to national parks has long been a fundamental tenet of indigenous activism. As a result, indigenous communities established themselves as pro-forest conservation but against creating a national park.

Environmentalists sought for mutual understanding and support from the indigenous communities, proposing a new initiative of 'co-management' on the part of both local indigenous communities and the government. Some indigenous activists regarded this proposal as a basis for the ongoing campaign for indigenous self-government, and agreed to negotiate with the environmentalist organizations. This resulted in significant agreements. Firstly, they renamed the national park "Maqaw", using the word that refers to the area in the local language. Secondly, they proposed a new national park, under the co-management of local indigenous communities and the government. In his May 2000 inauguration ceremony, President Chen announced his determination to set up the Maqaw national park.

2002 was a big year for the Maqaw campaign. Although some indigenous activists support the campaign, not all related communities are convinced that the promised ideal of co-management will be realised. There was harsh debate within the indigenous community at the beginning of the year. In general, the villages less influenced by modern political and economic structures have more confidence in their own ability to contribute to a practical co-management agenda. Those villages that are more incorporated into modern systems have developed some vital linkages with the loggers, and are hesitant to return to traditional ways of living.

Another influential factor was that an indigenous parliamentary member took the lead in the anti-national park campaign. Kao-Chin, daughter of a Han settler and a Tayal woman, did not claim her official indigenous identity before running for election to the parliament. As a former singer and actress, however, it was easy for her to attract media attention. She soon became the mouthpiece of her Tayal people.

To some Tayal elders, Kao-Chin's performance as a spokesperson was disturbing. Being brought up away from the community, Kao-

Chin's election was not based on recognition and respect from the Tayal community. She entered parliament only by the distorted electoral system for indigenous parliamentary members, which does not assign representatives based on community affiliation but rather treats all indigenous inhabitants the same and considers indigenous candidates as being capable of representing any indigenous communities.

For these reasons, the debate has become much more complicated. The positive aspect is that this intriguing situation inspires more thought on the promotion of a co-management system under the structure of a national park. At the same time, it sheds light on some critical issues that are unavoidable in the struggle for indigenous self-governance. The current indigenous society is a hybrid, influenced by its colonial legacy and the transformation from subsistence economy to market economy in the context of globalization, and is frequently placed within the context of cross-strait relations. The co-management initiative of the Maqaw may be only a small-scale self-government experiment. Nevertheless, the conflicts derived from the debate reveal a more insightful perspective on the upcoming challenges facing the path to self-governance.

Changes in draft law on indigenous self-governance

Another agenda item announced in President Chen's promise to bring about indigenous self-governance is the enactment of an Indigenous Self-government Act. The Aboriginal Peoples Council (APC), the highest administrative body for indigenous affairs under the Executive Yuan, [1] started drafting the act in 2000. The draft was highly contested within indigenous communities because it paid little attention to traditional political and social infrastructure, and adopting it could therefore cause greater assimilation.

Although the criticisms persisted, the APC did not change the framework of the draft. Before the final draft was settled, the APC sent it to other ministers for advice on revisions, and renegotiated certain articles with related ministries. The APC then came out with a shortened edition of the original draft, although the framework remained the same. To the people's astonishment, however, a few days before the draft was sent to the Executive Yuan Board, the APC came out with a second version of the Indigenous Self-government Act, which allows great flexibility for heterogeneity between different indigenous communities.

The change, however, was not made by the APC itself. The APC is generally reluctant to insist on radical positions for indigenous rights. The dramatic change was apparently the result of a phone call from an influential non-indigenous government member, asking the APC to come out with a more radical draft on self-governance. The APC then sent both versions to the Executive Yuan Board, and the second version was adopted at the preliminary examination.

This ironic development is positive to some extent, in that it allows greater freedom for indigenous communities to set up a government system that is more akin to their traditional practice. But the underlying difficulties should be addressed with great care. Such a system will inevitably result in more conflict with the existing local government system, and will require more efforts in negotiating with all related ministries. Such negotiations are never easy, and seem to be even more difficult in this case since the second version is the one that other ministries had never been informed of, let alone been given an opportunity to negotiate. If the Executive Yuan Board does adopt this second version, doubts and questions will inevitably be raised. The burden of negotiation will be on the APC, which has never been competitive in inter-ministry negotiations. The workload of negotiation will be impossible for either the APC or the indigenous communities to afford. ❑

Note

1 The Executive Yuan is the administrative body of the government. The Executive Yuan Board is the decision-making body of the Executive Yuan.

PHILIPPINES

The Philippines is the only Asian country to have officially adopted the term "indigenous peoples". According to estimates of the National Commission on Indigenous Peoples (NCIP), between 12 and 15 million of the total population of 70 million are indigenous. Roughly 60% of them live in southern island Mindanao, a third on the main island Luzon in the north, and the rest scattered over the other islands of the archipelago. In October 1997, the Philippine government passed the comprehensive Indigenous Peoples Rights Act (IPRA) as mandated by the Constitutional Provision, by which the Philippine state must recognize and promote the rights of indigenous peoples. However, more than five years after its promulgation, full implementation of IPRA still remains to be seen.

Implementation of IPRA

The National Commission on Indigenous Peoples (NCIP) continues to be faced with a host of internal and external problems, as described in last year's article on the Philippines (the *Indigenous World 2001-2002*). Compared to the previous year, however, there is more reason for optimism as several important steps have been taken. Under the new NCIP chairmanship of Atty. Rueben Dasay Lingating, the NCIP has finally drafted guidelines for surveying Ancestral Domains, as well as for the establishment and operation of the Consultative Body which, as a multi-layered institution, is supposed to comprise indigenous leaders from all the indigenous peoples of the country. Furthermore, the NCIP is in the process of a thorough internal re-organisation.

Powerful vested interests, especially at local level, either manage to block the implementation of IPRA or succeed in manipulating it to their advantage. One most revealing recent example was the suspension of the distribution of lands to the Maguindanaoan and B'laan communities in Barrio Apopong, General Santos City, South Cotobato, Mindanao, by Department of Environment and Natural Resources (DENR) Secretary Gozun in January 2003. She called for a review of the validity of a July 2001 Supreme Court decision recognizing the indigenous communities' ownership of 923 hectares of land. It appears that this call for review is in connection with the Alcantara Group, which had a Forest Land Grazing Agreement (FLGA) over the said land. According to the leaders of the communities, the Alcantara has already benefited from the said land for the past 30 years while they have been struggling to regain the land. The Commission on Settlement of Land Problems (Coslap), the Court of Appeals and the Supreme Court have all rendered decisions canceling the lease agreement in favor of the indigenous communities. It is puzzling, therefore, that Gozun should be questioning these decisions. What raises suspicion is the fact that Nicasio Alcantara, brother of newly appointed Public Estates Authority (PEA) Chair Tomas Alcantara, is involved in this case. Nicasio is also an appointee of President Gloria Macapagal-Arroyo and now president of oil giant Petron Corp.

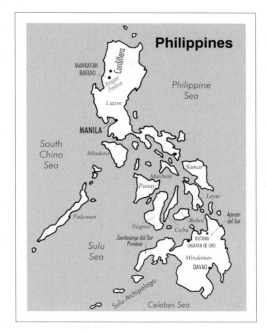

Conflicting laws are a major obstacle to a fully-fledged implementation of IPRA, such as the National Integrated Protected Areas Act and the Mining Act. On April 23, 2003, however, considering initiatives by which to harmonize the IPRA with environmental laws, the Department of Environment and Natural Resources (DENR), by way of memorandum, ordered the suspension of all issuances of licenses, resource use permits and clearances within areas covered by a Certificate of Ancestral Domain Claim (CADC) or Certificate of Ancestral Land Claim (CALC). The memo stated that no resource utilization instruments or clearances would be issued prior to issuance of Free and Prior Informed Consent (FPIC) statements from the communities involved. Appropriate coordination also had to be made with the NCIP office. In the same memo, the regional directors were also enjoined to submit a list of the status of licenses, permits and clearances within ancestral domains by May 15.

On face value, it is an important memo and supports IPRA section 59 on the certification pre-condition. It is significant as a regulatory tool, especially for forest concessions managed by outsiders or the government, or for large-scale projects intended to operate within ancestral domains. But the memo covers all permits and licenses, which means that even forest concessions owned or managed by indigenous people would also be subject to the stringent FPIC measures of NCIP Administrative Order number 3. The indigenous already find it very difficult and costly to acquire forest concessions (for rattan, almaciga resin, etc.). The memo therefore needs certain qualifications in order to avoid making it even harder for indigenous people to exercise their rights over the management of their domains and utilization of the forest products found within them.

The War in Mindanao

In February 2003, the war between the Philippine armed forces and the Moro Islamic Liberation Front (MILF) erupted again in Central Mindanao. President Gloria Macapagal-Arroyo even ordered the bombing of "embedded terrorist cells". According to government sources, more than 350,000 people, and among them a disproportional share of indigenous, generally known as Lumad, have been displaced, many living now under dire conditions in evacuation centers.

The government sees the new offensive against the MILF as part of the broader war against terrorism. In her state visit of late May 2003 to the USA, President Macapagal-Arroyo reaffirmed her support of the US led anti-terrorism coalition and stated that "we believe that US leadership and engagement with the US make the world a safer place for all of us to live in". US President Bush in return called the Philippines a special non-NATO ally, allowing the United States to respond more quickly to Philippine requests for military equipment, and President Macapagal-Arroyo received the assurance of 126 million dollars of military assistance. Macapagal-Arroyo is being heavily criticized for her iron-fist policy in Mindanao, both at home and abroad. The government is accused of trying to take advantage of the international "war on terror" to crush the MILF and the New Peoples Army (NPA), the armed wing of the Communist Party of the Philippines. According to newspaper reports in early 2003, the government is trying to speed up the passing of an anti-terrorism bill. Human rights organizations are extremely worried as they already observe democratic principles and human rights being rapidly eroded in the wake of the so-called anti-terrorism war the Philippines has joined in. Well-renowned human rights, humanitarian and legal aid organizations who are also known to be stout defenders of indigenous peoples' rights, such as the Legal Rights and Natural Resource Centre (LRC) and others, have been accused of being infiltrated by the NPA or being communist front organizations.

For many decades, the Lumad of Mindanao have found themselves caught up in the two wars that have ravaged Mindanao: the war against "Muslim rebels" and the war against the communist guerilla. In a most worrying recent development, the Lumad now appear to have been drawn into the war in a new way. According to news reports, the Armed Forces of the Philippines (AFP) are determined to draft Lumad into military service both as regular soldiers and as members of the Citizens Armed Forces Geographical Units (CAFGUs), the notorious vigilante units. In early April 2003, Defense Secretary Angelo Reyes told indigenous leaders in a meeting in Davao

City that the AFP would lower its education and height recruitments to accommodate high school graduates shorter than five feet and four inches. The AFP is even contemplating the idea of creating special units of battalion or company size composed entirely of Lumad. Indigenous organizations and their supporters are strongly opposed to such plans since the Lumad would be drawn even deeper into - and suffer even more from - a war that is not theirs. Only recently, three local government officials in an indigenous community in Tulunan who joined the CAFGUs were publicly executed by the NPA.

Ongoing struggle against development aggression

In April this year, the people of Sinakbat, Bakun Benguet in the *Cordillera* scored a major victory in their struggle to stop the drilling of a tunnel under their land for the Bakun AC project. This project is intended to divert water in order to supplement the water source for increased energy output from the existing Bakun mini-hydro plants. Because of the determination and consistent opposition of the people of Sinakbat to this project, which would potentially drain their water source, Pacific Hydro and HEDCOR, the project proponents, have decided to withdraw the project from their area, after two years of trying to convince the affected communities to give their consent. The people of Sinakbat have been supported by the Cordillera Peoples Alliance, which has brought their concern to the attention of the possible funder of this project.

In February this year, more than 1,300 mine workers (mostly indigenous workers from the different provinces of the Cordillera) of the Lepanto Consolidated Mining Company (LCMC) staged a month-long strike, resulting in the granting of their legitimate demands for better working conditions and benefits. In spite of military harassment, intimidation and the forceful dismantling of their picket lines, alongside an order to return to work, the workers and their families continued to block the different entry points to the mine sites. This action of the workers and their families paralyzed the operation of LCMC, causing them millions in losses. The only strike of Lepanto workers prior to this was 52 years ago, when a demand for the right to form a union was also successful.

Also in February this year, the communities near the Abra River formed a coalition to wage a campaign to stop the pollution of their sacred river by the Lepanto Consolidated Mining Company (LCMC). LCMC has been operating for more than 60 years, and had been dumping its toxic waste directly into the Abra river for more than 40 years before it built tailings dams. But mine waste is still seeping through into the Abra river. An Environmental Investigative Mission (EIM) was conducted in September 2002 by more than 60 participants coming from academic, medical and NGO backgrounds. The findings of the EIM illustrate the level of serious pollution of the Abra River due to LCMC's toxic waste disposal. More than 1,000 hectares of agricultural lands have already been damaged by siltation, and losses of aquatic, plant and bird life are great. Likewise, the affected people have been experiencing serious health problems, such as skin diseases, chest pains, cough, nasal and eye irritation resulting from exposure to the fumes from the polluted river or immersion in the river, along with contaminated rice fields.

Despite the fact that, in legislation, *Palawan* is considered an environmentally significant area, extractive, commercial mining has been ongoing in this pristine island for more than three decades. The Filipino-Japanese Rio Tuba Nickel Mining Corporation (RTN) is one company that has been in operation since 1967, engaged in Barangay Rio Tuba, Bataraza in mining, production and export shipment of beneficiated nickel silicate ore to Japan. It uses the surface strip-mining method, which involves removing the vegetation, soil, and rock layers to obtain minerals.

Although eight barangays (the smallest administrative unit of the Philippine State) and an estimated 500 families are affected by RTN's operations (ranging from health problems to siltation in agricultural fields, etc.) those of Barangay Iwahig and Sandoval are the most affected. More than 30 families of the Pala'wan indigenous community have long occupied the land forming part of the proposed quarry site of the proposed Hydrometallurgical Processing Plant (HPP) and are asserting their ancestral rights over their domain.

RTN disputes their claim on the grounds that the Pala'wan community of Sitio Gotok, bordering Barangay Iwahig and Sandoval, has no certificate of any kind to prove its claim. Contrary to the proponent's claim, the Pala'wan community's prior and long-term occupancy and beneficial use of the area are sufficient to establish their ancestral domain title or claim over such area. The IPRA law recognizes time-immemorial possession and jurisprudence supports the perspective that a certificate is only a means of validating title held since time-immemorial. The IP community has applied for a Certificate of Ancestral Domain Title (CADT) with the NCIP. Mt. Gotok in Barangay Iwahig is sacred to the Pala'wan and is also the source of spring water for the community there. In its desperate attempt to comply with social acceptability requirements under existing laws, the RTN secured the signatures of tribal chieftains representing various indigenous communities in the municipality of Bataraza. The manner by which such signatures were secured, however, is highly questionable considering that the community leaders were not fully aware of the nature, components and impact of the HPP project. The petition signed by the tribal chieftains is not in accord with the requirements of Free and Prior Informed Consent (FPIC). Under the IPRA law, FPIC means a consensus of all members of the indigenous communities, to be determined in accordance with their respective customary laws and practices, free from any external manipulation, interference and coercion, and obtained after fully disclosing the intent and scope of the activity, in a language and process understandable to the community.

A Senate inquiry has since been launched and an investigation team with members from the NCIP and the DENR is studying the case and the Environmental Compliance Certificate that was granted to RTN for the HPP project. ❑

Source

Environmental Legal Assistance Center (ELAC) Palawan – Position.

TIMOR LOROSA'E

On 20 May 2002, the independence of Timor Lorosa'e was celebrated in Dili and all over the country and, on 27 September, the country became the 191st member of the UN. Prior to these important events, a Constitution was finalized in March 2002 and, in April, the presidential elections were won by Xanana Gusmão, the supreme commander of Falintil (the armed resistance) for more than ten years until he was captured by the Indonesians in 1992.

The new Constitution[1]

The Constitution is the product of a joint national and international effort, in which the direct involvement of the United Nations is particularly noticeable in terms of its commitments to international law and to modern, individual human rights thinking. It introduces a system of parliamentary democracy with universal suffrage for citizens of 17 years and over; proportional representation in parliament; and separate elections for president and parliament. The powers of the president appear to be limited. He appoints the government but only after it has been nominated by the party or the coalition of parties that have a majority in parliament.

Observers, while commending the new Constitution, have also noted some deficiencies: the government has been given the power to make laws if the National Parliament authorizes it; there is nothing on local government and no reference is made to the status of the country's many ethnic and linguistic groups.

The new government

With independence declared, the Constituent Assembly elected in August 2001 (see *The Indigenous World 2001-2002*:253) transformed itself into the first national parliament and a government was formed. The Prime Minister is Mari Alkatiri, a representative of Timor Lorosa'e's small Muslim community and Minister for External Affairs in the first Republic of East Timor (28 November - 7 December 1975). The Foreign Minister is José Ramos-Horta, former UN representative from the same short-lived first Republic, and a Nobel Peace Prize winner in 1996 together with Bishop Carlos Belo. Mari Alkatiri and José Ramos-Horta both lived in exile during the Indonesian occupation.

Serious problems

But apart from these important steps towards nation building, there is not so much to rejoice about. Timor Lorosa'e faces a large number of serious social and economic problems. With a population of approximately 750,000, per capita GDP was US$ 378 in 2001, with more than 40 per cent of the population living below a poverty line of US 55 cents a day. The literacy rate is around 40 per cent, life expectancy is 57 years and there is high unemployment, especially among the youth of Dili. Coupled with this, there is a high incidence of disease, particularly tuberculosis, malaria, dengue and Japanese encephalitis, which are endemic. For every 1,000

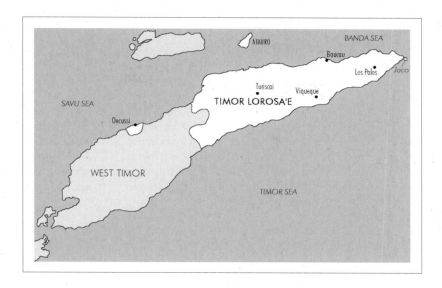

births there are 125 deaths, and the maternal mortality rate is 890 per 100,000 births. Malnutrition is rife, with 3-4 per cent of children aged between 6 months and five years diagnosed as acutely malnourished and 20 per cent chronically malnourished.[2]

In December 2002, Dili experienced the worst riots since independence. Two people were killed and several injured. In addition, there was some material destruction. According to the local NGO La'o Hamutuk:

> *There was no widespread looting, anarchy or civil disorder in Dili, escalating beyond what the authorities could contain. Rather, a few hundred people were manipulated by dissident political leaders to destroy selected property in an effort to destabilize the government. Responsible public authorities failed to act effectively, and the mob traveled around Dili for several hours, destroying buildings symbolic of the Prime Minister or of the unequal wealth of foreigners... Investigations will determine why the police and PKF [Peace Keeping Forces] were unwilling or unable to respond, but it is clear once again as in December 1975 and September 1999 the international community has failed in its responsibilities to the people of Timor Lorosa'e.[3]*

Help with strings attached

Timor Lorosa'e does have some sources of revenue (agriculture, fishing, tourism, oil and natural gas). that can provide the basis for a sound economy but they are far from fully developed. So, for the time being, Timor Lorosa'e is totally dependent on external help.

But some help seems to come with strings attached. British commentator Jonathan Steele explains how US Secretary of State, Colin Powell, before the new state had even been born "wrote to the incoming government ... warning them to give a written promise not to prosecute US citizens for crimes against humanity under the procedures of the newly established International Criminal Court [ICC]. Otherwise the US Congress would find it difficult to go on giving aid, he advised them." [4]

On 12 August 2002, Timor Lorosa'e's parliament ratified the Treaty of Rome establishing a permanent ICC that can hear cases of genocide, war crimes and crimes against humanity committed since 1 July 2002. At the same time, Timor Lorosa'e's government signed an "Article 98 immunity agreement" with the United States, in which Timor Lorosa'e agrees not to send any US government personnel to the ICC.

But this was not enough. The US demanded one more concession from Timor Lorosa'e and, once again, the Timorese gave in. On 1 October 2002, the two parties signed a Status of Forces Agreement (SOFA). SOFA will have wide-ranging consequences as it, in effect, gives US soldiers diplomatic immunity and places them above the law. It also exempts US Embassy personnel, as well as US soldiers and civilians working for the Pentagon, from Timorese taxes, contract regulations or criminal law. Nor can "Timorese authorities ... arrest or detain them, charge them with crimes, extradite them to other countries, compel them to testify in court, or hold them responsible for any half-Timorese children they might father. Their homes and personal property are "inviolable". They are immune from civil liability for actions related to their official duties." [5]

A long line of atrocities

Timor Lorosa'e also faces a serious problem in relation to justice. For 24 years, Indonesia committed a long line of atrocities against East Timor. During the first ten years, at least 200,000 people - almost one-third of the population before the invasion - lost their lives as a result of war, disease and starvation. It was one of the worst massacres the world has seen since 1945, both in absolute and relative terms, and many observers did not hesitate to use the term genocide to describe Indonesia's policies. In the following years, human rights violations continued, albeit on a smaller scale.

In 1999, the Indonesian military recruited a number of pro-Indonesian militias in East Timor in order to terrorize people into voting 'the right way' in the upcoming referendum on East Timor's future. When they realized they were going to lose the referendum, they arranged a final explosion of violence. They killed and tortured many people. They raped many women. In addition, they looted, burned and destroyed all over the territory. It was, in the words of American scholar Joseph Nevins, the making of "ground zero" in East Timor.[6]

All of these crimes were perpetrated by real people. Orders were given by the Indonesian government and they were carried out by the Indonesian military. It would be hard to find a single family in Timor Lorosa'e that was not adversely affected by these events. The Timorese cannot just forgive and forget. They do not want revenge. They understand that the killing has to stop. But they do want justice. Some of those responsible must be held accountable.

A dual approach

To deal with this crucial issue, the Security Council opted for a dual approach using domestic legal systems. Accordingly, the authorities in Jakarta set up an Ad Hoc Human Rights Court on East Timor to prosecute individuals in Indonesia, while UNTAET set up a Serious Crimes Unit to conduct parallel prosecutions in Timor Lorosa'e.

Timor Lorosa'e Serious Crimes Unit was established in June 2000 and the first trial began in January 2001. By May 2002, 101 persons had been indicted. Judgment had been handed down against 24 defendants, while a further 22 defendants were being tried or were awaiting trial. The statistics may look good. But the system suffers from serious flaws. In the first place, there is a lack of funds and qualified staff. Secondly, the Serious Crimes Unit can only prosecute people who are in Timor Lorosa'e. Only Timorese and only "small fry" have been indicted. Most of the "big fish" remain outside the court's jurisdiction.

Indonesia's Ad Hoc Human Rights Court did not start its work until March 2002, and it has a very limited mandate, covering only three of Timor Lorosa'e's thirteen districts, and only two months, April and September 1999, out of a 24-year military occupation. By

December 2002, the court had acquitted ten Indonesian officers. Only one Indonesian officer has so far been found guilty, and then only of having failed to prevent the violence committed by others.

The leaders are changing their tune

Many human rights organisations inside and outside Timor Lorosa'e have protested strongly against this way of dealing with the issue of justice. Instead, they are calling for an international tribunal similar to the ones set up for Rwanda and the former Yugoslavia, and with a wide-ranging mandate.

But the world's great powers - especially the five permanent members of the UN Security Council - do not seem to like this idea, and even the leaders of Timor Lorosa'e are beginning to change their tune: "Although former resistance leaders like Xanana Gusmão (now the country's president) and José Ramos-Horta (now the foreign minister) have forcefully spoken in the past about the need for far-reaching accountability for their country's plight, they almost never mention it now, instead stressing the need for 'reconciliation' and to concentrate on the future."[7]

Yayasan HAK, an important human rights organisation in Timor Lorosa'e, also denounces this development: "Some of our own leaders ... have dropped the demand for an international tribunal for fear of angering donor governments... Even our own leaders feed us nonsense about 'forgetting the past and looking to the future'."[8]

Will there be justice for Timor Lorosa'e?

Why do the great powers not want an international tribunal for Timor Lorosa'e? There are several reasons, as Sylvia de Bertodano writes:[9]

> The crippling cost of the existing International Criminal Courts, the embarrassing failures of the International Criminal Tribunal for Rwanda, and the US desire not to antagonize the world's largest Muslim country [Indonesia] while it is conducting a war on terrorism, means that no ad hoc tribunal is realistically going to be set up...In any event, even the existence of an ad hoc tribunal would not ensure that those in Indonesia would ever be prosecuted. As the International Criminal Tribunal for the former Yugoslavia discovered, arresting suspects who are protected by their state, even if the state is a relatively small one, is no easy task.

She concludes: "The real lesson, perhaps, is this: if a country defies the international community, flouts its commitments and obligations, and protects its criminals, the international community has a harsh choice between using force, and accepting that justice will never be done." ❏

Notes

1   This section is based on **Lars S.Vikør. 2003.** How will the country be ruled? *East Timor: Nation Building in the 21st Century,* ed. Gabriel Jonsson. Stockholm: Center for Pacific Asia Studies, Stockholm University.
2   **Thomas, Joe. 2002.** *HIV Australia.* November-December 2002.
3   **La'o Hamutuk.** "Disorder in East Timor: The International Community Must Accept Responsibility," 6 December 2002. http//www.etan.org
4   **Steele, Jonathan. 2002.** "East Timor is independent. So long as it does what it is told." *The Guardian,* 23 May 2002.
5   **Scheiner, Charles. 2002.** "East Timor Puts U.S. Soldiers Above the Law." *Estafeta,* vol. 8, no. 1, Winter 2002-2003. Published by ETAN.
6   **Nevins, Joseph. 2002.** "The Making of 'Ground Zero' in East Timor in 1999: An Analysis of International Complicity in Indonesia's Crimes." *Asian Survey,* vol. 42, no. 4, July/August 2002: 623-642.
7   **Nevins, Joseph. 2002.** "First the Butchery, Then the Flowers: Clinton and Holbrooke in East Timor." *CounterPunch,* Vol.9, no.10.16-31 May 2002.
8   Quoted by J. Nevins, *ibid.*
9   **Bertodano, Sylvia de. 2002.** *Justice for East Timor.* Report for the NGO *No Peace Without Justice.*

East Timor Action Network (ETAN): www.etan.org

INDONESIA

Mobilizing for the elections

There is still one year to go until the general elections of 2004 and yet the work of political parties in the regions, districts and sub-districts throughout Indonesia is already reflecting this upcoming event. "Internal Consolidation" is the expression used to describe these activities but sometimes it might be more appropriate to label the work as "mass mobilization". The electronic and printed media often describe the activities of political parties in some regions as "stealing the starting time". This means that, even though the government has not yet decided the timeframe for the political campaign, the "field work" of some political parties that is taking place at the moment could very well be categorized as political campaigning.

The situation in Aceh

National newspapers and the electronic media regularly expose the situation in Aceh and in Jakarta. At present, the situation in Aceh is far more critical than in any other place in Indonesia, and all government resources are dedicated to defending the territory from the GAM (*Gerakan Aceh Merdeka* or Aceh Liberation Movement). At the time of writing, the government of Indonesia is still offering the GAM time to consider the government's non-negotiable principles. That is, that all negotiation should be based on the fact that Aceh is a province of Indonesia. The option is therefore special autonomy or nothing. This means that if the GAM does not accept this principle, military operations will be the only way of settling the problem between the GAM and the government.

The sending of troops to Aceh has raised debate among Indonesian civil society. Military leaders argue that they have not sent new or additional troops but only replaced the division in the field with a new one, and yet civil society organizations question the truth of this statement, as well as the effectiveness of the military approach taken by the government. The Soeharto New Order regime demonstrated the failure of this approach to settling problems between communities and the state/government. Another concern is the Draft Bill on TNI (the Indonesian National Armed Forces). No sooner had the public debate on *Undang-Undang Penanggulangan Keadaan Bahaya* or the Law of the State of Emergency cooled down, than a new one arose, i.e. the debate on Article 19 of the TNI draft bill, which allows the Supreme Commander of TNI to take over authority from the government in an "emergency situation". Many people and organizations are questioning the meaning of this article. They are worried about the possibility of a military coup.

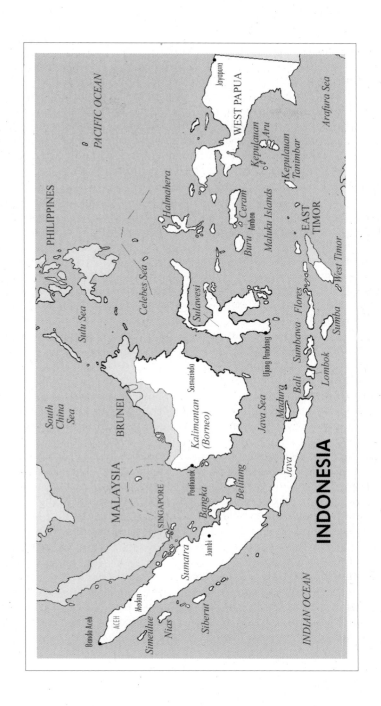

Village autonomy vs. district autonomy

Since the passing of Law No. 22 of 1999, there has been a growing tendency at community level to restructure and reorganize local institutions, including the governmental system. In Lombok, East and West Kalimantan, West Sumatra, South Sulawesi and Bali, the communities have been working on drafting their own village regulations.

Although there have been various responses to, and understandings of, the term "autonomy", there is a common expectation in the communities that they will gain more freedom to regulate their own matters. This is manifested in growing community activities throughout Indonesia in terms of practising and developing their autonomy as part of the broader political and governance reforms offered by Law No. 22 of 1999.

Many groups of people and parties – including the current ruling parties – have been trying to collaborate on this issue with the communities. Strengthening local organizations, raising political awareness and developing local business are some of the training activities that have been taking place at community/local level. The ruling party (PDIP) has been facilitating training on "raising political awareness", which has been seen by some political observers as more a mobilization of communities than training as such. For the civil society organizations, one of the main concerns of the past months has been to strengthen local organizations. AMAN (*Aliansi Masyarakat Adat Nusantara*) an umbrella organization for indigenous peoples and their organisations, for example, has been working intensively on this.

The focus of local government, however, has been on strengthening local business organizations and infrastructure. The example of the Sorong District, West Papua, shows that what is in fact happening is a concentration of the business sector and the economy in the hands of the district government (*Bupati*). Control over forests and land in Sorong district has been handed over to big corporations. This practice gives large sums of money to local governments and supports the political position of *Bupati*.

The tension between village autonomy and district autonomy (*kabupaten*) is reflected even more clearly in the cases of land reclaims. Some communities are now reclaiming land that has been used by companies (state or private) as forest concessions or other use rights given by the government. They have met with a hard response from local governments, for example, in Flores (in the districts of Manggarai, Kelimutu Ende and Flores Timur).

Another example is Deli in North Sumatra, which has a long history of agrarian conflict. The indigenous peoples' organization BPRPI (*Badan Perjuangan Rakyat Penunggu Indonesia*, Struggling Body of Indonesian Peoples) has been struggling for land by reclaiming, policy dialogue and participation in drafting local regulations, but relations with the local government are still very tense. Some land has already been taken back from the government, but this is not an indicator of a successful indigenous struggle for land, since most of it is unproductive, and amounts in total to only a very small part of what BPRPI actually requested. The situation of the indigenous communities has therefore not changed significantly.

New regulations and laws

Many regulations, local (*perda*) as well as village regulations (*perdes*) have been issued over the past two years. Bengkayang and Landak in West Kalimantan, Toraja and Luwuk in South Sulawesi, West Lampung and East Lampung in Lampung are all districts that have passed new local regulations. This is probably a sign of freedom and political awareness at local level.

More draft bills are waiting to be passed. In one way, this demonstrates the productivity of the *Dewan Perwakilan Rakyat* (DPR), the House of Representatives, and the government. But the main issue is not one of productivity. It relates to the substance as well as the process of formulating regulations and laws. Is it the peoples' needs that are stated in the law? Is it the peoples' demands? How do the government and the DPR (including the DPRD, or district or provincial DPR) carry out the process of formulating the laws and regulations? Civil society organizations therefore question the content of the new laws and regulations. As the main stakeholders, they question the legitimacy of the government and the legislature in their work of establishing new regulations and laws.

The Draft bill of the National Education System and Law No. 13 of 2003 on manpower have raised serious debates as to their content. The article on religious education in elementary and high schools emphasizes the obligation of every school to teach religion as a subject. The teacher should be from the same religion s/he teaches, i.e. teaching of Catholicism has to be undertaken by a Catholic teacher, of Islam by a Muslim teacher, etc. Schools that cannot fulfil this obligation will be fined one million *rupiahs* (approx. US$ 12,000).

Many are wondering why there is no article regulating the teaching of other subjects such as mathematics, biology, economics, history, literature, etc. The question is whether this law will be able to pave the way to sharpening people's minds as well as building a good moral basis among students, citizens and people? It is probably a good sign of democracy that the process of formulating a draft and the mechanism for establishing it as a law or regulation draws public attention and creates debate. But the extent to which the public interest is included in the new Law or Regulation is another important question. This issue may be reflected in the passing of Law No. 13 of 2003 and Law No. 32 of 2002 on Broadcasting. Article 5 of Law No. 32 of 2002 states that broadcasting is aimed at: supporting implementation of Pancasila (The Basic Principles of the Republic of Indonesia) and the Constitution of 1945; building and strengthening the moral base of the people of Indonesia; increasing the quality of human resources of Indonesia; ensuring the unity of the nation; and distributing information fairly. The *Komite Penyiaran Indonesia* (KPI), Indonesia Broadcasting Committee, has been established to monitor its implementation. This has created public debate, particularly because it falls within the mandate of the KPI to set the standard of broadcasting and to judge which broadcasting stations have broken the regulations. The KPI reports to the DPR. Some people are worried about the authority of the KPI, in that it could be a powerful institution just like the PWI (*Persatuan Wartawan Indonesia* or Indonesia Journalist Union) was in Soeharto's era, controlling information and communication in Indonesia. The argument is that there is no standard of fairness in information distribution. How then can it be judged whether a broadcasting station has crossed the boundaries of such fairness?

Broadening political participation

Since its formation in 1999, after the fall of Soeharto's New Order Regime, the national umbrella organization AMAN has played a major role in developing the indigenous peoples' movement in Indonesia. The increased political openness presents new opportunities for indigenous peoples' input into policy-making, and is a central theme in AMAN's work of broadening their political participation. This has created noisy responses in various regions. On the one hand, AMAN's members and its supporting organizations at local level have been working on this issue through organizational strengthening at community level. On the other hand, AMAN has to face its internal weakness in terms of community leaders or individuals who have been working within AMAN only to pursue their personal interest. This has created serious difficulties in AMAN's preparations for the upcoming elections.

Another interesting symptom to observe is that some activists are trying to form political groupings. Some try to become members of *Dewan Perwakilan Daerah* or the Local Representative Council, while others make efforts to gain good positions within political parties. Some of AMAN's members are a part of this game.

AMAN's overall preparations for next year's parliamentary elections therefore include work on consolidation. This means verification of members, organisational presentation, establishing regional/local indigenous organisations, strategic planning and selecting representatives to the AMAN Congress in July 2003, to be held in Lombok, West Nusa Tenggara.

The main objective of this organizational work is to ensure that AMAN will have a strong political bargaining position in the light of the 2004 general elections. It is clear enough that hundreds of political parties now need votes. If indigenous organizations, whether they join in AMAN or not, are well organized and consolidated, they can negotiate their platform with political parties. Put very simply: "We will give our vote to you, but you have to sign an agreement with us to implement our platform when you win or at least struggle for it when you have a position in legislative, executive or jurisdictional institutions."

In local government, this will involve more serious negotiations about natural resource management, indigenous rights, and about recognition of their existence in local regulations. As has been demonstrated, so far the main source of local government income has been natural resource exploitation. Over the last five years, for example, illegal logging has had a more serious impact than ever. This has happened because local government is opening up wide access to forests. The case of Sorong district is an example. Almost all the forest and land in this district have been handed over to the big forest concession holders.

Given this reality, indigenous peoples can do nothing but strengthen their organizations through alliances or other kinds of collaboration with civil society organizations in order to form a strong pressure group. This is the minimum target that has been set for 2004. ❑

MALAYSIA

The Federation of Malaysia consists of eleven states on the Malayan Peninsula and the two East Malaysian states of Sarawak and Sabah in northern and north-eastern Borneo. Indigenous peoples live both on the Peninsula and in the two states on Borneo. Those of the Peninsula are known as *Orang Asli* (Malay for "original people"). They comprise 18 ethnic groups and number about 96,000, roughly 0.6% of west Malaysia's population of 16 million or 0.5% of the Federation's total population of 20 million. In Sabah, there are about 39 different indigenous peoples who make up 65% of the state's 2.2 million citizens. Nationally, however, they are a minority of 7%. The indigenous peoples of Sarawak, commonly referred to as Dayak and consisting of 27 different ethnic groups, make up 30% of the 2 million people but, again, only 3 % nationwide.

Court victory creates precedence

The year 2002 saw some significant court cases related to indigenous land claims being filed or concluded in the three regions.

In *Peninsular Malaysia,* an epoch-making court victory for the Orang Asli became an important precedent for other communities in Malaysia and elsewhere. This prompted two other communities in Sabah and Sarawak to take two large companies to court for encroaching on their customary land.

In a landmark decision, the High Court in Peninsular Malaysia ruled that the Orang Asli have a proprietary interest in the customary and traditional lands occupied by them and that they have the right to use and derive profit from the land. In the case, seven Temuan Orang Asli sued the Federal and state governments, United Engineers (M) Bhd and the Malaysian Highway Authority for the loss of the their land and dwellings when their land in Kampung Bukit Tampoi, Selangor was acquired in 1996 to build a highway that connects to the Kuala Lumpur International Airport.

The Orang Asli plaintiffs sought a declaration that they are the owners of the land by custom, the holders of native titles to the land and holders of usufructuary rights to the land. They claimed that their customary and proprietary rights over the land, which their forefathers and foremothers have occupied and cultivated for many years, were not extinguished by any law. After reading his decision, the Judge urged all concerned to be consistent with current international

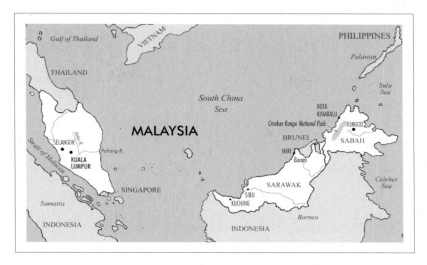

laws and practices, stating that although Malaysia had projected itself as progressive, it still refused to accept internationally recognised indigenous peoples' rights.

In *Sarawak*, four Penan communities in Upper Baram took up a case against the Sarawak Government and Syarikat Samling Timber and Samling Plywood (Baramas), two powerful timber companies operating in the area. The Penan, who to a large extent still depend on hunting and gathering in their forests, have suffered a great deal over the last decade due to logging operations. After a long wait, given that the communities filed their case at the Miri High court in 1998, the hearing scheduled to commence on October 24, 2002 in Miri was, however, adjourned mainly because of a last minute application by two Kenyah communities as defendants contending that the same land belonged to them.

Upon investigation, however, it was found that this was part of an elaborate plan by Syarikat Samling to block the case. Payments were paid to three Kenyah communities, in return for a so-called "Goodwill Agreement", to sign affidavits stating their claim over the Penan areas and allowing the Samling to log in their village area. Long Tungan, one of the three communities approached by Syarikat Samling, realised the implications of the agreement, backed out and refused to make the applications in court. Now the Penan and the Kenyah of Long Tungan have joined forces to work towards continued co-existence. The plaintiffs have filed an affidavit in opposition and produced papers from the Long Tungan representative's lawyers in order to expose Samling. The date set for the hearing in Miri High Court was 4th April 2003.

In *Sabah*, residents from seven communities in Tongod filed a case at the Kota Kinabalu High Court on October 11, 2002 against Hap Seng Consolidated Bhd and Asiatic Development Bhd, two oil palm companies, the Sabah Lands and Survey Department and the Sabah government.

The five plaintiffs representing the communities are now facing strong pressure from the government and company to settle the case out of court, especially in view of the forthcoming state elections. This is the first major case being brought before the court in Sabah, and would serve as a precedent for countless other communities facing the same problem. A Sabah legal support committee was formed after a meeting and sharing of information with lawyers involved in the cases in Peninsular Malaysia and Sarawak. While initially wide publicity was given to the case, the recent coverage of a press conference called by the communities was completely censored.

Other communities, encouraged by the action from the Tongod communities, continued to raise awareness about the native customary rights to land through community workshops. For the past two years, the communities – mostly of the Paitanic language family - have appealed to the government and companies to stop the encroachment onto their community lands, but no action has been taken. They started to actively prevent the opening up of their land for oil palm plantation by confiscating chainsaws belonging to the company. Seven of the village leaders were arrested and jailed, and their case is also pending in court.

Indigenous peoples and protected areas

Interest from both government and NGOs around collaborating with indigenous peoples living within and around protected areas increased in 2002. The active involvement of indigenous peoples in protected area management in Malaysia, let alone the subject of restitution, still lags far behind, despite the exposure of many government departments in international fora. Malaysia is now preparing to host the seventh Conference of Parties (COP7) to the Convention on Biodiversity (CBD) in 2004.

In Sabah, three projects by the Wildlife Department, Drainage and Irrigation Department (DID) and the Sabah Parks aimed at informing and involving communities with regard to laws and policies were facilitated by an indigenous organisation, PACOS Trust. The pilot and research project with the Wildlife Department involved several workshops and demarcation of community hunting areas. However, one of the two project sites, which overlaps with the Inarad community hunting area, was rejected by the Sabah Foundation - Rakyat Berjaya. Sabah Foundation was awarded this area under the Forest Management System by the state government for a period of 100 years. Another joint management effort is between the Dusun community in Tikolod and the DID. It involves workshops to inform communities about the categories of watershed areas and to work out community watershed management plans for areas within traditional territories of indigenous communities.

In 2002, in an effort to attract tourists to Sabah, the state government introduced homestay programmes and stepped up eco-tourism packages in existing national parks. One such programme included the opening of a tourist information centre in the Crocker Range Park by Sabah Parks (the state government's department in charge of protected areas). In conjunction with the launching of the centre, a community workshop was held at which the Sabah Parks explained its desire to involve communities in their tourism programme. The communities expressed concern about the expansion of the Park boundaries and also the threat of the Park's programme towards existing community eco-tourism activities. Such a workshop and other ongoing fora are important mechanisms by which communities can have more control over their traditional areas but, at the same time, find mutual benefits from eco-tourism programmes that do not go against indigenous resource management systems.

Garnering Suhakam's support

After the initial 100-day boycott of Suhakam, the Malaysian Human Rights Commission, indigenous organisations began to respond to Suhakam's effort to garner support. Indigenous representatives came in full force to the Commission's workshops and road shows organised all over Malaysia in 2002/3. For the past three years, several memoranda have been sent appealing for Suhakam's investigation of various human rights violations, particularly by logging companies, plantation companies and other agencies encroaching on indigenous territories in the name of development. Communities in Sabah have also complained about the ongoing appointment of traditional and other leaders by the government, resulting in corruption, a decline in good leadership and a breakdown of harmonious relations in villages. Sukham, however, did not respond to these appeals for a long time, hence the initial boycott of its campaign by the indigenous peoples.

Some recent, positive developments within Suhakam, such as the formation of an indigenous advisory group, the investigation into the Penan's complaints about incursion of logging companies onto their customary land and Suhakam's recognition of the seriousness of indigenous peoples' issues, have prompted many indigenous organisations to cooperate with Suhakam. The Commission has indeed managed to facilitate an investigation into the issues raised in the memoranda submitted by indigenous peoples. However, indigenous peoples are also concerned at the assimilationist attitude of some members of the Commission.

Pushing for international standards

In the meantime, indigenous organisations have stepped up their efforts to learn about and lobby for the implementation of international standards on indigenous rights. In February 2002, the Indigenous Peoples Network of Malaysia (IPNM), the Asia Indigenous Peoples Pact Foundation and the Office of the High Commissioner for Human Rights co-organised a training session on the United Nations and indigenous peoples. The International Labour Organization (ILO) also organised a training session on ILO Convention 169. More programmes and studies related to the CBD - in particular indigenous knowledge and biodiversity - are also being carried out in many communities through the UNDP/GEF Small Grants Programme and other donors and regional collaborations. In response to a campaign to get the Sarawak government to honour the international covenants and ILO Convention 169, the state government pointed out that Malaysia is not a signatory and therefore not bound by them.

The IPNM, which has continued to facilitate mutual support for indigenous organisations, also plans to take a more active role in international fora and has identified representatives to follow the work in the Permanent Forum on Indigenous Issues, CBD, human rights-related meetings and the UN Forum on Forest. The next assembly is planned to be held in June 2003 and will, among other things, strategize for the forthcoming COP7. ❑

THAILAND

Throughout the world, modern political boundaries have divided and regrouped culturally distinct populations into single nations, incorporating migratory populations, indigenous peoples and immigrants into discrete political entities now considered the legitimate form of governance and international interaction.

Thailand, in the center of the ethnically diverse states of Southeast Asia, is no exception and indeed its position at the convergence of a number of historical paths of trade and migration ensure that its population today reflects a range of peoples, cultures and histories. The government of Thailand, as in other countries, has struggled with internal cultural diversity and, since the first nationalist movement of the early 1930s, has instituted a process of assimilation through education that has created a society that almost exclusively self-identifies as "Thai".

The overwhelming majority of Tai Yai, many Khamu and Lua people, and large populations of Khmer and Lao incorporated into the Kingdom of Siam over centuries have become almost invisible within the current Thai population and even linguistic traces of cultural difference are diminishing. Yet this is not true for all peoples settled within Thailand. There remain a range of peoples, living predominantly in the northern region of the country, who maintain their cultural heritage and who self-identify as "Thai indigenous and tribal peoples". Within this group there is a great diversity of histories and cultures, with the Karen settlements pre-dating Tai settlements in the west of the country and the traditionally migratory Hmong and Mien peoples found throughout Southwest China and northern Southeast Asia. The major groups are shown below with recent population figures.

Indigenous-Tribal Peoples	Number of Villages	Number of Households	Population
Karen	1,986	81,090	411,670
Hmong	247	18,162	145,196
Mien	172	6,490	43,017
Akha	275	11,340	65,595
Lahu	412	17,034	95,917
Lisu	137	5,454	33,171
Total	**3,229**	**137,770**	**794,566**

Source: *Public Welfare Office, Thailand, March 2002*

Political situation

Despite very different histories, cultures and belief systems, these peoples face strong similarities in their dealings with the political state in which they live. They are viewed collectively by the government as *chao khao*, a term loosely translated as "hill people" and now rejected by the leaders of these peoples and communities. An alternative term *chon phao* is gaining acceptance within the government, and translates as "ethnic peoples" or "tribal peoples", importantly recognizing the reality of different peoples and cultural groups within the term. No matter which term in used, in practical terms indigenous and tribal peoples continue to occupy the same position in the Thai polity as they have historically, a position characterized by a view of highland communities as "threats" to national security (whether defined in terms of communism as in the late 1970s or in terms of drug trafficking as is the case today). This fearful stance has been augmented at times by periodic pushes for assimilation, historically visible in the earliest interest that the Thai government displayed towards indigenous and tribal peoples in the north, the Border Patrol Police policy of building schools and teaching Thai culture and language in remote areas. Assimilationist perspectives remain strong in current policy, and specific mention of indigenous and tribal peoples, or 'traditional communities' is rare. There is no government body in Thailand analogous to the Centre for Ethnic Minorities and Mountainous Areas (CEMMA) in neighboring Vietnam.[1] Assimilation has remained, along with a desire to control a perceived threat, the main discourse of Thai government policy towards indigenous and tribal peoples.

Land rights and the right to resources have complicated this situation. Since the National Parks Act in 1962 handed control of all forested lands over to the central Royal Forestry Department, the local struggle for control over traditional resources has been cast as a struggle against the government. However, in 1997 a new Constitution was promulgated by the Kingdom, and held within it the first legal protection in Thailand for the rights of "traditional communities". An avenue was opened with this Constitution, and one which civil society organizations in Thailand were not slow in taking up, shown most clearly in the development of the "Community Forest Bill", to be discussed later.

Even with these broad brushstrokes in place to describe the position of indigenous and tribal peoples in Thailand, the reality for the vast majority of communities is one of uncertainty. Historical trends in policy have little meaning at a local level where a given policy shift

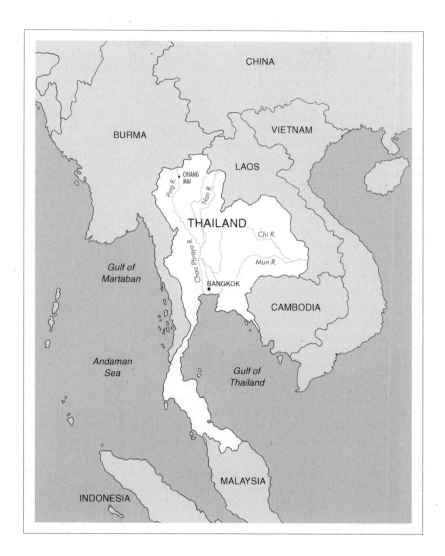

can mean the difference between the right to travel outside one's district or legal confinement to the district of residence. This uncertainty is best expressed in the terms of the Ministry of Social Development and Human Security of the Thai government, which released a report in late 2002 stating that "government policy towards minority [groups] is contextual and elusive ... changed according to situation, circumstance and public attitude".[2]

Recent developments

Unfortunately the "situation, circumstance and public attitude" in 2002 was characterized by factors not conducive to a sympathetic government attitude towards indigenous and tribal communities. There are two key issues of utmost importance to indigenous and tribal peoples in Thailand: the closely related issues of the basic right to citizenship in the land of one's birth, and the issue of the right to control and manage natural resources in the lands of indigenous and tribal communities. For both these issues, the highly bureaucratic nature of the Thai state requires that high-level policy change must occur if local practices are to change, and it is at this level of national lobbying that indigenous and tribal peoples in Thailand have gained experience and skills over recent years. National lobbying, and in 2002 direct negotiation with the government, is predominantly undertaken through the Assembly of Indigenous and Tribal Peoples of Thailand (AITT), a national assembly of indigenous and tribal peoples' organizations. This assembly was established in 2001 as a unified political voice with which to defend and articulate their position with the government, and again came to the fore in early 2002.

In April 2002, a massive rally of up to 4,000 people gathered in front of the Chiang Mai City Hall to bring local grievances to the government's attention. The rally began on the first of April and was a combined effort by the Assembly of Indigenous and Tribal Peoples of Thailand (AITT), the Northern Farmers Network, the Northern Assembly of Peoples Organizations and a range of smaller interest groups. The solidarity expressed across this range of social movements is a positive feature of political mobilization by indigenous and tribal peoples, for they are joined in the demand for local control over natural resources and the alleviation of the harsher effects of extreme poverty by a range of other marginalized groups. The two key issues of land rights and the right to legal status formed the central platform of the demands presented by the AITT to the government during this rally.

Community forests

The right to control and manage natural resources is one of the longest standing areas of political cooperation between indigenous and tribal peoples and lowland Thai communities, in the form of the "people's version" of a forestry law, the so-called Community Forest Bill, which would for the first time recognize the rights of 'traditional communities' to their lands. Senate consideration of this Bill, which had been planned since the Lower House passed the bill in 2001, was a key demand of the rally, and the Bill did pass before the Senate shortly after the rally finished.

The Community Forest Bill is an important piece of legislative history in Thailand as it is one of the first acts of legislation to be presented under a Constitutional provision that allows people to propose legislation for parliamentary consideration. A Bill under this provision may be presented if over 50,000 signatures are collected; the Community Forest Bill was presented in early 2000 with well over 52,000 signatures.

Despite strong public support and the support of the Lower House, the Senate significantly amended the Bill and, in doing so, stripped it of many of the protections and rights so painstakingly drafted in wide public consultations during the late 1990s. Notably, the Senate removed all "protected forested areas" from the scope of the Community Forest Bill, thus excluding the vast majority of indigenous and tribal communities in Thailand. After the amendments by the Senate, the Bill now returns for consideration by a joint committee of both houses of Parliament, expected to convene to consider the Bill in 2003. The amendments by the Senate have been declared as unacceptable by the AITT and lobbying continues to have the Bill returned to the form in which it was earlier passed by the Lower House.

Citizenship

The issue of citizenship is one of the most crucial for indigenous and tribal peoples in Thailand, and the problems that continue to plague highland communities with regard to their legal status in the Thai nation are the result of the "contextual" and shifting nature of Thai laws in relation to minority groups. In 2001, the Thai government declared that a period of one year remained for all people residing within the nation to apply for citizenship, and those without citizenship as of 28 August 2002 would be considered illegal residents. The Thai government (through the Department of Public Welfare) first surveyed remote areas in 1955 and, to the present day, serious barriers have existed in surveying, which have resulted in hundreds of thousands of indigenous and tribal peoples in Thailand being without citizenship. The Department of Local Administration placed the figure at 377,450 individuals at the beginning of 2002, a figure which Chutima Morlaeku, a Thai-Ahka human rights activist considers far lower than the reality. Whatever the true number, the position of these individuals and families is precarious and the AITT led the call for an extension of the grace period for citizenship applications.

After much work by local leaders, and direct negotiations with the government in April, the period available for citizenship applications was extended by a further year. This victory will only become a victory in reality if the process of application and consideration continues at district level. With the support of local NGOs and indigenous peoples' organizations, hundreds of thousands of applications were submitted, and many remain in district offices awaiting consideration. It is hoped that this problem, which has plagued communities throughout the north for decades, will be resolved soon. The establishment of a Sub-Committee on Solutions to Ethnic Issues in the middle of 2002, with Deputy Prime Minister Chavalit Yongjaiyut appointed the Chair of this Sub-Committee, is a step forward. However, the processing of applications at District level remains slow, and it is unlikely that the extra year granted will be sufficient.

Future

The closing months of 2002 did not bode well for the process of citizenship applications, with submitted applications remaining in district offices and Mae Aie district in the north seeing over a thousand successful applications withdrawn. At the same time, political pressure on the government to address drug trafficking across the border of Burma and Thailand meant that the perspective of tribal peoples as a threat to the nation again came to the fore in media and public perceptions of remote communities. The continuing lack of any real progress in consideration of the Community Forest Bill, now in front of Parliament for over two years, and stalling of citizenship procedures seems to indicate a lack of real commitment to solving these serious issues facing indigenous and tribal peoples in Thailand. They continue to lack concrete and permanent channels within the Thai political system through which to address problems arising at local level. If there is a shift in public attitude, for whatever reason, against the just calls of remote communities in Thailand for equality before the law, then certainty in life and property will again become a goal out of reach for the majority. These peoples and their communities remain at the mercy of a government policy that "is contextual and elusive". ❑

Note and reference

1   The term 'ethnic minorities' rather than 'indigenous' or 'tribal' is prefered by governments throughout Southeast Asia. In Thailand's case, this means that the Chinese diaspora, a sizable Vietnamese minority and indigenous and tribal peoples in the north occupy the same legal position.
2   **Satawat Sathitpiansiri. 2003.** *Minority Policy : a Case Study of Hilltribes in Thailand.* Bangkok: Ministry of Social Development and Human Security.

CAMBODIA

The peoples generally identified as indigenous peoples in Cambodia are usually referred to as "Khmer Loeu" ("Highland Khmer") or "highland peoples". Cambodia's indigenous peoples form a small minority of around 1% of the total population of 12 million. They live mostly in the eastern uplands and form the majority of the populations of the two north-eastern provinces of Ratanakiri and Mondulkiri.

In 2002, globalization and a lack of appropriate governance continued to impact on the lives of the indigenous peoples of Cambodia. In areas facing the highest rate of change, social problems are starting to arise. However, great efforts are being made to mitigate the effects of rapid change and its associated problems.

Land rights

Land rights and the arbitrary confiscation of ancestral lands remain one of the most pressing problems for indigenous communities throughout Cambodia.

Related to these problems, in 2001 the Royal Government of Cambodia passed a new Land Law that contains provisions for indigenous communities to gain title to their land, either in the form of individual titles for each family or as a communal title for the whole community. In this law, indigenous community land is open to be defined not only as residential and agricultural land but also including fallow plots left in reserve as part of the traditional crop rotation system.

As of early 2003, the new land law had yet to be supported by the necessary sub-decrees that define the requirements for legal recognition of communal land ownership. It would also appear that there is still space for more commitment, especially at national level, to fully allow the implementation of the intent of the new land law. This requires recognising that implementation of the intent of the law may contradict some other national laws and policies that seek to rapidly increase economic development in indigenous peoples' domains. There is a very real risk that these land law strategies will be implemented without sufficient consideration for the development priorities of indigenous peoples and the social situations prevalent in such areas.

At provincial level, there are a growing number of exceptions to the model of national-level policies being imposed on indigenous peoples. Whilst the national, regional and global levels are promoting alienation of ancestral lands, some of the provincial governments, notably the provincial government in Ratanakiri, have been following programs of promoting community-based natural resource management. In Ratanakiri, this has resulted in provincial recognition of community land natural resource management areas in 10 of 49 communes, with over 10 other communes progressing toward such provincial recognition. The challenge will now be to get these areas recognised at national level. This needs careful monitoring and support from the international community.

Forestry issues

Cambodia's forests continue to be rapidly degraded due to both commercial exploitation and infrastructure developments, which are increasing access to many areas of forest land traditionally utilized by indigenous communities. The Cambodian government has initiated reforms but these have mainly focused on the commercial aspects of forest exploitation and have been frustrated by the close linkages between government officials and logging companies. The Department of Forestry and Wildlife (DFW) has used the reform agenda to increase its direct control over the management and exploitation of forest resources. The new forestry law, approved in August 2002, contains provisions increasing the direct control the national DFW exerts over the forest estate, and has the potential to undermine the increasing role played by local government in community-based management of forest resources.

This situation has been further exacerbated by the design of some international projects aimed at promoting forestry reform in Cambo-

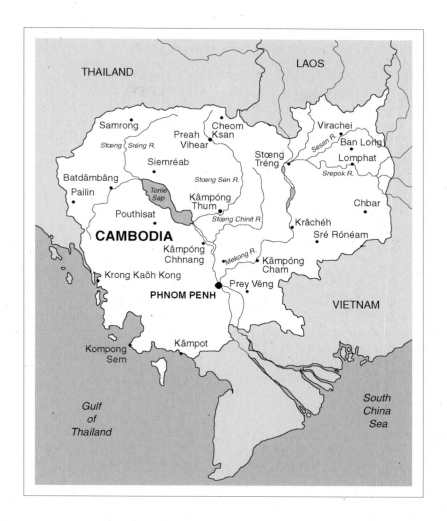

dia. In particular, the World Bank's Forest Concession Management and Control Pilot Project has been designed to increase the ability of the DFW to exert control over concession forest areas. However, the Cambodian government has used this to bolster the legitimacy of forest concessions and to undermine the ability of forest-dependent communities to make claims against forest areas controlled by logging concessions. This was demonstrated most obviously in November 2002 when the World Bank played a role in distributing Forest Concession Management Plans and Environmental and Social Impact

Assessments prepared by logging concessionaires as part of the government's forestry reform agenda. In doing so, the DFW was able to abrogate its responsibility to ensure transparency in relation to these documents. The staff of the DFW, while under the employment of forest concessionaires, had developed many of the plans. These plans were viewed as inadequate by almost all interested observers.

In response to these 'management plans', indigenous community representatives joined with representatives of other Cambodian communities in order to provide comments on these documents during the 19-day period allotted for public comment. The main theme of almost all submissions by communities was the claim for recognition and respect of the right to use and manage forest areas within logging concessions that had been granted by the national government. Representatives gathered peacefully at the DFW office in Phnom Penh waiting for a reply to their comments. In response, however, the Royal Government of Cambodia forcibly and violently broke up the gathering, during which one community representative died and others were injured.

These events have led to even more retaliations, including aggressive actions toward NGOs reporting the events surrounding forest concession management plans and their operation. While this continues, there remains much uncertainty that the promised reforms to the forestry sector will take place.

This echoes further concerns over the new Forest Law that was passed in 2002. This new law has been said by some observers to undermine community use of forests, which could greatly affect indigenous communities. An example of these problems is that the community use of trees to provide resin, a traditional form of economic livelihood for communities, was previously supported in the old forest law (the cutting of resin trees was prohibited). In the new law, this right is less strongly supported and the balanced development of a community forestry policy at national level has largely stagnated.

Education and health

Education reforms in Cambodia are, in general, progressing slowly. In the area of education for indigenous people, a number of both positive and disturbing trends can be seen. One positive aspect has been the support given to the development of bilingual education, a form of education that promotes the development of literacy in indigenous languages as a bridge to Khmer literacy. A CARE project is working closely with the Ministry of Education in the hope that a model for bilingual education will be produced that can be replicated by the Ministry.

Non-Formal Education (NFE) continues to return positive results, possibly reinforced by the deficiencies within the formal education system. This form of education remains literacy based and has had much success, as indigenous communities have been given the flexibility to manage classes at the time most suited to seasonal work patterns and daily lives (and because the teachers have been indigenous people.) Unfortunately, post-literacy NFE materials and classes remain seriously lacking.

In the formal education sector, many schools remain non-staffed and non-functional. In areas where there is no NFE, little or no effective education is available to indigenous peoples. This is within an environment of very rapid social and economic change and there is a very real danger that marginalisation will be further entrenched.

Health indicators among indigenous peoples in Cambodia are still among the worst in the country. Many of the attempts to rectify this situation have been frustrated by the almost total inefficiency of the public health system. Merely pouring in large amount of funds, as occurs with large donors, does not adequately address this problem. Indigenous people continue to report frequent incidents of corruption and abuse at the hands of non-indigenous health staff. This has led to indigenous people being very untrusting of the health system and less likely to follow its directions and services.

This spells further problems for the health status of indigenous peoples and has been part of the reason why there has been a national trend towards outsourcing health services to efficient health service providers, something that may not reform the national health system in the long term but may offer short-term relief.

Hydroelectric dams

In previous years, serious problems have been reported as a result of the hydroelectricity dams located on the Sesan River in Vietnam. This river flows through Ratanakiri in the north-east of Cambodia and the dams have resulted in deaths due to toxic water and irregular river flows. While these problems continue, such deaths are likely to increase since there are more dams under construction and being planned in Vietnam. These dams are going ahead despite the problems created by the existing dams downstream. International donor agencies and multilateral banks continue to support and validate their construction by supporting associated projects such as power line construction.

Tourism

Tourism is yet another outside globalization force that is beginning to have a very negative impact on indigenous peoples. Tourists are arriving in north-east Cambodia in ever increasing numbers. In Ratanakiri alone, tourist numbers soared from two thousand in 2001 to nine thousand in 2002. It has been predicted that up to 35,000 people will be visiting by the year 2010. These figures may even be underestimated given that the Cambodian, Laos and Vietnamese Governments have signed a "Triangle Development Plan", which includes opening up the north-eastern provinces of Cambodia to rapid and wide road access. In addition to this, the Asian Development Bank has funded, via loans, the development of an international airport in Ratanakiri, something done without any real consultation with indigenous community people, yet who are considered the tourist attractions and who will also suffer the negative consequences..

Despite the fact that the Asian Development Bank is to fund projects in "Pro-Poor Tourism" designed to allow communities more control, indigenous peoples will not have much success in this as new roads and airports are being built before they have developed the necessary social and human resources.

However, there have been a small number of programs in Ratanakiri that have begun to try and control the situation. One has been an English and tourism skills training program for a community that has lost a large proportion of its traditional lands and has had to receive a large number of tourists. Another has been the development of a provincial tourism steering committee that will try to co-ordinate efforts to ensure that tourism development is non-destructive.

Self-organizing

In the wake of these developments, indigenous peoples are starting to organize into associations and launch programs aimed at representation and cultural protection. Indigenous peoples have organised in a number of networks around issues such as the Sesan River hydroelectricity dams and natural resource management.

Some very positive results have already been achieved with regard to strengthening cultural identity. The Kui people in Preah Vihear and Kâmpóng Thom, for example, are now taking a greater interest in maintaining their identity, after they had almost given in to assimilation pressure. Similar developments are taking place among the Punong people in Mondulkiri and Kratie. The Kui and Punong peoples are also playing leading roles in the growing networks organized around natural resource management. In Stung Tréng, Preah Vihear, Kratie and Mondulkiri, indigenous peoples have also started to organize around community forest issues. They are now expressing their concerns at provincial and national levels to protect their interests with respect to natural resources.

In Ratanakiri, the Highlanders' Association, the Natural Resource Management Advocacy Network and the Sesan River Advocacy Network have been formed in recent years, with strong support from socially concerned NGOs. The Highlanders' Association has, among other things, conducted consultations and research into how indigenous communities could form strong and stable representation structures relevant to district, provincial and national development decisions.

The same issue is being addressed by the Ratanakiri Natural Resource Management Advocacy Network, a network of community representatives that aims to develop towards the goal of providing a strong and combined voice in the field of natural resource management policy and law, from community level up to provincial and government level. It also intends to provide a technical extension service in local languages to indigenous communities. ❏

VIETNAM

Vietnam officially recognises 54 ethnic groups. 'Ethnic Minorities' is the term used within both official and non-official Vietnam discourse, defined as those who have Vietnamese nationality, Vietnamese citizenship and live in Vietnam but who differ from the Kinh ethnic majority in terms of their language, culture, social cohesion, traditional wisdom, identity values and other basic characteristics. According to a recent estimate, ethnic minorities represented almost 14 percent of the total population.

Changes in national policy

The year 2002 saw many policies and programmes from the government, as well as from regional and international agencies that have striven to promote developments in the highlands, where most of the country's ethnic minorities live. Several of these programmes have been improved in order to meet the real needs of the peoples, but new challenges will still have to be met during future implementation processes.

Minority communities continue to be the most disadvantaged groups in Vietnam although the government is trying to tackle the problem. An example of this is national Programme No.135, which aims to reduce hunger and alleviate poverty in particularly remote and mountainous highland areas. During its first years, the Programme was blamed for the ineffectiveness of its implementation as well as for corruption scandals involving senior Vietnamese officials. Learning from these lessons, the government has made efforts to improve the Programme, whilst the National Assembly has taken strict action to discipline those responsible. The National Assembly co-operates with the government in the examination and investigation of the Programme's impact.

In 2002, members of the Vietnamese Communist Party signed a petition demanding that implementation of the Programme be more accountable and transparent. In addition, it requested that programme investments be increased with the objective of not only planting another five million hectares of forest but also helping those remote minority communities that are still without electricity to access the national power grid.

The government recently announced that a fund of Viet Nam Dong (VND) 600 billion (approx. US$ 40 million) would be created with the purpose of providing free health care to the poor. This nationwide fund is to be used to buy medical insurance and pay healthcare expenses, including hospital charges, for people living in particularly disadvantaged communes and for ethnic minorities in the Central Highlands region (Tay Nguyen). Approximately half of the fund will come from the Ministry of Finance, and the rest from provincial budgets, charity organisations and NGOs. Obviously, it is essential to enhance the health sector and improve the quality of health care nationwide. However, in order to do this, there also needs to be a way of ensuring that the fund is used in a practical and effective manner.

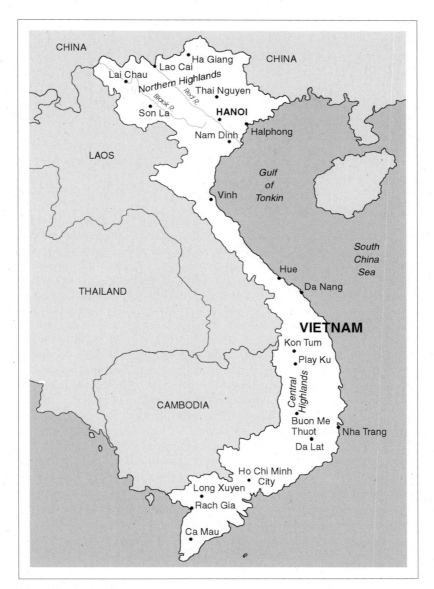

New approaches

Apart from establishing educational and health-care programmes, infrastructure programmes and projects such as road building, electricity, hospitals and schools, the National Assembly co-operates with the government, evaluation teams and civil society to improve the programmes' implementation processes. The previous approach for each particular stakeholder to do his own job and have his own sense of personal responsibility. However, on the other hand, there was no atmosphere of sharing a communal responsibility. In certain cases, no stakeholder was willing to be accountable for his actions. Within the current programmes, the National Assembly urges stakeholders to ensure that the investment goes straight to the community and that they apply participatory and co-operative approaches in order to avoid the existing dependency on the state. This new policy approach also addresses the problem of corruption by raising the sense of joint liability, equality and accountability.

A further change in policy at local, regional, and national level is the recognition of ethnic minority village elders and leaders within the decision-making and policy-making processes. Minority leaders and elders are made aware of and encouraged to get more involved in these processes. Minority female officials are being encouraged to take opportunities for their capacity building. Towards the end of 2002, the newly elected Vietnamese Communist Party General Secretary Mr. Nong Duc Manh (who himself belongs to the Tay ethnic minority) and many other government officials spent weeks visiting minority villages, talking to people and listening to their concerns, interests and expectations. At the same time, the National Assembly has opened the way for discussions on controversial ethnic minority issues in which traditional minority elders and leaders are invited to come and share and exchange their views. In the current 11th legislature (2002), 86 ethnic minority deputies, from 42 different minority groups, were elected and the number of minority deputies represented in the National Assembly has been constantly rising. Their presence and views will significantly contribute towards a better solution of their problems. It has been announced that the National Assembly intends to pass a new law on ethnic minorities that aims to improve minority peoples' standing and status.

Forest policy

Forestry has become a key element of government policies for ethnic minority peoples in remote areas, since a higher standard of living for ethnic minorities is one of the principle objectives in the coming year's forestry development plan of the Ministry of Agriculture and Rural

Development (MARD). The MARD Minister recently announced that their policies have now been adjusted so that any minority peoples living in remote areas will be allowed to live on and benefit from their local forest resources. It has also been announced that two million more hectares of forests will be allocated to local minority farmers.

The challenge for the government is to prove whether or not it has really learnt and understood the root causes of deforestation – i.e. logging, cash crop plantations, monopolised forestry, even the ineffectiveness of State-owned Forestry Enterprises – rather than just blaming minority highland peoples and their shifting cultivation. A government decision last year to gradually reduce the number of State-owned enterprises (which also include State-owned Forestry Enterprises) from over 12,000 in the 1990s to 5,000 in 2002 and to expect 3,000 by 2005 is encouraging.

The government has also implemented Decree No.163/CP in many villages, minority as well as majority villages. This decree allocates forestlands to individuals, households and organisations. Afterwards, individuals can acquire long-term and stable land use rights certificates (the so-called "Red Books"). In some places, the government has recognised and officially certified the entire community's communal forestland ownership. In the case of On Oc village, Muong Lum commune, in Son La province, the communal forestland was declared in the name of the Women's Union.

Hydropower projects

Great emphasis is being put on the 2001-2005 five-year plan, which focuses on economic growth, furthering modernisation and industrialisation while maintaining the political, economic, and social stability of the country. To increase the number of hydropower plants located in different regions throughout the nation is part of the national strategy to meet the demands of both demographic pressure and the process of industrialisation.

In October last year, the 215-metre-high Son La multi-purposes Hydropower Plant was approved. It not only aims to provide water to the lowlands, ensure public safety during the flood season, facilitate irrigation and river transport, and promote tourism but will also restructure the economy of the north-western region. This is populated by mainly black Thai and Hmong minority groups, soon to be displaced from the area. In order to benefit the nation as a whole, about 91,000 people, most of them Thai and Hmong, are to be resettled from 17 districts into new areas in the Son La and Lai Chau provinces. The government has dropped the earlier proposal to resettle them in the Central Highlands.

Many other large projects are also close to being approved by the National Assembly and the government, such as the Ca Mau gas electricity urea fertiliser complex, the 273 MW Se San Hydroelectric Power Station No.3 in Gia Lai and Kon Tum and the construction of the 300 MW Dai Ninh and Se San 3A hydro station.

A controversial apprehension has, however, arisen among academics and environmentalists: what will the future bring and what kind of future will the ethnic minority peoples be facing in terms of their local traditional knowledge, values, social cohesion and political institutions, once the Son La Hydro Power Plant has been constructed? Can sustainable development be ensured in these massive development projects?

The Central Highlands

Two years after the widespread demonstrations that triggered a heavy-handed response from the government, the situation remains tense in Tay Nguyen, the Central Highlands of Vietnam. Recent Human Rights Watch Briefing Papers (January and March 2003) report ongoing repression of ethnic minority Christian churches, prohibition of night gatherings, pressure to renounce their religion, land confiscation, detentions, physical abuse, tight border patrol and forced repatriation of indigenous who had fled to Cambodia. The reports cite numerous documents both from individual witnesses and from government sources supporting these reports.

The government of Vietnam has responded to the crisis by issuing a number of policy documents, such as on the long-term orientation of the five-year plan 2001-2005, on basic solutions to enhance the Central Highlands' economic and social development,[1] on solutions to resolve the lack of productive and residential lands for ethnic minorities in the Central Highlands[2] and on solutions to reinforce and consolidate the Central Highlands' local government over the period 2002-2010.[3]

However, at the same time, the government seems to continue with a repressive policy against those minority peoples in the Central Highlands who are considered to be linked to protests allegedly instigated by foreigners. Christians are apparently their main target. Better access to first-hand information on the ground is urgently needed, along with more transparent data-gathering and reporting procedures in order to be able to verify claims of both the victims of government repression and the Vietnamese government, which considers the protests as entirely instigated by anti-communist foreign groupings with the aim of destabilizing the country. Thus far, only cursory evidence for the latter allegations can be gathered. This exists mainly in the form of statements by individuals and Vietnamese NGOs which, at least until recently, had had access to the area. According to these sources, allegations of the role of the so-called "foreign hand" do not seem to be mere government propaganda. What has been repeatedly stated is that foreigners, i.e. mainly Central Highlanders who now live in the US and are usually devoted Protestant Christians of a more conservative political leaning, did play a crucial role in organising the uprisings. These, along with other radical Christian groups operating in the region, do pursue an anti-communist – and therefore anti-Vietnamese government – agenda. This largely explains the focus of repression on Christian churches in the Central Highlands.

Vietnamese NGOs are highly critical of reports published in the international media and by Western human rights organisations. Important to note is that they do not deny that injustice has been done to the ethnic minorities of the Central Highlands. What they criticize is the way the issue has so far been reported. They consider the reports to contain factual errors, be biased (mainly drawing on outsiders' information, i.e. refugees and expatriates living in the US), that people (like the indigenous leaders) are misquoted, and, to them one of the most crucial points, that the reports are generally written in an irresponsible way, i.e. without taking the culture and local political style (which means the way one can criticize the government in Vietnam) into account. After all, it is the Vietnamese NGOs, the emerging civil society in that country that face the consequences of the, in their eyes, unbalanced, incorrect and insensitive reporting. At present, Vietnamese NGOs cannot continue their work in the Central Highlands since the government has closed the area even to them. Furthermore, since the reports provoked even harsher interventions by the government, the consequences of such reporting ultimately have to be borne by the local people in the Central Highlands. The Vietnamese NGOs that have tried to improve the situation of the indigenous peoples in the Central Highlands and bring about policy changes see all the gains they have achieved in previous years lost. On a more general level, the slow opening-up of the government with respect to allowing the growth of a civil society in the country has come to an abrupt end.

Some NGOs have recently even come under investigation by the government as suspicion has grown in response to the reports published internationally.

Notes

1 Resolution No.10 NQ/TW dated January 18 2002 of the Politburo; Decision No.168/2001/QD-TTg dated October 30 2001 of the Prime Minister.
2 Decision No.132/2002/QD-TTg of October 08 2002.
3 Decision No.253/QD-TTg of March 05 2003.

LAOS

L ao is home to one of the most ethnically diverse populations in South-east Asia. The largest politically and economically dominant ethnic group, the Lao, comprises approximately 30% of the 4.8 million inhabitants of Lao (far more Lao live in the north-east of present-day Thailand than in Laos). The remaining 70% encompass more than 230 different ethno-linguistic groups. It is the latter that are generally considered as Laos' indigenous peoples. The term 'indigenous peoples' is increasingly used by international development agencies working in Laos. Officially, the terms "ethnic groups", "ethnic peoples" or *Lao son phau* ("non-ethnic Lao") are used.

2002 was an eventful year for indigenous peoples but, unfortunately, Laos' diverse peoples continue to be threatened as a result of various government policies and development projects, a number of which are described and reviewed here.

Large hydropower dams

2002 saw increased activity in large hydropower dam development in Laos, particularly in areas inhabited by indigenous people. In September, the Australian company Statecorp Holdings announced that it had received the go-ahead from the Lao government to conduct an 18-month feasibility study of the 80-metre high US$ 150-200 million Nam Pha Hydropower Dam in the northern province of Bokeo,

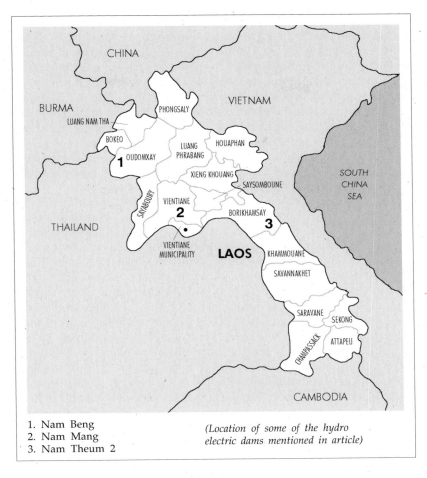

CHINA

BURMA

LUANG NAM THA

VIETNAM

PHONGSALY

BOKEO

OUDOMXAY

LUANG
PHRABANG

HOUAPHAN

1

XIENG KHOUANG

SAYSOMBOUNE

SOUTH
CHINA
SEA

SAYABOURY

VIENTIANE

2

BORIKHAMSAY

3

THAILAND

VIENTIANE
MUNICIPALITY

LAOS

KHAMMOUANE

SAVANNAKHET

SARAVANE

SEKONG

CHAMPASSACK

ATTAPEU

CAMBODIA

1. Nam Beng
2. Nam Mang
3. Nam Theum 2

*(Location of some of the hydro
electric dams mentioned in article)*

near the border with Luang Nam Tha Province. The project is reportedly being developed for both local power generation and for export.
In addition, in December, the International Braster Group announced
plans to build another large dam in the northern Lao province of
Oudomxay. The Nam Beng dam has reportedly already had a 20-
month feasibility study completed on it, and the 45-50 MW capacity
dam is expected to be built over a three to five-year period at a cost of
between US$ 50-60 million dollars. The investor has reportedly received
a 30-year concession from the Lao government to operate the dam.

Apart from the newly conceived northern Lao dams, considerable
debate continued regarding the merits of constructing the long-de-

layed Nam Theun 2 dam in central Laos which, if built, would be Laos' largest dam by far. The dam-building consortium, Nam Theun 2 Power Company (NTPC), which is largely controlled by Electricité de France International, plans to move ahead on the project by obtaining a financial guarantee from the World Bank. NTPC continued its aggressive public relations campaign to try to build up international and Lao support for the project. However, at the end of 2001, the Lao PDR/Canada Fund for Local Initiatives released a report regarding livelihood issues along the Xe Bang Fai River.[1] Although the report does not actually mention the dam by name, it clearly illustrates the situation along the river at present, and helps to show what might be lost, in terms of livelihoods, if the project proceeds.

In December 2002, the construction of infrastructure for the 40 MW Nam Mang 3 Hydropower station was announced. This dam, which is widely believed to be a bad deal for Laos, and is not expected to generate significant economic benefits for the country, is being constructed in Thoulakhom District, Vientiane Province, inside Phou Khao Khouay National Biodiversity Conservation Area. The project is estimated to cost US$ 63 million, and is a joint venture between the China International Water and Electric Company (CWE) of the People's Republic of China, which holds 80 per cent of the shares in the project, and Electricité du Laos, which holds the remaining 20 per cent. It has been reported that the dam will be completed by 2004. Most significant is that it is the first large hydropower dam project that China has become involved with in Laos. However, it has been reported by various sources that the Hmong people living inside or near the planned dam reservoir are very unsatisfied with the relocation and compensation plan associated with the project and, in November 2002, a number of Hmong villagers living in the planned reservoir area protested at the dam-site, carrying sticks and guns. They told the Chinese contractors to return to China. At the time of writing, the situation in the project area remains very tense.

Apart from being relocated as a result of large hydropower dams, indigenous peoples have also suffered serious relocation problems due to other types of water projects, such as the large Nam Tine Irrigation Project in Houay Xai District, Bokeo Province. As reported in *Khao San Pathet Lao*, the Labour and Social Welfare Service of Bokeo Province admitted that the resettled villagers had faced considerable "hardship from the resettlement", and provided the resettled ethnic minority peoples in four villages with a consignment of rice and clothes.[2]

Swidden agriculture under continuous attack

As in the previous year, 2002 saw the Lao government continue with its policy to eradicate swidden agriculture. The government policy states that it will stop all swidden agriculture by 2005. In May 2002, the Ministry of Agriculture and Forestry announced that "slash-and-burn" agriculture had declined by 28,000 ha compared to the previous year. The Agriculture Department reported that 73,000 ha are still utilized for swidden agriculture, mostly in the northern provinces. The southern and central provinces are said to have made the most progress in eradicating shifting agriculture. However, considering the pressure being put on local governments to follow the central plan to eliminate shifting cultivation, it seems likely that estimates regarding the amount of land that has been taken out of swidden agriculture production are exaggerated. In 1990, the total area under swidden agriculture was reportedly 245,800 ha.

There are indications, however, that the program cannot be fully implemented. Mr. Vannakon Phommahasit, Head of the Agriculture and Forestry Extension Unit in the Ministry of Agriculture and Forestry, also acknowledged at a workshop last year that, "The priority plan so far has not been completely successful due to many factors encouraging slash and burn cultivation, such as geographical location, traditions, socio-economic bases, and the technical and professional comprehension of people in the local and mountainous areas."[3]

Upland peoples have certainly suffered a great deal due to the government's swidden agriculture eradication program (see *The Indigenous World, 2001-2002*) but many donors, including the Asian Development Bank (ADB), are apparently oblivious to the past problems associated with eradicating shifting cultivation. For example, the ADB is continuing to fund a pilot project "for the termination of slash-and-burn cultivation in Sam Neua District, Houaphan province". The project covers 48 indigenous villages with a population of 12,600 people and includes 1,130 ha under swidden agriculture.[4] The United Nations Drug Control Programme is also supporting these efforts, since many of the project's target villages are also involved in opium production.

Despite the continuing efforts to eradicate shifting agriculture, there are at least some people in the Lao government who are beginning to question the wisdom and feasibility of their plans, and some are redefining government policy in order to make it fit with what is actually feasible. For example, the Deputy Governor of Savannakhet Province now classifies shifting cultivation areas into two categories:

pioneer swidden cultivation and rotational swidden agriculture. Others in the government have also begun doing the same. Conveniently, they say that the government policy is to eradicate pioneer swidden agriculture but that there may still be a place for rotational shifting cultivation in upland areas. In fact, most of the ethnic groups in Laos have long practiced various forms of rotational swidden cultivation, so this redefinition of government policy is potentially very good news for them. It however still remains unclear as to the practical impact that these subtle changes in policy will have over the coming years.

It has also been reported that the Lao government's controversial Land and Forest Allocation Program may already be undergoing a critical review by the government, at least partially due to recent reports that the program has actually contributed to increasing poverty as well as environmental and social degradation, especially in areas where swidden agriculture has long been the main component of local production systems.

Relocation programs

Efforts to eradicate shifting cultivation have, unfortunately, also been closely linked to forced - or at least strongly encouraged - relocation of indigenous peoples from mountainous and remote areas to the lowlands, along the roads, although the government claims that all resettlement in Laos is "voluntary".

Of particular concern, one of Laos' last hunter and gather groups was reported to have been resettled in Khamkeut District, Bolikhamxay Province, Central Laos in April 2002. The official Lao news service, *Khao San Pathet Lao*, reported that this group of "Tong Leuang" people,[5] who were described as being a small and unique ethnic group living deep in the forest and in mountainous areas along streams, was "resettled in their best interest". The KSPL also reported that the authorities of the province had urged the Tong Leuang to remove themselves from their traditional way of life. The people were promised better living conditions in areas where they could live along newly developed roads. 52 families in two villages were reportedly relocated.[6] There have been no reports regarding the impact on the livelihoods of the people but various studies conducted in recent years suggest that indigenous people resettled to the lowlands from mountainous areas often suffer serious health problems soon after being relocated, and that they often have a difficult time adjusting their livelihoods.

In *The Indigenous World 2001-2002*, it was reported that there were plans to relocate a large number of indigenous peoples from northern Laos to the southern province of Attapeu but that local authorities were not in favour of the plan. In 2002, most of the 20 or so ethnic Hmong families that had initially moved to Phou Vong District were asked by the ethnic Brao-dominated local government to return to the north. Despite initially resisting attempts to orchestrate their return, most of the Hmong had left Attapeu for the north by the end of 2002.

Push for industrial tree plantations

Apparently related to the swidden agriculture eradication program, and the rapid decline of natural forests due to heavy logging in recent years, which is often associated with large-scale exports of raw logs to neighbouring countries, the government of Laos has stepped up its interest in large industrial tree plantations. These plantations are generally monocultures dominated by non-indigenous trees species, particularly pine and eucalyptus. They are environmentally and so-cially destructive since they often replace diverse natural forests and displace indigenous peoples from their ancestral lands. Despite this, some aid agencies have fallen into the trap of supporting these initia-tives. Recently published research regarding industrial tree planta-tions in Laos does not support the assumption that such develop-ments are benefiting local people.[7]

Sepon gold and copper mine moves ahead

In 2002, the Australian company Oxiana Resources, and Lang Xang Mineral Company, moved forward with their joint-venture gold mine in Sepon District, Savannakhet Province, an area populated mainly by indigenous Brou people. In 2002, the associated and larger copper project was the subject of an intensive feasibility study but concerns remain regarding the potential for project-related social and environ-mental impacts. Concerns are especially strong regarding the fate of the ethnic Brou communities living within the concession area, as well as in relation to the potential negative impacts that will be caused by mine-related pollution of the Kok River. Despite these concerns, the project is being supported with a US$ 30 million debt-financing package pro-vided by the International Finance Company (IFC), the private finance division of the World Bank. Production is expected to begin in 2004.

Important Hmong leader visits Laos

Amid continuing reports of intermittent rebel conflicts in northern Laos, it is significant that in late 2002 the prominent Hmong community leader in the USA, Dr. Yangdao, visited Laos on invitation from the Lao Minister of Foreign Affairs. It was his first visit to Laos in 27 years. The invitation seemed to be linked to efforts by the Lao government to gain preferential trading status with the USA, which is often opposed by anti-Lao government groups based in the USA, many of which are run by Hmong people. In fact, Dr. Yangdao has long been associated with moderate Hmong elements and, according to the *Vientiane Times*, "Yangdao does not like Vang Pao's ideas".[8] Vang Pao is the Hmong leader in the USA who is most strongly associated with anti-government rebel activities in Laos, and is despised by the Lao government.[9]

New list of ethnic group names obtains further recognition

One positive development for Laos' indigenous peoples in 2002 was the increased recognition of a new list of names for ethnic groups in Laos. As reported in *The Indigenous World 2001-2002,* the Lao Politburo adopted the new list of names in late 2001. The list recognises 49 ethnic groups as being present in Laos, including at least 149 subgroups. As expected, in 2002 there was continued progress in the full adoption of this list. The Lao Front for National Construction officially announced the new list at its annual plenum on March 27, 2002 and, later in the year, the Government fully adopted the list. It is expected that it will be presented to the National Assembly for final approval in February or March 2003. It is widely accepted that the National Assembly will adopt the list, and that full acceptance will represent an important step forward in recognising ethnic diversity in Lao PDR. ❑

Notes and references

1   Shoemaker, B., I.G. Baird and M. Baird. 2001. *The People and Their River.* Lao PDR/Canada Fund for Local Initiatives.
2   *Khao San Pathet Lao.* February 15, 2002. "Aid for relocated villagers in Bokeo".

3   *Vientiane Times*. August 6-8, 2002. "Upland Agriculture: new alternative to slash and burn cultivation".
4   *Khao San Pathet Lao*. February 5, 2002. "Laos, ADB discuss swidden cultivation in Houaphan".
5   It is unclear what the actual name of the ethnic group is but it is certainly not Tong Leuang, which is a pejorative used by Lao people to describe all hunter-gatherers.
6   *Khao San Pathet Lao*. April 2, 2002. "Tong Leuang ethnic group moves to new settlements".
7   **Lang, C. 2002.** *The Pulp Invasion. The International Pulp and Paper Industry in the Mekong Region*. World Rainforest Movement, United Kingdom.
8   *Vientiane Times*. December 10-12, 2002. "Expat leader in Laos to see for himself".
9   See **Gary Yia Lee. 2000.** "Bandits or Rebels? Hmong Resistance in the New Lao State". Indigenous Affairs 4/2000. Copenhagen: IWGIA.

Other sources

International Rivers Network. 2003. "New Lao Dam Embroiled in Controversy. Report from a Fact-Finding Mission to the Nam Mang 3 Hydropower Project". March 2003, Berkeley, CA, USA, 16 pp.
Khao San Pathet Lao. 2002: February 20 and 25, May 22, and December 13.
Khao San Pathet Lao. 2003: January 1, and 2.
State Planning Committee. 2000. *Poverty in the Lao PDR: Participatory Poverty Assessment*
Vientiane Times. 2002: March 29-April 1, May 28-30, June 11-13, June 28-July 1, September 13-16, and December 20-23.

BURMA

T he non-Burman ethnic groups of Burma are estimated to make up 60% of Burma's total population. However, they have been ruled by successive Burman-dominated military regimes since 1962, despite the Panglong Agreement signed in 1947, which aimed to unite the ethnic nationalities to form the Union of Burma. It is the non-Burman ethnic groups, generally referred to as "ethnic nationalities", that are considered to be Burma's indigenous peoples.[1]

Building confidence?

During 2002, the ruling military regime, the State Peace and Development Council (SPDC), released several hundred political prisoners to deflect growing impatience from the UN and the international community with the delays in taking steps towards democratisation. On May 6, the regime's powerful and politically-connected US public relations firm, DCI, made their début for the regime, announcing the release of the popular National League for Democracy (NLD) leader Daw Aung San Suu Kyi following over 19 months of house arrest. The SPDC declared that a "new page" had been turned, that the confidence-building stage was over and substantial dialogue could begin, which renewed hope for progress on democratisation and national reconciliation. However, the "dialogue" was only to be between the SPDC and the NLD, as the SPDC would not agree to a tripartite dialogue with representatives from the ethnic nationalities of Burma.

Indicative of what was to come, on the same day Daw Aung San Suu Kyi was released, the SPDC destroyed villages in Karen State. In the latter part of 2002, the SPDC began open harassment of Daw Aung San Suu Kyi, the NLD and human rights defenders in ethnic nationality areas and re-accelerated their rate of arrests of ethnic nationality and pro-democracy defenders. To date, no "substantial dialogue" has begun, and is unlikely to, as the SPDC is calling for people to rise up against these "destructive elements" and promising never to bow to international pressure.

Growing alliances

While the SPDC continues to pursue a path of divide and conquer, ethnic nationality groups are forging greater alliances and understanding among themselves as well as with the nationwide democracy movement. In July, the United Nationalities Alliance (UNA) was formed by 7 ethnic nationality groups as a "temporary measure", to represent ethnic nationalities should there be a tripartite dialogue in the future. The SPDC has refused to acknowledge the UNA as a legal organization. The National Democratic Front (NDF), comprising 11 ethnic nationality groups, has also reiterated its call for tripartite dialogue and a genuine nationwide cease-fire. Most ethnic nationalities have stated their desire to be a part of a legitimate form of federalism and continue to develop their constitutions.

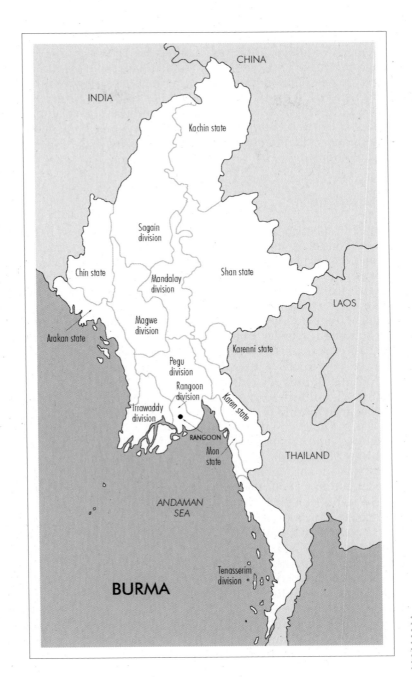

CHINA

INDIA

Kachin state

Sagain
division

Chin state

Mandalay
division

Shan state

LAOS

Magwe
division

Arakan state

Karenni state

Pegu
division

Rangoon
division

Irrawaddy
division

Karen state

RANGOON

Mon
state

THAILAND

ANDAMAN
SEA

Tenasserim
division

BURMA

There has been intentional effort focused on uniting the opposition movement, of which ethnic nationalities are an integral part. Daw Aung San Suu Kyi and some NLD members have travelled around the country to re-vitalize the party as well as increase dialogue with other ethnic nationality political parties, and this has been generally well received. The Committee Representing People's Parliament, formed in 1998, has begun accepting applications for new members. Those eligible are individuals and parties that were elected in the 1990 democratic elections.

Militarisation

The SPDC subscribes to the belief that a strong military and tight military control is the way to create "stability" and "unification" throughout Burma. There have been 17 cease-fire negotiations but more than 10 armed groups remain. Using the pretext of "fighting terrorism in the post-September 11 world", the SPDC has increased its military action against these groups. It has secured its second arms shipment from India and received several shipments of arms, missiles and armoured vehicles from China. The military forces in ethnic nationality areas aim to end ethnic armed opposition, gain control of resources and to create a more homogenous culture that is in line with SPDC "approved" cultural traditions.

Burma's military force is the second largest in the region and actively growing and developing more capabilities. The SPDC military has the ability to deal with internal uprisings and ethnic "insurgencies" and can more effectively fight on multiple fronts at the same time.[2] In 2002, the SPDC expanded, upgraded and created new military bases throughout ethnic nationality regions. This raises concern not only about their planned military offences but also the human rights violations that are implicit in SPDC occupation. For example, in Mon State, where cease-fires have been signed, the SPDC has confiscated more than 2,000 acres of land to build heavy artillery bases.

Another growing concern are the SPDC's border security forces, NaSaKa, which are concentrated in Arakan State, where the majority of Rohingya and Rakhine people live. NaSaKa forces are notorious for using forced labour and extortion to construct their compounds. Their powers extend beyond "security" as they have become thoroughly intertwined in Rohingya and Rakhine communities. They have to approve any NGOs working in Arakan State, have consistently harassed UNHCR officials, placed humiliating restrictions on marriage and are reportedly raping women with impunity.

The widespread use of landmines continues to terrorize and maim civilians. Since 2001, the SPDC has had a plan to "fence the country" with landmines. NaSaKa forces and 13 ethnic nationality and armed groups also use landmines to protect their business interests, and narcotics production, from military intrusion.[3]

Economic domination

Ethnic nationality areas are being suffocated by the SPDC, not only by military infiltration but also by economic dominance. In Arakan State, NaSaKa forces have been "successful" in achieving a monopoly over nearly all trade and commerce. In Shan and Arakan States, resettlement of ethnic Burmans in SPDC "urbanization projects" is furthering the economic domination and dependency of the indigenous people in those states.

Food security has reached near crisis levels in many areas, yet the NaSaKa and SPDC banned the trading of certain staple foods in several ethnic nationality states in order to manipulate trade and provide more food for the city centres. The food crisis was created by the regime closing the border with Thailand for five months and forcibly increasing rice exports to a rate that makes it impossible for farmers to retain enough for domestic consumption. Furthermore, farmers are forced to sell rice to the regime at prices that leave them with no profit and land is being confiscated without compensation in order to cultivate more rice.

Many ethnic nationality states have been identified as 'prime sources' of precious gem mining and regional tourism. The SPDC is offering 42 blocks to foreign companies for gem exploration, mainly in ethnic nationality areas. The regime is also working with Thailand's Prime Minister Thaksin on tourism development in Kachin State. A proposed project for a gas pipeline from Arakan State to India and Bangladesh is being orchestrated by regime forces, and many people from Arakan State fear that forced labour will be used on the pipeline.

Forced labour

Resolution 2002/67 of the United Nations Commission on Human Rights called for the end of "institutionalized human rights abuses" and "military offensives against the ethnic minorities," including the wide-scale use of forced labour. Despite the SPDC's minimal cooperation with the International Labour Organization and the appointment in October 2002 of an ILO Liaison Officer to Burma, forced labour continues unabated in ethnic nationality areas, particularly in highly militarised areas. EarthRights International showed that forced labour continues to be linked with beatings, torture, stabbings, rape and extra-judicial, summary and arbitrary executions. The SPDC has officially created Order No. 1/99 outlawing the use of forced labour but has done little to implement the order, such as creating local reporting centres, protection for victims or information in local languages on ways victims of forced labour can seek justice.

It is hoped that the appointment of an ILO Liaison Officer to Burma will improve the situation.

Abuse of women

On June 19, the Shan Human Rights Foundation (SHRF) and Shan Women's Action Network (SWAN) released a detailed and gruesome report entitled *License to Rape*. The report "gives clear evidence that rape is officially condoned as a weapon of war" against the civilian population in Shan State. The report involves 625 cases of sexual violence between 1996 and 2001, committed by soldiers, 83% by officers.[4]

The SPDC launched two sham 'investigations' into the rape allegations, which were carried out with threats and intimidation. It forced people to sign documents denying the existence of rape by SPDC soldiers. Since the release of the report, the systematic rape of women in other ethnic nationality communities is continuously being reported. The SWAN spokesperson said it was impossible to address the causes of the systematic rape without democratic reforms and called on the international community to withhold all forms of aid to the regime until irreversible changes are made towards democratic reform in Burma.

Burma was again classified by the annual *Trafficking in Persons 2002 Report* published by the US State Department as not complying with the US Anti-Trafficking of Persons Act (2000) and denounced for not making significant efforts to comply with previous recommendations. While many people are victims of trafficking, women from ethnic nationality communities are particularly vulnerable, either unknowingly being sold or being sold by their parents due to the extreme economic conditions being perpetuated by the military regime.

Displacement

Millions of people from Burma are refugees or migrants in neighbouring countries or internally displaced within Burma. A large percentage of these people are from ethnic nationality communities and are fleeing desperate economic conditions, grave human rights violations such as forced labour, forced eviction or rape, and military invasions or clashes with ethnic resistance groups. To illustrate the magnitude, the Free Burma Rangers estimated that, in Karen State, between January and July 2002, more than 470 villages were burned down or forcibly relocated by SPDC forces.

More than two million people from Burma are estimated to live in Thailand. When the SPDC slammed the border shut between May and October, many Thai officials expressed the opinion that Thailand's tolerance of ethnic resistance forces and human rights organizations operating out of the country were the reason why relations between the SPDC and the Thai Government were hitting an all-time low. To assist in reconciliation with the SPDC, Thailand issued new restrictions to hinder activities of pro-democracy organizations working in Thailand, primarily by using immigration laws to deport or repatriate people to Burma.[5] In early August, the Thai Defence Minister ordered the leaders of Burmese and ethnic nationality groups to be monitored and arrested if found in Thailand without legal documentation.[6] Thai officials have since been raiding offices and arresting and deporting people from ethnic nationality and human rights organizations, as well as undocumented migrant workers, even after the border was reopened.

The Bangladeshi government has continued to press the SPDC to accept the repatriation of nearly 20,000 asylum seekers, mostly Rohingya, but the SPDC has refused, at times claiming that the Rohingyas are not citizens of Burma. The asylum seekers have held numerous protests and hunger strikes to demand UNHCR status, even threatening "to fast until death". Malaysia has taken the strongest stance, with a "zero-tolerance" policy on undocumented migrants. While persecution of ethnic nationalities in Burma continues to escalate, their options for asylum are rapidly dwindling. The SPDC is working to prevent the exodus of people from Burma by tightening border policies with neighbouring countries as well as by threatening severe punishments to citizens caught leaving Burma.

Religion

For the third year in a row, Burma was labelled "a country of particular concern" by the US State Department's annual *International Religious Freedom Act Report*, which highlighted Burma's practice of forced conversion of Christians and Muslims to Buddhism. Non-Buddhists must apply for permission to hold religious events, which are often cancelled without justification. Restrictions are placed on religious publications, building new churches, and the SPDC has banned the building or repairing of mosques. It has been reported that anti-Muslim literature is being openly sold in central Burma and Muslim shops are being boycotted.

After the SPDC signed the US-ASEAN Joint Declaration for Cooperation to Combat International Terrorism, the SPDC announced that Muslim-based terrorist organizations were operating on its border with Bangladesh.[7] By classifying all the Rohingya as terrorists, the regime is attempting to legitimise offences committed by the SPDC against them. ❑

Notes

1   "Burman" refers to the dominant ethnic group while "Burmese" refers to all the citizens of Burma.
2   **International Crisis Group.** 27 Sept. 2002. "Myanmar: The Future of the Armed Forces".
3   **International Campaign to Ban Landmines. 2002.** "Landmine Monitor Report".
4   The full report can be found at:
    www.shanland.org/shrf/License_to_Rape/ license_to_rape.htm
5   *Forum Asia*, 10 Sept. 2002. "Border Update: Fears of Crack Down on Pro-Democracy and Human Rights Groups Still Prevail."
6   *ibid.*
7   *Myanmar Times* 26 Aug. - 1 Sept. 2002. "Myanmar to Investigate 'Terror Tape' Allegation."

NAGALIM[1]

Naga leaders make an historic trip to India

For the first time in 37 years, Naga leaders Isak Chishi Swu and Thuingaleng Muivah, Chairman and Secretary-General of the National Socialist Council of Nagalim (NSCN-Isak Muivah faction) formally set foot on Indian soil on January 9, 2003. Thousands of Nagas, who had come to Delhi in anticipation of their visit, and Naga students in Delhi received them at the Indira Gandhi International Airport with a traditional welcome dance and waving of the national Naga flag. Their visit, the first in more than fifty years by the top Naga leadership, came at the invitation of the Prime Minister of India, Mr. Atal Bihari Vajpayee. It was loudly hailed in the Indian media.

The primary aim of the visit was to strengthen the confidence building process. Apart from the meetings with the Prime Minister and members of his Council of Ministers, and the meetings with the Indian Opposition leaders and MPs, they were also able to meet with civil society organizations. In a unique gesture of goodwill, the former Prime Ministers of India V.P. Singh, Chandra Shekhar and Dev Gowda hosted an "All Party" dinner in honour of the Naga leaders. All these were reported in the media with enthusiasm.

The extensive media coverage of their arrival and departure, the numerous meetings, interviews and media speculations on the future of the Nagas, it appears, made visible impact on the general public in terms of their perception of who the Nagas are. It seems like the general public in India has been encouraged by the visit to take a fresh look at the Nagas instead of clinging on to the old perception that holds the Nagas as some kind of savages.

The visit was preceded by an important development in the official negotiation table. In July 2002, the Indian and Naga peace teams took up the Preamble of the Naga proposal, an outline of the history of the Nagas as a distinct people. After several days of consultation with Delhi, the Indian team consented to the Preamble. The Joint Communiqué of the teams issued on 11 July 2002 stated that India recognized the uniqueness of the Naga issue. The agreement on the Preamble of the proposal was considered fundamental to the future negotiations as the preambular section sets out the historical context of the issues to be resolved.

Six years of cease-fire

The government of India has taken some difficult decisions, including lifting the ban on the NSCN-IM and withdrawing all the criminal cases registered against its top leaders, including Thuingaleng Muivah and the Chief of Staff of the Naga Army, Major General Hanshi Ramson. The lifting of the ban is not just about free movement for NSCN-IM members. More importantly it means the NSCN-IM can no longer be easily branded as a "terrorist" organisation. The almost six-year-long cease-fire has also been extended for one year.

India and the NSCN faction under the leadership of Khaplang (NSCN-K) have also announced a one-year extension to the cease-fire between them, as well as to their decision to fight against "terrorism" in Nagaland. Although no political talks have been held, or proposed, both sides were so far satisfied with the cease-fire.

One most significant development is that NSCN-K has issued a statement condemning the 16-point agreement of 1960 signed between the government of India and the Naga People Convention (NPC), and has said that the agreement, "brought seeds of hatred and division among the Nagas".[2] This refers to the Memorandum of Understanding between NPC and the Indian government. The State of Nagaland was created in 1963 on the basis of this Memorandum, which has brought about deep divisions and ultimately fratricide among the Nagas. Mr. S.C. Jamir, the deposed Chief Minister of Nagaland State and a known ally of NSCN-K, has often claimed credit for drawing up the Memorandum. However, it is not clear whether the statement of condemnation issued by NSCN-K is a sign of strain in relations between Jamir and the NSCN-K following Jamir's departure from power. In any case, the statement is a major shift in the position of the organisation which, since their split, has been a major adversary of the NSCN-IM.

Most units of the Indian Army in Naga areas are observing the spirit of the cease-fire. NSCN-IM leaders and their army commanders are able to move around openly in almost all parts of their ancestral homeland. Many senior leaders of NSCN-IM, including its Army Chief, openly participated in a five-day public meeting at Khambi, Ukhrul, Manipur. Many Manipuris made demands that the meeting should be banned and NSCN members "captured", but the Indian Army seems to have prevailed over the Manipur State Police.

There has been an improvement in the overall situation. However, the army has not been fully withdrawn from operating in civilian areas. And they have not given up their taste for action. Harassment

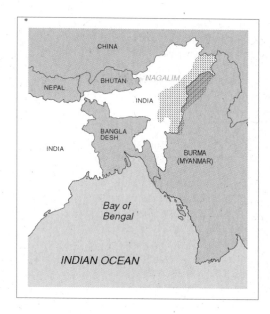

of civilians at check points is still prevalent and they have often singled out civil society activists for humiliation whenever they have the opportunity to carry out "security" checks.

Furthermore, the peace talks between the government of India and the NSCN-IM are being watched with apprehension by the state governments of Assam, Arunachal Pradesh and Manipur, which have sizeable Naga populations. They vehemently oppose the recognition of Nagalim as this would imply a loss of state territory. Likewise, some ethnic groups in these states see the recognition of Nagalim as a threat to their own integrity and identity, and, consequently, present territorial counterclaims (see section on the Northeast in the chapter on India).

Nagaland State freed from Special Powers Act

The new State government formed by the Democratic Alliance of Nagaland has decided not to renew the Disturbed Areas Notification. This Notification is a formality the civilian administration has to declare before activating the Armed Forces Special Powers Act, which gives the armed forces a virtually free hand for arbitrary action against anyone arousing their suspicion. Nagaland State stands to benefit greatly from this bold and rightful decision. The new State government has also formed a Consultative Peace Committee composed of elected members and leading members of the civil society organizations to facilitate the peace process. The Committee, however, faces enormous challenges as it has to deal with deep political and tribal divisions among the Naga people, and the wounds created by inter-factional fighting among them are not yet healed. But with some of the basic preconditions now in place, there is more reason for hope than during the past decades. Much of this hope rests on the Naga civil society organisations and the Naga *Hoho*, the supreme all-tribal council of the Nagas, which have committed themselves to an encompassing reconciliation initiative.

Illegal immigration

The rising population of illegal immigrants in the Indian part of Nagalim is becoming a threat to the reconstruction and survival of Naga society. They come from the South Asian subcontinent, about 230,000 from India, 220,000 from Bangladesh and 50,000 from Nepal. For Nagalim, with less than three million people, even under normal conditions it would require great social strength to take in half a million immigrants in less than twenty-five years.[3] Interestingly, the Bharatiya Janata Yuva Morcha (BJYM), the youth branch of the ruling Party in India, has stated that "the main causes of the influx of illegal migrants are cheap labour, a lack of proper co-ordination in issuing and monitoring Inner Line Permits (ILP) and a lack of suitable administrative infrastructure to handle the issue specifically".[4] Although the immigrants stand out from the local population because of their stark difference in physical appearance, there is no official record of their presence in Nagalim.

Imposing state religion

In Eastern Nagalim, across the Indian-Burmese border, the military regime in Rangoon has been intensifying its Burmanisation program. Recently, many Nagas were killed at Loikha village. In the nearby Layshi village, a teenage girl was raped by a military-sponsored Buddhist monk. Mr. L. Longsa, Secretary of the Naga League for Democracy, informed the press that the military regime in Burma had been sending its army into the Eastern Naga Hills for several years, trying to forcibly convert Nagas, who are mostly Christian, to Buddhism. Punishment for non-compliance is reportedly forced labour.❏

Notes and sources

1   Nagalim means "Naga ancestral land" and encompasses all Naga inhabited areas, both in India and Burma. It replaces the term 'Nagaland'

which has formerly been used and which is also the name the Indian government gave to the Union State it created in a limited part of Nagalim in 1963.

2 *NET News Network*, 17 May 2003.
3 Illegal immigration has been taking place ever since the military occupation of Nagalim in 1960. It was, however, limited in numbers. Large-scale immigration commenced in 1981, beginning with people fleeing the mass ethnic cleansing killings in Assam in the wake of the Assam student movement.
4 *NET News Network*, 19 May 2003.

NET News Network. Dimapur. 29 November 2002, 6 April 2003, 28 April 2003, 30 April 2003, and 7 May 2003.

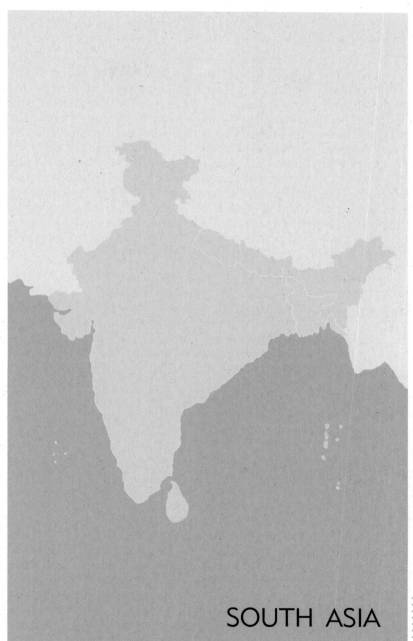

SOUTH ASIA

BANGLADESH

The situation of indigenous peoples in Bangladesh has not improved over the past year. The Bengali Muslim majority continues to encroach on their land forcibly, supported both directly and indirectly by the government. The Chittagong Hill Tracts region in the southeastern tip of Bangladesh, home to the indigenous Jumma peoples, continues to be an area beset with tension and violence. The 1997 Peace Accord,[1] whereby the indigenous armed movement led by the Parbattya Chattagram Jana Samhati Samiti (PCJSS- United Peoples Party of the Chittagong Hill Tracts) and the Bangladesh Government ceased hostilities and agreed a framework for indigenous autonomy, remains largely unimplemented. Five years on, much remains unchanged with self-determination an elusive challenge. This chapter presents some of the most important developments in the Chittagong Hill Tracts (CHT) as well as the Northern hills, home to the Khasi and the Garo peoples.

The Chittagong Hill Tracts

Political developments

An implementation committee was established to oversee progress on the Accord but, five years on, the committee no longer exists and the Accord remains largely unimplemented. Mr. Larma, Chairperson of the PCJSS and member of the now defunct committee, has been openly critical of the lack of progress in implementing the Accord, and has even gone as far as to question the sincerity of the government in this regard. Most of the provisions, such as the formation of the Land Commission for settling land disputes, rehabilitation of returnee Jumma refugees and internally Jumma displaced families, withdrawal of temporary camps of security forces and military administration, preparing a voter list of the permanent residents of CHT only, effective enforcement of the three Hill District Councils and CHT Regional Council Act, rehabilitation of the Bengali settlers outside CHT etc. have either been left unimplemented or only partially implemented.[2]

Dates have been set by the High Court Division of the Bangladesh Supreme Court to hear petitions that challenge the legality of the Hill District Council's laws of 1989.[3] In these petitions, it is alleged that the provision of the Local Government Council Act of 1989 requiring

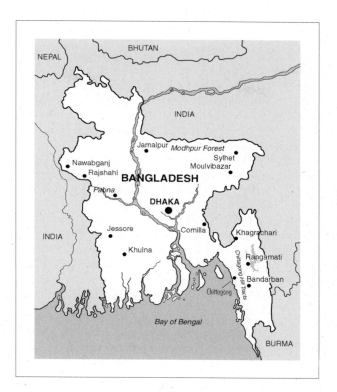

the mandatory consent of the district councils prior to allotment and transfer of lands in the concerned district (section 64), and the provisions that the chairpersons of the regional council and the three district councils are to be held by indigenous persons, discriminate against the Bengali inhabitants of the CHT and are therefore contrary to the equal rights clauses of the Bangladesh Constitution.

The situation is tense now and it is uncertain what the outcome of these cases will be, or the repercussions on the Peace Accord and the CHT as a whole. The situation is aggravated even further by the continuing conflict between the PCJSS and the UPDF (United Peoples Democratic Front), which was formed by a group of dissident students in 1998. The UPDF argues that the Peace Accord does not meet the indigenous people's demands for self-determination. The conflict continues, despite attempts by indigenous leaders to get the two parties to resolve their differences and work together to protect and strengthen the rights of the indigenous Jummas.

Land rights issues

The main question in the CHT is that of land rights. Traditionally an indigenous region, with an indigenous system of land ownership and natural resource management, colonization and development projects have taken their toll on the land rights of the indigenous peoples. The current situation is as follows:

Settlement programme

Migration to the CHT, historically an area closed to outsiders, intensified soon after Bangladesh gained independence. A government-sponsored settlement programme aimed at diluting the indigenous composition of the CHT and integrating the indigenous peoples into the majority Bengali population was implemented from 1979 onwards. Gradually, indigenous people have been forced to relocate to hilltops with little or no means of making a living. It is feared that unless steps are taken to protect the indigenous identity of the CHT, it will become like any other district in Bangladesh, with the indigenous peoples as a minority in their own homeland. The current population ratio of indigenous people to settlers is 51:49 - a far cry from 1947 when the indigenous peoples made up 98.02% of the Hill Tracts population.

There are reports of continuing migration of plains settlers to the CHT, and of forcible take-overs of land from indigenous peoples. One such case is that of the settlers from Barunachari and nearby areas in Subholong, who are forcibly grabbing land from Jummas in Billachari village of Barkal sub-district and constructing houses on these lands. It is reported that both Mr. Larma, Chairperson of the Regional Council and Mr. MS Dewan, Deputy CHT Minister ordered the local officials concerned to return the land to the indigenous peoples, but this has not been implemented. In addition, settlers are being included on the CHT voter lists although they are not 'permanent residents' in the CHT, another attempt to ensure their presence in the CHT on a long-term basis.

The question of the settlers remains in abeyance, and constitutes one of the main obstacles to resolving the CHT issue. With reference to the crucial nature of finding a solution to this question, the European Union has offered its financial assistance in rehabilitating and resettling the settler families to areas outside the CHT,[4] although the Government has not yet accepted this timely and necessary support.

Forest policy

In earlier times, the CHT hills and mountains were forest covered but today little remains.This is the effect of deforestation and logging, although successive governments have carried out a policy of creating "government forests" – for the purposes of "afforestation and environmental protection." This policy has served to limit and/or restrict the access of indigenous peoples to the forests and their resources, a right they have exercised according to traditional methods of use and management of the forests and their produce.

The government has different categories of forests, with increasing levels of restrictions applied: Reserved Forests (approximately 1,977.43 sq. kms.) - strictly off limits and any incursions a criminal offence; Protected Forests (87.21 sq. kms.) - some use allowed; and the residual Unclassified State Forests (6,215.90 sq. kms.).[5] Begun in the 1920s, this forest policy continues to be implemented to this day, with serious socio-economic consequences for the indigenous peoples who are steadily being deprived of their ancestral lands and are criminalized for accessing and using the forests and their produce once they are designated as government-owned. The Ministry of Environment and Forests has initiated a process expanding the existing reserved forests through a series of gazette notifications (1992, 1996 and 1998). The Committee for the Protection of Forests and Land Rights in the CHT, created to mobilise support to prevent the affected indigenous peoples (approximately 200,000) from being evicted off these lands, is against these orders. It believes they will convert forests and grazing commons, homesteads and agricultural lands into industry-oriented plantations with the effect of destroying the biological and cultural diversity of the region. The indigenous peoples will receive no benefits whatsoever. The proposed areas amount to 7,411,286.30 acres (Bandarban: 7,280,917.17 acres; Khagrachari: 41,907.50 acres; and Rangamati: 88,461.63 acres).[6] These notifications remain in force despite repeated demands by the Forest Committee for their repeal.

Conflicts between the forest department, which is responsible for managing and administering the government forests, and the local people, are numerous. There are reports of wide-scale harassment and criminal actions against innocent villagers by forest officials. Of special concern is the practice of charging local people with the theft of forest produce on a large scale. A local NGO has claimed that the vast majority of these cases are baseless, and point to examples of cases against blind and severely disabled and even dead people![7] The situation continues, and the Forest (Amendment) Act of 2000 perpetuates the forest policy of exclusion and control as conceptualised by the British in the CHT with little recognition of the lands rights within reserved forests.[8]

The Asian Development Bank is the major partner of the Bangladesh Government in the forestry sector. Recent projects have included a component for "social forestry", which has been criticized as being neither "social" nor "forestry" as all decision-making power remains with the forest department, and civil society has little or no scope for participation in the management of the forests. There have been demands for the draft rules on social forestry to be revised to include a more participatory approach.

Internally displaced persons and refugees
There are a large number of internally displaced persons in the CHT (approximately 60,000)[9] many of whom have been displaced twice – (i) by the Kaptai dam and (ii) due to the civil war when many of them were placed in government created cluster villages. There are also approximately 55,000 refugees who fled to neighbouring countries, mainly India, and have recently returned under rehabilitation agreements concluded with the government in 1992 and 1997. A Task Force was created to oversee the repatriation-rehabilitation of the internally displaced and the refugees, and a new problem emerged when the then chairperson of the task force, Mr. D Talukdar, included 38,156 settler families as 'internally displaced' despite strong objections from other members of the task force and indigenous leaders.[10] This matter also continues in abeyance and a new chairperson of the task force has not yet been appointed.

Land allocations
The Hill District Councils have primary responsibility for land and resource rights administration as per the Hill District Council Acts and the Peace Accord. However, in actual practice, it is the civil servants and bureaucrats who exercise this authority as land has not been transferred to the Hill District Councils. There are reports of the deputy commissioners in the three districts transferring land to non-indigenous peoples. After receiving repeated complaints from various sources, the Ministry of CHT Affairs instructed the deputy commissioners to act in accordance with Section 64 of the Hill District Council Acts of 1989 i.e. to transfer land only with the consent of the Hill District Councils.

Continued military presence

The armed forces are the chief tools of the government's policy of assimilation and control of the Hill Tracts and its indigenous peoples. In 1972, soon after Bangladesh gained independence from Pakistan, the armed forces took charge of the Hill Tracts (Operation Uttaran), and this has been the status quo since. Since its arrival in the Hill Tracts, the military has taken an active role in all matters relating to the CHT, including civil administration and development.

There are explicit provisions in the Accord for the phased withdrawal of all temporary camps of military personnel, Ansar and Village Defence Party,[11] with the exception of the border security forces (BDR) and six permanent cantonments (one each at the district headquarters of Bandarban, Khagrachari and Rangamati, and at Alikadam, Dighinala and Ruma). This was to have commenced on the signing of the Accord but, five years on, the military remains in the CHT and there are no indications of their withdrawal. On the contrary, the armed forces have taken out leases in the Hill Tracts, including 30,000 acres in Bandarban district for an artillery training camp, which will displace 25,000 indigenous peoples. Of 500 camps in the CHT, some 35 camps have been dismantled so far. Despite repeated demands from the indigenous peoples for the armed forces to withdraw from the CHT, there have been no credible signs that the military authorities plan to do so in the near future.

A result of this is human rights violations against the indigenous peoples, with the armed forces being the chief perpetrators, often in collaboration with the settlers. There are numerous reports of the army attacking, torturing, assaulting and arresting indigenous peoples, including in Baghmara Union, Roangchari Thana (30 September 2002), Baghichara Para (24 September 2002), Amtoli (9 September 2002) and Sao Para (7 September 2002), among others.[12] The military also continues to be engaged in activities outside their sphere of operations, including road maintenance, general administration, law and order, and admission of indigenous students to higher educational institutions.

Development programmes resumed ·

Following the abduction and holding to ransom of three aid workers in February 2001, international development activities in the CHT ground to a halt. In June 2002, a joint government-UNDP (United Nations Development Programme) risk assessment team visited the

Hill Tracts. The team classified the 27 *upazilas* (sub-districts) in the CHT in three categories according to their risk potential: (i) low risk – 22 upazilas; (ii) medium risk – four upazilas; and (iii) high risk – one upazila, namely Mahalchari in Rangamati district, and recommended a resumption of development aid for most areas of the CHT with the exception of the high risk area, and with security precautions for the medium risk areas. The team stressed that the situation was dynamic and would need to be monitored on a regular basis. Priority areas were environmental management, poverty alleviation and job creation for local communities - UNDP has assigned a total of US$ 4.3 million for a sustainable environment management programme and US$ 3.5 million for poverty alleviation. Initial steps have been taken to commence operations in the CHT.

The Asian Development Bank, World Bank and other major donors are also implementing projects in the CHT, as are some international non-governmental organizations such as CARE. However, taking advantage of the renewed interest in the Hill Tracts, and the flow of funds to the region, a number of national NGOs are also active in the CHT. They are engaged in implementing projects in different areas of the CHT many if not most of which are settler-oriented. Of the few that are targeted at the indigenous peoples, they take little or no account of the special characteristics of the indigenous peoples and apply the same approach as in other areas of Bangladesh, with deleterious effects on indigenous people's society and culture. One result is an increasing reliance on micro-credit, an issue alien to the indigenous peoples, with an emphasis on a cash economy. Also active in the CHT are international Islamist organizations including the Bangladesh Islamic Foundation and the Al Rabeta organization, which are engaged in strengthening the presence of the settlers in the Hill Tracts, and in building more Islamic schools and mosques. There are also reports of forced conversions.

The Japanese Government is another major aid contributor to Bangladesh. There are plans to use some of these funds to build a new turbine at the Kaptai hydroelectric project. This would increase the water level of the Kaptai Lake and flood low-lying areas used by the indigenous peoples to harvest rice crops (known as fringelands). Representatives of the indigenous peoples met with the State Minister for Power to protest against this proposed project and were assured that the government would not install the turbine at the cost of the fringelands. An inquiry team was to be established to look into the matter. There has been no further information on the inquiry team or any report, and the matter remains pending.[13]

Indigenous peoples have taken an active lead in efforts to maintain and strengthen their culture, identity and rights in the CHT. There are a large number of indigenous organizations, including the umbrella organization, Hill Tracts NGO Forum, but their activities are closely monitored and they lack the necessary funds to work effectively. This is due to the refusal of the NGO Bureau to give indigenous organizations the necessary certification to receive foreign funding. This certification can be obtained only if state security and intelligence agencies, including the National Security Intelligence (NSI) and the Directorate General of Forces Intelligence (DGFI), recommend that the NGO Bureau does so. Many indigenous organisations have been refused certification, while national NGOs such as the Bangladesh Rural Advancement Committee (BRAC), Proshika and the Islamist organizations operate freely in the CHT. The CHT is the only area where NGOs are required to obtain clearance from the DG FI. Many perceive this as yet another example of military interference and control. Moreover, the NGO Affairs guidelines contain various provisions that clearly discriminate against organizations run by indigenous peoples and those seeking to protect the cultural heritage of indigenous people. The Hill Tracts NGO Forum has continued to protest at these discriminatory practices of state agencies.

The Peace Accord lays down the basics for a move towards peace and development in the Hill Tracts. It is a step forward but only when it is fully implemented, in letter and in spirit, with the indigenous peoples in full control of their destiny, can there be meaningful peace in the CHT.

Indigenous peoples of Garo and Khasi Hills

The *Garos of Modhpur Forest* have long been facing endless violations of human rights and harassment. They have lost their homeland in the name of "reserve forest", "national park", "training ground for the Air Force", "social afforestation" and finally in the name of "ecotourism". The Forest Department has filed thousands of false cases against indigenous peoples of the forest and continues to do so. Besides this, thousands of Bengali Muslim settlers have occupied the forestland with the direct and indirect help of the Government. Many Garos have left their motherland and migrated to India.

The murder of the young Garo women's leader Gidita Rema (see *The Indigenous World 2001-2002*) by Muslim settlers in 2001 was followed by mass protests by indigenous peoples. This forced the police to arrest the killers but the Garos did not get justice.

In early 2002 a young Garo, Sentu Nokrek, was abducted and killed in the Modhpur forest by a group of Bengali Muslims. The killers have never been arrested. Indigenous people organized a big protest rally and a strike in the area but the killers are threatening them to force them to withdraw the case.

In the *Khasi Hills*, Moulvibazar area, 1,000 Garo and Khasi families are currently facing eviction due to the Government's plan to develop an Eco-park in their ancestral homelands. Bangladesh Indigenous Peoples Forum, a national forum representing 45 indigenous peoples, has started a democratic movement against the eco-park project. The present government had declared it would cancel the eco-park project in the first parliament session in November 2001 but this did not happen.

On 26 July 2002, a gang of Bengalis attacked the Fultola Khasi villages with help from the forest department. Forest guards shot one person dead. The assailants raped women and destroyed the village. They looted and later burned the houses. A murder case was filed but the police did not arrest the killers although they are living in the area. The criminals are supporters of the present government.

On 14 July 2002, a group of Muslim assailants attacked the Balarma Khasi villages at Kulaura in the Moulvibazar district. They wanted to evict more than 40 Khasi families from their land. The Khasis protected themselves with bow and arrows, and the assailants did not succeed with their plans. The Khasi headman went to the police station to file a case against the criminals but the police did not co-operate.

At present, some Bengali settlers use a new strategy when they want to grab the land of indigenous peoples. First they show a false land ownership document and order the indigenous peoples to leave. If the latter do not agree, the Bengali forcibly build a mosque on their land. Afterwards it will be difficult, if not impossible, to get rid of this mosque and, after a while, the indigenous people will be forced to leave their lands.

Notes and references

1   See *The Indigenous World 1997-98, 1998-99* and *1999-2000* for more de-
    tails on the Peace Accord.
2   *"The CHT Issue and its Solution"* by **Jyotirindra Bodhipriya Larma**,

Chairperson of the CHT Regional Council, President of the PCJSS and Member of the CHT Accord Implementation Committee. Paper presented at the "Regional Training Program to Enhance the Conflict Prevention and Peace-Building Capacities of Indigenous Peoples' Representatives of the Asia-Pacific", Chiang Mai, Thailand from 7-12 April 2003, organized by the UN Institute for Training and Research (UNITAR).

3   Acts No. XIX, XX and XXI of 1989, and the Regional Council Act of 1998. One of these is Writ Petition No. 2669 of 2000 – Mohammed Badiuzzaman vs. the Govt. of Bangladesh and others.

4   European Parliament Resolution on Bangladesh, adopted on 17 January 2001.

5   Figures adapted from **W.E. Webb & R. Roberts. 1976**: "Reconnaissance Mission to the Chittagong Hill Tracts, Bangladesh: Report on Forestry Sector", Vol.2, Asian Development Bank, Manila, 1976 and quoted in **Raja Devasish Roy. 2002.** *Background Study on the Chittagong Hill Tracts Land Situation*. Dhaka: CARE-Bangladesh.

6   **Committee for the Protection of Forests and Land Rights, CHT. 2002.** *Mobilise Support to Stop the Eviction of Indigenous Peoples from Ancestral Lands in the Chittagong Hill Tracts, Bangladesh in the name of Afforestation and Protection of the Environment*. Dhaka.

7   **Raja Devasish Roy and Philip Gain. 1999.** "Indigenous Peoples and Forests in Bangladesh." In *Forests and Indigenous Peoples of Asia*. Minority Rights Group International. Report No. 98/4. London.

8   **Raja Devasish Roy and Sadeka Halim. 2001.** "A Critique to the Forest (Amendment) Act of 2000 and the (draft) Social Forestry Rules of 2000." Philip Gain (ed.), *The Forest (Amendment) Act, 2000 and the (draft) Social Forestry Rules, 2000: A Critique*. Dhaka: SEHD.

9   **Amnesty International. 2001.** *Bangladesh – Human Rights in the Chittagong Hill Tracts*. London, UK.

10 This brought the total number of internally displaced in the Hill Tracts to 128,000 (New Country Profile on Internal Displacement in Bangladesh, June 2001.)

11 These are vigilante teams formed in the settler villages, and provided with arms by the military.

12 **PCJSS Information and Publicity Department. October 2002.** *Increasing military atrocities on the Jumma People*. Report.

13 For more details see **Raja Devasish Roy. 2002.** *op.cit.*

NEPAL

On January 29 2003, Maoist insurgents and the government declared a cease-fire and announced that they were ready for peace talks. After 7 years of armed conflict, peace talks are now underway.

The peoples' war was originally declared in early February 1996 when an overground and registered organization of the Nepal Communist Party (Maoist), the United Peoples' Front, presented a 40-point programme of demands to the Prime Minister. Of the 40 points, secularization of the state, linguistic equality and autonomy for ethnic minorities were the points relating to indigenous peoples/nationalities. 59 ethnic groups of Nepal are officially recognized as "indigenous nationalities". 48 of these are represented in NEFEN (the National Federation of Nationalities) through formally organized indigenous peoples' organizations.

During the 7 years of war, the Maoists have caused significant turmoil and indigenous peoples have suffered tremendously. Their national umbrella organization NEFEN has recently made its own input into the ongoing peace talks.

Political and legislative developments

On October 4, 2002, His Majesty King Gyanendra Bir Bikram Shah Dev dismissed Prime Minister Sher Bahadur Deuba. With this move, the king assumed executive power under Article 127 of the constitution, until alternative arrangements are made. The king assured the people that the "takeover" would in no way damage the constitutional system, and that the civil and military authorities should continue to discharge their usual responsibilities without any fear.

Prior to the King's October 4 move, Prime Minister Deuba had dissolved the Parliament and set the date for elections to the House of Representatives as November 13, 2002. Nevertheless, with the consent of an all-party meeting, the government proposed that the king should postpone the general election for one year in response to a commonly shared fear that peaceful elections would not be possible because of the Maoist Insurgency.

Peace talks

After the cease-fire agreement and the subsequent start of peace talks in April 2003, both parties agreed on a 23-point code of conduct for the peace dialogue, and decided to form a monitoring committee consisting of 13 members, of which one is a representative of NEFEN.

Compared with the original 40 points presented by the Maoists in 1996, their current presentation of issues to be discussed only mentions the secularisation of the state, and not the issue of indigenous ethnic groups' autonomy. However, it is obvious that an important reason behind the involvement of many young people from the indigenous peoples/nationalities in the insurgency was the fact that secularisation of the state, as well as indigenous peoples' autonomy and right to self-determination, were on the Maoists' agenda.

Many people do not have high expectations of the peace talks. It is feared that the guerrillas will be reluctant to give up their arms, and that a peace agreement reached in Kathmandu will not bring an end to the conflict in rural areas. Indigenous women further complain of the serious under-representation of women in the peace talk teams. The Maoist team consists of 5 men, whereas the government team has one woman and 4 male members.

"One of the worst democratic constitutions"

The constitution promulgated in 1991 promotes just one language, one religion and one culture and is biased towards other cultures and groups. In the preparation of the constitution in 1990, the drafting committee threw out suggestions made by Nationalities to protect indigenous languages and cultures and declare a secular state. Instead, the 1991 act constitutes Nepal as a Hindu state.

Scholars and Indigenous Peoples' activists call the present constitution "racist" and "sexist" (Lawoti 2003).[1] The declaration of the state as Hindu is racism in its most fundamental form. According to Dr Mahendra Lawoti, a University of Pittsburgh scholar, the constitution discriminates against non-Hindus, as the state institutions and policies are imbued with elite male Hindu norms and values. How can people whose language and religion are not recognized compete on an equal footing with the dominant group whose religion, language and culture are promoted by the state? And how can women expect to be treated equally, both legally and socially, when patriarchal Hindu thought has shaped the laws?

Dr Lawoti recently stated that,

> The constitution paves the way for exclusion of a majority of the population in almost all important realms of society: politics, administration, education, media, security forces, political parties, human rights, business, industry, the private sector and so forth. The oppressed socio-cultural groups suffer from poverty, illiteracy, a high infant mortality rate, low life expectancy, and lack of basic services.

Lawoti claims that those supporting the constitution are its beneficiaries, that is, mainly male Bahuns (Brahmins). He further observes that the constitution may be "one of the worst democratic constitutions in the world".

Government policy in the tenth five-year plan

His Majesty's Government of Nepal (HMG) recently completed its 10th five-year Plan.[2] There is a separate article no. 5.9.2 addressing indigenous issues under the heading "Aboriginal and Ethnic People". The article states:

The major challenges of this sector relate to the underestimation of the skills and capabilities of ethnic groups as a national asset in formulating a development approach; weak implementation of targeted programmes; lack of involvement of ethnic groups in development programmes; lack of protection and conservation of culture, language and knowledge remaining at the phase of being extinct; etc. The following policies and programmes will be adopted to resolve the problems and challenges related to aboriginal and ethnic people:

1. Policy will be adopted to preserve and promote aboriginal and ethnic peoples' different cultures, languages, knowledge, and skills according to their proper study and research.
2. An ethnic academy will be established and strengthened by the Act with a view to protecting and preserving the rights of aboriginal and ethnic people, as well as their culture, language, and diverse knowledge.
3. A strategy and action plan, based on a long-term vision derived from the analysis of problems and opportunities of the aboriginal and ethnic people, will be implemented.
4. Existing programmes targeted for aboriginal and ethnic people will be effectively implemented through structural and institutional improvements.
5. Priority will be given for the admission of aboriginal and ethnic students in higher education and in technical schools. Similarly, at school level, scholarship programmes targeting the children of such communities will be expanded and made effective.
6. Establishment of schools and health centers will be prioritised in such communities and areas to enhance the access of education and health services.
7. Programmes implemented by different agencies of the Government will be targeted to those places and communities. Special arrangements will be made to monitor and evaluate the investment targeted for the upliftment of aboriginal and ethnic people.

International Indigenous Peoples' Day

NEFEN marked International Indigenous Peoples' Day on August 9 2002 in Kathmandu. Various programmes were conducted from August 7 to 9, including an exhibition of books, photographs and audio-visual materials, a literary meet, a seminar, the inauguration of NEFEN's website and a special ceremony that included a procession with cultural demonstrations and had the Prime Minister as the chief guest.

On the occasion of the celebration of the eighth Indigenous Peoples' Day in the country, His Majesty the King, in a message to mark the day, stressed the multi-ethnic, multi-lingual and multi-cultural nature of the country. The Prime Minister, in his address during the special ceremony, pointed to the diversity and heterogeneity prevailing in the country. He emphasized the importance of the development of indigenous peoples/nationalities for the overall development of the country, and further remarked that NEFEN had a special responsibility during these critical times. The Vice-Chairperson of the National Planning Commission, in his address during the seminar on August 8, elaborated on the policies and programmes incorporated in the government's Tenth Plan of benefit to indigenous peoples/nationalities, and stated that the National Planning Commission was carrying out substantial activities in this regard. During the August 8 seminar, the Resident Representative of the United Nations Development Programme, the Director of the International Labour Organization, the Resident Representative of UNESCO and the Country Director of the World Bank all spoke about international commitments to indigenous peoples around the world. They elaborated on the initiatives and activities taken on behalf of indigenous peoples, with special reference to the Nepalese context. They also stated that their respective organizations welcomed the possibility of further initiatives vis-à-vis indigenous peoples in Nepal and around the world.

Indigenous issues and the peace dialogue

NEFEN recently organized a seminar to highlight the issues that indigenous peoples/nationalities have been raising as relevant to the present process of peace talks. In the seminar, Dr. Lawoti stressed the fact that the political institutions in Nepal are promoting exclusion. In his opinion, the country has not one single inclusive institution. Federalism, proportional electoral procedures, proportional distribution of resources and minority protection all need to be included in the constitution of Nepal.

In the same meeting, Dr. Krishna B. Bhattachan, advisor to NEFEN, presented their demands for the peace talks, which included: state secularisation, equal status for languages, respect for the right to self-determination or ethnic autonomy, for example, through a federal government structure as mentioned above.[3] He also criticized the biased collection of census data,[4] and called for better procedures in the future. In addition, the right of all peoples to access resources such as land, forest, water and pasture, and the need for affirmative action or positive discrimination (both remedial and preferential) should be included in the peace talks.

The following input for the dialogue between Maoists and government was agreed upon in the seminar:

1. *Ensure representation of the issues as well as the institutions of indigenous peoples/nationalities during the peace talks, the round table conference and the creation of a national government, in order to reach a solution in the context of the new political situation that has developed following the announcement of the cease-fire;*
2. *Form an independent commission with the objective of carrying out a judicial inquiry of all the extra-judicial killings perpetrated against indigenous peoples/nationalities collectively or individually during the course of the violent conflict prior to the cease-fire;*
3. *Release immediately all indigenous peoples arrested on the basis of suspicion and kept unlawfully since the outbreak of the Maoist insurgency;*
4. *Make arrangements for compensation and appropriate treatment of indigenous peoples/nationalities, especially women and children who were killed, injured or disappeared during the conflict;*
5. *The state to make all arrangements for the necessary security and reconstruction for rehabilitating indigenous peoples/nationalities displaced from their traditional lands by the conflict; the rebels should also respect the right of the indigenous peoples/nationalities to live in their own lands;*
6. *Declare the country secular, in place of the present Hindu state, since it is against democratic principles to associate the state with one particular religion in a multi-religious country;*
7. *Recognize the linguistic rights of all language communities, implement an equal language rights policy and end linguistic discrimination; implement a trilingual education policy;*
8. *Although the indigenous peoples/nationalities constitute the majority in the country their presence in various state institutions is minimal, which has led to their falling behind in development. Since it is not possible for them to compete on an equal footing due to lack of qualified human resources (created by the historical discrimination and mistreatment carried out against them) arrangements should be made for reservation or affirmative action in education, government service and other employment opportunities;*

9. Make arrangements, when drawing up a new constitution in the future or amending the present constitution, for proportionate representation or special representation of indigenous peoples/nationalities in the legislative, executive, judiciary and other state bodies, given that their representation in decision-making levels or policy-making levels is necessary for their well-being;

10. Guarantee indigenous ethnic self-rule to indigenous groups in accordance with the principle that indigenous peoples/nationalities have the right to self-determination so they can carry out their own development on the basis of their historical homeland, population and linguistic density;

11. Sincerely address, while looking for a political way out of the country's present impasse, the fundamental issues related to the indigenous peoples/nationalities enshrined in international human rights instruments and identified and raised by the indigenous peoples' groups of the country themselves, such as the rights to self-determination, ethnic self-rule, right to land and natural resources, ethnic proportional representation system, and equality of language, ethnicity, religion, culture and region; and

12. Create a multi-party democratic constitution mindful of the international human rights instruments and a political system inclusive of the way of life, condition and norms and values of the country's indigenous peoples/nationalities.

Strategies to be adopted

1. Carry out discussions, seminars and raise public awareness at the local, regional, and central levels through the Indigenous Peoples' Organizations;

2. Organizations associated with NEFEN should participate in the discussions and seminars organized by NEFEN at local, regional, and central levels and make them a success. NEFEN should also carry out joint activities by coordinating with the organizations of other indigenous peoples/nationalities;

3. Raise the issues of indigenous peoples/nationalities effectively, through all kinds of national-level political, intellectual, professional and social organizations and associations or their networks; and

4. Take initiatives for the effective presence of indigenous peoples/nationalities as well as for solving their problems through appropriate international and diplomatic and bilateral and multilateral aid agencies.❑

Notes and references

3   **Lawoti, Mahendra. 2003.** "Inclusive Democratic Political Institution for Nepal." **in Bhattachan, Krishna (ed).** *Expected Model and Process of Inclusive Democracy in Nepal.* Social Science BAHA: Kathmandu.

2   **HMG. 2003.** National Planning Commission. Shinghadurbar, Nepal.

3   These ideas are presented thoroughly in **Bhattachan, Krishna** (*op.cit.*)

4   The census data continues to show a clear majority of Hindus in the population, even though many indigenous peoples do not identify themselves as such.

INDIA

Over the past year, India's indigenous / tribal peoples or *Adivasis,* as they are called in mainland India, faced both the expected and unexpected consequences of last year's policy developments. Forest-dwelling indigenous peoples are under threat of eviction from their homes nation-wide, and some have already suffered violent evictions. The Prevention of Terrorism Act (POTA), which was passed last year, has caused serious harassment of indigenous peoples, and the peace process in the North-East is still moving at a slow pace.

Threat of violent mass eviction from forests

The frenzy of activity evicting "encroachers" from the Reserve Forests nation-wide began with a letter from the Inspector General of Forests dated 3 May 2002. The letter claimed to be in furtherance of an order of the Supreme Court on 23 November 2001 as a result of the Public Interest Litigation by T.N Godhavarman Thirumulpad of Kerala (Writ Petition 202 of 1995). G. Thirumulpad once owned vast tracts of forest granted to his family, who now fell in the Nilgiri District of Tamilnadu. The petition protested the illicit felling of timber from forests that his family had protected for generations but which had been decimated since the forest department took them over. The Supreme Court expanded the scope of the case on its own initiative to cover all forests in the country, with the dictionary meaning of "forests" being understood, that is, irrespective of the category of land or ownership. As a result, some 1000 interlocutory applications (IA) from all over the country, from the North-east and central India to the Andamans, have been filed in the Supreme Court. The court has since been issuing orders in their regard.

However, the order to which the letter of the Inspector General of Forests of May 2002 referred does not exist. The only order that is available on record for 23 November 2001 runs thus: "The Chief Secretaries of the State of Orissa, West Bengal, Karnataka, Tamilnadu, Assam, Maharashtra, Madhya Pradesh, Chattisgarh and Kerala are directed to file a reply to the IAs, insofar as they concern the said States in relation to the steps required to be taken by them to prevent further encroachment of forest land and in particular the land in the hilly terrains, national parks and sanctuaries, etc. It should also be indicated as to what steps have been taken to clear the encroachments from the forest, which have taken place at an earlier point of time. Affidavits be filed by the said states and the Union of India within four weeks..."

In June 2002, the Supreme Court appointed a 5-member Central Empowered Committee. Pending interlocutory application in the writ petitions, the Committee has been designated with the power to examine the reports and affidavits of the States and to place their recommendations before the Court for orders. The Committee's recommendations were a calculated effort on the part of the Forest Department to eliminate all the rights of tribals that have been recognized by the governments and courts after long struggles. The Committee did not invite any Adivasis to the proceedings. The recommendations were unilateral.

With the flurry of activities that followed the case, Adivasis are in danger of being evicted.

With the irresponsible order of 3 May 2002 on the part of the Ministry of Environment and Forests (MoEF) directing all states to vacate all encroachment of forestland by 30 September 2002, the state governments commenced issuing eviction orders on a large scale in some places, and in many places launched summary evictions. Tension and conflict have spread throughout the country. Hundreds and thousands of homes have been destroyed or are in the process of being destroyed. There have been widespread protests as the evictions were made in complete violation of the 1990 orders from the Ministry. These orders pertain to guidelines regarding encroachment on forestlands; reviews of disputed claims over forestlands arising out of forest settlement; and conversion of forest hamlets into villages and settlement of other old habitations. On 30 October 2002, the Ministry of Environment issued a clarification to all the states that the 1990 orders should be adhered to with regard to the rights of Adivasis. However, the influence over and control of forests by global capital inter-

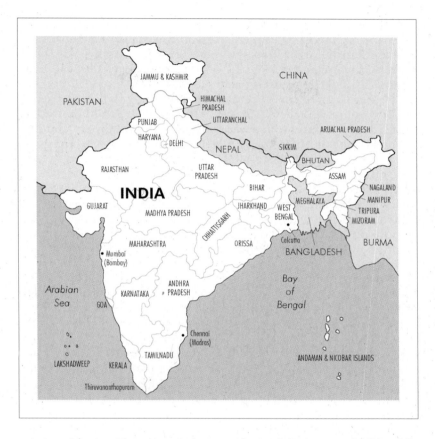

ests is evident, with economic interests becoming more and with additional economic dimensions having been opened up in the form of biodiversity, intellectual property rights and carbon sinks to name but a few. Investment for future profits and global futuristic trading in forests are literally in operation. Consequently, the government's approach to the peoples whose livelihood is based on the forests is to exclude them totally, with the use of violent repressive regimes in the name of tackling security.

National Biodiversity Strategy and Action Plan

The National Biodiversity Strategy and Action Plan (NBSAP) was supposed to be finalized by May 2003. The Draft Action Plan, which was prepared in October 2002, is currently under discussion.

The NBSAP process is the outcome of a consolidated report on the direction that India should take in terms of conservation, and the sustainable and equitable use of biodiversity and biological resources, and of the country's commitments under the UN Convention on Biological Diversity (CBD). India became a signatory to the CBD in June 1992.

The need to re-orient development policies and practices and decentralize governance of natural resources are key thrusts of the draft action plan. The draft recommends a series of measures relating to environmental conservation and the security of livelihoods of biodiversity-dependent communities, tenure rights, controlled commercial development in some areas and an absolute ban on development projects in ecologically fragile areas, protecting the rights of Adivasis/i ndigenous tribal communities, joint and participatory management of natural resources, and it calls for a major re-orientation of the process of economic development and governance of natural resources in such a way that the components of biodiversity conservation become central to planning and local communities become central to decision-making.

However, apprehensions have been voiced by a group of civil society organizations, movements and alliances. In a letter to the Ministry of Environment and Forest (MoEF) dated November 25, 2002, these organizations accused the government of pushing the action plan through and obtaining a hasty endorsement since, in its letters to several organizations, the MoEF gave only fifteen days in which to respond and send comments on the massive draft. Their letter to the ministry demanded that the NBSAP should be put on hold until communities were given an opportunity to address issues that concerned their livelihood and urged the Ministry instead to provide: (i) the executive summary of the NBSAP in various Indian languages for nationwide dissemination for people to comment; (ii) the full report of the NBSAP across the country for people to see, get copies and respond where necessary; (iii) a functional process in all the states to disseminate the report and seek views from various communities; and (iv) a credible mechanism that would take the various comments received into consideration.

These organizations also felt that unless the safeguards enshrined in the Constitution and laws were enacted in advance, and a more complete picture presented of the implications of NBSAP to local communities, any haste in finalizing the strategy without a democratic debate would be a great injustice to the communities and a violation of constitutional responsibilities.

The draft plan has given priority ratings to various strategies and actions recommended. While integration of biodiversity concerns into existing national and state policies, foreign investment mechanisms and international treaties to be signed by India and, accordingly, the subsequent review of national laws have been accorded a top priority rating, the amendment of incompatible national laws and policies has not been prioritized. Similarly, the strategy of integrating the right to information into the action plan for making government information and records on biodiversity accessible to the public has been kept open-ended.

Strategies covering important issues of livelihood, tradition, knowledge, control over resources and governance of local and indigenous communities have not been accorded a clear priority. On the other hand, the protection and conservation of Protected Areas, Reserve Forests, National Parks, Sanctuaries and related issues such as encroachment of forest lands, prevention and mitigation of wildlife-human conflicts, promotion of awareness and understanding of eco-tourism, have been given foremost priority in the national action plan.

Jharkhand

Demonstration on forest rights

The indigenous peoples living inside or on the fringes of currently degraded forest lands staged an impressive demonstration for the first time in Ranchi on 24 November 2002. The demonstrators, under the banner of the *Jharkhand Jangal Bachao Andolan* (Jharkhand Save the Forest Movement), marched through the thoroughfares of the capital city of Jharkhand, assembled at the main gates of the Legislative Assembly and held a public meeting. A memorandum was delivered to the Chief Minister for immediate fulfilment of the popular demand for restoration of ownership rights over the ancestral forests and unconditional access to the Reserved Forests, as well as the adoption of the concept of Community Forest Management in the place of the hitherto practised policy of the Joint Forest Management, which left no room for people's control over the forest and people's participation in the decision-making process.

Santhal struggle to protect land and identity

The contradiction between the judicial and administrative systems of the country on the issue of so-called "development" has led to a sharp conflict between the state and indigenous peoples. Jharkhand has been one such place where the people have been struggling hard against the onslaught of the notorious Land Acquisition Act, which flouts the land tenure acts that uphold the inalienability of tribal land, such as the Chotanagpur Tenancy Act of 1908, the Santhal Pargana Tenancy Act of 1949 as well as the recent Supreme Court Judgement on the well-known Samata case (see *The Indigenous World 2001-2002*), which bans the transfer of 'tribal' land to 'non-tribals' for mining purposes.

A case in point is the land acquisition spree of the Bharatiya Janata party-led government in the Santhal Parganas, against which the Santhal have risen in revolt. The government has started acquiring land in the Pachwara central block, which measures roughly 13 sq. km, covering 9 villages. The block has a coal reserve of 562 million tons. The coal will be extracted, but not to remove the darkness of the area's Santhal villages; on the contrary it will be handed over to the PANEM Coal Mines Ltd. for electricity genera-tion in Punjab, an affluent province in north India.

The Santhal of the district, facing massive displacement, are resisting the government move under the banner of the "*Rajmahal Bachao Andolan*" (Save the Rajmahal Hills Movement). Several pro-testers have already been arrested and are languishing in jail, but the community is unwavering and states that they are waging a battle for both the survival and protection of their cultural identity.

Struggle against World Bank-funded project

The struggle of tribals against a World Bank-funded coal project has been vindicated by the World Bank's own Inspection Panel. For over five years, Santhal and Turi tribals of the Parej East open cast project in Jharkhand had been campaigning against the project on the grounds of its failure to restore income, to recognise customarily held land, to offer genuine consultation and information sharing, to provide a legal right to resettlement land and more. They claimed that the promised rehabilitation ("to share in the benefits of the project") had not taken place, that the majority of the people had been turned from subsistence land owners into landless casual labourers, and that the Bank had failed in many of its promises and commitments.

Eventually, the people filed a case with the Inspection Panel, supported by networking with local and international NGOs. The Inspection Panel of three persons visited the site twice, and in early December 2003 released its report. It found that the World Bank had breached its own policies on 31counts, with several other counts of "serious failures". The Inspection Panel upheld many of the claims made by the people. Furthermore, the Report indicated a disturbing gap between the Bank's claims and the reality on the ground, namely that the Bank had used gross oversell and exaggerated claims to present the benefits of the project at the planning stage, and that, when the chips are down, it will violate its own stated policies.

The Bank has to come up with a remedial action plan - but the people have prepared their own and presented it to the Bank. The outcome remains to be seen.

Indigenous peoples harassed under POTA

The Prevention of Terrorism Act, 2002, commonly known as POTA, was passed by the Indian parliament to prevent terrorist activities in the country, especially in Jammu and Kashmir. It gives immense power to the police to arrest and detain suspects without trial. However, it has so far been used mostly in Jharkhand with the avowed objective of curbing communist revolutionary struggles. But in reality only innocent indigenous people, Dalits and other downtrodden people are being booked and harassed under this draconian law. A team of eminent citizens including lawyers, journalists, human right activists and an ex-army man visited the state and produced a report that revealed shocking facts. Indiscriminate use of the act has meant that mostly young men and women have been arrested. The police have not even spared minors. No terrorist threatening the national integrity was booked under POTA in Jharkhand. Not one of the 3,000 odd people named under POTA in less than a year seemed to merit the use of POTA, as there were no anti-nationals among them. Only cases that merit sanctions under ordinary law were brought under POTA.

The report was presented to the National Human Rights Commission and the Union Home Ministry. It was then that central government asked the Jharkhand government to send a report on its use of POTA. The Director General of Police of Jharkhand appointed a high-level police committee to review all the POTA cases, and found that over 50% were ill-founded. Now the state Central Intelligence Department has come up with the specific figure of 83.

When POTA was passed in a joint session of Parliament (despite opposition from all the opposition parties), the Union Home Minister gave a solemn assurance that it would be used only against extremists who posed a serious threat to the security of the nation.

But the way it has been used/misused by the Bharatiya Janata party-led Jharkhand government is inexcusable. In fact, as the Investigative Team remarked, "In Jharkhand all the laws of the land are replaced by POTA."

Demystifying Bengal

The cherished belief, nourished and popularised by the ruling left of West Bengal, that discrimination along the lines of caste and ethnicity has no place in the "progressive" nature of the state, has received a jerk. A rigorous empirical study conducted by the Pratichi (India) Trust[1] reveals that discrimination against people of so-called lowly background, the Scheduled Castes (SC) and Scheduled Tribes (ST), forms an integral part of the social, economic, political and cultural oppression that continues to marginalize these people. Children of the SC and ST communities face multi-layered deprivations in the existing education system, which have enormous social implications. Firstly, the economic status of their parents (most of the SC and ST families surveyed were occupationally agricultural wage earners) did not allow them to afford the extra cost of private tuition (private tuition is widespread and, in general, those who do not take private tuition cannot even write their names properly). Secondly, at primary school, the teachers reportedly gave children of the SC and ST communities almost no attention. Absenteeism among the teachers was found to be very high in schools with a majority of SC and ST students. Many, including some teachers, even believed that "the SC and ST children are not fit for acquiring education for they are less intelligent." Teachers at one primary school went as far as to seat tribal children apart from the others. Thirdly, the language barrier is a major hindrance to the school success of children from tribal communities, particularly Santhal and Kora children. It seems that the protagonists of "class war" have failed to protect the real "lower class" people of the state from malicious discrimination and gross injustice.

Kerala

The Government fails to comply with agreement

Consequent to the 38 starvation deaths in July-August 2001, and the successful protest of the *Adivasi-Dalit Samara Samithy* (Adivasi-Dalit

Struggle Committee) and the *Adivasi Gothre Mahasabha* (Grand Council of Adivasi, AGMS), the government entered into an agreement with the struggle committee on 16 October 2001 – the C.K. Janu – A.K. Antony "agreement" (see *The Indigenous World 2001-2002:335-339*). The agreement consisted of providing up to 5 acres of land to those Adivasi families who were landless or possessing less than an acre of land and development plans for sustainable land use. In addition, another key provision was a cabinet resolution to include all Adivasi hamlets under Schedule V, which would confer on them the right to a high degree of self-governance under the Panchayat Raj Act (Extension to the Scheduled Areas), 1996. Adivasis in Kerala, unlike those in 10 other states, have to date not been included in Schedule V. The government also agreed to abide by the outcome of pending Supreme Court of India cases on land transfers to scheduled tribes in Kerala (see *The Indigenous World 1999-2000* and *2000-2001*).

By 1 January 2002, the government had identified 53,472 families eligible to receive five acres of land, of which 22,491 were landless, while the remainder had less than one acre. Concurrently, the state has identified 59,452 acres for distribution. So far 843 families have been given 1,747.62 acres. This works out at 1.6 percent of the identified beneficiaries getting some 3 percent of the total land, averaging roughly 3 acres per beneficiary. At this rate, it will take another half century to distribute the identified lands to the beneficiaries.

It was clear that the economic lobbies around the forest and the plantations had sufficient influence and control over the mainstream political parties as well as the bureaucratic machinery to subvert the agreement, as it did with the law pertaining to the restoration of alienated lands. The AGMS' success in gaining legitimacy through the agreement in 2001 and following up with the initiation of a participatory democratic process not only threatened the economic lobbies that stood in the way of implementing the agreement but also upset the delicately deceptive politico-administrative system that so beautifully passed itself off as a "democracy".

Police force on the rampage

Around 1,000 heavily armed police officers stormed the Muthanga range of the Wayanad Wild Life Sanctuary in the Nilgiri Biosphere in Wayanad district of Kerala on the morning of 19 February 2003. Approximately another 100 non-Adivasi locals joined the police, baying for the blood of Adivasis. These people included local politicians of all hues, henchmen of the powerful forest mafia and members of *Wayanad Prakrithy Samrakshana Samithy*, a so-called environmental group.

Adivasis had been occupying the Muthanga range since 4 January 2003. In a meeting in August 2002 convened by the AGMS, it had been decided to take this action if the government did not distribute the land promised to Adivasis according to the C.K. Janu – A.K. Antony "agreement" before 31 December 2002, as they had officially agreed. The Muthanga occupation was thus part of the AGMS' decision to implement the "agreement" on their own. By February 2003, about 1,100 landless Adivasi families had settled in the Muthanga range on deforested barren and eucalyptus plantation land, which was officially registered as forest. This part of the forest was earlier leased out to a private contractor and, at the same time, forms the corridor for a powerful inter-state forest mafia.

When the police clashed with the Adivasis on 19 February, around 5 Adivasis, one forester and a policeman were injured. The police went on the rampage, brutally slaying the Adivasis, including women and children. Huts were set on fire and the Adivasis' meagre worldly belongings smashed, accompanied by the firing of tear gas and guns. An Adivasi fell victim to the firing. According to official reports there were 18 rounds of firing. The journalists present were beaten and driven away lest they document and report the brutalities. However, some managed to bring back pictures and eyewitness accounts of what really took place. Over the next 16-18 hours, the area was subject to a mysterious cordoning off from the outside world. The brutal hunt by the police spread to all the nearby Adivasi villages and, in the subsequent days, it reached other districts of the state. Hundreds were arrested and tortured. 143 people were reported arrested, including a large number of women and children. A month and a half later, the exact number of people arrested, taken into custody, tortured, injured, dead or missing is still not known. Many have abandoned their villages and taken shelter in the neighbouring states of Tamilnadu and Karnataka.

On 23 February, C.K Janu and M. Geethanandan, both prominent Adivasi leaders, emerged from the forest and handed themselves over to the police, holding high the spirit of the tradition of democratic struggle. They faced brutal custodial torture.

The attack in Muthanga sent shock waves across the state. The Congress-led United Democratic Front (UDF) congratulated itself on cracking down on a "fully armed violent terrorist group" linked to the banned Peoples War group of Andhra, as well as the Liberation Tigers of Tamil Elam. The Chief Minister revealed with much aplomb that the

AGMS had established a "parallel" government, basing his accusations on alleged intelligence reports. Within days, the theories and allegations against AGMS crumbled. The officials agreed that there was no credence to the allegations of an armed uprising or links with banned groups. The brutal actions of the state that were initially welcomed, if seen to be too harsh, were soon widely condemned by many. The declaration of Adivasi habitation as scheduled area under the Vth Schedule of Article 244 would give the Adivasis the constitutional right to self-rule. However, both the ruling and the opposition fronts have quietly and collectively relegated this issue, declaring that autonomous processes such as the AGMS' have no legitimacy in a democracy. Both regard the participatory democratic process unleashed by a section of Adivasis as threatening democracy in its current form. The international discourse on self-rule among indigenous peoples has begun to anger sections of non-tribal society that had otherwise been opposing globalisation's influence on the national and local political debate.

The North-East

Increasing and heightened political aspirations fuelled by the discourse on self-determination has set the tone for indigenous and tribal politics in the North-East region of India. This genre of politics hit a new zenith of conflicting territorial claims and demands in 2002-2003 as tribes and indigenous communities struggled for their rights. The year was no different to the previous as inter- and intra-tribal clashes, intra- and inter-armed groups clashes, as well as clashes with the Indian army and paramilitary forces took a deadly toll on lives and displaced thousands of women, children and men.

While a total figure is not available for the region as a whole, newspaper reports stated that over 83 persons belonging to the United Liberation front of Asom (ULFA) and the National Democratic Front of Bodoland (NDFB), the former an armed group fighting for a free Assam and the latter an armed organization seeking an independent homeland for the Bodos, had been killed in encounters with the Indian army and state police forces. According to the annual Indian Home Ministry report, the total number of civilians killed in the crossfire of encounters between the Indian forces and the various armed organizations during the year was around 454. It could in fact be much more, as many such deaths go unreported. An almost equal number of members of the security forces have died in the numerous violent encounters during the year.

Looking for peaceful solutions

The government of India (GOI) is hard put to assemble a workable policy to handle the complicated situation in the North-East. Its policy of negotiating with the various armed organizations fighting for various tribal causes and hammering out a peaceful agreement within the framework of the Indian Constitution in its present form has been outgrown by the problems and issues presented by the region on the ground. Its overtures for peaceful negotiations with some of the armed tribal groups have only served to set off a series of counter-claims or demands on other fronts. At the moment, the GOI is holding negotiations with the National Socialist Council of Nagaland, Isak Muivah faction (NSCN-IM) (see article on Nagalim). It has furthermore signed an agreement to form the Bodoland Territorial Council (BTC) with the armed Bodo organization, the Bodoland Liberation Tigers (BLT), as well as ceasefire agreements with the Dimasa armed group, Dima Halam Daoga (DHD) and a Karbi armed group, the United People's Democratic Solidarity (UPDS). All these agreements have resulted in either counter-claims from other tribes and communities or factional feuds, as in the case of the BLT agreement and the UPDS, which have strong anti-talks factions.

The talks between the GOI and the Nationalist Socialist Council of Nagalim-IM, which were held in Delhi last January, were hailed as a watershed heralding a new dawn for peace for the Naga and thereby the rest of the region (see article on Nagalim). For the first time, the leaders of the NSCN-IM Thuingaleng Muivah and Issac Chishi Swu came to India for the talks. But these much-vaunted talks may remain a mere incident and gesture unless the struggle for peace among the Naga continues within their fold. Last year, the hopes for bringing forth a reconciliation among the different factions of the Naga remained a mere chimera as the year saw one of the fiercest factional fights between the different factions of the Naga, in which more than 100 people allegedly died. In this context, S.C. Jamir, who led the Nagaland state apparatus for nearly a decade and a half, is considered one of the factions. With the disposal of Jamir in the recent state elections of February 2003 and with the new coalition government's commitment to the peace process, there is again hope for reconciliation among the Naga (see article on Nagalim, *this volume*). However, the NSCN-IM's demand for a "Nagalim", uniting all Naga inhabited areas, has resulted in a domino effect of demands and counter-demands as the neighbouring tribes and communities have commenced a scramble to safeguard their own "historically" claimed areas, thus spreading tension across the ethnic fabric of the region. The Dima Halam Daoga, an armed outfit of Dimasa tribes of the North Cachar Hills district of Assam, has laid claim to "Dimasaraji", their historical kingdom, which they claim spans into the areas claimed by the NSCN-IM as Nagalim territory. Like the Naga groups that have entered into a ceasefire agreement with the GOI, the Dimasa armed cadres are free to wander around at will. The agreement is that they cannot carry their arms or weapons with them but this clause is not totally implemented.

New frictions

These kinds of ceasefire agreements have spawned a new brand of problems for the people as some members of the respective ethnic groups have taken these as a virtual licence to brow-beat the smaller tribes or communities living in and around the areas concerned, or the major tribal group has used the ceasefire as an opportunity to absorb smaller communities within its fold in order to legitimize its territorial claims. This has resulted in serious friction along tribal lines. Resistance to this has caused an outbreak of feuds and killings. The most recent outbreak of clashes was between the Hmar and Dimasa people in the North Cachar Hills District of Assam where more than 40 people died in separate incidents during the months of March, April and May 2003. Dozens of homes were burnt and ransacked and thousands of people had to flee. The state governments of Assam, Mizoram and Meghalaya, where the people fled to, are still trying to rehabilitate these displaced persons or convince them to move back home.

The hardening of tribal boundaries and the intra-tribal factionalism is taking a massive toll on the people. Among the Kuki tribe of Manipur, for example, more than six different armed groups and organizations claim to be speaking on behalf of the "Kuki people". This new layer of emerging conflicts has created a totally different and even more perilous security scenario for the ordinary people of the region. At each step, the ethnic issue comes up.

The Bodoland Territorial Council's agreement with the Bodoland Liberation Tigers (BLT), an armed group of the Bodo tribe, is yet to become fully operational. One of the contentious issues arising out of this agreement is the fact that it also seeks to give the Bodo living within the Karbi-Anglong Autonomous District Council, an area of the Karbi tribe, the status of a scheduled tribe, which alone would entitle them to franchise, land ownership and other rights on an equal standing with the Karbi within the Karbi-Anglong Autonomous District. The Karbi are vehemently opposing this with *bandhs*[1], protest rallies and strikes. Tribes and communities are thus lined up in mutually conflicting positions. Even if the political demands can be justified in every sense, the slide into criminalisation to support the movement has spawned a flourishing network of extortion and a racket based on kidnapping for ransom. During 2002, more than 450 people from across the region were kidnapped for ransom. As 2003 unfolds, analysts predict more clashes unless the government of India and the north-eastern states, intellectuals at all levels and civil society organizations, both national and international, work together to invoke a dynamic new vision for the people of the region that may have to be based on values and concepts other than those of ethno-cultural nationalism and of carving out ethnic homelands alone.

The politics of dams

The North-East region of India has been identified as one of the areas that can provide hydropower. There are more than one hundred dam projects for hydroelectricity generation in the pipeline. These projects have the potential to displace a large number of people and destroy the unique biodiversity of the land. The people who will be affected are in a catch 22 situation. They need the development that these dams symbolise. On the other hand, some may lose their land to the rising waters. NGOs are campaigning against the dams. In January, a memorandum of understanding was signed between the government of Manipur and the North-Eastern Electric Power Corporation Ltd (NEEPCO) to build the Tipaimukh Hydroelectric (multipurpose) Project. The proposed 162.80 metre-high dam has the primary stated objective of preventing the frequent flooding of the Cachar plains of Assam and of generating hydropower. NGOs campaigning against the dam say that it will destroy the lands on which several indigenous tribes live.

Andaman and Nicobar Islands: removal of settlers

On May 7, 2002, the Supreme Court of India issued an unprecedented order: settlers on the Andaman Islands were ordered to be removed from tribal reserves, the Andaman Trunk Road to be closed, and all logging on the islands to be halted immediately. The court ruling

followed a petition regarding logging on tribal land filed by the Society for Andaman and Nicobar Ecology (SANE). Activists and observers celebrated the landmark ruling in May last year and regarded
it as a turning point, giving the isolated indigenous Jarawas on the
South and Middle Andaman Islands as well as the Onge of Little
Andaman Island the best chance of survival for years. For more than
150 years, the indigenous peoples of the islands have suffered from
exploitation by outsiders who have settled on their land, taken over
their forests for timber extraction, etc. To date (May 2003), however,
the court orders have only been partially implemented by the Andaman & Nicobar Administration. According to Survival International, most settlers who had recently moved into the Jarawa reserve
have been removed, whereas the closure of the trunk road has yet to
be implemented.

On the other hand, the court ruling is having an impact in neighbouring Nicobar Islands, where the indigenous islanders' own organization, the Nicobar Youth Association, has filed a Public Interest
Litigation case against illegal settlers modelled on the Andaman experience.   ❏

Note and reference

1   **Rana K et al. 2002.** *The Pratichi Education Report.* With an introduction by
    Amartya Sen. Delhi: TLM Books in collaboration with Pratichi (India)
    Trust.
2   *Bandh* means closed, and in its political meaning a bandh is an organized
    closure of all businesses with the purpose of calling attention to a specific
    problem. Bandhs are a common form of political protest in South Asia.

SRI LANKA

The last 2,000 Wanniyala-Aetto (often still called *Veddah*) are the descendants of the aboriginal people of Sri Lanka. Under difficult conditions, they still attempt to continue their traditional life as hunter-gatherers. They are poorly prepared to defend their right of self-determination - a right which, for them, simply means looking after their own families, speaking their own language, maintaining their religion, marriage and funeral customs and pursuing their foraging subsistence economy without harassment.

Not yet assimilated into the country's mainstream (Singhalese) society, they have not accommodated themselves to northern-based education and acculturation. European languages are still not spoken by any of them, Roman orthography is unknown. Hence there is no written communication with outside societies. They lack experience in dealing with the bureaucracy of the modern state, and have no tradition of representative democracy and elections. They deal with local issues only and do not devise plans on behalf of *all* Wanniyala-Aetto.

It was only in connection with the United Nations meeting of the Working Group on Indigenous Peoples (WGIP) in 1996 that the Wanniyala-Aetto became aware that they were the first people of the country. Hence, they were not the descendants of evil *Yakkhas* or demons[1] as educated people and Buddhist monks had told them, quoting from the holy Chronicle, the *Mahavamsa*. There has been insufficient resistance, if any, to the major changes imposed by government. There is no history of war, feuds or opposition to rulers in the past. In spite of the blank promise that they were free to return to their forest, made by the President, the Wanniyala-Aetto raised no specific objection when this written assurance was broken. Both national media and the WGIP witnessed the promise in 1997.

The Wanniyala-Aetto, which means 'forest-dwellers', still attempt to hunt and gather in their old settlements, not for the sake of resistance but in order to survive. They meet overwhelming and sometimes deadly opposition from the government. As their numbers dwindle, the issues that confront these hunter-gatherers seem ever more quaint and irrelevant to the parliament in Colombo, which is so remote from the daily challenges of life in government resettlement villages. There is no organization in Sri Lanka that defends the rights of the Wanniyala-Aetto or champions their cause. As time passes, increasingly few remain among the relocated Wanniyala-Aetto who remember the old life, and fewer still attempt to live in their old village sites near the forests.

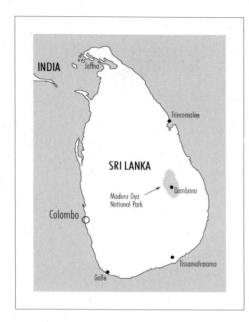

December 2001 elections

In June 2001, changes began to occur inside the parliament building. Ministers and government members from the ruling Peoples Alliance (PA) switched to the opposition, the United National Party (UNP). This latter governed the country from 1977 to 1994 when the Peoples Alliance was elected. The UNP is remembered for the Mahaweli Development Project, a hydroelectric and irrigation project which, among other things, caused the eviction of the Wanniyala-Aetto from their forest in order to make way for the Maduru Oya national park.

Once the PA came to power, they decentralised the presidential powers and focused on human rights. Mass graves were unearthed and former ministers and government officials were put on trial. The PA government allowed the Wanniyala-Aetto to participate in the WGIP in 1996, something they had been denied in 1985 during the UNP regime.

The UNP won the elections in December 2001- the most violent ever in the history of Sri Lanka. Road mines and huge trees functioned as roadblocks in several districts, preventing people from voting. Those that reached the polling stations unharmed were, in many districts, threatened, shot or killed with their ballot papers in their hands. In some instances, international observers even removed their signs from their vehicles, fleeing with bullets whistling above their heads.

"Family problems"

The Wanniyala-Aetto are not used to representative democracy. It is of no consequence to them who works with what in the provincial or national capitals. Both political parties know this, and try to motivate the indigenous people to vote for them.

The UNP campaigners targeted young Wanniyala-Aetto men as campaign leaders. The argument was that the UNP were the ones who had taken away the land from the Wanniyala-Aetto in 1983 and moved them from the jungle to Rehabilitation Villages hence they, and only they, were the ones who could resolve it. Ever since the Wanniyala-Aetto returned from their 1996 UN participation, they have been criticized for bringing their problems out into the open. They were discouraged from seeking further assistance from international fora. As commented by a visiting UNP member, "The issue should be resolved within the family".[2] Convinced by the campaigners, the Wanniyala-Aetto now pin their hopes on the new UNP government.

One hundred days

Economic development is a high priority for the new administration. Soon after the UNP's victory, each province was given the incentive to start development projects where they were most needed. The idea was to raise the country to its feet in one hundred days. Two weeks after the election, engineers came to Dambana, a village with a relatively large Wanniyala-Aetto population, to survey the road. Rumour had it that the road would be widened and that they would establish jeep routes inside the park for safaris. It was said that the Maduru Oya National Park, created in 1983, had not yet been developed to its full capacity. There was a lack of infrastructure, vehicles, certified tourist guides, resorts and accommodation. Development of the Maduru Oya National Park was one of many one-hundred-day projects. The process was, yet again, undertaken without the prior and informed consent of the Wanniyala-Aetto.

Fear of setting a precedent

Given the ethnic conflict between the Singhalese and the Tamils, the government is reluctant to formally recognize its indigenous people as a minority. Government sources have repeatedly stated that they might have been more lenient toward the 2,000 Wanniyala-Aetto if the other minority, the Tamils (three million) had not fought for their political, economic, cultural and social rights. There is a fear, it was said, that a benevolent approach toward the indigenous people could set a precedent for other minorities, one that might lead to drastic, unwanted political change. The best thing was therefore to make all citizens equal in Sri Lanka, without claiming different treatment based on ethnicity.

Part of the plan was to absorb the Wanniyala-Aetto into mainstream society. The government imposed regulations stating that all Wanniyala-Aetto women should bear their husband's name and that the children should bear the name of their father. This is the norm in both Singhalese and Tamil societies. Since marriage customs are less formalized among the Wanniyala-Aetto in comparison with those of the Singhalese, Tamils and/or Muslims, the local authorities were astonished to find, when writing new ID cards, that the Wanniyala-Aetto were not *legally* married.

In 1989, Sri Lanka therefore decided that all forest-dwellers had to obtain a marriage certificate and register their marriage with the state. The government arranged mass ceremonies to "legalize" previous Wanniyala-Aetto alliances[3] so that sometimes life-long unions between couples could be "officially" recognized as marriages. Today, because of the government's requirement for official registration, the younger generation do not consider themselves married unless they put their fingerprint or signature on an official marriage certificate.

Having completed that reform, in 2002 the government initiated yet another way of integrating the Wanniyala-Aetto into the norms of mainstream society: through their funeral traditions.

The Wanniyala-Aetto regard themselves as creatures of the forest who share a complex moral universe of visible and invisible fellow-beings in an environment in which everything is alive. They believe that their dead live in another dimension, yet are always with them. For them, no one really dies until those who knew and loved them are also dead. This is why they bury their deceased family members at the edge of the vegetable garden, close to the house so that they can be near and participate in daily life. Their ancestors are a part of the upbringing of the children.

In January 2002, at a village meeting by the main road in Dambana, there was a proposal from the Singhalese majority to change the Wanniyala-Aetto funeral customs. They should find a confined area, in the village, where all deceased would be buried together; a cemetery. Having lost their forestland, living in the buffer zone between the borders of the national park and the main road, their first concern was the land. Whose land was going to be taken? Some hesitated, watching the "more advanced" Singhalese people advocating for the cemetery. Others wished to prioritize the living over the dead. Once the Wanniyala-Aetto had a place to live, they meant, they would provide for the dead as prescribed by their tradition.

Since this was a village meeting with mostly Singhalese participation, (the Wanniyala-Aetto are not accustomed to such get-togethers), a majority vote overruled the Wanniyala-Aetto traditions. Hence, with this democratic process, another step was taken to absorb the Wanniyala-Aetto into mainstream society.

The paradox

If the Wanniyala-Aetto are going to survive as a culture, they need to have the self-confidence to speak out on their own, even in the presence of what they have been made to believe are 'more advanced' people (Singhalese, Tamils, foreigners from the North). This can be achieved if they learn to critically examine government statements and legal documents. To gain this knowledge they need to have financial resources, excel at school and advance to higher education, maybe abroad. Human rights and capacity building on indigenous issues is not on the agenda in Sri Lanka.

And herein lies the paradox. If the Wanniyala-Aetto wish to raise their children according to their traditions, teach their language, share their beliefs and way of life, they first have to send them into mainstream (in this context, Singhalese) society. In addition, when abroad, the adult students may acquire customs alien to the ones practised by their own forest people. They may dress, talk and smell strangely and become distanced from their people in the compound. Chances are that they will not choose their future spouse from the native settlement. The paradox lies in this conversion: the Wanniyala-Aetto have first to acquire an alien culture, maybe even two (national and international), if they are to maintain their own. ❑

Notes and references

1   **Geiger, Wilhelm (trans.). 1950.** *The Mahavamsa, or The Great Chronicle of Ceylon.* Colombo: Ceylon Government Information Department.
2   **Uru Warige.** Personal communication. Wanniya, 11 Dec. 2001. Notes in author's files.
3   **Weerasinghe, Chadrasiri.** "Historic day for Veddahs." *Daily News*, May 19, 1989. Colombo, Sri Lanka.

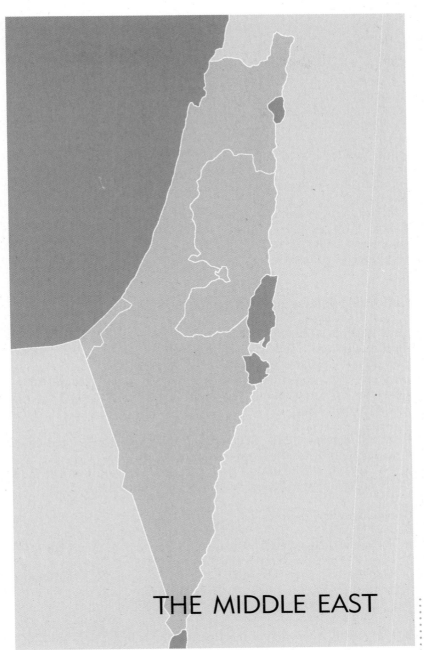

THE MIDDLE EAST

THE BEDOUIN OF ISRAEL

The Arab Bedouin are the indigenous inhabitants of the Negev Desert and represent approximately 12% of the Palestinian Arab minority in Israel.[1] The Negev comprises 2/3 of the total land area within the green line (the 1948 border of Israel). Prior to 1948, the Bedouin lived from agriculture and livestock raising. During the 1948 war, the majority of the Negev's Bedouin were driven out or fled. The remaining tribes were rounded up and spent the next 18 years under military rule in a closed military zone. Throughout this period, a number of laws were used to dispossess them of their traditional lands.

Today, approximately 130,000 Arab Bedouin live in the Negev, half of them in 7 "recognized" townships, which rate among the poorest localities in Israel. The other half in villages that are not recognized by the state.

Land dispossession and sedentarisation

Since the mid-1960s, the Bedouin of the Negev have been subjected to a process of forced sedentarisation in urban townships. This relocation policy, designed to "modernize" the Bedouin, has been conducted without consultation and in a manner that is culturally inappropriate. Like policies enacted on other indigenous peoples, it has had two main aims:

- To concentrate the Bedouin and make their traditional lands available for settlement programmes for Jews only;
- To domesticate the indigenous Bedouin economy and create a cheap source of wage labour for the Jewish economy.

British mandate records list 12,600,000 dunams[2] in the Negev as Bedouin lands. Today, the Bedouin are struggling to avoid eviction from the estimated 900,000 dunams[3] that remain to them. The state of Israel's sedentarisation policy has been accompanied by a legal process that has made Bedouin land claims invisible. The Land Rights Settlement Ordinance (1969) classified all *mawat* lands as state property unless a formal title could be produced. *Mawat* land was defined as untilled and more than 1.5 miles from the nearest settlement. The category became a major means of expropriation in the Negev because

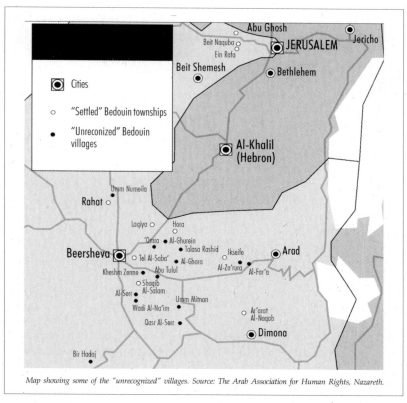

Map showing some of the "unrecognized" villages. Source: The Arab Association for Human Rights, Nazareth.

although Israeli courts acknowledged that Bedouin had been living in the areas they claimed, they did not recognize Bedouin tents as constituting settlements in terms of the law. Further, they defined working the land as changing it; and pastoralism was an unrecognised way of life. Later, the Negev Land Acquisition Law (1980), following the peace treaty with Egypt, facilitated a large-scale confiscation order of Bedouin lands in order to build military bases and an airport. Much of that land, however, was later turned over for use by Jewish farmers.

Denial of traditional employment

Prior to 1948, approximately 90% of the Bedouin in the Negev earned their living from agriculture and 10% from raising livestock. Today over 90% earn a living from wage labour. According to the Arab Association for Human Rights, the policy in effect makes the Bedouin's traditional lifestyle unworkable by:

- Restricting their access to land and water: while handing over large areas of former Bedouin land to Jewish farmers on long-term leases, the state will only lease lands to Bedouin farmers for brief periods, usually not the same land twice in a row, and will not permit any permanent cultivation. Bedouin farmers are either not given water quotas, or are charged at high domestic rates. No assistance is given for drought years.
- Restricting their goat flocks. The Plant Protection (Damage by Goats) Law (1950) requires Bedouin shepherds to obtain a permit from the Ministry of Agriculture to graze their goats outside their privately-owned land, on surrounding state lands (mostly military areas). Permits are issued on the condition that the state is not responsible for any casualties and at the discretion of Ministry officials. Since the mid-70s, it has been policy to seize unregistered flocks which has resulted in a significant reduction of the registered flocks – some statistics indicate as high as by 10-15% per annum.
- Creating the Green Patrol. The Green Patrol is an environmental paramilitary unit established by Ariel Sharon when he was Minister of Agriculture in 1978. It mobilises for special operations to demolish Bedouin tents, seize flocks and destroy crops. Physical coercion of Bedouin farmers has led to hospitalisation and a number of deaths. In 1997, the Green Patrol was expanded to help speed up the sedentarisation process.

Townships and unrecognised villages

Approximately 55,000 Bedouin live in 7 townships in the Beersheva area. Listed as the poorest municipalities in Israel, they have no sewage systems, few paved roads, and lack any kind of local employment opportunities. Unlike the facilities offered to neighbouring Jewish communities, there is no provision for maintaining livestock or engaging in agriculture. Five townships have government-appointed councils and only two are able to elect their own local representatives.

Another 70,000 Bedouins live in 46 'unrecognised' villages, many of which are located next to municipal waste dumps, military zones, polluting factories or – in the case of Wadi Na'am, a toxic waste incinerator. Although most of these villages existed before the establishment of the state of Israel, they became illegal as the result of the Law of Planning and Construction (1965) when the lands on which they sit were retroactively re-zoned as non-residential (i.e. agricultural) and partial ownership was claimed by the state. The villages, whose population ranges from 600 to 4,000 inhabitants, are afforded no official status: they are not on the map of Israel, they have neither local councils nor belong to other local governing bodies; they receive little or no rudimentary government services. All buildings erected are illegal and potentially targeted for demolition. It is estimated that there are currently 22,000 unrecognised houses in the Negev.

House demolitions and crop destructions

The strategy to remove the Bedouin of the unrecognised villages from their land and concentrate them in townships has, for many years, therefore consisted of house demolitions. In 1986, the Markovitz Committee recommended the demolition of 6,601 existing homes and all new buildings in the Negev. Subsequent governments have maintained this policy, and an average of 100 houses are destroyed each year. From May to July 2002 alone, the Green Patrol - accompanied by policemen and soldiers - bulldozed some 50 houses in 4 different villages, and approximately 1,700 cases are currently being prosecuted in court.[4] Defendants – i.e. people who have resisted the order to demolish their house - are not only fined but also have to pay the costs of the demolition, which as recommended by the Committee is double the cost of the house. 2003 has already seen tens of demolitions. In early February, a mosque in Tel al Milah was razed. This was the first incident of damage to a holy site. The mosque was the only one in this unrecognized village of 3,000 inhabitants and had been built with money collected from its residents. In March 2003, some 17 houses were demolished in different villages; in May, 11 structures were demolished.

In early 2002, the government strategy took a nasty turn by introducing the poisoning of the land of the unrecognized villages. In February 2002, without any prior notice, eight airplanes from the Israel Land Authority (ILA) sprayed toxic chemicals on the land of 10 villages, destroying approximately 12 sq. kms of crops allegedly planted illegally on state-owned land.[5] In order to quell any protests from the residents, a large ground force from the Police and the Green Patrol accompanied the airplanes. The operation also targeted farmers who were in their fields during the act, and a school. Two similar events have also occurred this year (2003). The first was in March, when some 500 acres of crops belonging to the residents of Abda were sprayed. Again, the toxic chemicals also fell on elderly people and children who were in the fields, and 12 people had to be hospitalised. Although a "recognized" village, Abda has never enjoyed the benefit of this recognition, which was conceded in 1992 after a 6-month sit-in in front of the Knesset (the Israeli parliament) as a protest at having been evicted from their old village and moved some 4 km away. The eviction was part of the government's plan to turn the village and the surrounding area into a National Park, due to the presence of Nabatean ruins (3rd century BC). The third herbicide spraying, which lasted one hour, took place in April and destroyed around 1,500 acres.

The Sharon Plan

It appears that these repressive measures are marking the onset of the Negev Development Plan whereby residential, grazing and agricultural Bedouin land currently in use will be claimed by the government and converted into some 17 Jewish neighbourhoods and 30 single-family farms, in order to alter the demographics of the Negev and "Judaize" the area.

Indeed, in early 2003, the Israeli government revealed a budget of US$250 million and a 6-year timeframe for implementing a plan to remove the indigenous Bedouin living in unrecognized villages and concentrate them into 7 recognized townships. The plan allocates 56 million ILS (or some US$ 12.8 million) to the Green Patrol whose authority will be expanded, and more funds for the creation of a new police unit. Part of the 27 million ILS (US$ 6.1 million) offered to the ILA will go towards crop-dusting airplanes, most likely to monitor Bedouin development and agriculture. The allocation of massive funds to patrol the desert with police in the midst of massive budget cuts points to the influence of the Transfer Party in the coalition government. Member of the Transfer Party[6] and Minister of Tourism, Beni Alon has been quoted as saying, "We will make their lives hard until they will ask to leave."

The preparation of this plan is being accompanied by frequent racist news items in the Hebrew printed and electronic media warning of "a Bedouin threat to take over the Negev" and urging an accelerated demolition of "illegal Bedouin homes". Another common theme is reference to the practice of polygamous marriage, still practiced by some Bedouin communities, and which is declared to be "a demo-graphic danger" or "time bomb".

Resisting the Plan

The Bedouin leaders and their main lobby organization, the Regional Council for the Palestinian Bedouin of the Unrecognized Villages,[7] have characterized the plan, which has never been discussed with any of the population or their representatives, "as a declaration of war on the Bedouin community of the unrecognised villages." They are supported by a coalition of 30 NGOs – many of them Jewish Israeli NGOs –who are working with different kinds of support projects in the unrecognised villages of the Negev. They have organized several protest demonstrations and are fighting this Development Plan with ferocity but agree that it is becoming increasingly clear that the effi-cacy of protesting against the Israeli establishment today is extremely limited. There is a great need for international support. ❏

Notes and references

1   The Arab minority within Israel numbers 1.2 million and represents 19% of Israel's total population (Israel's Central Bureau of Statistics; www.cbsgov.il).
2   Approx. 700 hectares (4.5 dunams = 0.4 hectare). Unlike the rest of mandatory Palestine, no formal registration process of Negev lands was undertaken during the mandate period.
3   This is a rough estimate. Much lower figures (240,000 dunams) are given by the Arab Association for Human Rights.
4   These figures do not include those houses demolished by the owners themselves after having been served with an administrative order to do so.
5   See also *Washington Post Foreign Service*, 20 March 2002. Daniel Williams: "Another Arab population group grows angry at Israel". www.washingtonpost.com.
6   The Transfer Party (*Moledet* or "homeland" in Hebrew) embraces the idea of population transfer as an integral part of a comprehensive plan to achieve real peace between the Jews and the Arabs living in the land of Israel.
7   The Regional Council of the Bedouin Palestinian Unrecognized Villages in the Negev was established in 1997 as a community movement (grass roots representation) for Palestinian Bedouin equality in the Negev.

The Arab Association for Human Rights: www.arabhra.org.
The Regional Council of Unrecognized Villages in the Negev (RCUV):

www.arabhra.org/rcuv

Bustan L'Shalom, a grass roots human rights organisation. They publish a
network bulletin and have a website: www.bustanlshalom.org

The Legal Center for Arab Minority Rights in Israel: www.adalah.org

The Association of the Forty: www.assoc.40.org

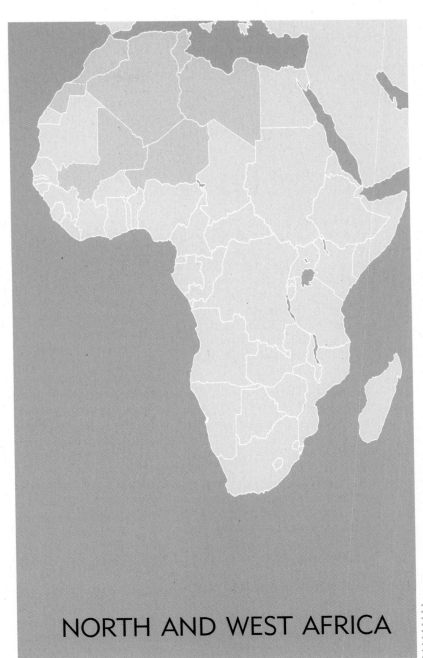

NORTH AND WEST AFRICA

THE AMAZIGH PEOPLE

D uring 2002 and early 2003, the Amazigh cultural movement, which is the movement of indigenous peoples in North Africa, continued its struggle for constitutional recognition of the Amazigh people with all its dimensions (as an identity, language and civiliza-tion). However, the situation of the indigenous Amazigh continued to vary greatly from one country to another.

In **Tunisia, Libya, Egypt** and **Mauritania,** the governments are thus still repressing indigenous peoples and they are, to a large extent, prohibiting the founding of associations defending the Amazigh culture and Amazigh rights.

In **Algeria,** the military regime has, over the past few years, introduced some positive measures such as the establishment of the High Commission for Amazigh and the constitutional recognition of the Amazigh language. Yet the actual policy adopted by this regime violates these stated principles and all international conventions. During 2002, the situation deteriorated due to the refusal of the Algerian regime to initiate a serious dialogue with the Amazigh Movement. Peaceful demonstrations and strikes were organized but instead of fostering dialogue and listening to the demands of the protesters, the Algerian regime responded by arresting a great number of activists, about forty of whom are still being detained.

MOROCCO

I n Morocco, some progress towards more democracy was made during 2002. The results of the legislative elections on 27 September were not rigged; the voting age was lowered from 20 to 18 thus opening the path to a wide category of youth; and detainees arrested arbitrarily over the past 40 years are receiving compensation. In December 2002, one former political detainee was appointed Secretary-General of the Consultative Council for Human Rights, the official body for human rights.

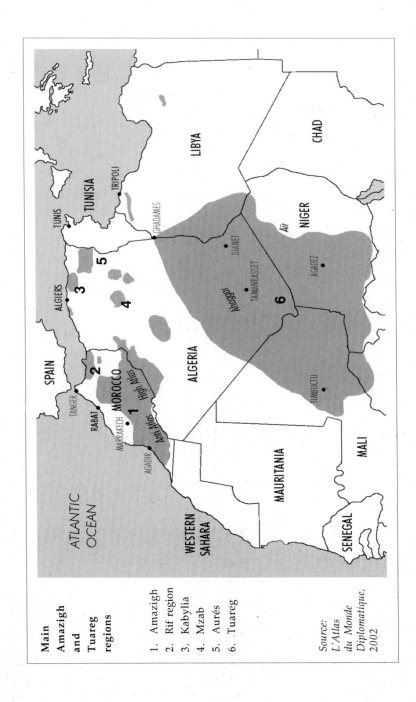

Main
Amazigh
and
Tuareg
regions

1. Amazigh
2. Rif region
3. Kabylia
4. Mzab
5. Aurés
6. Tuareg

Source:
L'Atlas
du Monde
Diplomatique,
2002

Struggle for recognition and rights

After the royal and collective recognition of the Amazigh identity in all of its dimensions in the address delivered by His Majesty King Mohammed VI in Agadir in October 2001, and the promulgation of the Royal Decree ordering the foundation of the *Royal Institute for Amazigh Culture* (see *The Indigenous World 2001-2002*), the first meeting of the administrative council of this Institute was held at the end of July 2002. This administrative council comprises 32 members, seven of whom are government representatives (ministries and universities) and the rest activists belonging to the Amazigh Movement or individuals supporting this movement. For the first time, this has paved the way to dialogue at a higher level. The decisions of the Royal Institute will be taken by a 2/3 majority and its recommendations will be submitted to the King for ratification, as the King is the supreme constitutional body in Morocco.

Another positive element is that the civil registry system has been changed to allow the registration of Amazigh names, something that had been prohibited for the last decade. However, in many regions the civil registry offices are still following the departmental note from the former Minister of the Interior, and refusing to register Amazigh names, which are considered as the harbingers of a rise in the Amazigh Movement in North Africa.

Despite the change in the official discourse coming from the official bodies in Morocco, a policy of integration and assimilation still prevails, notably in the fields of education, mass media and administration whereby the Amazigh language and its three dialects remain excluded, although they are spoken by a majority of Moroccans.

Arrests in Imilchil

On March 6-7, 2003, the population of Imilchil protested against the unfulfilled promises of the Moroccan government to build roads and schools and provide water, electricity and medical care to the tribes of Aït Haddou. In fact, instead of initiating dialogue and fulfilling its promises, the entire region was surrounded by all kinds of forces and twenty-one protesters were arrested, four of whom were brought before the court in Errachidia. Many Amazigh mountainous regions suffer from the same conditions as Imilchil, lacking necessary infrastructure and suffering from bad living conditions. Illiteracy rates for women are over 90%. Among the protesters were many jobless graduates belonging to Aït Haddou tribes. Most of the youth and men fled in order to escape arrest, leaving the women and children at home. The authorities did not initiate any dialogue with these protesters.

Dialogue with the Minister for Human Rights

As government institutions did not comply with the demands of the Amazigh cultural associations, the Tamaynout Association sent a note to the Prime Minister, the Minister of Justice, the Minister of the Interior and the Minister of Communications on December 31 2002. In this note, it called for the abolition of all forms of discrimination against the Amazigh people prior to Morocco's presentation of its reports on the International Convention on the Elimination of all Forms of Racial Discrimination (CERD) and the Convention of the Rights of the Child (CRC) in March 2003.

For the first time, three representatives of the Tamaynout Association held talks with the Minister for Human Rights and discussed the need to abolish all forms of discrimination against the Amazigh people in Morocco. These discussions were fruitful as the Minister for Human Rights undertook to implement urgent measures based on the aforesaid note and on principles of human rights.

Morocco and Tunisia before the CERD Committee

Morocco and Tunisia are to present their periodic reports on the implementation of the International Convention on the Elimination of all Forms of Racial Discrimination (CERD) to the CERD committee. In this connection, several Amazigh associations, together with the International Federation of Human Rights, presented unofficial reports and provided important information to experts investigating the rights of indigenous peoples in Africa.

In this context, the Moroccan and Tunisian governments had to answer a series of questions concerning discrimination against the Amazigh people. This is the first time that countries from North Africa are due to appear before the CERD since publication of the Durban Declaration (from the UN World Conference Against Racism, Racial Discrimination, Xenophobia and Related Intolerance), which abolishes racial discrimination.

From the official reports of the two governments and from the unofficial reports of the non-governmental organisations, it can be said that, in spite of adherence to the CERD Convention, the actual policy that had been adopted and implemented right up to the end of 2002 was a policy of integration and assimilation.

Obviously, the report presented by Morocco referred to recent positive events, including the foundation of the Royal Institute for Amazigh Culture and the decision of His Majesty King Mohammed VI to rehabilitate and use the original Amazigh characters known as *Tifinagh* in schools and in all documentary systems. However, the policy of discrimination is apparent in the report, through the *Pact on Education and Teaching,* which establishes discrimination against the Amazigh language when it states in paragraph 110 that the Amazigh language can only be used to improve the learning of classical Arabic.

The struggle of the women's movement

The struggle of the women's movement for equal rights between men and women in Morocco resulted in the creation of a committee charged with revising the Civil Status Law. In this connection, protest marches were organized on March 8, 2002 and 2003. However, intense disagreements among the members of this committee led to the appointment of a former conservative and right-wing minister as president of the committee. Apparently, the work of this committee will not now move forward due to the many reservations expressed by Morocco following its ratification of the Convention Against All Forms of Discrimination Against Women. The women's movement is likely to demand the withdrawal of these reservations.

Amazigh New Year

For many years, Amazigh New Year was celebrated almost secretly within families. Today, and thanks to the Amazigh Movement, it has increasingly become a collective event in all regions of North Africa. Thus, 13 January 2002, which corresponds to the beginning of the year 2952, and 13 January 2003, which corresponds to the beginning of the year 2953 according to the Amazigh calendar, were celebrated collectively in North Africa, particularly in Morocco and Algeria, and among Amazigh immigrants in exile all over the world, especially in Europe, Canada and the United States of America.

In order to enable all categories of society to take part in these celebrations, the Amazigh cultural movement has called for Amazigh New Year to be officially celebrated as a National Day in order to revive all forms of ancient Amazigh celebrations in North Africa.

International prize awarded by Holland

During 2002, Amazigh culture was honoured by Prince Claus of Holland, who awarded the highly acclaimed international *Prize for Culture and Development* to the Amazigh researcher and Dean of the Royal Institute for Amazigh Culture, Mr. Mohamed CHAFIK. This event was considered by many international observers as the start of a process of recognition of the Amazigh language.

In addition to its symbolic importance, this prize has a communicative dimension. Amazigh immigrants form one of the major minority groups in Holland and they have founded Amazigh cultural associations to fight for recognition of the Amazigh language. They have advocated that Amazigh should be taught in Dutch schools for Amazigh immigrants, who participate actively in the development of the Dutch economy.

Conclusion

The past year witnessed a number of positive measures in Morocco as well as a number of violations of human and indigenous rights. It also witnessed a clear rise in the struggle of the Amazigh movement, particularly in Algeria. with an escalation of repression. The common denominator in North Africa continues to be integration and assimilation policies in the fields of education, mass media and administration. Moreover, the provisions of international conventions related to basic freedoms and human rights have not thus far been put into effect, and the action plan annexed to the Durban Declaration aimed at abolishing racial discrimination fell on deaf ears in North Africa as a whole. ❑

THE TUAREG PEOPLE

Positive indicators

Efforts to accommodate former Tuareg rebels and returning refugees in both Niger and Mali, following the Tuareg revolts in both
countries in the 1990s (see *The Indigenous World 2001-2002*), have continued to make good progress. The Aïr (est. pop. 200,000) in particular, the
redoubt of the Tuareg rebellion led by Mano Dayak, can now be regarded
as having achieved a high level of regional autonomy, with former rebels
now seemingly well integrated into the local security and government
services. The region, especially in the wake of the excellent late summer
(2002) rains, has a renewed air of prosperity. Agricultural production,
especially in the traditional gardening regions of Timia, Iferouane, Oued
Bargot, Tabelot, Abardokh, In Tedeini, etc., is of an increasingly high
quality, as too is the state of livestock (goats, sheep, camels and a few
cattle). The winter (2002-2003) salt caravans to Bilma are provisionally
assessed as numbering as many as 10,000 camels. The region's agro-
pastoral base should be made more secure through the series of barrages
currently being constructed with the assistance of international aid.
Agadez, the regional capital, is currently being ably served by a highly
regarded Mayor, a woman who originates from the Tuareg Tegehe-n-Efis
'tribe' of the Ahaggar region of southern Algeria.

Tuareg regions threatened by insecurity

In spite of such positive indicators, two potentially problematic issues
remain. The first is the need to undertake a full evaluation of the
refugee resettlement programme, especially the extent to which initial
grievances and the fundamental causes of the revolts have been resolved and are perceived to have been resolved. Moreover, and quite
apart from local needs, the UNHCR needs to know the shortcomings
of and longer term problems emanating from its returnee assistance
programme. The second and most serious issue, however, is the fact
that any such 'follow-up' assessment, along with the future redevel-
opment of both northern Mali and northern Niger, is effectively pre-
cluded by the prevailing insecurity throughout the region.

A 'zone of insecurity' now stretches across almost forty degrees of
longitude from the Sudan, through southern Libya and Chad, northern Niger and northern Mali, southern Algeria and southern Mauri-

tania to the Senegal valley area. Until recently, insecurity in this zone was associated with the Toubou/Teda rebellions in Chad and north-eastern Niger and the Tuareg revolts in Niger and Mali. With the exception of Chad, this is no longer the case. As was described in last year's issue, various forms of "banditry" have become increasingly prevalent in these regions over the last 4-5 years.

The causes of this "banditry" are multiple and complex and partly self-perpetuating to the extent that, as the state and international organisations withdraw from these areas in the face of such insecurity so these regions become increasingly more attractive to outlaw elements. Much of this insecurity is attributed to trans-Saharan smuggling, of which there is a long history, particularly between the richer northern countries of Algeria and Libya and the poorer countries of the Sahel. However, in the space that opened up in the wake of the Tuareg revolts in Niger and Mali, new outlaw elements have taken root in these regions.

Warlords, bandits and smugglers

The most notorious of these outlaws is probably Mokhtar ben Mokhtar, whose establishment in the region and main activities were described in last year's issue. Reports of his death or capture are perennial. The latest report of his arrest at Adrar in southern Algeria in March 2003 was denounced by Mohammed Jai, chief of police in El Golea (Algeria), as unfounded and simply a rumour. "Banditry" is an oversimplification of what is becoming an increasingly complex situation. In addition to the "war-lord" syndrome established in the western end of this region by Mokhtar ben Mokhtar, there are a range of other "illegal" activities that all add to the region's insecurity. These include an unspecified number of "copycat" elements, some of whom are clearly nothing more than simple criminals, often ishumar or former rebels, who have taken to raiding trans-Saharan traffic – usually tourists. A small number of these people, such as Aboubacar Alambo (various spellings), a former Tuareg rebel who was incorporated into the Niger army before undertaking a series of "hijacks" in 2002, including an attack on local security forces in Aïr in July 2002 in which three policemen were killed, are well known to the authorities. According to the authorities, Alambo and his ten accomplices have been captured. According to local people, they are still at large. A number of attacks, usually denied by the authorities, such as the hijack of four vehicles carrying French tourists near Chirfa (Djado region of north-east Niger) in November 2002, in which the women were raped, the men beaten up and the vehicles stolen, may have been the work of Alambo or one of a number of such "bandits" operating in this extensive region. It is significant that Alambo's killing of the three policemen immediately sparked rumours of the commencement of a new Tuareg revolt.

More serious for the long-term security and stability of the region is the professional smuggling of cigarettes, arms and stolen vehicles (mostly 4WDs), which now seems to be in the hands of a few war-lords such as Mokhtar ben Mokhtar and a complex network of agents and alliances that spreads over much of the Sahara. While one of the key focal points in the vehicle-arms trade is southern Mauritania and the Senegal valley area, the cigarette trade runs more or less south-north, from the Benin region into Mali and Niger and then across Algeria to the large North African markets and on into Europe. While the major international cigarette companies must be held ultimately responsible for the huge scale of this contraband trade, there is now clear evidence to suggest that government elements in Niger, Mali and Algeria are complicit in it.

"Terrorist" rumours

Many of these "bandits" are believed to have links with armed Islamic "terrorist" groups in northern Algeria. Mokhtar ben Mokhtar, for example, is believed to have been associated for some time with Hassan Hattab, who broke recently from the Armed Islamic Group (GIA) to form the Salafist Group for Call and Combat (*Groupe salafiste pour la prédication et le combat* - GSPC). Among its many attacks on the Algerian state, the GSPC was held responsible for the ambush of a military convoy at Teniet El-Abed, in the Aures mountains south of Batna on January 4, 2003, in which 43 soldiers were killed and 19 wounded. According to official Algiers sources, the GSPC is affiliated to Al-Qaeda. The alleged "infiltration" of many of the mosques in northern Mali since September 1,1 2001 by Islamic fundamentalists of Pakistani origin is thought by many local people to give further credence to an Al-Qaeda presence in the region. This has given rise to much local hearsay. For instance, it was rumoured in December 2002 that the American Ambassador had recently been in Timbuktu and had got lost for ten days in the desert with twenty men and two helicopters while allegedly setting up a military base to counter Al-Qaeda activities! Although rumours such as this will probably never be verified, their mere existence is an indication of the level of insecurity now perceived to extend over much of the Tuareg's northern territories. Indeed, it is now regarded as extremely dangerous to travel anywhere in the vast sector from southeast Mauritania, through northern Mali above a line drawn roughly from north of Timbuktu to Kidal and down to Manaka and including most of the Azaouagh valley in both Mali and Niger. In 2002, local authorities in Gao put the chances of driving from there to the Algerian frontier at either Timaouine or Tin Zaouatene without being hijacked by "bandits" at 50-50. In Niger, vehicles have been attacked on an intermittent basis right across the north of the country from Tamesna in the north-west, through northern Aïr and the Tenere to the Djado-Mangeni region in the north-east. Until the state can reassert itself in these vast "border" regions, it is unlikely that their scant populations will see the benefits of any major development initiatives.

The situation in Algeria

While the problems for Tuareg south of the Algerian frontier are currently more closely associated with the state's inability to establish it presence in the face of the insecurity described above, the main problem for Algerian Tuareg in 2002 came from what they perceived as the state's attempt to "sabotage" the political stability and economic development of the south. The Tuareg of Algeria (est. pop. 30,000) are small in number compared with those in Niger, Mali and Burkina Faso. However, their territory extends over an area the size of France, and in a country whose economy and infrastructure are substantially more developed than its southern neighbours. Algerian Tuareg territory falls within the two administrative regions (wilaya) of Tamanrasset (est. pop. 220,000) and Illizi (est. pop. 36,000). Public demonstrations against the government's representative (wali) in Illizi in the summer of 2001 led to his replacement. By 2002, the Tuareg in the Tamanrasset wilaya had experienced three years of what they perceived as ineffective and incompetent government by the wali. Behind the accusation of "sabotage" that they levelled at the government in a letter to the Prime Minister and relevant Ministers in November 2002 was the belief that the state had not only done nothing during these three years to help the Tuareg in developing what they regard as "their industry", namely tourism, but had been actively impeding its development.

Sabotaging the tourist industry?

The bizarre events that led Tuareg to accuse the government of sabotage came to a head in October 2002. For the three preceding tourist seasons, following the effective re-opening of Algeria's south to tourism in 1999-2000, local Tuareg tourist agencies felt, quite correctly, that the government – especially through the personage of the wali - had been impeding rather than assisting their attempts to re-establish "their industry". Indeed, he had been putting one administrative obstacle after another in their way. In 2002, good summer rains had continued intermittently into the early autumn with massive rains over much of the central Sahara in early October. These rains cut the main north-south road at Arak, leading to two strange incidents. The first involved a group of 4 Swiss tourists, accompanied by 17 Algerians who, while waiting for the road to become passable at Arak, were hijacked and taken hostage by a group claiming to be Islamic fundamentalists. In spite of local rumours, no official communiqué was issued by any government office to any of the responsible parties, notably local (predominantly Tuareg) travel agencies who learnt about the hijacking through Internet communications from Switzerland. The hostages were eventually released or escaped with the hijackers being tracked by the gendarmerie to Tin Gherghour, more than half way to Mali, where they were apprehended. However, according to local hearsay, the gendarmerie received orders to release their captives. No arrests were made. The international media reported the incident as a "put up job" by the Algerian authorities!

The second incident was the wali's imposition of further fuel rationing on local people, notably Tuareg tourist agencies, on the highly questionable pretext that fuel supplies from the north were restricted by flood damage to the road. For several weeks, the two fuel stations of Tamanrasset were surrounded by angry (mostly local) drivers who were forced to wait days for fuel while losing precious business and in the knowledge that the town held massive strategic reserves and that other supply trucks were reaching Tamanrasset.

At the same time, the authorities, without any explanation, refused visa applications to Niger citizens wishing to enter the region from the south and effectively stemmed the inflow of Europeans from the south by imposing lengthy delays on the issuance of tourist visas.

Improving Tuareg-government relations

It will probably never be known why elements in the Algerian government tried to create the impression of an Islamic fundamentalist attack on foreign tourists at the same time as restricting local fuel supplies and effectively closing the southern frontier. Those Tuareg who were aware of these strange actions believed that it was an attempt by "hard-core" elements within the government to provoke them into reacting in order to justify an even greater military presence in the south of the country. Others saw the moves as an expression of resentment against the Tuareg on the part of certain government elements in the north of the country for their being the only people in the country in a position to develop tourism successfully. The reaction of the Tuareg was one of "no reaction"! Believing that elements within the government were wanting them to "revolt", they did just the opposite. Instead, on 1 November 2002, the Association of Travel and Tourist Agencies of Tamanrasset (*Association des Agences de Voyages et de Tourisme de la Wilaya de Tamanrasset*) sent a four-page letter to the Prime Minister, with copies to the Ministers of the Interior, Tourism, Transport and Energy, listing examples of how the government had been damaging local tourism interests, accusing the government of sabotage and reminding it that the consequence of bad government in the bordering countries of Niger and Mali had been rebellion. The Prime Minister's office responded by sending a senior director of Sonatrach (the national oil company) to Tamanrasset to inform the wali that Sonatrach was a commercial company and none of the wali's business. Fuel restrictions were lifted immediately.

Four months later (March 2003), the wali of Illizi organised a Programme of Conferences on Tourism in the Tassili and Ahaggar (*Programme de Journées d'études sur le tourisme dans Le Tassili et L'Ahaggar*) in Djanet. This 3-day event is likely to become a milestone in both the immediate development of southern Algeria and Tuareg-government relations. The outcome of the Programme was extraordinary in that there was unanimous agreement from all delegates on measures to protect both the future of tourism, the environment and the region's patrimony – three issues of major concern to the Tuareg. The political significance of the event was threefold:

1. The only representatives of the Tamanrasset wilaya to accept the invitation were two Tuareg: the President of the National Union of the Associations of Travel and Tourist Agencies (*Union Nationale des Associations des Agences de Tourisme et de Voyages*) and a member of the Association of Travel and Tourist Agencies of Tamanrasset. Government representation in the personages of the wali, Director of the Hoggar (Ahaggar) National Park and the Director of Tourism, was noticeable by its absence. This abdication

of responsibility on the part of the Tamanrasset wali (following the accusations of "sabotage") is such that a shake-up in government representation in Tamanrasset is now seen as inevitable.

2. The performance of the newly appointed wali at Illizi demonstrated to the Tuareg that the government was prepared to appoint administrators of the highest calibre to the region, an act that will merely fuel the demand for the replacement of the Tamanrasset wali.

3. The impressive contribution of the Ministry of Culture and Communication (compared with the noticeable absence of any contribution from the Minister of Tourism) has led local Tuareg to realise that they do have a "champion" in central government in the personage of the Minister, Madame Khalida Toumi.[1]

In short, the Programme went a long way to improve Tuareg-government relations in the wake of the bizarre events of the previous autumn. Nevertheless, one disturbing situation currently facing the Tuareg of Algeria, along with people in almost all other parts of the Sahara, is that several groups of Europeans, mostly Germans, are looting huge quantities of archaeological antiquities from the Sahara for commercial purposes. Tuareg, who regard these artefacts as part of their patrimony, have submitted full details of these criminal organisations to Madame Khalida Toumi and now await their arrest.

More camels to the Sahara

A final comment worth noting is that the nomadic community throughout the Sahara now appears to be benefiting substantially from the gift of money made by the Saudi Arabian government to strengthen camel stocks in the Sahara. Amongst the Algerian Tuareg, for example, after overcoming the many administrative and veterinary difficulties, the owners of each female camel that has produced offspring has received a cash payment of Dinars 20,000 (approx. £200). One outcome of this exercise is that the head count of camels in Ahaggar, which was assumed to be around 12,000, is now put at 90,000! ❏

Note

1 Many local Tuareg now speak jokingly but respectfully of Mme Toumi as "the only man in the government."

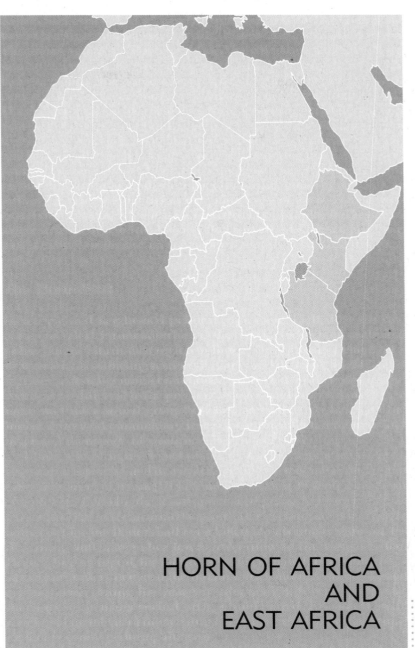

HORN OF AFRICA
AND
EAST AFRICA

ETHIOPIA

The main indigenous peoples in Ethiopia, as in most countries in the Horn of Africa, are pastoralists who live by rearing livestock. The pastoralist population is estimated to be 12% of the country's population, roughly five million, living in the harshest environment, namely in arid and semi-arid climatic zones. Made up of 29 different ethnic groups, Ethiopian pastoralists have livelihood systems that correspond to the specific environment and climate in which they live. The majority are Somali, Afar, Borena and Kereyu (Oromo), with Nuer and other smaller Omotic-speaking groups in the south. Other indigenous peoples include a very small hunter-gatherer group in southwest Ethiopia. Some of the pastoralist communities, such as the Somali, Afar, Borena and Nuer find themselves in different countries, whose borders were artificially demarcated by European colonization.

The regions inhabited by pastoralists are rich in natural resources, with the largest livestock population in Africa and other natural resources such as surface and ground waters, minerals, fisheries and energy such as gas and geo-thermal energy. Wide rivers cross these regions, providing sufficient water and pasture. These regions are also endowed with wildlife and the two largest national parks, Awash and Omo, are located in pastoralist areas.

Marginalization

Despite the rich natural resources with which they are endowed, Ethiopian pastoralists are subjected to the worst forms of political, economic and social marginalization and subjugation. For more than a century now, since a centralized autocracy was established in Ethiopia, pastoralist communities have been subjected to various forms of marginalization characterized by social, ethnic, religious, political and economic inequality. One aspect of marginalization reinforces the other. Cultural stereotypes serve to advance the irrational policy of political marginalization while the political in turn "rationalizes" the economic marginalization.

Pastoralists have been considered as uncultured, uncivilized and barbaric. In fact, the word *zelan* in Ethiopia's official language Amharic - literally meaning uncultured and unruly - has been used to describe pastoralists. Their culture and way of life has been looked

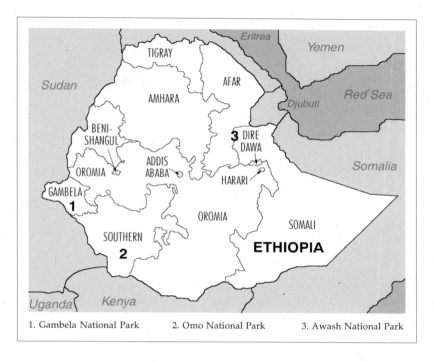

1. Gambela National Park   2. Omo National Park   3. Awash National Park

down upon for such a long time that such hegemonic perceptions have almost appeared to be the "norm". These stereotypes have given way to two forms of inequality. The first is that they are used to rationalize the confiscation of grazing areas and eviction of pastoralists from their ancestral land. This land has in a number of places been taken over by private and absentee landlords as well as 'modern' commercial farm "developers". The second form is that they have informed the macro-economic policy very negatively in the sense that they have contributed to the prevailing notion that "development" in pastoralist regions has to start with the settlement or sedentarization of pastoralists. As such, pastoralist communities have been completely marginalized from the official macro-economic policies of the various governments in Ethiopia. In fact, there has never been a pastoralist development strategy or policy as such. The sad thing is that this is still the case.

On top of all this, the prevalence of conflicts in pastoralist regions has added more fuel to their marginalization. The artificial division of pastoralist communities into a number of countries/states such as the Somali, who find themselves in Somalia, Djibouti, Ethiopia and Kenya; the Afar who are found in Eritrea, Djibouti and Ethiopia or the

Nuer in Ethiopia and Sudan, has been utilized by various ethnic political under-currents fanned mainly by urban elements. As such, political movements in the name of nationalism have come and gone in these regions. In the armed conflicts that have ensued, and the government's backlash, civilian pastoralists have been greatly affected as they have been accused of harbouring guerrilla fighters. The involvement of neighbouring states has also complicated conflicts, as such interventions generally prolong the lives of movements.

This state of affairs has created an atmosphere of mutual suspicion between pastoralist communities and the government. Outright political repression has been the norm in pastoralist regions for many decades. Even now, when the new Constitution grants full political freedom for "citizens", an atmosphere of political intimidation still prevails. Rulers in pastoralist regions rule arbitrarily, with no tolerance of dissenting views. They rule with no accountability whatsoever and with an iron fist against civic groups. As a consequence, tyranny, corruption, embezzlement, violation of the rule of law, violence against women and destruction of the environment are rampant and unchecked.

The issue of land

Eviction of pastoralists from their ancestral land is a huge problem that has besieged their communities for a long time. Pastoralist land is passed on to commercial farmers as "developers" and large tracts are also turned into wildlife reserves and game parks. This in itself has caused conflicts between the communities and the government. The case of the Awash National Park, as well as the commercial farms along the Awash River, are typical examples of this systematic eviction of pastoralists from their own land. Other areas, such as the Kereyu and Borana in the Oromia region and other places in the South can also be mentioned.

Land eviction - on top of the sheer neglect of pastoralist development policies and strategies - has greatly exacerbated the poverty of pastoralists. It has deprived them of the development of alternative or additional means of livelihood systems. Because the communities are neglected, they do not even have a mechanism to facilitate the sale of their animals on the domestic market. As a result, pastoralist communities constitute the poorest of the poor.

As if to add insult to injury, natural disasters such as droughts and floods cause immense destruction in terms of lives and property. The current drought, (i.e. during the period of 2001-2003) has hit the pastoralist regions very hard and has been the cause of a massive catastrophe for the communities. It is estimated that the Afar pastoralists have lost more than 90% of their cattle, not to mention the unknown figure as far as human casualties go. The year 2002-2003 marked a dark year for Ethiopian pastoralists as famine broke out on top of devastating poverty. Pastoralist communities heavily affected by the famine situation are the Afar, Somali, Borana and those in the southern region.

The Pastoralist Forum Ethiopia

It was against this backdrop that the need for policy advocacy on pastoralist development became a crucial issue for all those involved in pastoralist development. Twenty NGOs got together in 1998 and formed a loose network called the Pastoralist Forum Ethiopia (PFE). Later on, as the PFE saw the urgency of policy advocacy, it started to organize annual conferences on pastoralist development issues. The first conference was held in 2000 and looked at the previous decades of "development" initiatives in pastoralist regions undertaken mainly by three post-war governments. The conference in 2001 was devoted to the issue of Poverty Reduction Strategy Plans (PRSP). The Ethiopian government came up with an interim PRSP, which contained literally nothing on pastoralist communities, although the pastoralists of Ethiopia are indeed the poorest of the poor. The 2001 national conference was so successful that the government that introduced a new macro-economic policy in the autumn of the same year gave pastoralist development a high priority. The PFE succeeded in developing a chapter on a poverty reduction strategy for pastoralist regions and suggested it to the government for inclusion in its final PRSP document to be submitted to the World Bank. A sub-chapter on pastoralism was indeed included although the substance of the government's strategy on pastoralism still fell short of the PFE's expectations.

With the outbreak of the current famine, the PFE organized a round table last December on the relationship between pastoralist life systems, drought and famine. The round table brought development practitioners and government officials face to face with representatives of the various pastoralist communities in the country. It was emphasised that drought, though undesirable, could not cause famine by itself, as pastoralist communities living in environmentally harsh areas have been able to cope for centuries using their own indigenous knowledge and environmental management systems. However, along with the decline of pastoralist power, the prevalence of their indigenous knowledge system has also gone. This is especially so for the environmental management systems that were destroyed or undermined by modernity passing as development. At the end of the day, pastoralist communities were left with neither their knowledge system nor any "development", for this never materialised.

Prompted by these developments as well as the amount of work needed to be delivered on pastoralist issues, the PFE decided to continue to develop by registering as a national network. Its application is still being processed. In the meanwhile, the forum is active in regional as well as continental networking, representing the pastoralist communities of Ethiopia. Its representative also takes part in the annual session of the UN Working Group on Indigenous Populations in Geneva.

The Pastoralist Day

In 1998, a pastoralist NGO called Pastoralist Concern Association of Ethiopia (PCAE) introduced the idea of marking a pastoralist day. The man behind this was Abdi Abdulahi, the director of PCAE, and it was quickly endorsed by the pastoralists in an area called Filtu, Somali region. Pastoralist Day then began to be celebrated every year from 1999 on. In 2002, the PCAE passed the responsibility of organizing the event over to the PFE. By 2002, the Federal Government of Ethiopia had already adopted a new policy on pastoralist development. This gave way to cooperation between the PFE and regional governments of areas where pastoralists predominate. The 4th Pastoralist Day was therefore organized by the PFE and hosted by the Afar regional government, where the celebrations took place. In 2003, the PFE co-organized the event with the regional government of the Southern Nations and Peoples. Pastoralist Day serves as an important advocacy event, whereby the government's policy is questioned, thus generating discussion. In 2004, Pastoralist Day will be celebrated in the Oromia region as a national day and it will also be marked in the other pastoralist regions.

Pastoralist Commissions

A major incident in 2002 of benefit to pastoralists was the establishment of the Pastoralist Standing Commission within the Ethiopian

Federal Parliament. Led by a prominent head of a pastoralist NGO and a founding member of the PFE, this commission is expected to contribute greatly towards advancing the cause of pastoralists at the level of policy formulation and legislation.

With the Federal Government's changed policy on pastoralism, some regional governments have gone ahead and formed pastoralist commissions in their respective regions. The Oromia, Afar and Southern Peoples' regional governments have all formed pastoralist commissions that will specifically work towards pastoralist development. The PFE is actively cooperating with these regional governments. However, misguided perceptions about pastoralism still linger on within government circles. The policy of sedentarization, for instance, is still being advanced. The PFE, for its part, has suggested the formation of consultative policy fora and policy councils among stakeholders in pastoralist development, in order to come up with policy recommendations both for the federal as well as regional governments on pastoralist development. The pastoralist commissions of the regional governments mentioned above are currently studying the proposal.

Conclusion

The years since 2001 have marked a shift in the Federal Government of Ethiopia's policy in terms of recognizing the pastoralist communities and pastoralist development. Verbal allegiance and devotion to pastoralist development is now given prominence. However, a major problem, which is a problem of perception, still prevails. The government has not yet recognized pastoralism as a viable traditional way of life in the same way as it recognizes farming. This is fundamental to pastoralist development as this requires recognition of the pastoralists' right to development, as universally recognized in, for example, Agenda 21. The government still clings on to the idea of settlement and sedentarization as the solution to pastoralist problems. However, pastoralists and experts of pastoralist development emphasize that settlement policies will only exacerbate pastoralist poverty. Nevertheless, the new policy adopted by the government has at least opened the door to cooperation with NGOs. Pastoralists still have a long way to go but at least the first step has been taken. ❑

KENYA

2002 was an important year in the history of Kenya for two reasons. Firstly, it was an election year, which also signaled the end of an era for the political party that had been in power since the country gained independence in 1962. Secondly, it also saw the retirement of a president that had ruled the country for twenty-four years. These two factors, as well as the constitutional review process, which has been in progress for several years, have in various ways presented opportunities as well as challenges for indigenous peoples.

The general elections

The fact that the incumbent president chose and vigorously campaigned for his preferred presidential candidate created a great deal of animosity toward the ruling KANU party and the preferred candidate, and ultimately sealed the fate of both. It also influenced the realignments of parties, the merger and eventual coalition of major opposition parties and the formation of the National Alliance Rainbow Coalition (NARC), which eventually delivered defeat to KANU.

Pastoralists and hunter-gatherers were not immune to all this political activity. North Eastern Province ended up voting in their majority for KANU, largely through fear of the ensuing repression should it win the elections, which it always seemed to do. In other areas, the defections of candidates also influenced the voting patterns, with people voting for or against candidates rather than parties and vice versa. This tended to split pastoralist districts among political parties. One factor remained constant, however, and that was the fact that, although parties prepared quite comprehensive manifestos as campaign tools, few of their candidates seemed to use them. Instead, individuals simply sold themselves or their party sold them. This weakness seems to be most common in the districts occupied by indigenous pastoralists and hunter-gatherers.

The constitutional review process

The general elections falling as they did at the same time as the constitutional review process affected both processes in different ways. The constitutional review process struggled on with great difficulty

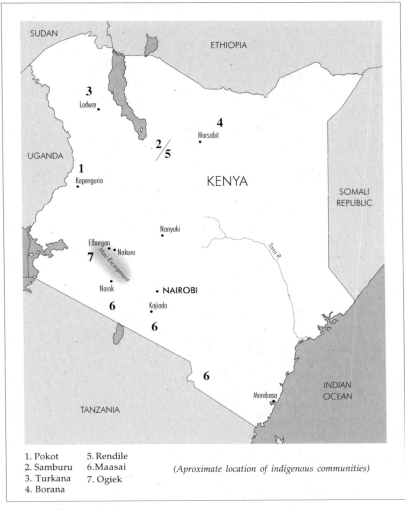

1. Pokot	5. Rendile
2. Samburu	6.Maasai
3. Turkana	7. Ogiek
4. Borana	

(Aproximate location of indigenous communities)

until the end of the year 2002. The main activity of the commission was to conduct and facilitate civic education so as to stimulate public discussion and awareness of constitutional issues. Following this, the Commission collected and collated views from the public on what they wished to be reflected in a future Constitution. Thereafter, a Bill was drafted, which embodied the proposed changes, and which was to be discussed at the National Constitutional Conference, after which it would be presented to the National Assembly.

The Bill was published by September 2002 but the National Constitutional Conference was not held because Parliament and the local authorities (who comprise the bulk of the delegates to the constitutional conference) had already been dissolved due to the upcoming elections. The election campaign period then ensued and the whole constitutional review process was put on hold, to be re-started after the new Parliament was in place.

Despite its deferment, all political parties made promises to the effect that they were committed to the constitutional review and even pledged a timetable for its revival and completion. One hundred days was the minimum pledge.

During the presentation of views to the Commission, indigenous communities were all very active to ensure that their views were heard and the process stimulated a high level of mobilisation. Many memoranda were prepared and presented by indigenous communities and organizations highlighting the grievances that were common to all of them.

Top of the list were the injustices relating to land and resources, which they had hoped the new constitution would address and offer safeguards against. Many also emphasized the demands for a federal system of governance, which was perceived by most pastoralists as a means to self-determination. This was reflected in many memoranda submitted to the Commission. The Maa Pastoralist Council presented the views of the Maa-speaking communities from six districts (Kajiado, Narok, Transmara, Laikipia, Samburu and Baringo). The Pokot did the same through their Centre for Peace Traditions (TOMWO) and the Ogiek through the Ogiek People's National Assembly, and so forth.

The Maa Pastoralist Council (MPC), including many of its member organizations, worked hard to prepare its people to present their views to the Commission. As a result, people arrived in large numbers way before the centres - where the presentations of views were going to take place – had opened and presented their views and proposals on how they wished the grievances addressed. They had, however, two complaints: that the coordinator for one of the districts was not indigenous and that Maasai views were not passed on to the commission in one of the constituencies. These two issues will be raised with the Commission in early 2003.

For their part, the Pokot also held several workshops in preparation for presentation of views, which were quite similar to the other pastoralists. They shared the view of multiple citizenship since they, too, have been split between Kenya and Uganda.

Basically, all memoranda presented by indigenous peoples took into consideration issues expressed by women. Among these are issues of equity, particularly in inheritance of family property.

The northern pastoralists, mainly Somali and Borana from four districts (Wajir, Mandera, Garissa and Isiolo) had some demands that were different from their southern counterparts. They criticized the draft constitution of the Kenya Review Commission for leaving out pastoralists and demanded an affirmative action plan to be included in the draft report. They also wanted a future Constitution to allow them to acquire Ethiopian and Somali nationality while retaining their Kenyan citizenship. This is because the Somali community straddles the three nations and their nomadic lifestyle requires that they move between the three countries. Under the current Constitution, a Kenyan loses citizenship when he or she acquires another country's nationality.

The demand for a federal system of governance is not supported by the northern pastoralists. This is because, unlike their southern counterparts, their worry is not that their resources are being alienated by the dominant communities. Being far from dominating influences, they have never faced this threat. Their main concern is the fear of being even further marginalized than they presently are.

The final draft constitution is yet to be finalized through a constitutional conference scheduled to take place in May 2003. The recommendations are to be agreed upon by all stakeholders.

The Ogiek case

The Ogiek have continued their demand for ancestral land at the Mau East Forest and the courts have similarly continued to deny them this right. As it is, the Trust Land Act Cap 288, Forest Act Cap 285, and Government Lands Act Cap 280, while safeguarding the forests and the resources, do not address the reality that the Ogiek are a forest-dwelling community. Besides this, the Kenyan courts are too rigid to open up to debate the possibility that indigenous land rights issues may be a part of Kenyan law. Apart from being a specialized field, which is not readily understood even by some judges, there is a discernable unwillingness on the part of the authorities in Kenya to uphold the rights of the Ogiek to their ancestral land. This unwillingness, including the fear that the government of the day may not approve recognition of ancestral rights, has unfortunately permeated court judgments. In other words, there seems to be an unwritten rule that the issue of ancestral rights is too serious for any administration to accept. If a case touching on ancestral rights is allowed to go through, it would set a serious precedent for all those whose ancestral rights have been violated. There are potentially many cases of this nature in Kenya. For example, in April 2002, the High Court sitting in Nakuru denied the Endoroi their rights to their land, including benefits from the Lake Bogoria National Reserve. The court ruled that, "the law does not allow individuals to benefit from such a resource simply because they happen to be born close to the resource". This means that there is a fear that the present government may not approve recognition of ancestral rights because the law does not provide for communal sharing of rights and that, if they recognize them for one community, all the other communities, and not only the indigenous people, will demand their ancestral rights.

The quest by the Ogiek of Tinet for recognition of their rights met a similar fate in the year 2000 when their case was thrown out by two judges. They ruled that, "there is no reason why the Ogiek should be the only favoured community to own and exploit natural resources, a privilege not enjoyed or extended to other communities."

As it is, the government is unable to come up with any policies to save indigenous peoples' land from environmental degradation and alienation by third parties.

Although indigenous rights have been recognized under the UN Draft Declaration on the Rights of Indigenous People, the issue of indigenous rights is still a contentious one in Kenya, as in most of Africa. Marginalised communities are denied valuable natural resources within their midst, for the benefit of others. As a result, poverty, illiteracy, unemployment and soaring health problems still plague many indigenous communities in Africa.

Pastoralists sue the British Army

The indigenous Samburu and Laikipia pastoralists, who had sued the British army for damage caused by unexploded ordinances left in their area following military manoeuvres, finally received compensation of over £540 million. The claims for compensation, which the British preferred to settle out of court to avoid embarrassment and possibly a protracted court battle, were to cover bodily harm such as loss of limb or incapacitation. It may be recalled that the British government is a signatory to international human rights agreements, including the European Union's protocols on protection of minorities.

In the Kenyan context, the case has prompted questions on the nature of foreign military agreements, and on whether the safety of Kenyans was covered in the agreements. When the question was raised, the Attorney General indicated that he would make the content of the agreements public "when and if necessary". One would have thought the court case would have been reason enough.

In Kenya, the problem came about because certain areas were designated as military training zones without the informed consent of or appropriate safeguards towards the residents. Both the Kenyan army and the provincial administration, which relocates people out of proposed training grounds or warns them to keep off certain areas during training seasons, failed to do so. They also declined to assist the victims in any way. Instead, they secretly collected and hid away some ordinances. They even barred the experts from accessing key areas.

The administration and the police have also declined to give useful information to victims when requested. Information on issues such as training schedules and areas and types of explosives used is usually provided to the administration and the police when being instructed to evict communities from certain zones. The two are also withholding death and injury reports – which are very accurate as regards date, place, time and cause, and date back many years.

While more claims may be pending, the case has so far created an important historical precedent that may have significant implications for the region and the Commonwealth as a whole. The very fact that small indigenous communities in a largely forsaken part of the world even dared to take soldiers of a former colonial power to court and win is shocking to most but quite encouraging to other indigenous communities in similar circumstances. The case is being perceived as a landmark case, and many more such plaintiffs are bound to emerge. Unexploded munitions left in pasture fields have killed many people, particularly pastoralists, and maimed many more. Livestock step on them or children pick them up thinking they are playthings, only to be blown up. The British Army has been training in Kenya for the past 50 years. The training continues to this day, with approximately 3,000 British soldiers coming to Kenya every year. Many other parts of the continent have similar experiences.

It is expected that the case will highlight the need for troops to clean up after their military exercises in order to safeguard the security of all peoples, including indigenous peoples.

It is also hoped that the case will prick the conscience of the Kenyan media dominated by the majority communities who have an anti-pastoralist bias. It may be recalled that, despite pleas by the local community to the local media to gain publicity by having their story printed, the local print and electronic media all turned them down. It was the foreign media that first highlighted the issue. The local media is now freely printing the story, albeit with the usual typical trivializing, exaggerations and pure lies.

Land dispossession

The issue of land dispossession has over the years remained a major problem for hunter/gatherers and pastoralists. Their hope and expectation, but also their fear, is that even the new government, like the previous one, will see itself as having too much at stake to agree to revise land laws and possibly accept responsibility for violations relating to land grabbing all over the country. The new government, like the previous one, still comprises individuals from majority ethnic groups who benefited from gifts of land and other resources during previous administrations. Pastoralists and hunter/gatherers consider it the greatest challenge of all if the new government were to agree to right all wrongs relating to land dispossession since independence and beyond. All their memoranda focused primarily on land and resources.

Gender

The previous government was always perceived as being gender insensitive. But by the end of its tenure, women held a number of important positions in the government. These included the head of the civil service and secretary to the cabinet, director of education, several permanent secretaries, eight judges of the high Court and Court of Appeal, Chief of Protocol and six ambassadors and high commissioners. However, this has been seen as mere tokenism since the appointments were made at whim by the president and could be revoked in the same manner (except in cases where security of tenure protected the appointee). Despite this tokenism, the appointments have raised the visibility of women in positions that had hitherto been assumed to be the preserves of men. In the process, this has helped to break prejudices and perceptions that only men can hold positions of responsibility in the public domain. Following this, more women have stood for parliamentary and civic seats, even though only few have been successful.

The constitutional review process also offered the opportunity for women to air their views on the changes they would like to see reflected in the new constitutional order so as to correct the gender imbalance. One important proposal was that one third of parliamentary and civic seats should be reserved for women candidates. If this proposal were to be accepted, it would also positively affect indigenous women. To have their voices felt in the political sphere, indigenous women seem to depend largely on outside intervention but all indigenous women supported gender sensitive proposals in their own submissions.

The year also saw the creation of the Family Court among the Divisions of the High Court. This court is bound to be beneficial to all women, including indigenous women.

Female Genital Mutilation (FGM) has been illegal for a long time now. However, it is still very much practiced, mainly in indigenous peoples' areas – among hunter/gatherers and pastoralists. This means that public pronouncements and use of force has done little to change social practices that are not performed in the public sphere. This is all the more so if the people have little faith that the government is truly concerned with their welfare, rather than simply interfering with their lives. This has been the perception of indigenous peoples toward the government. Were the government to show a different face, the issue of FGM might perhaps be resolved administratively and through legal channels. So far, the hope for young girls lies in the efforts of local indigenous women's groups working together with the parents of young girls and in league with nurses and circumcisers to gradually introduce positive changes that would either replace the practice or do away with it altogether in socially acceptable ways.

Regional events

The East African Community (EAC) celebrated its first anniversary since it was launched a year ago with much pomp but has had few tangible benefits for indigenous peoples. Its overriding aims are to create regional integration, customs union, trade and industry, harmonization of investment, monetary and fiscal policies, etc. The promise to improve the infrastructure in marginalized areas of the region, however, could create better accessibility for indigenous peoples to social amenities that are presently few and far between. A regional workshop on harmonization of livestock policy in the EAC was also held in August 2002 to define the current situation with regard to policy and legislative development for animal health services. This could have the potential of creating awareness on the plight of indigenous pastoralists with regard to livestock markets, livestock drugs and the right to free movement across borders, which is presently a nightmare. ❑

TANZANIA

Tanzania is praised in various international publications for having recorded development in a number of sectors during 2002. Economically, Tanzania is seen as a success story by the Bretton Woods institutions, and it is a recipient of various lending and aid programmes. Its population is currently 36 million and official statistics show that 80% of this population have access to basic health care. Economic growth is estimated at between 5.8% and 6.5% and per capita income is estimated at US$ 220.

However, the indigenous peoples of Tanzania have not benefited from this economic growth and socio-economic development, and their socio-economic conditions seem to be going from bad to worse: the Rural Development Strategy (RDS) developed by the Tanzanian government over the last two years with the purpose of harmonizing different policies adopted since 1995 under the Structural Adjustment Programmes is strongly biased against indigenous peoples' modes of production, whether they are hunter-gatherers or pastoralists, and states that the official policy is to settle pastoralists permanently since movements of people and livestock are destructive to the environment. Indigenous communities are thus not only not benefiting from different national development programmes, they are also losing access to natural resources in their ancestral territories, resources that are critical for their survival, the security of their livelihood and their cultures.

This is the case of the indigenous hunter-gatherer communities of Hadzabe and Ndorobo, as well as the indigenous pastoralist Barbaig and Maasai,[1] who have continued throughout 2002 and into 2003 to experience various challenges and threats, some of which threaten the very sources of their livelihood, culture, identity and well-being.

The situation of hunter-gatherers

The recently introduced guidelines and regulations for wildlife policy and wildlife management areas (WMAs) give priority to commercial hunting and other forms of utilisation of wildlife resources, which have led to a loss of sources of livelihoods for indigenous hunting communities in Tanzania. Through a loss of land and subsistence hunting rights, the Hadzabe and the Ndorobo now experience systematic deprivation of their own livelihoods. An example of this is the displacement of the Hadzabe people - who inhabit the area near the Lake Eyasi in Arusha, Shinyanga and Singida regions - in order to give hunting rights and licenses to Tanzania Game Trackers, a company formerly owned by Mr. Robin Hurt, a Kenyan Briton who owns several hunting blocks in Tanzania.

The new policies and regulations further stipulate that if the Ndo-robo and the Hadzabe, like any other Tanzanians, want to hunt, they have to apply for and secure a hunting permit, with wildlife officials allocating quotas of game meat to applicants.

To make matters worse, the revenue generated from sport hunting is not used to benefit indigenous peoples or to offset losses caused to the communities by damage from wildlife. Instead, indigenous hunt-ing communities are experiencing multiple deprivations of land, re-sources and identity. This multiple deprivation has negatively im-pacted on these communities, whose livelihoods are dependent on game resources, wild berries and honey.

Food insecurity and livelihood insecurity are features commonly experienced by Hadzabe and Ndorobo and parameters that mediate their livelihood have come under severe threat from wildlife conser-vation policies. Both the Hadzabe and the Ndorobo are now more vulnerable and unable to cope with environmental uncertainty. Indig-enous hunter-gatherer communities have been experiencing displace-ment by the government, farming communities, agro-pastoralists and pastoralists alike.

The support from human rights organisations and development NGOs that have tried to work with hunter-gatherers in Tanzania has always been too little too late and, in many cases, short-lived.[2]

The situation of pastoralist communities

Indigenous pastoralist communities continued to experience mar-ginalisation and exclusion from local and national development pro-cesses. The losses they experienced included: loss of land, loss of livestock, loss of primary production systems and loss of cultural identity.

The Barbaig

Most of Hanang district, which is situated in the newly created Ma-nyara region and has been the traditional territory of the indigenous pastoral Barbaig people, is now given over to small and large-scale farming. In the 1970s, the parastatal National Agricultural and Food

Corporation (NAFCO) took 100,000 acres of land from the Barbaig and put it under wheat production. This massive alienation of prime Barbaig pasture lands forced the Barbaig community to move to other areas in search for water and pasture for their livestock. They migrated to Singida, Dodoma, Morogoro, Shinyanga, Iringa, Rukwa, Mbeya and Ruvuma. The Barbaig never found a place they could call home in the areas they moved to, as they were considered intruders with no respect for other peoples' property or cultures. Perceived by mainstream groups as "loose foot herders", the Barbaig are constantly discriminated against and exploited.

Land use conflicts between farmers and agricultural pastoralists are a recurrent feature and are intensifying. The mainstream dominated media is biased against pastoralists in its coverage of issues related to conflicts. It often reports pastoralists as the aggressors and the pastoralists' view are rarely put across. There have been calls from mainstream groups for pastoralist Barbaig and Maasai to be sent back to where they came from: their traditional territories, most of which are at present under other uses such as wheat and other grain production or which fall within protected areas.

NAFCO, like many other parastatals has failed miserably in its performance. In spite of abundant capital from Canadian CIDA and heavily mechanised farming methods, wheat production has always been too low to justify the level of investment. The degree of environmental destruction is recorded as being one of the highest in the country and the cost of human suffering for the indigenous Barbaig has reached intolerable levels. The loss of huge tracts of pasture has, for instance, meant alienation from their holy sites. This alienation of holy sites, ancestral graves and sites of cultural significance has had deep spiritual and cultural significance for the community. Sources say that talks started recently on selling Hanang's wheat farms in Basuto to a private investor and, like many other privatised public utilities, the deal has not involved any consultation with the Barbaig community, who are the true owners of the land. Worse still, there is no discussion about returning land to the indigenous Barbaig for their own use as pasture.

The Maasai

The Maasai have experienced alienation of their lands, further marginalisation and multiple forms of deprivation, all of which has led to increased vulnerability and impoverishment. In 2002, more lands were taken away from them and put to other uses, such as small and large-scale farming, wildlife conservation, tented camps, sport hunting and mining.

Wildlife conservation and the tourist industry remained key threats to the livelihood of the indigenous pastoralist Maasai in Tanzania. Different policies, regulations and guidelines that were conservation-wildlife-tourist related were introduced and they all re-enforced the *"scramble for Maasailand"*. The wildlife policy (1998) has been seen as a radical move as it speaks for the first time of the need to empower local communities and give them user rights to wildlife resources. However, the regulations and guidelines for establishing Wildlife Management Areas (WMAs) are demanding, costly and cumbersome and it becomes very difficult for villagers to meet all the requirements and ultimately be able to benefit from wildlife resources. Instead, people and companies from outside local communities benefit the most. This has been the case so far and there is no likelihood that things will change soon.

The wildlife policy has two other inherent limitations; 1) it lacks political will; and 2) it does not recognise transhumance pastoralism and other tracking strategies of resource utilisation and management that pastoralists use in arid and semi-arid environments in order to maximise resource use while allowing soil nutrients and vegetation to regenerate. Wildlife policy intentions have remained largely rhetorical as the reality on the ground has not changed. In some cases, the situation is getting worse because of market economics that places profits above livelihood security.

Emerging issues, analysis and discussion

Indigenous peoples, both pastoralists and hunter-gatherers, have continued to experience multiple forms of deprivation that have systematically led to further loss of sources of their livelihood. Land alienation continued unabated during 2002, causing further loss of key pastoral and game resources, alienation or depletion of wild berries, roots and honey. As a result, a host of other problems have beset the communities, such as increased levels of vulnerability and poverty and chronic food insecurity. The future of the communities now seems more uncertain than ever before. Land losses inevitably contribute to a loss of the key resources that indigenous communities need for their subsistence and for their cultural survival.

Intensification of resource based conflicts

The shrinking resource base and encroachment of crop farming into pastoral areas has intensified resource-based conflicts. In 2002, violent conflicts between pastoralists and farmers intensified, leading to deaths in some areas. Indigenous resource owners such as the Barbaig, the Maasai, the Ndorobo and Hadzabe clashed with the migrant farming communities. In Kiteto district, for example, clashes broke out in the villages of Kimana, Namelok and Katikati. In all these villages, these clashes led to loss of lives. In Simanjiro, Monduli, Hanang and Babati districts conflicts frequently occurred in the traditional territories of indigenous peoples. These conflicts were caused by farms blocking stock routes to water points and by the location of farms in grazing areas.

These resource-based conflicts often resulted in pastoralists' animals being poisoned, animals legs cut and some cows, sheep or goats being killed by farmers. Such resource-based conflicts have increased in both frequency and intensity, displacing people in different areas.

Indigenous pastoralist women

Pastoralist societies are going through social changes that impact on gender relations. The Maasai pastoralist society traditionally organised work along gender, clan, age and territorial section lines, with men's primary responsibilities being herding, management of pasture, water points, building and maintaining fences for settlements and protecting the herd against predators.

The role of women was traditionally managing the homes and provisioning their households. Women's work included: building and maintaining houses, milking, cooking and feeding the household and visitors, fetching firewood as well as water. In their roles as managers of livestock, women had an extra task of rearing and domesticating animals.

Because of different social changes taking place, the situation is increasingly changing and gender labour relations are being redefined. First, the decrease in pastoral lands has led to a reduction in livestock numbers, with young Maasai men moving to the cities in search of waged employment. An absence of young men at home has increased the workload for women, as they have had to assume the work previously done by the young men. School has also taken most of the children, and the roles that children used to play, such as looking after the livestock, now also fall to women.

In addition to increasing workloads for women, social changes have further changed property relations, with women losing access and control over the resources they traditionally controlled. Commoditization of livestock and livestock products has upset the balance that existed between men and women.

Gender relations in terms of acquisition, disposal and exchange of livestock have changed, widening the scope of men's control while narrowing that of women. The concentration of cash into the hands of men almost to the exclusion of women has intensified age and gender gaps, largely making women more vulnerable economically and socially.

The diminishing number of livestock and increased articulation of market relations have changed gender relations, with men's roles as managers being transformed into that of owners and controllers of family property i.e. livestock. In the process, women are increasingly losing out not only in terms of ownership rights but also the user rights that social institutions such as marriage guaranteed them in the past. Women have therefore found themselves the producers but not the owners of the product of their own labour and, indeed, dependent on their male counterparts for subsistence.

Other socio-economic changes have constrained the ability of women to benefit from the commoditization process in the same way that men have. Women would traditionally have gained in the sale of what they "traditionally" controlled, which is milk, milk products such as butter and ghee, as well as hides and skins. However, non-Maasai and young Maasai men now dominate trade in livestock products such as hides and skins and this has denied women any potential benefits that could have accrued to them.

Women's responses to these processes have varied. They have sought other ways of supplying their households with food and kept their roles as providers of sustenance. In performing these roles, many marginalized women have involved themselves in different activities ranging from manufacturing artefacts for the tourists market to brewing and selling beer, etc.

Changes in men's activities have also somewhat increased women's workloads, while the difficulties involved in marketing livestock have also increased that of the men. The implications of this is that men are finding themselves away from home for long periods of time and their previous roles have ended up being performed by women. This is in addition to the numerous domestic chores already performed by these women.

Grain now forms an essential part of the diet of indigenous pastoralists. The procurement of grain, grinding of maize, fetching water and fuel wood for preparing grain-based foods have all added to the already heavy workloads of women. It is the women who carry maize to the mill for grinding, fetch fuel wood, fetch water and cook food. Although there are grinding mills in various trade centres, they are located very far from where most pastoral women live.

Most of the activities performed by women are both laborious and monotonous, unrelenting and quite taxing, whereas most of the tasks performed by men, such as herding and watering the animals, are seasonal and can be done with different men taking turns.

Indigenous children working in the Mererani mines

Increasing poverty levels have forced many children from the indigenous pastoral communities to go and work in the mines in Mererani. Mererani, a mining town near Arusha in northern Tanzania is famous worldwide because of its tanzanite, the precious and highly lucrative gemstone mined there. The area was once a grazing land for the pastoralist Maasai and it is now home to big international mining companies as well as millions of small miners from East Africa and beyond.

For many years, Mererani was predominantly populated by male adults. However, its wealth and fame attracted people from all walks of life. Some people left their diplomatic careers, or their white and blue collar jobs to work in the industry. Young Maasai men and women left pastoralism, indigenous Maasai children left school and some left home to work in the mines. As the saying goes, "all roads lead to Mererani and indeed they do."

Children in Mererani are engaged in a number of activities. Some work as domestic workers, others work in the commercial sex industry. However, the majority of children work in the mines either underground or sieving sand to extract small pieces of tanzanite. Those who work in the mines are called *Nyoka*, a Swahili word which means a snake, because of their ability to move fast and swiftly through dark tunnels just like a snake in a hole.

Living and working conditions in Mererani are difficult and dangerous. This is the case for many people but children are more vulnerable. Children die from malaria, TB, HIV / AIDS related complications and respiratory infections.

The level of exploitation of these children is very high and many dealers feel that they should not employ children since it is against the law. Instead, they only give them a little money to cover their food and accommodation. Many children stay because what they get is better than what they have at home but many stay because of the hope that they will one day become rich, for they see themselves as being on the road to riches.

Maasai youth as security guards in the cities

It is common knowledge that, in both Kenya and Tanzania, most of the security guards are young Maasai men. Many indigenous Maasai youth leave home and go to the big towns where they work as security guards. This has been found to be an alternative form of income and probably the only one for people with low levels of literacy and professional skills looking for waged employment.

In towns such as Mwanza, Arusha, Tanga, Morogoro, Dodoma and Dar es Salaam, you see Maasai youth in their hundreds working as *Walinzi*.[3] They are called *Mbwa Mwitu* (meaning *wild dogs*). The money they get is insufficient and living conditions are often bad.

The presence of such young men in towns is a reflection of a society in crisis and the decreasing ability of pastoralism to absorb its own populations. Many pastoralists who have been pushed out of pastoralism often have none of the skills needed in the formal sector due to a lack of formal education. The departure of able-bodied youths further undermines the viability of pastoralism since it deprives it of its vital labour.   ❏

Notes

1 Discussion about other groups in Tanzania that may claim the identity of indigenous peoples is beyond the scope of this paper.
2 Oxfam UK and CUSO did some work with the Hadzabe but they both discontinued their involvement after a short time.
3 A Swahili word meaning security guard.

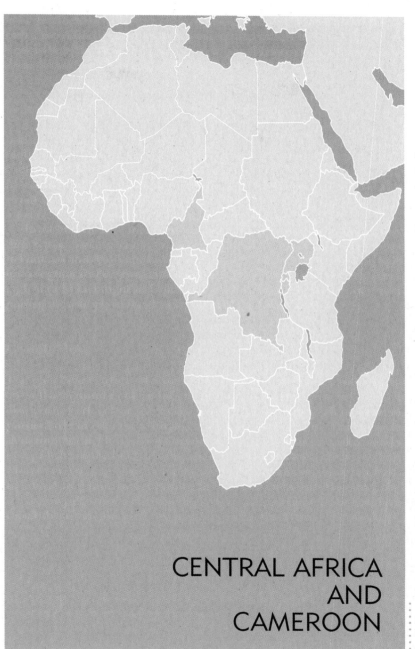

CENTRAL AFRICA
AND
CAMEROON

THE GREAT LAKES REGION

The political situation

A rmed conflict continued in the **Democratic Republic of Congo** (DRC) between forces of the Kinshasa government and its allies, and rebel groups operating in the east of the country. Much of the current conflict stems from the violence and mass displacements unleashed by the 1994 Rwandan genocide, when over two million people, including many of the *Interahamwe* militia responsible for the genocide, spilled into Tanzania and the DRC. They were accommodated in refugee camps close to the Rwandan border, from where the Interahamwe continued to mount insurgency operations. Since then, the conflict has grown into a battle between political and military elites, including warlords of various militia groups, for control of the DRC's mineral wealth.

During 2002, following international diplomatic pressure on all parties, the DRC reached separate agreements with eastern neighbours Burundi, Rwanda and Uganda, resulting in the near total withdrawal of their forces from the DRC. The Peace Accord signed between the DRC and Rwanda in Pretoria, July 2002, committed the DRC to demobilise and repatriate Rwandan Hutu Interahamwe militias and former armed forces, who sought refuge in the DRC following the Rwandan genocide. However, by the end of 2002, the DRC had made little progress in fulfilling this commitment, with only 3% of ex-combatants repatriated. Meanwhile, Kinshasa allies Angola, Namibia, and Zimbabwe - which have supported the Kinshasa government since 1998 against rebel forces backed by neighbouring Rwanda and Uganda - also withdrew their forces from the DRC.

In December 2002, all parties to the inter-Congolese dialogue signed a comprehensive peace deal under which current DRC President Kabila will remain in office and four new vice-presidents will be drawn from the government, rebel groups *Rassemblement congolais pour la démocratie-Goma* and *Mouvement de libération du Congo* and opposition groups. This paves the way for a transitional government and finalisation of a new constitution ultimately leading to national elections. Donors resumed aid to the DRC and made provisions for rescheduling and cancelling some of the country's huge debts.

Despite progress towards peace, the conflicts continued unabated in eastern DRC, particularly in the provinces of Equateur and the Kivus, where huge numbers of people were displaced and massacres, rape and torture occurred on a daily basis with impunity. In Ituri

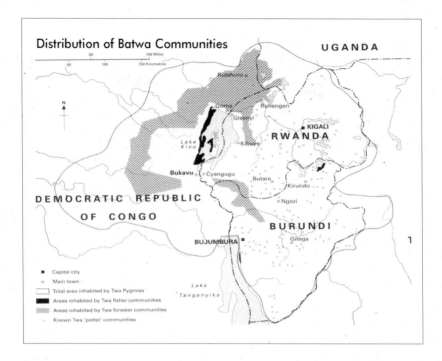

Distribution of Batwa Communities

UGANDA

RWANDA

KIGALI

DEMOCRATIC REPUBLIC
OF CONGO

BURUNDI

BUJUMBURA

Lake
Kivu

Lake
Tanganyika

■ Capital city
○ Main town
▭ Total area inhabited by Twa Pygmies
▨ Areas inhabited by Twa fisher communities
▨ Areas inhabited by Twa forester communities
○ Known Twa 'potter' communities

District, an economically-fuelled ethnic conflict was aggravated by advancing rebel groups (some backed by Uganda) battling for control of mineral resources, including gold and diamonds. The situation deteriorated to such a barbarous level that many humanitarian agencies issued warnings of genocide (see DRC report below).

In October 2002, a report by the UN Panel of Experts on the Illegal Exploitation of Natural Resources and Other Forms of Wealth of the DRC, in the five eastern provinces of the DRC, found that the Rwandan and Ugandan occupation had caused more than 3 million further deaths since the outbreak of war. The report highlighted the involvement of dozens of multinationals based in Europe, Canada and the USA who are extracting minerals from eastern Congo in violation of OECD guidelines on ethical working practices in conflict zones.

In **Burundi**, the first direct peace talks for nine years were held between the Tutsi-led transitional government and Hutu rebel groups. By the end of the year all but one of the Hutu parties and their various factions had signed a ceasefire agreement. However, an African mission due to monitor the application of the ceasefire and set up canton-ment camps for the former rebels was delayed and the ceasefire remained largely un-enforced. The political fractures and military manoeuvrings continued into 2003 and are likely to increase as the date set for the transfer of power from a Tutsi to a Hutu president (1st May 2003) approaches.

In the **Republic of Congo**, initial hopes in early 2002 for an end to civil war were short-lived. Following the agreement of a new constitution and elections for the national assembly, the senate, and the president, fighting erupted in the Pool region in late March between government forces and Ninja rebels. Tens of thousands of people were forced to flee. Fighting continued during the year and by December the instability in the Pool region remained unresolved, and the country was struggling with a staggering debt burden and diminishing international donor confidence in the government's questionable fiscal management - particularly of its enormously lucrative petroleum sector.❑

RWANDA

Although conflict continued outside Rwanda's borders, the internal security situation during 2002 was stable.

In March 2002, the largest Twa organisation, CAURWA (*Communauté des Autochtones Rwandais*) was legally recognised as an indigenous organisation working to promote Batwa rights. This signals an important shift in attitude by the Rwandan government, which previously had opposed reference to indigenous peoples and to specific ethnic groups in an attempt to overcome the ethnic tensions that led to the 1994 genocide. CAURWA has decentralised its activities through a network of provincial Twa volunteers who inform communities of their rights and help them claim these rights and seek solutions for their land, education and housing problems with the local government authorities. CAURWA is now supporting 50 local Twa associations to increase their food security and develop income-generating activities. Forty Twa secondary school children have received bursaries and five adult literacy centres have been established. Sixty houses have been built for Twa communities in three provinces. These activities will be further extended during 2003.

Briefing session at CAURWA. Photo: Dorothy Jackson

Twa organisations met with the Constitution Commission to press for their rights in the new constitution, calling for increased representation of Twa at all administrative levels in the country, inclusion of Twa in land distribution, recognition of Twa as a disadvantaged group needing particular attention, and support for Twa education. The draft constitution has allocated 2 senate places, to be nominated by the President, for representatives of people "disadvantaged by the historical process." Twa could therefore be eligible for these seats. A referendum on the new Constitution will be held in mid-2003, followed by parliamentary and presidential elections to replace the current transitional government.

CAURWA has opened a dialogue with Rwanda's Poverty Reduction Strategy (PRS) – which is intended to be a framework for pro-poor development activities in the next 5 years, under the IMF's Highly Indebted Poor Countries (HIPC) initiative. CAURWA has briefed communities about PRS-funded community projects, to try to reduce the possibility that marginalised Twa communities will be left out of the process of planning community projects or the benefits of those projects. CAURWA is collecting socio-economic data on Twa communities to compare with official government poverty statistics, which will be used to support advocacy on rights and entitlements for Twa communities.

A new land code being developed proposes various measures for land concentration and formal land titling, which could have serious implications for the largely landless Twa. The Twa organisation, AIMPO, produced a study of the Twa land situation in four provinces. Preliminary data collected by CAURWA from Cyangugu province shows that 88% of Twa households lack agricultural land, compared with 11% of the general population.

Twa activists have received training on Rwanda's *Gacaca* (village court) process, which will try people accused of categories 2, 3 and 4 genocide crimes, and which was piloted during the latter part of the year. They encouraged Twa communities to attend local meetings on *Gacaca*, stand for election to *Gacaca* committees and to participate actively in the process. The concern is that Twa, as marginalised members of Rwandan society, will be scape-goated by others seeking to conceal their crimes, and will not be able to find witnesses to testify for them.

The Twa increased official and public awareness of Twa issues by stepping up their national and international advocacy work through meetings with government ministries, the Unity and Reconciliation Commission, donors, embassies, NGOs and civil society networks. CAURWA organised meetings between Twa representatives, conservation bodies and local authorities to discuss the rights of Twa people who have been evicted from the Volcanos National Park, Gishwati Forest and the Nyungwe Forest. Conservation agencies are beginning to listen to the Twa voice and respond to the development needs of evicted communities, but implementation of the modern conservation guidelines that recognise indigenous rights and promote co-management is lagging far behind. Twa activists used the media to support their advocacy work, including TV and radio reports about Twa concerns. During August, Ayitegau Kouevi, the indigenous member for Africa of the United Nations' Permanent Forum on Indigenous Issues, visited Rwanda to meet Twa communities and Rwandan government authorities. ❑

BURUNDI

In Burundi, the Twa continued to suffer as a result of the civil war. A Household Livelihood Security assessment carried out by CARE in Muyinga Province, NE Burundi, revealed how the country's insecurity enabled the rich to exploit the poor, including the Twa, and called for Twa rights to access land to be guaranteed and measures to be taken to secure Twa lands against expropriation.

In August, the Association of Action Batwa organised a seminar in Gitega to inform Batwa about their rights, democracy and the country's peace process.

Despite the grave humanitarian situation in Burundi, the government has taken steps to increase the political representation of Twa. The senate, whose role is to scrutinise legislation and promote peace and reconciliation mechanisms, has three seats for Twa representatives. One of the members of parliament is a Twa woman, Mme Libérate Nicayenzi, who has been pressing the government to allocate land to the Twa. Tragically, one of the Twa senators, Jean-Bosco Rutagengwa, was killed in a rebel ambush in May 2002. Twa representatives from Rwanda and the DRC attended his funeral.

Twa activists made contact with a group of young Twa refugees from Kigoma, Tanzania, who were urgently seeking help to further their education.

The Batwa NGO, UCEDD (*Union Chrétienne pour l'Education et le Développement des Déshérités*), continued to support Twa communities through agro-pastoralist programmes and the Nyangungu Hope School, a kindergarten which supports 150 Twa children. They intend to expand the school to benefit both primary and secondary school children. ❑

UGANDA

In 1991, the Twa Pygmies of southwest Uganda were forcibly evicted from their forests following the establishment of the Bwindi and Mgahinga National Parks. The closure of the forests caused many of the Twa to move from a fairly independent existence to being landless, impoverished squatters, forced to survive by working for local farmers. Since 2000, the Twa and their organisation, UOBDU (United Organisation for Batwa Development in Uganda), have been seeking better dialogue with the Mgahinga and Bwindi Impenetrable Forest Conservation Trust (MBFICT). The Trust was mandated by the Global Environment Facility to protect the two forest parks and had a specific component for rural development activities with Twa communities, including land purchase. However, erosion of the stock market led to the Trust eliminating its Batwa programme in mid-2002. The programme was partly reinstated after protests by the Twa and support organisations, but will be finally closed down in February 2003. This is extremely serious for the Twa, who have no other means of securing land or livelihoods.

The Ugandan Twa continued to dialogue with district officials and conservation authorities in order to discuss policies and programmes aimed at Twa people and, in particular, to call for new rules of forest access that take into account the Twa's special attachment to the restricted forests in the Bwindi and Mgahinga National Parks. Conservation authorities have begun to openly acknowledge the increased role Twa should play in the parks' management. Two workshops were held, with the result that:

- Government authorities and development organisations agreed to collaborate better in their work with the Twa;
- NGOs working with Twa agreed that they need to design and implement their programmes more effectively;
- The problems with the Trust fund were aired to a wider audience, although no solutions were found;
- Plans for concrete actions relating to Twa forest use were proposed by the Uganda Wildlife Authority and CARE's multiple forest user programme.

A student from Glasgow University has begun researching the oral histories and traditional knowledge systems of the Twa living around the Mgahinga and Bwindi Impenetrable Forests. Twa dancers from Kisoro Town and Nyarusiza represented UOBDU at an International Festival in Kampala organised by the Uganda Development Theatre Association. The Twa Cultural Dancers were awarded two medals. ❑

DEMOCRATIC REPUBLIC OF CONGO

The eruption in January 2002 of Mt. Nyirangongo, near Goma in north Kivu, caused widespread destruction. Several Twa organisations provided emergency assistance to Twa communities disrupted by the volcanic eruption, fearing that relief services would not reach these marginalised groups.

The civil war in the DRC continued to wreak its toll on Pygmy communities in the east of the country, who are caught between warring factions that loot, rape and murder with impunity. Many communities leave their villages to hide in the forests at night, or move into the towns, to avoid being attacked.

In late 2002, news began to emerge of atrocities against local populations, including Pygmy communities, in the Ituri District. Reports claimed that Ugandan-backed rebel groups, the Congolese Liberation Movement (MLC) and Congolese Rally for Democracy-National (RCD-N) had been forcing their captives to eat human flesh in Mambasa, Koanda and Teturi. Mambasa covers an area of 37,860 km^2 and Mbuti Pygmies are thought to comprise 50% of the population.

The total number of hunter-gatherer Mbuti who live in the Ituri tropical forest is not known, although it has been estimated at 30,000. Their existence is already extremely fragile: their land rights are not recognised either in law or in the customary rights systems of neighbouring peoples, the authorities of the 13,000 km^2 Okapi Wildlife Reserve no longer permit them to hunt large game, and they survive by hunting small animals and bartering labour, firewood and game with the surrounding Bantu in exchange for food. They have little or no access to healthcare facilities and suffer from many preventable diseases such as river blindness and malaria, while their children suffer disproportionately from measles and polio. The forest, and therefore the Mbuti's food supply, is under increasing threat from the rapidly spreading commercial plantations of Ugandan timber companies and the increasing number of coltan mines.[1] Although relations between the Mbuti hunter-gatherers and the traditional Bila fisher- farmers (who practice sustainable shifting cultivation) are generally sustainable and involve sustainable forest use, the forest has also been under increasing pressure from incoming gold panners. This has involved incomers clearing the forest to create large permanent fields to grow produce to sell to the gold panners at exorbitant prices, upsetting both the local economy and local ecology.

After a 6-day investigation, the UN mission in DRC – MONUC – confirmed allegations of rape, child rape, abduction, torture and summary executions. The summary executions were perpetrated by the rebels, primarily against the Nande in Mambasa, the Mbuti Pygmies, and populations in villages around Mambasa and Beni, in an operation called *"Effacer le tableau"* (Operation Clean Slate). Eye witnesses provided horrific accounts of babies' hearts being torn out and eaten, small children being killed and mutilated, and people being executed in front of their families. Bukavu-based Twa organisations travelled to the region to provide support and conduct their own assessments.

A delegation of Pygmy peoples who travelled to Kinshasa in late January gave eyewitness accounts of acts of cannibalism being committed by MLC soldiers. They demanded that the government create a tribunal to investigate the crimes committed against them. The DRC state prosecutor confirmed that an investigation into allegations would begin.

The UN Security Council has condemned the rebels, and the High Commissioner for Human Rights called for sanctions against them. The Congolese authorities have asked the Security Council to establish a UN criminal court to try the rebels accused of cannibalism, and confirmed they will file a complaint at the International Court of Justice in The Hague.

The conflict in Ituri has caused massive population displacement. More than 10,000 refugees from Ituri have crossed the border into Uganda, and a reported 100,000 people have taken refuge in Beni. Recent reports suggest at least 3,000 pygmies have fled the forest, an extreme step for them to take. A group of at least 1,000 have sought shelter in the village of Mangina, while other camps of the displaced are located between Mambasa and Beni. The poor security situation has prevented humanitarian agencies from working in Ituri, leaving the Mbuti without adequate food, shelter or security.

PIDP-Kivu (*Programme pour l'Intégration et le Développement des Pygmées du Kivu*) continued publication of its quarterly bulletin, *Bambuti*, which reports on its activities in the region. PIDP also organized training for Pygmy community representatives in basic journalism techniques, water management and human rights. Some non-Pygmy representatives also participated. PIDP continued its support of Pygmy communities with agricultural inputs and training in farming methods.

In August, PIDP held its annual celebration of the International Day of the World's Indigenous People, to increase awareness of Pygmy rights and culture through public meetings, Pygmy dancing and craft exhibitions, and discussions of PIDP's work.

In association with CAURWA, PIDP collaborated on a consultation and feasibility study organised by the Forest Peoples Project into low-cost solar energy applications for Batwa communities in Rwanda and the DRC. The results of the study strongly indicate that DIY solar energy technologies would bring practical benefits and opportunities to the communities.

In June, the *Centre d'Accompagnement des Autochtones Pygmées et Minoritaires Vulnérables* (CAMV), *l'Action d'Appui pour la Protection des Droits des Minorités en Afrique Centrale* (AAPDMAC) and *l'Union pour l'Emancipation de la Femme Autochtone* (UEFA) sent a stark message to the "World Food Summit: 5 Years Later", organised by the United Nations Food and Agriculture Organisation (FAO) in Rome. Their statement noted that the Batwa in eastern DRC have been driven from their land and rendered homeless by the creation of the two national parks, Kahuzi-Biega and Virunga. CAMV continued its regional food security programme, with the distribution of seeds to over 200 Pygmy households. In July, CAMV organised a meeting for Pygmy NGO representatives from the DRC, Rwanda and Burundi to discuss communications techniques and methodology. ❑

REPUBLIC OF CONGO

A cross the border from the DRC, in the Republic of Congo, fighting between government forces and Ninja rebels has forced thousands to flee from the disputed Pool Region, including over a hundred Pygmies from the village of Nko. Nevertheless, UNICEF was able to vaccinate Pygmy children against polio in a cross-border, synchronised polio vaccination campaign in July. In the northern Sangha region, UNICEF is currently developing integrated basic services within Pygmy/Bantu villages to allow better access to health, education, water supplies and food production. The project plans to expand to benefit 50,000 Pygmy families (250,000 children) in the Likoula, Lekoumou, Bouenza and Plateaux regions of the Congo.

The US State Department's Country Reports on Human Rights noted the unequal treatment of Congo's tens of thousands of Pygmies, their severe marginalisation in the areas of employment, health and education and their lack of political voice. The US Embassy in Brazzaville announced a human rights training programme for 120 Baka people in the regions of Likouala, Sangha, Plateaux and Lekoumou over one year.❑

CAMEROON

The Bagyeli

The 4,000 or so Bagyeli 'Pygmy' people live in the south-west of Cameroon, where their traditional lands are traversed by the controversial Chad-Cameroon oil pipeline project, underwritten by the World Bank. The pipeline project set up the Foundation for Environment and Development in Cameroon (FEDEC) fund, as part of the compensation package to communities affected by the pipeline. The fund is mandated to finance an Indigenous Peoples Plan (IPP), to be developed in consultation with the Bagyeli community. However, so far there has been no Bagyeli involvement in the IPP. FEDEC is also charged with funding the protection of Campo Ma'an National Park (which overlaps Bagyeli traditional areas) and Mbam Djerem National Park, as part of environmental mitigation for the pipeline construction. Ironically, the establishment of these environmental mitigation measures will curtail Bagyeli hunting and livelihood activities, and therefore actually worsen their situation.

International and local NGOs raised concerns about the FEDEC programme through letters to FEDEC board members and the International Advisory Group (IAG) set up by the World Bank to monitor project implementation. As a result, the IAG visited Cameroon to gather information about the pipeline's impacts on the Bagyeli, and discuss FEDEC.

International NGOs are working with the Bagyeli and local support NGOs to support Bagyeli to gain more control over the pipeline process and to protect their lands and livelihoods. This work includes building the Bagyelis' information base, skills and confidence; helping Bagyeli to secure access to their natural resource base, including community mapping of Bagyeli land use; and supporting the development of new institutional mechanisms that promote informed and equitable dialogue between Bagyeli and their Bantu neighbours.

The Baka

In July, an exhibition at an animal park at Yvoir, Belgium, of Baka Pygmies from the Djoum area in southern Cameroon caused international outrage. Cameroonian NGOs denounced the exhibition as an intellectual, financial and political swindle that was undermining the dignity of the Baka and causing social disruption in their communities.

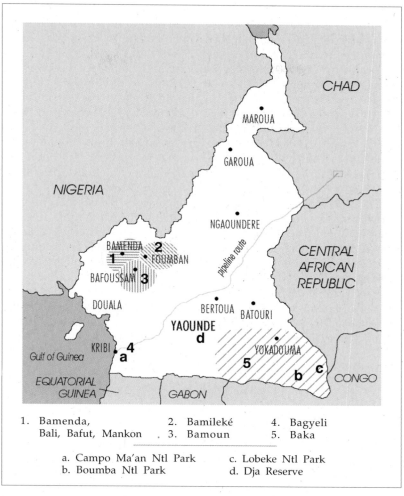

1. Bamenda,	2. Bamileké	4. Bagyeli
Bali, Bafut, Mankon	3. Bamoun	5. Baka

a. Campo Ma'an Ntl Park	c. Lobeke Ntl Park
b. Boumba Ntl Park	d. Dja Reserve

Baka people in south-east Cameroon faced increasing threats to their customary land rights from the new forest conservation rules devised for Lobeke and Boumba National Parks, and the protected areas around them, which were established in 1999 without Baka involvement. The area is home to many communities engaged in farming, hunting, fishing and gathering for mainly subsistence purposes. Most conservation managers in the region agree that subsistence hunting by Baka does not pose a serious threat to biodiversity. The greater threat is from commercial safari companies exploiting the sport hunting areas that were established around the Lobeke Park, several large logging companies, illegal commercial bushmeat hunters and traders and trophy hunters, who pay hefty fees to local safari companies to hunt and smuggle out ivory and rare bird species.

In many parts of this region Baka are in the majority, yet they face persistent and significant marginalisation by government and the local conservation authorities in decisions about the allocation of forest rights. Exploitation of flora and fauna by local communities is supposed to be controlled in each communal management zone by a local committee. These committees are overwhelmingly dominated by established local elites, and the committee selection methods and criteria, including the need for French literacy, make it difficult for Baka representatives to get onto these committees.

The consequence of this lack of participation by Baka is that decisions of the communal forest management committee, for example, to allow safari companies access to prime forest hunting areas in their zone for a small fee, can come into direct conflict with the subsistence hunting needs of Baka. Rather than targeting commercial trade in bushmeat and backing it up with strong enforcement measures, the protection measures now in place penalise those with the most to lose. The paradox is that they are doing this in order to protect the resources and habitats that local people, especially Baka, already cherish but are powerless to protect because they do not have secure rights to their forests.   ❏

REGIONAL EVENTS

In November 2002, the UN Office of the High Commissioner for Human Rights (OHCHR), ILO and UNESCO organised a joint consultation and training seminar on indigenous and human rights for Pygmy representatives. Meetings were held in Yaoundé and at Mekas, in the Dja Reserve, Cameroon, the traditional territory of Baka Pygmies. It provided a valuable opportunity for Pygmy representatives from seven central African countries to meet and exchange information and experiences and propose follow-up actions to the UN bodies, such as developing a network of Pygmy NGOs; assisting then to seek funding from the UN Voluntary Fund and to use the African system of human rights protection.

A regional workshop was held by Minority Rights Group International in Kigali, December 2002, on the subject of *Promoting the Rights of Batwa Pygmies: Recognition, Representation and Cooperation*. Twa representatives from three of the four Great Lakes countries attended, as well as government officials. Amongst the 24 recommendations were that governments should protect, promote and respect Batwa human rights; that international NGOs and United Nations agencies should support the Batwa in their struggle for rights and that the Batwa themselves should unite to claim their rights.

A new economic development and conservation initiative for six Central African countries (Cameroon, the Central African Republic, the DRC, Equatorial Guinea, Gabon and the Republic of Congo) was announced at the Sustainable Development Summit in Johannesburg, South Africa, in September 2002. Known as the Congo Basin Forest Partnership (CBFP), the initiative is backed by northern donors, conservation agencies and private sector groups, including forestry and timber organisations. The aim is to:

- Provide people with sustainable means of livelihood through well-managed forestry concessions, sustainable agriculture and integrated ecotourism programs.
- Improve forest and natural resource governance through community-based management, combating illegal logging and enforcing anti-poaching laws.
- Help countries develop a network of effectively managed national parks, protected areas and corridors.

African environmental and indigenous NGOs have written to the CBFP to convey their concerns about the lack of civil society participation in the process, lack of access to information, the involvement of agencies that are major players in the destruction of central Africa's forests and the poor record so far of conservation agencies with regard to the rights of local and indigenous communities. The concern is that, once again, the interests of forest-based communities and indigenous peoples will be overridden. ❏

Note

1   Coltan is used to make pinhead capacitors – an essential component in mobile phones. 80% of the world's reserves of coltan are found in the DRC (ed.note).

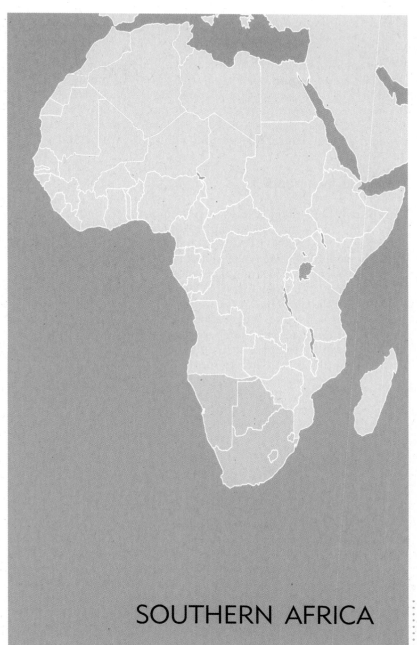

SOUTHERN AFRICA

NAMIBIA

The San (Bushmen) of Namibia are indigenous peoples who, as of 2002, number some 34,000 people in a country of around 1.8 million. Like the indigenous peoples of other countries in southern Africa (Angola, Botswana, South Africa, Zambia and Zimbabwe), the San of Namibia face a variety of human rights issues related to land, natural resource access, poverty, cultural rights, leadership and political representation.

Land and livelihood

Only a small percentage of the San in Namibia have control over their own land. These include the approximately 4,000 Khwe in West Caprivi and the 1,800 Ju | 'hoansi in Tsumkwe District East. The majority, however, were dispossessed of their land and resources over past centuries by encroaching populations, not only Europeans (especially Germans and Afrikaaners) but also Africans, including Ovambo, Kavango, Mbukushu, Herero and Damara. There is a major problem of land intrusion and land degradation due to growing populations of humans and livestock in a number of areas where San reside today. This is the case, for example, in Tsumkwe District West and Tsumkwe District East (the region known formerly as Bushmanland).

The Namibian San vary in terms of their adaptations and livelihoods. Many Namibian San reside in small settlements, earning their living through a combination of foraging, agriculture, livestock raising, small-scale industries (e.g. handicraft sales) and wage labor. Others, like the Hai//om, who number some 11,000 people, have their homes on freehold farms belonging to other people, where they work as herders and laborers, or live in small communities scattered across northern Namibia and on the outskirts of sizable towns such as those in Ovamboland. There are a number of San from various groups who have gone to neighboring countries in southern Africa for the purposes of work or education. Only a few San, estimated at around 20, live in the Namibian capital of Windhoek.

A significant proportion of the San live below the poverty line, and malnutrition and under nutrition are problems in some areas. Some San households receive food provided by the government, and they earn some income through working for government institutions. In 2001, for example, it was estimated by the government of Namibia's Emergency Management Unit (EMU) that between 17,000 and 22,000 of the country's estimated 34,000 San were dependent on food aid.[1] According to

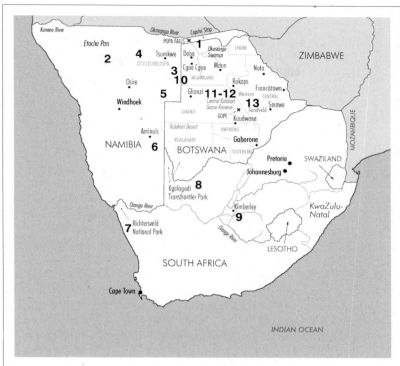

NAMIBIA

1. Khwe (West Caprivi)
2. Hai//om
3. Ju|'hoansi
   (Tsumkwe District East)
4. !Kung, Khwe, and Vasekele
   (Tsumkwe District West)
5. Ju|'hoansi (Omaheke),
6. !Xoo (Aminuis)

SOUTH AFRICA

7. Nama
8. ‡Khomani
9. !Xun, Khwe

BOTSWANA

10. Ju|'hoansi
11. G||ui, G||ana, Kua
12. Bakgalagadi
13. G||ui,G||ana, Tshassi, Teti

San organizations, leaders and community members, however, the San see their dependency on the government and outside agencies to be a major problem and something that they would like to change, promoting instead economic self-sufficiency. The question facing the San today is whether or not such goals are realistic given the high unemployment rate and the lack of formal education amongst the San.

Plans for new refugee camp shelved

A significant concern of San and other peoples residing in north-eastern Namibia over the past few years has been the possibility of the establishment of a large refugee resettlement facility, with as many as 21,000 refugees in the M'Kata region of Tsumkwe District West. The proposal to move the refugee camp from Osire in central Namibia stems from complaints by commercial farmers in the area. In 2001, a survey of the potential impact of the Osire refugee resettlement was undertaken by a consultant for the United Nations High Commissioner for Refugees.[2] There were also investigations of the reaction of stakeholders to the Osire refugee resettlement by a WIMSA consultant. San leaders from Tsumkwe District met with then Prime Minister Hage Geingob on the issue of Osire, and there were efforts to disseminate information and carry out human rights education in Tsumkwe District West by consultants working with WIMSA.

In March, 2003, the Representative of the United Nations High Commissioner for Refugees based in Namibia met with donors who have supported refugee programs in the country. At an earlier stage, donors had indicated that they might withdraw funding if the Namibian government went ahead with its plans to undertake resettlement of the Osire refugees. The UNHCR Representative informed the donors that there had been a change in the refugee situation in Namibia, brought about by the end of hostilities in Angola and the signing of a Peace Accord between the government of Angola and UNITA, the main opposition group that has been involved in armed struggle in the country. Most of the 21,000-plus refugees in the main UNHCR refugee camp at Osire and in the smaller camp at Kasava had said in interviews carried out in February 2003 that they wished to be repatriated to their former homes in Angola (UNHCR, 2003).[3] It is anticipated that the repatriation of the Angolan refugees would be initiated in June 2003. This process will lessen the pressure to establish a new refugee camp in Tsumkwe District West, where the majority of residents are San.

Struggling for their rights

Since the early 1990s, the San of Namibia have sought to gain government recognition of their land and natural resource rights. They have also sought to have the Namibian government recognize their traditional authorities, something that is still a contentious issue. While the Ju | 'hoansi leader of Tsumkwe District East in the Otjozondjupa Region, Tsamkxao =Oma, has been recognized, as has John Arnold, leader of the !Kung, Khwe, and Vasekele in Tsumkwe District West, other San leaders, such as those of the Hai-om of northern Namibia, the Khwe in West Caprivi, the Ju | 'hoansi in Omaheke, and the !Xoo of Aminuis have not been as fortunate. Efforts continue on the part of San groups and support organizations such as WIMSA to ensure that San leaders receive official government recognition.

Challenges continue to face the San in 2002-2003 with respect to land and resource rights. An innovation in Namibian development is the concept of the conservancy. A conservancy is an area of communal land where communities have some control over natural resource management and utilization. They do this through a statutory body that is recognized officially by the government of Namibia, a conservancy committee. While there have been over a dozen conservancies established on communal land in northern Namibia, some of which are in the hands of San communities, there are threats to the long-term viability of these conservancies because of population growth, in-migration of other groups and possible changes in land tenure.

Such a situation can be seen in West Caprivi, for example, where the Namibian government announced in 2002 that the West Caprivi Game Reserve would be turned into a national park, the Bwabwata National Park. There will be restrictions placed on where people can live in the national park and on the kinds of activities they can pursue there. For example, people will not be allowed to keep cattle in some parts of the new national park, and there will be limits placed on agricultural activities. The Khwe and !Xu (Vasekele) of West Caprivi are concerned that they will not receive the benefits they have been promised by the Ministry of Environment and Tourism's Vision for Caprivi plan and that they will potentially be excluded from decision-making in the new national park.

The !Kung community of Tsumkwe District West submitted its application for the N/a Jaqna Conservancy to the Ministry of Environment and Tourism (MET) three and a half years ago. As of mid-2003, the MET had still not allowed this conservancy to be registered officially. This lack of official recognition poses risks for the populations residing in Tsumkwe District West. Currently, other groups are moving into the region and utilizing the natural resources. Some non-San water point owners in Tsumkwe District West are preventing other people from gaining access to water, which is a serious threat to the well-being of people and their herds of domestic animals. There are also commercial operators entering Tsumkwe District West in search of 'devil's claw' (*Harpogophytum procumbens*), a popular medicinal plant that is used by local healers and which is also harvested and sold by local people in order to generate income.

Another potential threat facing the Khwe, !Xu, and other San in Namibia is the proposed construction of a dam on the Okavango River, near Popa Falls. This dam would potentially would have a significant impact on down-stream populations and habitats, not only in Namibia but also in the Okavango Delta region of Botswana, which has sizable numbers of people, including many San. At present, the plans for building this dam are on hold for economic reasons, but the Namibian government hopes to go ahead with the facility at some point in the not-too-distant future. The governments of Angola and Botswana and various non-governmental organizations have protested about the Namibian government's plans for the dams and other water projects on the Okavango and the Cunene Rivers in Namibia.

Organizing for strength

As many San say, "We are people who suffer." The San feel that they are marginalized minorities who have less access to rights and resources than other groups in Namibia. They are concerned about the trends, even in community-based natural resource management in Namibia, which they see as being of potential benefit but which to them appear to be increasingly overseen by other groups or individuals who reap the majority of the rewards.

If current trends continue in Namibia, some San believe, they will face further problems in terms of lack of access to natural resources and development programs. It is for this reason that the San of Namibia have sought the assistance and support of organizations such as the Working Group of Indigenous Minorities in Southern Africa, which collaborates with them in efforts to promote San rights.[4] Without collaborative, participatory, community-based development and education programs in Namibia and the support of groups such as WIMSA, the San will continue to be marginalized, dispossessed and poverty-stricken, facing a future with little hope. ❑

Notes and References

1   See **Suzman, James. 2001.** *An Assessment of the Status of the San in Namibia.* Windhoek, Namibia: Legal Assistance Center.
2   See **Hitchcock, Robert K. 2001.** *Anthropological Study on the Potential*

Impact of Refugees in M'Kata, Namibia. Windhoek, Namibia: United Nations High Commissioner for Refugees.

3   **United Nations High Commissioner for Refugees. 2003.** "What Next for Osire Refugees?" *Newsletter of the United Nations in Namibia*, Issue 1, May, 2003. Windhoek, Namibia: UNHCR. '

4   **Working Group of Indigenous Minorities in Southern Africa. 2002.** *Working Group of Indigenous Minorities in Southern Africa (WIMSA) Report on Activities April 2001 to March 2002.* Windhoek, Namibia: WIMSA.

BOTSWANA

There are some 48,000 San (Basarwa) in the Republic of Botswana, the largest San population in the six countries of southern Africa in which San peoples currently reside.[1] While the San of Botswana faced a variety of different situations in 2002-2003 in terms of lifestyles and living standards, human rights, political participation, development and health, some generalizations can be made.

Insecurity of land and resource rights

The problem for most San in Botswana is that they have not been able to obtain secure land and resource tenure rights. The reasons for this situation are complex, but they are due in part to the fact that the Botswana government has been unwilling to grant land rights to groups that make claims on the basis of customary rights and traditional livelihoods. The efforts to lay claim to ancestral territories on the basis of 'indigenousness', the notion that San peoples were 'first comers' or were 'native to the areas in which they lived,' have been rejected by the Botswana government, which does not accept the argument that the San or any other group is indigenous.[2]

An example of this situation can be seen in the case of the Central Kalahari Game Reserve (CKGR), the second largest game reserve in Africa, where the G/ui, G//ana, and some Kua San, along with Bakgalagadi, a non-San population, had resided for generations. For years, the Botswana government had been trying by different means to get these people to move out of the reserve[3] but, until last year (2001), some 700 people were still holding on to their traditional land and lifestyle. However, as mentioned in *The Indigenous World 2001-*

2002, the Botswana government finally decreed that all services (water, health and food distribution) in the CKGR would stop by 31 January 2002, thereby virtually forcing people to abandon their homes. Despite the attempts of the Negotiating Team of CKGR residents and supporters to engage the Botswana government in discussions, by early 2002, nearly all of the residents of the reserve had been relocated by the Botswana government and the District Councils to a few, large settlements in areas on the periphery of the reserve, where they rejoined people who had been resettled on earlier occasions and who have been eking out an existence and living on government rations ever since.[4]

In February 2002, the G/ui and G//ana San and Bakgalagadi of the CKGR filed a legal case in the High Court of Botswana in an effort to get the Botswana government to reverse its decisions and resume services so that people could return to their traditional territories. The High Court dismissed the case on a technicality, arguing that it had not been filed properly. The case is currently being appealed.

The Diamond issue

One of the most contentious issues in the CKGR case has revolved around diamond mining. For many years, some international organizations have claimed that the main reason the San and Bakgalagadi were being relocated involuntarily outside of the CKGR was because of the mining interests of the De Beers group, which has found diamond deposits at Gope, in the western part of the reserve. The Botswana government, for its part, has always argued that the reason for the resettlement was to ensure that local people in the Central Kalahari could benefit from the development opportunities provided by government and could participate more easily "in the life of the nation".

Groups inside Botswana, including many of those involved in the CKGR Negotiating Team, have also maintained that diamond mining was not the reason for the relocation but rather the government's ill advised "development policy" and its fear that tourists would believe Botswana to be a backward and 'primitive' country when meeting the residents of the CKGR. Finally it should also be said that, unlike in Canada and Australia, Botswana law regarding mineral rights is such that the presence of indigenous peoples does not in any way compromise the government's right and ability to extract and benefit from the minerals on the land they occupy.

"May I speak?" San standing between a representative of Survival International and Mrs. Nasha, Minister of Lands and Government. *The Botswana Guardian*, Gaborone, 22 February 2002.

In late 2002 and early 2003, the diamond issue came to the fore again when it became known that another diamond prospecting group – Kalahari Diamonds Ltd – had been granted exploration licenses in different places in Botswana, including the CKGR, and that they had received a loan from the International Finance Corporation (IFC), the private sector development arm of the World Bank Group and a multilateral development and finance institution that, along with the International Development Association (IDA), the World Bank and the International Monetary Fund, makes up part of the United Nations family of agencies.

However, as pointed out by several observers, there is a big difference between "exploration" and actual "mining".The whole of Botswana is, and has been for decades, apportioned into prospecting blocks (apart from cemeteries and national parks) for which licenses are granted for a period of time, after which they can be reallocated to other companies who may, for instance, be using newer technology (which seems to be the case here). But even if diamonds are found, mining will hardly be undertaken unless it is economically viable. Right now the diamond market is not very lucrative, and this is believed to be one of the reasons why De Beers, despite costly prospecting and development input, has never undertaken any mining activity in Gope.

However, the situation should be closely monitored. The mineral prospecting licenses allocated by the Botswana government for areas inside the Central Kalahari Game Reserve have expanded considerably since the time of the relocation of the resident populations out of the CKGR. There was no consultation with the CKGR communities prior to the loan agreement between the IFC and the mining company. The IFC and Kalahari Diamonds Ltd. should be required to follow the World Bank standards on indigenous peoples, and there should be close monitoring of the activities of the company as it carries out its explorations in the concession areas in the Central Kalahari. Should any decisions be made about opening mining operations in the Central Kalahari, detailed social and environmental impact assessments must be required.

The Western Sandveld

San in other parts of Botswana have also experienced problems in gaining access to land and resources. The Western Sandveld region of Central District, the largest commercial ranching area designated under the Tribal Grazing Land Policy (TGLP) and the National Land Use planning exercises in Botswana in the 1970s, contains sizable numbers of San peoples, most of them Kua, along with some /Gui, G//ana, Tshassi, and Teti. In 2002, it was announced that the government of Botswana was going to allow people in the Western Sandveld who had boreholes and cattle posts to obtain rights over the water points and grazing areas. The problem is that many of the people living on the cattle posts, many of whom work for the borehole owners, face the possibility of eviction from their ancestral lands. In the past, efforts were made to establish communal service centers and Remote Area Dweller settlements at places such as Maletswai but now even these places will be leased out to individual cattle owners. The possibility of large-scale dispossession of the resident populations of the Western Sandveld exists, and no plans are in place for alternative places for people to live or compensation to be paid to people who may lose their rights to their land, resources, homes and fields. There will be forced relocation of as many as 4,000-5,000 people, four times as many people as lost their homes and ancestral lands in the Central Kalahari Game Reserve case. The San and other groups in the Western Sandveld have sought the assistance of San support organizations and have called upon the Botswana government to revise its plans for the Western Sandveld region to include land and water allocations for San communities.

Water festival

In December 2002, a water festival was held at Shaikarawe, a community in which the majority of residents are San. This was the community
where, only a few years before, the Tawana Land Board and the North
West District Council had ruled that the land on which the San lived
at Shaikarawe was no longer theirs but rather belonged to a non-San
(Mokgalagadi) man who had taken over the water point there with his
livestock. With the support of the Trust for Okavango Cultural and
Development Initiatives (TOCaDI), a San support organization, the San
appealed to the government and, eventually, with the help of DITSH-
WANELO, the Botswana Center for Human Rights, they were granted
the right to return to Shaikarawe, where they immediately began to dig
a well. Water was struck in late 2002, and the people of Shaikarawe
were granted a water right by the Tawana Land Board. TOCaDI is also
helping San in other communities in Ngamiland to drill boreholes and
seek water rights, and it is hoped that the North West District Council
and the Botswana government will allow these communities to obtain
de jure (legal) rights over water, grazing and land.

Health and well-being

Botswana is considered by the United Nations and the World Health
Organization to have one of the highest – if not the highest – rates
of HIV / AIDS infection in the world. While they appear at present to
have somewhat lower HIV rates than other groups, in part because of
their living in remote locations, the San are being increasingly exposed to HIV / AIDS and other sexually transmitted diseases. "It is
only a matter of time," one health worker in Ngamiland said in 2002,
"before the San will see the losses of sizable numbers of adults and
an expansion in the number of AIDS orphans." Clearly, more work
must be done on HIV / AIDS prevention and treatment, including
making antiretroviral (ARV) drugs available to people not just in the
cities and towns of Botswana but also in remote rural areas.

New directions in San development

An innovative activity of the San of southern Africa, including those
in central and north western Botswana, in the new millennium has
been the mapping of ancestral territories and culturally and histori-

cally significant sites using Geographic Positioning Systems (GPS) instruments and the creation of maps through the application of Geographic Information Systems (GIS) technology. The impacts of the community mapping efforts on San communities have been profound. They have helped awaken a sense of collective identity among community members, and have helped instil in people the desire to learn more about past land use and resource management patterns.In North West District, the detailed maps of community areas have been introduced as exhibits in land and resource claim efforts at meetings of the Tawana Land Board and Sub-Land Boards. These maps have also been used in the planning of cultural and nature-based tourism routes in areas where San and other groups live. According to local people, the mapping work gave people the hope that they could gain secure rights to their own land and greater access to the benefits that tourism and business could generate.

The community-based natural resource management (CBNRM) programs in Botswana have seen the establishment of over 60 community-based institutions that have the right to utilize the wildlife and other natural resources in their areas. The problem is that the government of Botswana continues to be reluctant to allow the community-based institutions to control their own funds and to disburse the income they receive from safari companies, businesses and tourists as they see fit. Nevertheless, some community-based organizations have been able to generate income and jobs for their members, sometimes in substantial amounts. Unless they are able to participate in Botswana's community-based natural resource management and land allocation programs, the San will continue to live, as one Ju | -'hoan San woman put it, "in a sea of poverty." ❏

Notes and references

1   See **Suzman, James, ed. 2001.** *An Introduction to the Regional Assessment of the Status of the San in Southern Africa.* Windhoek, Namibia: Legal Assistance Center.
2   **Saugestad, Sidsel. 2001.** *The Inconvenient Indigenous: Remote Area Development in Botswana, Donor Assistance, and the First People of the Kalahari.* Uppsala, Sweden: The Nordic Africa Institute.
3   For more background information see *The Indigenous World 1996-1997* and onwards.
4   **Hitchcock, Robert K. 2002.** "We Are the First People": Land, Natural Resources, and Identity in the Central Kalahari, Botswana. *Journal of Southern African Studies* 28(4): 797-824.

SOUTH AFRICA

I ndigenous peoples in South Africa strengthened their national civil society structures during 2002. The government of South Africa made slow progress on a number of fronts related to indigenous peoples' rights, possibly edging towards signing ILO Convention 169.

Indigenous organisations gain strength

Two important national umbrella structures consolidated themselves during the year. The National Khoi-San Consultative Conference (NKCC) groups together all Khoe, San and revivalist Khoesan groups in the country. Its focus is primarily cultural, tipping over into economic development themes. After representation by San groups, the NKCC agreed to place a hyphen between the words Khoe and San to recognise the right of self-determination of San peoples in southern Africa. The NKCC held regular executive meetings and played an important role in co-ordinating indigenous groups participating in the all-important UN World Summit on Sustainable Development (WSSD) held in Johannesburg in August.

The leaders of the !Xun, Khwe and ‡Khomani San peoples strengthened the capacity of the South African San Council (SASC). The SASC was formed in November 2001 as a South African "chapter" of the Working Group of Indigenous Minorities in Southern Africa (WIMSA). The council comprises two elected leaders each from the !Xun, the Khwe and the ‡Khomani groups, and is bound by the terms of a constitution. The formation of SASC as a formal organisation was prompted by the need to negotiate an agreement on the Hoodia case in particular, and to take a hand in San people's rights and interests in general.

Defending intellectual property rights

For the past year, SASC has assumed responsibility for negotiating the Hoodia deal on behalf of all San. It threatened legal action against the Centre for Scientific and Industrial Research (CSIR), which had concluded a lucrative deal with international pharmaceutical companies for the exploitation of a chemical compound found in a local desert plant, known to the San. SASC, in partnership with WIMSA and the

South African San Institute (SASI), was finally successful in securing a landmark out-of-court deal recognising the collective intellectual property of the San over exploitation of the desert succulent, *Hoodia Gordonii*, or *!Khoba*. The settlement was signed in March 2003. It is dependent on Pfizer's successful marketing of a weight-loss drug derived from the !Khoba's hunger-suppressing compounds, and which could potentially see the San earning millions of Rands worth of profits. Funds are to be channelled to San-controlled regional poverty alleviation and development initiatives.

The other major battle for SASC has been its challenge to the Province of KwaZulu-Natal, which attempted to open a major tourism venture exploiting ancient San rock art, while excluding any presence of, or benefits to San communities. The negotiations are continuing in 2003 but the presence of an organised San leadership structure laying claim to their collective heritage is an important warning to government officials who continue to think of the San as extinct in South Africa.

Land claims victories

The government of South Africa took the opportunity of the UN World Summit on Sustainable Development to rapidly hand over the new !Ae!hai (Oryx Tail) Heritage Park to the ‡Khomani San people of the southern Kalahari. !Ae!hai is part of a land claim settlement process that saw 25,000 has of land previously in the Kgalagadi Transfrontier Park restored to the original owners of the land, the 1,000 surviving ‡Khomani San.[1]

The Richtersveld issue involving the Nama people of the West Coast took a new, positive turn in February 2003 when the Bloemfontein government conceded in the Supreme Court of Appeal in Bloemfontein that the Richtersveld community retained ownership of their land after British annexation of the area in 1847.

The Richtersveld community is reclaiming around 85,000 has of its ancestral land, which is now registered in the name of government-owned diamond mine Alexkor. The government earlier argued that it was entitled to transfer ownership of the claimed land to Alexkor during the 1920s because it was crown land belonging to the government under the terms of the former colonial power's Crown Lands Act. It has also held to the argument that the Richtersveld claim was not valid in terms of the Restitution Act because the Richtersvelders were not dispossessed as a result of racial discrimination. The Richtersveld community disputed this, arguing that it was assumed for decades that the Richtersveld people had no right to their land simply because they were an indigenous people.

Judgment by the Appeal Court will now follow. According to the government, a ruling in favour of the claimants may put the owner- ship of all colonised land in South Africa in dispute. A ruling in favour of the Richtersvelders may also be followed by a claim against the privately-owned Transhex diamond mine. Transhex is mining under the terms of a lease agreement with the government on around 40,000 has along the Orange River, within the boundaries of the Richtersveld Reserve. The reserve comprises the eastern part of the area which, by the early 19th century, was being occupied by the Richtersvelders' forebears. After alluvial diamonds were discovered along the West Coast, the community was gradually moved east- wards and ultimately confined to the reserve, where they live to this very day.[2]

Standardizing Khoe and San languages

There were a number of advances on the language front. The Northern Cape government expanded its pilot Khoekhoegowab early primary project from one school in the Richtersveld to a second school on the Orange River. Khoekhoegowab is a language spoken by San and non- San and it has been standardised for over a century.

Khwe speakers from three countries (South Africa, Namibia and Botswana) entered into discussions with the African Studies Institute of the University of Cologne about an alphabet for their language, Khwedam. The University of Cologne has been actively involved in researching the Khwe language for decades and linguists are produc- ing a dictionary of the language and training Khwe activists in the writing system. A degree of conflict emerged when academics insisted that the alphabet include a series of special symbols not available in ASCII on regular computers. This would have made the Khwe de- pendent on special software and would prohibit use of emails and Internet. Khwe activists took a policy decision at a WIMSA-sponsored workshop to adopt an alphabet based on the detailed work of Cologne but technologically appropriate and usable on any computer. Co- logne academics eventually accepted that there would be two ver- sions of the alphabet. The conflict, however, raised the issue of how much say indigenous people have over the work of linguists and in whose interest such work is conducted.

Khwedam is only the third San language to be standardised, the first two were Ju | 'hoansi and Naro. Efforts are still underway to standardise !Xun. Most of this effort is coming from community activists with no government support, despite constitutional guarantees for language development.

The Khoe and San National Language Body helped convince two municipalities to adopt original indigenous names for their urban districts. This is the first time in modern South African history that indigenous place names with clicks are in use on maps. Upington is now part of | | Harahais municipality, and Keimoes is within Kai !Garib municipality. San and Nama leaders would like the government to engage in a wider programme of place name restitution.

Political lethargy

Whereas San and Khoe groups made progress in their struggles, the South African government continued to show slow progress and a lack of political leadership on indigenous issues. The Department of Provincial and Local Government released the research document on the claims to indigenous status of various interest groups around the country. Overall the quality of the research was uneven, with particularly poor coverage of San issues. The language issues of the indigenous peoples, which are considered central by Nama and San groups, were barely discussed in the report.

The final recommendation of the research document called for the government to adopt a policy framework that would marry the domestic constitutional context with the mechanisms of the international system. The concept of "indigenous peoples"' would be modified to become "vulnerable indigenous peoples"', thus avoiding a conflict with the traditional leaders of the Black, Bantu-speaking majority peoples. The authors recommended that this status be allocated to the ‡Khomani San and the Nama peoples. The principles by which this recommendation were made were not apparent in the document, and it seemed to be influenced by the SA Human Rights Commission Report of two years previous, which is still embargoed by the Department.

The San Council resolved to support the principle of identifying "vulnerable indigenous peoples", but to contest the criteria and link it to language rights, which are already explicit and particular in the constitution. This would then bring the !Xun and Khwe into the same framework.

Executive Committee members of the Indigenous Peoples of Africa Co-ordinating Committee (IPACC) met with government officials from Foreign Affairs and the Dept.
of Provincial and Local Government. Civil Servants were keen to highlight that the government, once it has adopted a domestic policy on vulnerable indigenous peoples, would be well-placed to provide more vocal support to the UN Draft Declaration on the Rights of Indigenous Peoples and to sign ILO Convention 169. President Mbeki may be looking to fulfil his obligations on this front in the final year of the UN Decade.

On the international front, the Commonwealth Policy Studies Unit (CPSU) organised a high profile meeting of African Commonwealth experts to discuss the situation of indigenous peoples in Africa. The October 2002 meeting was held in Cape Town, with the co-operation of the IPACC Secretariat. The Canadian High Commissioner hosted a reception for the guests, who included the African members of the UN's Permanent Forum on Indigenous Issues, Dr Ayitegan Kouevi and Mrs Njuma Ekundanayo. Mrs Ekundanayo later travelled to the southern Kalahari to visit !Ae!hai Heritage Park and the ‡Khomani elders. ❑

References

1   For more information on the ‡Khomani situation see:
    www.sanculture.org.za
2   www.news24.com February 18, 2003.

PART II

INDIGENOUS RIGHTS

8TH SESSION OF THE UNITED NATIONS WORKING GROUP ON THE DRAFT DECLARATION ON THE RIGHTS OF INDIGENOUS PEOPLES

The 8th session of the Working Group on the Draft Declaration on the Rights of Indigenous Peoples (WGDD), held in Geneva from 2-13 December 2002, was of great importance because its work plan included the core articles of the draft Declaration – a cluster dealing with the right of self-determination (articles 3, 31 and 36), and a cluster dealing with land and resource rights (articles 25-30). The agenda also included a third group of articles relating to the right of indigenous peoples to cultural integrity and to protection from ethnocide and cultural genocide (article 7), the right of indigenous peoples to identify as indigenous and to be recognized as such (article 8) and the right to protection in times of conflict (article 11).

This report summarizes the debates of the 8th session. Although slight shifts can be detected with regard to the first cluster of articles in that governments are increasingly prepared to use the term "indigenous peoples" and to acknowledge collective rights, the discussion on indigenous land and resource rights revealed that state and indigenous positions remain incommensurable.

A large part of the discussions at the 8th session of the WGDD occurred in the light of an informal governmental meeting held 3 months earlier in September 2002. At this meeting Norway proposed amendments to the Declaration's text which, for the first time in the history of the WGDD, were considered a possible basis for discussion by a sizeable group of governments and some indigenous delegations. At the same time, pressure on the WGDD to adopt the Declaration, or at least show some progress by the end of the International Decade of the World's Indigenous Peoples in 2004, is strong and its future remains uncertain.

Attendance and procedure

The meeting was attended by a total of 298 people, including representatives from 36 governments, 2 UN organizations and 55 indigenous and non-governmental organizations.[1] African states were completely absent, with the exception of Morocco. Asian countries were either absent, as in the case of Bangladesh, Indonesia, India and Nepal, or silent, as in the case of the Philippines, Vietnam, Malaysia and Thailand.

The WGDD consisted of 3 formal meetings and 13 informal meetings. On the second to last day of the WGDD, the chair also convened a so-called "informal informal" meeting, which he co-chaired with the chairperson of the indigenous caucus, Alberto Saldamando from the International Indian Treaty Council (IITC). Government meetings, chaired by the Canadian delegate and Permanent Forum member Wayne Lord, were also held every morning. They consisted of attempts, mainly on the part of the CANZUS bloc (Canada, Australia, New Zealand and the US), to redraft the Declaration. Central and South American states were largely absent, while "friendly" states such as Norway and Denmark attended but where much less eager to redraft.

Self-Determination: Articles 3, 31 and 36

State proposals and amendments

The meeting started off with Mexico, Guatemala, Ecuador and Cuba all stating that they would accept the Declaration as currently drafted, including articles 3, 31, and 36 under debate:

Article 3. Indigenous peoples have the right of self-determination. By virtue of that right they freely determine their political status and freely pursue their economic, social, and cultural development.

Article 31. Indigenous peoples, as a specific form of exercising their right to self-determination, have the right to autonomy or self-government in matters relating to their internal and local affairs, including culture, religion, education, information, media, health, housing, employment, social welfare, economic activities, land and resources management, environment and entry by non-members, as well as ways and means for financing these autonomous functions.

Article 36. Indigenous peoples have the right to the recognition, observance, and enforcement of treaties, agreements and other constructive arrangements concluded with States or their successors, according to their original spirit and intent, and to have States honour and respect such treaties, agreements and other constructive arrangements. Conflicts and disputes which cannot otherwise be settled should be submitted to competent international bodies agreed to by all parties concerned.

However, the attention of the meeting was soon steered towards the Norwegian proposal, which was made in light of the fact that most governments are concerned about two elements of the right of self-determination. The first is whether the right of self-determination entails a right to secession. The second is whether indigenous peoples' right to land and natural resources is to be regarded as integral to the right of self-determination. The Norwegian proposal was an attempt to address these concerns and bridge the gap between both government and indigenous delegates and amongst governments, while at the same time maintaining the right of self-determination as "the cornerstone of the Declaration". It was made up of three moves, and proposed a way of keeping article 3 of the Declaration intact. The first was to have paragraph 15 of the Declaration's Preamble include a reference to the 1970 Declaration on Friendly Relations, so that it would read as follows:

"Bearing in mind that nothing in this Declaration may be used to deny any peoples their right of self-determination, yet nothing in this Declaration shall be construed as authorizing or encouraging any action which would dismember or impair, totally or in part, the territorial integrity or political unity of sovereign and independent States conducting themselves in compliance with the principle of equal rights and self-determination of peoples."

The second move was the reorganization of a number of the Declaration's articles so that articles 3, 31, 19, 20, 21 and 36 would form an interrelated cluster. This move, together with the new preambular text, would enable Norway to accept articles 3, 31 and 36 as currently drafted, although its delegation still reserved the right to present amendments to articles 19, 20, 21 and 30. The third element of the Norwegian proposal comprised the suggestion that the remaining text of article 31 be deleted after the phrase "local affairs." This proposal was supported by the governments of Costa Rica, Cuba, Denmark, Ecuador, Finland, Guatemala, Mexico, Norway, Peru and Spain. As a way of 'supporting and supplementing' the Norwegian proposal, Finland suggested alternative language for the Declaration's article 45 in ways that explicitly granted states an absolute right over territorial integrity, regardless of whether they recognize the right of self-determination of their peoples or not. Most CANZUS states and the Russian Federation, however, could not accept the Norwegian proposal or the Finnish addition and argued that articles 3, 31 and 36 as currently drafted needed to be specified. In the 'informal informal' session, New Zealand however noted that it would "give very serious consideration to the Norwegian proposal". Canada proposed to shift parts of Norway's proposed preambular text into operative article 3 of the Declaration, and also stated that it could not accept article 36 in its current form.

The US reiterated its well-known position that it wished to combine articles 3 and 31 and use the concept of "internal self-determination". This proposal was vehemently opposed by indigenous delegates as well as a number of governments, including the South and Central American countries present (Guatemala, Mexico, Peru, Ecuador, Costa Rica and Cuba), and the Nordic states. Even Australia stated that "internal" was "possibly discriminatory," while Japan stated that 'internal' was unnecessary in the light of the proposed inclusion of aspects of the Friendly Relations Declaration. Most of the arguments marshalled against "internal self-determination" stated that the US proposal was blatantly in conflict with the universal principles of non-discrimination and equality. In fact, the insertion of "internal" would create a new category in international law. Finally, Cree representative Willie Littlechild reminded the WGDD that the concept of "internal self-determination" had also been brought up at the 2002 meeting of the Organization of American States (OAS), and rejected there. Both indigenous and some government delegates reiterated time and again that the drafting should aim to produce an international, aspirational Declaration that should serve to guide further developments in domestic law.

Indigenous reactions to the Norwegian proposal

Indigenous reactions were varied. No consensus was forthcoming, let alone strategically articulated in the plenary. What all indigenous delegates were agreed on was that they would not accept a dilution of the right of self-determination. What they could not agree on was whether the proposed preambular changes actually dilute this or not. The Norwegian government insisted that the inclusion of a new preambular text was a 'purely tactical move' to prevent governments from endlessly amending article 3. Their move would not, Norway's delegation argued, dilute the right of self-determination in the text because the right of self-determination is already qualified in international law. The Saami delegation, like the Haudenosaunee Nation and the Indian Law Resource Center, also came to this conclusion, and stated that the new preambular text was redundant but non-discriminatory. In their eyes, the proposal's value lay in the fact that it preserved article 3 as it stands, while simultaneously assuaging state fears. The Saami delegation felt that the Norwegian proposal could create a momentum in the discussion by moving an increased number of states into accepting article 3 without amendments.

Many indigenous delegates, however, were more ambivalent about the Norwegian proposal, although ready to consider it. Dalee Sambo Dorough from the Inuit Circumpolar Conference, for example, noted that its potential lay in the fact that the Friendly Relations Declaration puts states under the obligation to be democratic, and to respect the right of self-determination of all peoples. Mililani Trask from Na Koa Ikaika O Ka Lahui Hawaii argued similarly that the preambular addition implies that those states that recognize their peoples' right of self-determination have the right of territorial integrity, whereas those that don't, do not. At the same time, Dalee Sambo Dorough warned that the addition in the preambular text, as proposed, pertained to the entire Declaration and could be construed as meaning that every single right contained in the Declaration could be read as encouraging the territorial break-up of states. In other words, *any* action on the part of indigenous peoples, even if not even remotely linked to secession, could be taken as violating the territorial integrity of the state. Some indigenous delegates were also unsure about the implications of the proposed clustering of articles, while Mohawk representative Kenneth Deer reacted to the proposed deletion of text after "local affairs" in Article 31 by arguing that it would make unclear exactly what "internal" and "local" entail.

South and Central American delegations as well as the IITC strongly opposed the Norwegian proposal, and argued that it would open the floodgate to other amendments. These delegations were in a particularly difficult position because the Norwegian proposal comes right at a time when an increasing number of states from their region have significantly shifted position and are explicitly arguing for an adoption of the Declaration as it stands. Andrea Carmen from the IITC said that while the Norwegian proposal might keep article 3 intact, it would encourage more and more amendments to what is really at stake in the Declaration – the rights of indigenous peoples to their land and natural resources.

The term "peoples"

For the first time, both the US and the UK conceded that they were "willing to consider the usage of 'peoples' in the appropriate places".

While they disagreed that the term "peoples" underlies the entire Declaration, they nevertheless acknowledged that the term "peoples" applies to some articles of the Declaration that contain collective rights. When prompted by indigenous delegates, the US and UK were unable to specify which articles contained collective and which individual rights. Instead, they insisted on an article-by-article discussion of the Declaration, and stated that they would only be able to determine the articles pertaining to collective rights once their language was finalized. However, discussions at the "informal informal" meeting led the Chair to summarize that, in fact, no states, not even the US, disagreed in principle with the term "peoples". Chávez stated explicitly that "the US objection to 'peoples' is not about objecting to the rights of peoples in principle, but about an article-by-article look at the applicability of the term." Disagreement thus exists over the general applicability of 'indigenous peoples' to the entire Declaration but not over whether it should be used at all.

Land and Resource Rights: Articles 25-30

In the "informal informal" session on the second to last day of the WGDD, Australia proposed a new text as a basis for the discussion of articles 25-30, and as a reflection of what its delegate called "the basic common ground amongst States." This proposed text was explicitly backed by Canada, New Zealand and France. The proposal merged and completely reformulated the articles as they currently stand. It also suggested the rewriting and fusion of articles 26-28 by diluting strong wording, erasing controversial language and diminishing the rights of indigenous peoples while entrenching those of states. Indeed, while many states seem ready to negotiate the meaning and practice of self-determination as a political right that could entail autonomy or self-government, the land and resource question seems unsolvable at present. In fact, as Les Malezer from the Foundation for Aboriginal and Islander Action stated, there exist such wide gaps between proposals on land and resource rights that "positions are at present incommensurable." Amendments to article 25 were exemplary of the changes envisaged by the CANZUS group.

Article 25, which reads:

"Indigenous peoples have the right to maintain and strengthen their distinctive spiritual and material relationship with the lands, territo-

ries, waters and coastal seas and other resources which they have traditionally owned or otherwise occupied or used, and to uphold their responsibility to future generations in this regard."

was rewritten in the Australian proposal to read:

"Indigenous peoples have the right to have their distinctive relationship with the land recognized."

This reformulation not only explicitly denies the materiality and spirituality of indigenous peoples' relationship with the land, replacing it with the much more opaque "distinctive", it also moves emphasis away from indigenous peoples as rights-bearing subjects in international law, and towards states "recognizing" indigenous peoples. All explicit references to specific rights to territories have been removed in view of the many problems the states have with the text. One is the "retrospective nature" of articles 25-30 and their prescriptive wording. Another is the states' worry that a strong wording of articles 25-30 would impinge on so-called "third party" [i.e. state and corporate] rights. A third is the Declaration's broad conceptualization of territory as a "total environment", including its natural resources, and the calls for "compensation". Canada, France, Australia and the US also insisted on the need to "recognize existing private property rights," saying that it was unrealistic to return to pre-colonial land rights, and that instead contemporary private ownership of land needed to be recognized, including lands "that had been voluntarily alienated or expropriated."

Indigenous representative Minnie Degawan asked for just one example of where "third party rights" had been violated by the recognition of indigenous rights. Mathias Åhrén from the Saami Council noted that the WGDD could not go below already established international standards, especially in light of the fact that ILO Convention 169 refers to the collective rights of indigenous peoples without referring to "third party rights". The IITC reminded the government of Australia that the UN Human Rights Committee (HRC) had previously instructed this government (as well as the governments of Norway, Mexico and Canada) to do justice to the indigenous right to land and self-determination.[2] Indigenous delegates, as always, urged states to take into account recent developments in the jurisprudence of UN treaty monitoring bodies such as the HRC and the CERD (Convention on the Elimination of Racial Discrimination) Committee. The representative from Na Koa Ikaika O Ka Lahui Hawaii and Permanent Forum member Mililani Trask stated that the WGDD, as a human rights standard setting body, was in fact required to take into account the decisions of the HRC, and to base its work on existing and evolving human rights standards. Tim Coulter from the Indian Law Resource Center reminded the plenary of the recent, legally binding and precedent-setting decision by the Inter-American Court of Human Rights that had ruled that the right of the Mayagna Indian community of Awas Tingni to its lands, natural resources and environment had been repeatedly violated and needed to be addressed by Nicaragua. The Guatemalan government also strongly objected to attempts to domesticate international law, and pledged for a "fearless" reading of the Declaration. The Chair added that the job of the WGDD was to establish international standards that should eventually be reflected in domestic legislation – and not the other way around. He also stressed explicitly that it was in the nature of human rights work to establish standards that would protect victims and not States.

The debate surrounding article 29 on indigenous intellectual property rights started with calls on the part of New Zealand, Australia, Russia and the US to postpone the discussion until the World Intellectual Property Organization (WIPO), currently dealing with traditional and indigenous knowledge, had come to a resolution. Indigenous representatives such as Maui Solomon strongly protested because the WIPO process was predicated on the eurocentric nature of the current intellectual property regime. Instead, he went on to argue, there was a need for a human rights framework to deal with these issues. Nevertheless, some indigenous delegates felt that the article had been drafted so long ago that significant changes in the way indigenous peoples and specialists conceptualize this issue had occurred. Organizations such as the Saami Council thus proposed new wording that would do justice to contemporary situations.

Many state proposals revealed that their basic intent was to shift emphasis from indigenous peoples' rights to 'states' rights and obligations. In all of the articles pertaining to land and resource rights, states made attempts to deprive indigenous peoples of their status as actors equal in rights and duties to states and other third parties. The US explicitly stated in this regard that indigenous peoples do not have rights under domestic law but rather obligations. As Dalee Sambo noted, debates at the WGDD continuously evoked worst case scenarios in which indigenous peoples would claim absolute rights to their natural resources, whereas it was, in reality, states who were claiming this absolute right. As they had done many times before, indigenous delegates challenged obstructive states to support their arguments with reference to contemporary human rights law, something the latter were unable to do. Instead, and despite the fact that the WGDD must produce a document founded on international human rights law, states argued time and again solely on the basis of domestic problems, while ignoring both the universal principles of equality and non-discrimination and the progressive work of the UN's human rights treaty bodies.

Articles 7, 8, 11

Article 7, dealing with the right of indigenous peoples to cultural integrity and to protection from ethnocide and cultural genocide, had already been debated at the 7th WGDD session. Positions were more or less reiterated at the 8th session. The CANZUS states in particular were unhappy with the terms "ethnocide" and "cultural genocide", both of which they said were not recognized in international law. Norway thus proposed replacing "ethnocide and cultural genocide" with "genocide, forced assimilation or the destruction of their culture." Some indigenous delegates felt that they could support the changes proposed by Norway, as well as other minor ones proposed by New Zealand. Others argued that the terms "ethnocide and cultural genocide" were contained in the Declaration of San José, produced in 1991 by experts on ethno-development and ethnocide, and could thus be said to be founded in international law. They also argued that the individual right to life is enshrined in many international instruments, while the collective right of peoples was not addressed in any instrument other than the Convention on the Prevention and Punishment of the Crime of Genocide. The Chair closed the discussion with the remark that no common ground had been reached, as had been the case at the 7th session. The Chair did, however, feel that the Norwegian suggestion had produced possibilities for agreement.

Debate surrounding Article 8 on the right of indigenous people to self-identification was dominated by a Canadian proposal to substitute "indigenous peoples" with "indigenous peoples and individuals". The governments of Australia, Denmark, Ecuador, Finland, Mexico, New Zealand, Norway, Russia and Switzerland aligned themselves with the Canadian proposal, while a number of indigenous delegations, including the Saami Council, the American Indian Law Alliance and some Asian indigenous delegates said that they could live with this change. They either felt that the Canadian proposal was redundant and did not change the substance of the article, or that the emphasis on individual and collective rights was acceptable in light of the fact that it did treat both individual and collective rights as equal. They also noted that individual and collective rights would in any case be balanced according to local situations and contexts. Other delegations, such as the International Indian Treaty Council, Na Koa Ikaika O Ka Lahui Hawaii, the Indigenous World Association and the Consejo de Todas Las Tierras Mapuche strongly argued that Canada's proposal did change the article's substance, elevating the rights of individuals to those of the collectivity, whereas it was the latter that was supposed to be protected in this Declaration. The Chair, in his summary statement, noted that this was the first time that a proposal for alternative language had found a significant amount of support amongst both government and indigenous delegations, and that "great progress had been made here".

The discussion of article 11 on the protection of indigenous peoples in periods of armed conflict was postponed by the Chair after it became clear that states were insisting on tinkering with the text and that no agreement could be reached. Once again, however, a number of indigenous delegates stated that they could live with changes if they were minor and non-discriminatory.

Summary and conclusions

This meeting confirmed the strong stance increasingly being taken by some South and Central American governments. The meeting also, however, confirmed the intransigence of the CANZUS states, none of whom made proposals that were acceptable to indigenous delegates. In fact, some of the proposals made by this group were unacceptable to a number of government delegates, as the debate surrounding "internal self-determination" clearly showed. This increased polarization amongst governments was matched by an increased polarization amongst indigenous delegates. For the first time in the history of the WGDD, however, a governmental proposal - the Norwegian proposal – seemed to have the potential to become a basis for discussion for a number of governments and some indigenous delegations.

This meeting also revealed the fundamental disconnection that exists for most states between the political and economic aspects of the right of self-determination. While the South and Central American governments in particular spoke of their domestic efforts to promote pluri-nationalism, decentralization and autonomy, and while it seemed that some other states such as Sweden, Finland and Norway were ready to consider self-determination as the right of a people to freely determine its relationship to the state, the question of land and resource rights remains extremely difficult and contested. Even though some countries were able to accept articles 25-30 as drafted others, including Guatemala, repeatedly mentioned "third party rights". Indigenous delegates, in the meantime, acted unanimously when it came to the protection of their rights under article 25-30, largely because the "summary" proposal made by Australia did not even remotely cover any of the rights to lands and resource that indigenous peoples claim.

One way forward might be to draw on the expert advice of an advisory group. During the meeting of the Permanent Forum in New York in May this year, a number of indigenous persons present decided to establish such a group to consider the drafting of the Declaration, provide advice to the caucus and lend legal support in other ways. This decision was taken in anticipation of a situation in which governments would start to speed up the drafting process and thus force the indigenous delegates present to take a position on a number of issues. This was precisely what happened in Geneva in December 2002.

The advisory group, however, did not manage to meet before the Geneva session and was only able, to a limited extent, to work as a body during the meeting. This is partly explained by the fact that a number of indigenous persons were opposed to such a group because they did not want this group to speak on behalf of the caucus and because they distrusted its legitimacy. The immediate implication of this was that the indigenous caucus was unable to present a unified strategy during the WGDD. Instead, they openly contradicted each other in the plenary. The long-term implications may be that the different opinions in the caucus between those who oppose any changes to articles and those who would consider changes (without violating the fundamental right of self-determination) will develop into a devastating cleavage. An advisory group, in contrast, might enable indigenous delegates to discuss the exact legal and political implications of some of the government proposals within the caucus, in order to find some common ground and avoid openly contradicting each other in the plenary. ❑

Notes

1 For attendance list and report, see E/CN.4/2002/92 on the website of the Office of the High Commissioner for Human Rights: www.unhchr.ch

2 See UN documents CCPR/C/79/Add.112, CCPR/C/79/Add.109, and CCPR/C/79/Add.105.

THE FIRST SESSION OF THE UN PERMANENT FORUM ON INDIGENOUS ISSUES

The first session of the Permanent Forum on Indigenous Issues took place at the UN headquarters in New York from 13 to 24 May 2002.

More than 600 people participated in this historic event, including more than 300 indigenous representatives, State delegations, UN bodies and agencies.

At its first session, the expert members of the Permanent Forum chose Ole Henrik Magga (a Saami from Norway) to be President for the first year. Four Vice-Presidents were also elected: Antonio Jacanamijoy (Colombia), Njuma Ekundanayo (Democratic Republic of Congo), Parshuram Tamang (Nepal) and Mililani Trask (USA). Willie Littlechild (Canada) was elected as the Permanent Forum's rapporteur.

Two main issues

There were two main issues on the agenda of this first session:

- The general declarations of observers
- A review of the activities of the UN system.

Under the agenda point "General Declarations", the Permanent Forum heard state and indigenous delegates speak on a wide variety of issues. Some of the declarations from indigenous representatives were of a general nature, presenting a wide range of issues relating to the difficulties and discrimination faced by indigenous communities and peoples, whilst others made specific recommendations to the members of the Permanent Forum.

The discussions on a review of the activities of the UN system focused on the following issues: economic and social development, environment, health, education and culture, and human rights.

A large number of UN specialised agencies and other bodies were invited by the President of the Permanent Forum to present their work and programmes in relation to indigenous peoples. There were interventions, among others, from the World Bank, UNDP, ILO, UN-Habitat, UNEP and the Secretariat of the Convention on Biological Diversity, the UN Population Fund, UNICEF, WHO, UNESCO and OHCHR. These interventions were followed by a brief "dialogue" of questions and answers between the members of the Permanent Forum and the representatives of the UN agencies and bodies, which gave rise to a constructive dialogue on how to strengthen the UN agencies' programmes in relation to indigenous peoples.

One of the issues that was repeatedly raised by indigenous representatives and members of the Permanent Forum was the need for the Forum to have its own Secretariat, adequately financed out of the regular budget of the United Nations. This secretariat, according to the interventions made, should be directly linked to the ECOSOC Secretariat and not to the Office of the High Commissioner for Human Rights. The main argument given for this was that the Permanent Forum has a mandate to deal with issues not only related to human rights but also economic and social development, the environment, health, education and culture. The majority of indigenous interventions indicated a desire to see a Secretariat made up of a team of indigenous professionals.

The lack of financial resources for the Forum, both for activities and for the running of its own secretariat, made it quite difficult for this first session to draw up a real plan of work. Until then, the only budget granted by the UN to the Forum was that which was strictly necessary for holding the first and second sessions.

Priority issues

The following are some of the priority issues that can be found in the meeting's report:

- The need for an adequately constituted and financed Secretariat, linked directly to the ECOSOC Secretariat.
- The need to gather information within the UN system in order to promote coordination of its work on issues directly affecting indigenous peoples.
- The need for strengthened communication with other UN bodies.
- The gathering of information on indigenous organisations. In this regard, the reports of the Permanent Forum recommend that a UN publication be produced every three years on the status of the world's indigenous peoples.
- The need for indigenous children's and young people's issues to be a central issue, separate and permanent, in the agenda and work plan of the Permanent Forum.

Indigenous rights in the areas of, among others, health, intellectual property, human rights and genetic resources also received special consideration from the Permanent Forum. Access to education systems and language learning were also the object of special consideration, along with conservation of the environments upon which indigenous peoples' lives depend.

The Forum also urged the countries to ratify a number of international instruments such as International Labour Organisation (ILO) Convention 169 and encouraged the states to adopt the UN Draft Declaration on the Rights of Indigenous Peoples before the end of the Decade.

With regard to the location and date of its next session, the Forum recommended that ECOSOC decide to hold it once more at the UN headquarters in New York during the period April-May 2003.

After two weeks of deliberations, the first session of the Permanent Forum came to an end with a declaration from the UN Secretary-General. In his speech, Mr. Kofi Annan began by welcoming the indigenous peoples into 'the family of the United Nations' and said to all indigenous peoples of the world, "You have a home in the United Nations". The indigenous peoples, he said, have hopes, rights and aspirations that could and must be addressed by the Organisation, as well as knowledge and skills that could help the international community in its goals of development and peace.

Recent developments

The efforts of the indigenous peoples, and particularly the members of the Permanent Forum, to ensure that this new body will, like other UN bodies, have its own Secretariat with which to implement its mandate adequately, have borne fruit.

Following the recommendations made by the Permanent Forum to ECOSOC, in December 2002, the General Assembly decided to ask the Secretary-General to establish a Secretariat within the Department of Economic and Social Affairs (DESA) to assist the Permanent Forum on Indigenous Issues and with the aim of enabling this body to carry out its mandate.

The General Assembly also asked the Secretary-General to establish a Voluntary Fund for the Forum with the aim of funding implementation of the recommendations made by the Forum through the Economic and Social Council.

Following these recommendations of the General Assembly, the Vice Secretary-General of the United Nations for Economic and Social

Affairs finally established, in February 2003, the Secretariat of the Permanent Forum on Indigenous Issues as a dependent office within the Division for Social Policy and Development of DESA.

It is the Secretariat's job to provide technical and administrative assistance to the Permanent Forum on Indigenous Issues in order to enable it to implement its mandate.

In addition, the Secretariat will administer the Voluntary Fund for the Permanent Forum and will coordinate the activities of the work programme of the Permanent Forum.

The Secretariat is in the process of establishing its offices and communication networks and already has a Web site. It will be responsible for organising the second session of the Permanent Forum, to be held in New York from 12 to 23 May.

With the Secretary-General's establishment of the Permanent Forum's own Secretariat, the United Nations has re-affirmed its commitment to indigenous peoples and to the Permanent Forum and has taken a hugely important step towards ensuring that this new body enjoys the conditions necessary to fulfil its role within the system.❏

For anyone wishing to communicate with the Permanent Forum's Secretariat, its contact details are the following:

Secretariat of the Permanent Forum on Indigenous Issues
Department of Economic and Social Affairs
DC2-1772
United Nations Headquarters
New York, NY 10017
USA
Telephone: + 1 917 367 5100 / Fax:
Email: indigenouspermanentforum@un.org
Web site: www.un.org/esa/socdev/pfii/

THE SPECIAL RAPPORTEUR VISITS THE PHILIPPINES

"I cannot promise you anything but to bring your message through..."

T his was the assurance given to indigenous peoples by Dr. Rodolfo Stavenhagen, the United Nations Special Rapporteur on the situation of human rights and fundamental freedoms of indigenous peoples, when he visited the Philippines from December 2 to 11, 2002.

The Special Rapporteur (SR) has kept his promise. On March 5 2003, on the occasion of its fifty-ninth session, Dr. Stavenhagen submitted his final report to the Commission on Human Rights. Having travelled with the entourage of the SR's mission, I can confidently say that the report vividly and truthfully captures the testimonies of the indigenous peoples that he met during his rigorous ten-day visit. The document itself is a compelling chronicle of the human rights situation of indigenous peoples. On reading the report, one can virtually hear the voices of the people who have so long been silenced by the dominant forces of state, military and big business corporations.

This article has two objectives. One, to explain the process that led to the successful visit of the SR to the Philippines and the role of indigenous peoples in this process. By doing so, we hope that indigenous peoples from other countries may learn and draw lessons from our experience. Second, to validate the report of the SR, which unfortunately has been brazenly and maliciously dismissed by the Philippine government as nothing more than "fabricated facts". This article contains narratives from the indigenous peoples who met with the SR.

Making it happen

The Special Rapporteur's visit to the Philippines was made possible by the invitation of the government of the Republic of the Philippines. Indigenous peoples' organizations also undeniably played a significant role in making the visit happen.

The idea was born during the "National Indigenous Peoples' Workshop on Indigenous Peoples' Rights Act and Development", which was held in February 2002 in Cagayan de Oro City in Mindanao. Indigenous participants in the workshop reported several cases of human rights violations. This pushed the workshop to form a resolution asking the Philippine government, through the National

Commission on Indigenous Peoples (NCIP), to invite the SR to undertake a mission here.

Subsequently, the Philippine government, through the Philippine Mission in Geneva, issued an official invitation in around May 2002 to visit the country. Preparations promptly began. The SR clearly wanted to fulfil his mandate, which included, among other things:

[T]o gather, request, receive and exchange information and communications from all relevant sources, including government and indigenous people themselves and their communities and organizations, on violations of their human rights and fundamental freedoms.

In July 2002, during the session of the UN Working Group on Indigenous Populations, the SR met with the delegation from the Philippines and discussed the preparations for the mission. The indigenous delegation included Victoria Tauli-Corpuz (Kankanaey), Jimid Mansayagan (Manobo), Onsino Mato (Subanen) and Jojie Carino (Ibaloi). Dr. Stavenhagen expressed his desire that an NGO in the Philippines should be involved in the preparations. The Philippine delegation assigned this role to Tebtebba, the (Baguio) Philippine-based Indigenous Peoples' International Centre for Policy Research and Education.

When the Executive Director of Tebtebba, Victoria Tauli-Corpuz, returned to the Philippines, she immediately held several meetings with indigenous peoples' organizations and civil society groups to determine which areas the Special Rapporteur should visit. Having been informed that the United Nations budget for this kind of missions was limited to the immediate expenses of the SR and his assistant, she also approached the International Work Group for Indigenous Affairs (IWGIA) who responded positively to provide the funds to be used to bring the mission to the communities and to hold regional and national consultations.

Victoria Tauli-Corpuz was also in constant communication with the SR and the UN Office of the High Commissioner on Human Rights, Indigenous Peoples' Unit, as well as the National Commission on Indigenous Peoples (NCIP). The NCIP prepared a travel itinerary for him. This itinerary was later revised on the basis of the indigenous peoples' request, as they found the NCIP proposal rather "touristy".

The first areas proposed by indigenous peoples' organizations were Dalupirip, Itogon in the province of Benguet and Siocon, Zamboanga del Sur. These were rejected by the Philippine government because, according to them, these were subjects of the Special 1503 procedure.[1] The Office of the High Commissioner for Human Rights (OHCHR) consulted the legal department and was told that there was no ruling preventing a Special Rapporteur from visiting places subject to SP 1503. The Philippine government questioned this opinion and asserted that these places could not be visited. In consultation with indigenous peoples' organizations, Tebtebba changed the places to Mankayan, Benguet and Agusan del Sur. This was acceptable to the Philippine government. Preparations by the Tebtebba and indigenous peoples' organizations therefore continued. The Philippine government procrastinated.

The Indigenous Peoples' Unit waited for the final official letter from the Philippine government to give the go-ahead for the Special Rapporteur to proceed. But, until November 22, 2002, no such letter arrived. Ms. Tauli-Corpuz followed this up with Mr. Dennis Lepatan, the person assigned to deal with these matters at the Geneva Philippine Mission, on November 18, 2002. Mr. Lepatan said that until he got a letter from the capital he could not give the go-ahead to the OHCHR. It turned out that the NCIP's Executive Director, Atty. Evelyn Dunuan, had written to the Department of Foreign Affairs (DFA) suggesting that the mission be postponed, mainly on the basis that "they have not been involved in the whole process".

Ms. Tauli-Corpuz immediately wrote to Atty. Evelyn Dunuan and Ambassador Delia Albert, Under-Secretary of Foreign Affairs, requesting that the Philippine government should give the go-ahead. Ms. Tauli-Corpuz said that all the necessary preparations had been made, from the local indigenous communities to the OHCR in Geneva. Ambassador Albert favorably responded to the request of Ms. Tauli-Corpuz. On November 26, 2002, the DFA convened a meeting with various government agencies and Tebtebba to thrash out the issues and coordinate the activities. The Philippine government decided to push through with the mission.

The Mission

The Special Rapporteur's mission to the Philippines was unprecedented. This was the first time that a UN Special Rapporteur's visit had been coordinated not only by the government but also by an indigenous peoples' organization (Tebtebba). The involvement of an NGO/IPO in the whole process facilitated the direct dialogue between the SR and the indigenous peoples, especially the victims of human rights violations themselves. This resulted in a series of fruitful consultations, ultimately leading to a straightforward report. This would not have been the case had the mission followed the usual government itinerary of mainly showcasing its 'good practices' and taking the SR to tourist areas.

The mission was quite hectic and thorough. The SR visited the key cities of Manila and Baguio, as well as Mankayan in Benguet Province and Butuan in Mindanao. In Manila, he met with senior government officials, including the Secretary of the Department of Environment and Natural Resources, the Under-Secretary of the Department of Justice, the Under-Secretary of the Department of National Defense, the Co-Vice Chair of Task Force 63, the Presidential Adviser on Peace, the Chair of the Commission for Human Rights, the Commissioners and Executive Director of the National Commission on Indigenous Peoples (NCIP), and the Chair of the Commission on the Role of Filipino Women. The SR also met with the Catholic Bishop of Butuan, the President and members of the academic community of the University of the Philippines and other academic institutions, and the President of the Chamber of Mines of the Philippines.

Findings

The Special Rapporteur's main finding was that indigenous peoples have, for a long time, been ignored by mainstream Philippine society. The Philippine nation-state has done little to improve the standards of living of its indigenous cultural communities or to overcome the high rates of poverty and low levels of human development that characterize these populations. During the press conference held on December 11, 2002, Dr. Stavenhagen revealed that, "indeed, far from being full and equal partners in the construction of the modern nation, the indigenous peoples have been largely excluded, discriminated against and marginalized."

Legal deception

The Philippines is the only country in Asia that has a law on indigenous peoples, the Indigenous Peoples' Rights Act (IPRA). But the SR found that its adequate implementation is still an unfulfilled promise, particularly because it may enter into conflict with other laws (such as the Mining Act of 1995) and because IPRA itself contains laws that do not favor the indigenous peoples entirely.

During the meeting with KAMP on December 4, 2002, Mr. Windel Bolinget, Secretary General of the Cordillera Peoples' Alliance (CPA) told the SR that the IPRA was flawed on three counts. First, it continues to uphold the Regalian Doctrine, a colonial legacy and legal fiction that assumes that Philippine lands are owned by the King and, subsequently, the State. Second, the IPRA does not repeal oppressive land laws and third that, based on the experience of indigenous communities in the Cordillera, the IPRA has proved to be a problem rather than a solution to the historic problems of indigenous peoples.

Atty. Marvic Leonen, a legal luminary on indigenous peoples' rights, said during the National Consultation on Indigenous Peoples' Rights held on December 10, 2002 that the IPRA was a "heavily compromised law". He gave three reasons for this analysis. One, the IPRA inherited a (huge but largely inefficient) bureaucracy from the defunct Office of Northern Cultural Communities (ONCC) and Office of Southern Cultural Communities (OSCC). Two, it does not offer any fundamental solution to the conflict between customary law and state law. Three, "IPRA is an analgesic. It directs attention away from the significant issues confronting indigenous peoples".

The SR aptly observed that the National Commission on Indigenous Peoples (NCIP), the primary government agency responsible for the formulation and implementation of policy, plans and programmes to promote and protect the rights and well-being of indigenous peoples, "has not been able to live up to the expectations and aspirations of indigenous peoples regarding the full implementation of IPRA. This results in part from insufficient funding, bureaucratic hitches, and the inexperience of NCIP itself, as well as delays in implementation."

Development aggression

The SR reports that many communities resist being forced or pressured into development projects that destroy their traditional economy, community structures and cultural values, a process that has been described as "development aggression".

The SR received reports of serious human rights violations regarding the implications for indigenous communities of economic activities such as logging, mining, the building of dams, commercial plantations and other development projects.

The testimonies of several indigenous peoples that I heard during the meetings support the SR's conclusion. I was witness to an extensive interview by Dr. Stavenhagen of a 70-year old Ata Manobo woman, who walked for three (3) days just to be able to make her testimony. Ba-e Leonora (not her real name) lamented that Alcantara and Sons, a logging company, had first grabbed and then deforested their 29,000 hectares of ancestral land. After denuding the Ata-Manobo land, Alcantara and Sons obtained money from the Asian Development Bank (ADB) to reforest the land, under the Integrated Forest Management Agreement (IFMA). In the process, the Ata-Manobos were again displaced from their land. To ensure there was no indigenous resistance to the project, the company, in connivance with the military, brought in the dreaded Ala Mara, a paramilitary 'indigenous' (but not Ata-Manobo) army that has wrought fear and terror on the Ata-Manobo.

Serious human rights violations

From one meeting to another, the Special Rapporteur listened intently to the harrowing and moving testimonies of arbitrary detentions, persecution and summary executions of community representatives; of coercion, forced recruitment, and also rape, perpetrated by individuals pertaining to the armed forces, the police or so-called paramilitaries within the framework of counter-insurgency activities. These allegations are documented and substantiated, and yet the victims claim that they do not receive due process and justice in the courts or by the relevant government agencies when they file their complaints about such alleged violations.

The militarization of a number of indigenous areas was repeatedly mentioned to the SR, including the practice of hamletting (congregating indigenous peoples into specified locations against their will). There were also reports of indigenous people being accused of and prosecuted for terrorist activity simply because of their involvement in legitimate protest or the defense of their rights, in violation of national legislation and international human rights law.

Militarization has adversely affected indigenous women and children. For example, extensive research and documentation undertaken by the Cordillera Women's Education and Resource Center (CWERC) and submitted to the SR revealed that, from 1986 to the present, there have been 99 women and 119 children abandoned by soldiers in the provinces of Kalinga and Abra alone. There have also been 25 cases of "sexual opportunism," including two gang rapes, seven rapes by individual soldiers and three attempted rapes.

Impoverishment

The Special Rapporteur also received numerous reports of indigenous peoples not being able to receive the social service benefits to which they have a right. Various surveys and studies also report that human development indicators are lower, and poverty indicators higher, for indigenous peoples than the rest of the country. In many indigenous communities, basic health services are simply not available, and preventable disease abound. Access to basic education is severely restricted.

The SR's report is not mere speculation. His findings are even supported by poverty assessments undertaken by the World Bank and the Asian Development Bank. A World Bank study, for instance, reveals that in Mindanao, 11% of the respondents said that the lack of government facilities forced them to use private clinics and hospitals. In education, 41% of school-age children in Mindanao do not attend school. Mindanao is a region with one of the highest concentrations of indigenous population in the country.

Inadequate access to justice

According to the Special Rapporteur's report, there is a looming "protection gap" in the human rights protection system for indigenous peoples in the Philippines. This conclusion is based on several complaints about insufficient measures taken by the national authorities to remedy human rights violations. The SR further writes, "Indigenous peoples believe that their voices have not been adequately heard nor their situation remedied by the authorities."

The response of the Philippine government, through its Philippine Mission representative in Geneva, Mr. Dennis Lepatan, reflects its callousness to indigenous issues and demands. This state arrogance is precisely the cause of the alienation of indigenous peoples from the Philippine nation-state. It should be noted, however, that during the debriefing for the government of the Philippines by the SR, held on December 11, 2002, government officials - including the then NCIP Chairperson Evelyn Dunuan, and Ambassador Howard Dee, the Presidential Advisor on Indigenous Peoples Affairs - lauded the SR presentation as a "very precise, accurate and comprehensive" report.

Recommendations

The Special Rapporteur made several recommendations to various actors for the better promotion and protection of the human rights of indigenous peoples in the Philippines. The most fundamental and 'courageous' recommendations included the following:

- *Resolving land rights issues should at all times take priority over commercial development. There needs to be recognition not only in law but also in practice of the prior right of traditional communities;*
- *The government of the Philippines [must] carry out a prompt and effective investigation of the numerous human rights violations committed against indigenous peoples, which have been documented by human rights organizations and special fact-finding missions;*
- *Given the severity of the various alleged human rights abuses and the divisive effects on indigenous communities caused by irregular military units or paramilitary groups, the Special Rapporteur urges that the Citizens' Armed Forces Geographical Units (CAFGUS) be withdrawn from indigenous areas altogether, within the framework of a national programme to demilitarize indigenous peoples' territories. Furthermore, the Special Rapporteur recommends that the government of the Philippines take maximum caution to protect indigenous peoples' rights during its military operations, in accordance with international humanitarian standards;*
- *That the government of the Philippines request the United Nations High Commissioner for Human Rights to establish an office in the Philippines to provide technical cooperation in the field of the promotion and protection of the human rights of indigenous peoples.*

The Special Rapporteur's recommendations dealt with the basic structural problems that oppress and exploit indigenous peoples in the Philippines. The question now is whether the Philippine state will even acknowledge the issues raised and recommendations made by the UN Special Rapporteur.

Lessons learned

For Tebtebba and the rest of indigenous peoples in the Philippines, the engagement with the UN Special Rapporteur left enduring lessons. Foremost is the realization that this instrument of the United Nations System can be used by indigenous peoples' organizations in articulating their issues, concerns and aspirations. Indigenous Peoples' Organizations can play a pro-active role in influencing the process. Of course, the aim of such active intervention is to ensure that the SR is able to receive data and information directly from indigenous peoples' themselves.

The SR's visit to the Philippines was able to gather together several actors and stakeholders - the academe, Church, human rights and indigenous peoples' organizations, including the government and military officials - to discuss the problems of indigenous peoples. Such a rare opportunity has provided a space for deliberating on how Philippine society in general should resolve the historical and lingering marginalization of indigenous peoples.

The SR visit also encouraged various indigenous peoples and non-government organizations in the Philippines to systematize and document their experiences. These organizations have no doubt used their data in their own advocacy and campaigning, even beyond the framework of the SR visit.

The Philippine government's refusal to deal with the issues raised by the indigenous peoples through the UN Special Rapporteur confirms the indigenous peoples' conviction that they can only rely on no-one but themselves to confront the forces that further marginalize them. ❑

Notes

1 The Special 1503 Procedure is a complaints procedure in the Commission for Human Rights which an individual or a representative of a community can use to file a complaint against a government for human rights violations.

THE AFRICAN COMMISSION ON
HUMAN AND PEOPLES´ RIGHTS

The human rights of indigenous peoples in Africa have remained on the agenda of the African Commission on Human and Peoples' Rights during 2002 and 2003. The Working Group on the Rights of Indigenous Populations, established under the African Commission, submitted its final report and recommendations to the African Commission during the 33rd Ordinary Session held in Niger in May 2003. The report analyses the human rights situation of indigenous peoples in Africa as compared to the rights provided for in the African Charter on Human and Peoples' Rights. It analyses the African Charter on Human and Peoples' Rights and the jurisprudence of the African Commission, especially relating to the collective rights of "peoples". It discusses criteria for identifying indigenous peoples and it makes recommendations to the African Commission.

The report was presented during the Niger session and was received positively by those commissioners who took the floor. The report will be discussed and hopefully adopted during the next session of the African Commission, to be held in Cameroon in October 2003. When adopted, the report will be published as a co-production between the African Commission and IWGIA.

Prior to the finalization of the report, a draft report was discussed at a consultative workshop in Nairobi in January 2003. Around 30 indigenous representatives and African human rights activists participated in this workshop and made an important input to the draft report. The workshop also served as a forum for informing indigenous representatives and other human rights activists about the ongoing process in the African Commission.

Indigenous representatives have been participating actively in the ordinary sessions of the African Commission held in 2002 and 2003. The 32nd session was held in the Gambia in October 2002 and around 6 indigenous representatives participated and made statements in the public session.

Around 12 indigenous representatives participated in the 33rd session in Niger in May 2003 and the human rights concerns of indigenous peoples were voiced clearly during this session. During the Niger session, indigenous organizations were for the first time granted observer status with the African Commission. The three organizations that applied for and were granted observer status were the *Indigenous Peoples of Africa Coordinating Committee* (IPACC) based in South Africa, *Mainyoito Pastoralist Integrated Development Organization* (MPIDO) based in Kenya and the *Centre for Minority Rights Development* (CEMIRIDE) based in Kenya. This sent a clear signal regarding the interest of indigenous peoples in having their concerns addressed by the African Commission and it is important that more indigenous organizations apply for observer status before the next session in October.

During the Niger session, some commissioners raised questions about the human rights situation of indigenous populations during the examination of state reports. A human rights seminar and a report on the human rights situation of the Pygmies of the Democratic Republic of Congo had been prepared by the Pygmy organizations PIDP-KIVU and the report and specific questions were handed over to a number of commissioners to raise these issues with the DRC government delegation. Unfortunately, the DRC government delegation did not attend but it is hoped that the issues will be raised next time.

During the Niger session, indigenous representatives presented statements regarding the alarming situation of the Pygmies in the DRC, the Twa in Rwanda, the Maasai in Kenya, the Peul[1] in Niger and the Tuareg in Niger and Algeria.

A few government delegations reacted negatively to statements from indigenous representatives. Others – such as the government representative of South Africa in particular – were very supportive towards the process. The sessions of the African Commission provide a good platform for lobbying and dialogue with government delegations.

The Niger session was unfortunately the last session of Commissioner Barney Pityana. He has been a strong advocate for the inclusion of the protection and promotion of the rights of indigenous peoples in the work of the African Commission and it is to be hoped that the process can maintain its momentum after his departure. ❏

Note

1   Also known as Fulani or Fulbé (ed.note).

FRENCH GUIANA:
MAKING GOOD USE OF THE UN SYSTEM

French Guiana comprises six indigenous peoples: the Kali'na, the Lokono, the Pahikwaki, the Teko, the Wayampi and the Wayana. Since 1984, when Félix Tiouka - as the first indigenous leader from Guiana - started to question the State and the regional authorities,[1] the indigenous peoples of Guiana have multiplied their actions in order to achieve a true recognition of their rights.

The Federation of Indigenous Organisations of Guiana (F.O.A.G.) has thus, from the very start, set itself a certain number of goals. One of these is to establish and coordinate relations with the various governmental and non-governmental bodies, at national as well as international level. Another is to encourage contacts and exchanges with like-minded organisations worldwide. This is why, in 1995, F.O.A.G. decided to participate on the international scene in order to respond to the total disinterest of the French state with regard to the issue of the rights of indigenous peoples living on French territory. Since then, F.O.A.G. has assiduously maintained its struggle at international level by participating in the different UN working groups under the Commission on Human Rights: the Working Group on Indigenous Populations, the Working Group on the Draft Declaration on the Rights of Indigenous Peoples and the *ad hoc* Working Group on the possible establishment of a Permanent Forum on Indigenous Issues.

Our objective is to negotiate at a higher level than the French state and denounce the lack of concern of successive French governments with regard to this issue. We thereby hope to force the French state to react and reply to our repeated demands for recognition of our rights.

This participation has resulted in a noticeable change in the French state's attitude towards the indigenous population of Guiana. The politicians now know that they can no longer ignore our presence on the territory of Guiana. Since 1999, we have been able to observe a clear improvement in the state's position towards the indigenous peoples. The international context is gradually influencing decisions taken at the national level. Since October 2000, we have seen the results of this new development: today F.O.A.G. is able to get support from French representatives in international fora: the barriers we felt in the beginning are no longer there, and French diplomacy is far more willing to listen to our demands. Moreover, the clear improvement in attitude towards indigenous peoples in the international context as a result of the International Decade of the World's Indigenous Peoples (1995-2004), is gradually impacting on decisions at national level.

International discussions between indigenous peoples and States are thus bearing fruit. France now takes positive decisions with regard to indigenous peoples, as was the case in Nairobi in 2000, with the Convention on Biodiversity. The International Decade has also promoted a raising of international awareness. The indigenous issue is thus very often mentioned in the press or on French television and the French are now beginning to learn that there are indigenous peoples in Guiana. The State itself talks more openly about these questions. President Jacques Chirac thus wrote a letter on the problem of mercury pollution in which he affirmed the need to recognize the rights of indigenous peoples, referring to the United Nations' report on biodiversity. France now belongs to the states that are in favour of creating an international permanent body on indigenous issues. It is the first time that such an attitude has been observed on the part of the French state's representatives. Before that there was an almost total refusal to sign anything that might entail the risk of giving weight to the demands of indigenous peoples. The situation in New Caledonia has also played a fairly important role in this area, and it is now possible to influence the state by referring to the situation out there. In more general terms, it can be seen that the attitude of the French state is changing with respect to the indigenous populations overseas.

In December 2002, during the last session of the Working Group on the Draft Declaration, we were able to see new progress. The French delegation thus declared that, "France recognizes the right to self-determination." This is real progress in French rhetoric even if certain issues remain unclarified, notably regarding the notion of territory, since the French representative added, "France considers that the right of self-determination should benefit everybody in a given population." In that case, the question is whether or not France's concept of self-determination can be applied to the indigenous peoples of Guiana. Does the state thereby mean the entire Guiana territory – and in that case populations other than the indigenous are implicated – or is it ready to restrict this definition to a limited territory claimed by a particular indigenous people?

Where France, on the other hand, really positions itself is when its representative declares that, "France naturally recognizes the indigenous peoples" basing himself on a declaration made by the President of the French Republic during his intervention before the Commission on Human Rights on 30 March 2001, "Victims of History, the indigenous peoples are the depositaries of a priceless part of the common heritage of mankind. These peoples and their knowledge are threatened. Let us recognize what we owe them and what they can contribute to us."

These various declarations suggest a true change in French policy towards indigenous peoples. After having successively experienced colonialization, near extinction, 'French-ization' and assimilation, we can now hope that a true will to recognize the rights of the indigenous peoples of France will be forthcoming. But much remains to be done. We must therefore continue our actions, continue to make our voices heard at all possible levels, at departmental, national and international level. The state will no longer be able to disregard our demands and our rights if constant pressure is put on it by other states.

To conclude, we think we have acted these past years according to the objectives we had set ourselves. We can now consider ourselves as recognized negotiators at the level of the state and the international institutions, this notably thanks to our actions at the level of the United Nations and in other international meetings. The defence of customary rights seems to have partly born fruit since, from now on, in state and regional speeches, reference is often made to customary authorities and the need to take them into account, even though some issues remain very problematic such as, for instance, the land issue, which is far from being resolved. ❏

Note

1   It was on this occasion that the Amerindian Association of French Guiana (A.A.G.F.) was created. AAGF later became the Federation of Indigenous Organisations of Guiana (F.O.A.G.).